THE FIFA WORLD CUP

THE FIFA WORLD CUP

A History of the Planet's Biggest Sporting Event

CLEMENTE A. LISI

ROWMAN & LITTLEFIELD
Lanham • Boulder • New York • London

Published by Rowman & Littlefield
An imprint of The Rowman & Littlefield Publishing Group, Inc.
4501 Forbes Boulevard, Suite 200, Lanham, Maryland 20706
www.rowman.com

86-90 Paul Street, London EC2A 4NE, United Kingdom

British Library Cataloguing in Publication Information Available

Library of Congress Cataloging-in-Publication Data

Names: Lisi, Clemente Angelo, 1975– author.
Title: The FIFA World Cup : a history of the planet's biggest sporting
    event / Clemente A. Lisi.
Description: Lanham, MD : Rowman & Littlefield, 2022. | Includes
    bibliographical references and index. | Summary: "In The FIFA World Cup:
    A History of the Planet's Biggest Sporting Event, Clemente A. Lisi
    chronicles the full history of the tournament, providing vivid accounts
    of individual games, controversies, and innovations from 1930 to
    today"—Provided by publisher.
Identifiers: LCCN 2022001221 (print) | LCCN 2022001222 (ebook) | ISBN
    9781538156438 (cloth) | ISBN 9781538156445 (epub)
Subjects: LCSH: World Cup (Soccer)—History.
Classification: LCC GV943.49 .L569 2022 (print) | LCC GV943.49 (ebook) |
    DDC 796.334/66809—dc23/eng/20220114
LC record available at https://lccn.loc.gov/2022001221
LC ebook record available at https://lccn.loc.gov/2022001222

CONTENTS

Acknowledgments

I AM GRATEFUL FOR A GREAT NUMBER OF PEOPLE. NO BOOK CAN BE written without the support of others. This book would not be possible without the patience and backing of my wife Kate and children Grace and Mark. They make everything I do worth the effort.

I would also like to thank my parents Franco and Rachele for their love and helping to make me the person I am today.

Special thanks go to my colleagues at The King's College in New York and the entire team at the McCandlish Phillips Journalism Institute. In particular, I want to thank Paul Glader for supporting my work and encouraging me to take on new projects.

A thank-you also goes to Terry Mattingly, who was always open to having a conversation about the U.S. national team and the growth of American soccer.

Extensive research went into putting this book together. A special thank-you to Lucas Drumond. His knowledge of Portuguese and love of soccer were an immense help, particularly when it came to providing information and photographs for this book from Brazil's National Archives.

Much of the information on World Cups past would not have been possible for me to access if not for the many journalists who wrote newspaper articles and books on the subject in decades past. Journalism is indeed the first draft of history, and without those drafts, so many of the games and personalities that made this game so great would have been forgotten to history.

There are too many players to name here, but special thanks to those who sat for interviews and gave their time to tell their stories. I would

like to highlight Carlos Alberto, Eusébio, Teófilo Cubillas, Bora Milutinović, and Paolo Maldini. All of them provided wonderful insight into
their playing days and World Cup experiences.

Finally, this project would not have been possible without the support and hard work of my editor, Christen Karniski, at Rowman &
Littlefield. She championed this project, and without her it would not
have become a reality. A big thank you also to editor Nicole Carty and
proofreader Matt Seccombe. Their fact-checking skills and meticulous
work made this a better book.

INTRODUCTION

THE WORLD'S LARGEST RELIGION IS CHRISTIANITY, WITH 2.4 BILLION adherents. I often joke that the biggest religion on earth is soccer.

Yes, soccer.

No matter where you live—or whether you call it football, *fútbol*, *futebol*, or *calcio*—it is extremely likely that you are a fan of the game or know someone who is. For example, an estimated 1.1 billion people watched the 2018 World Cup final won by France against Croatia. A total of 4 billion watched at least one game at that tournament either on TV or streaming on their phones.

In his book, *How Soccer Explains the World: An Unlikely Theory of Globalization*, author Franklin Foer makes the following astute assessment: "Soccer isn't the same as Bach or Buddhism. But it is often more deeply felt than religion, and just as much a part of the community's fabric, a repository of traditions."

I can attest to that very profound statement. I fell in love with this game in the summer of 1982. I was just six years old. I was on vacation in Italy with my family, and just two countries over, in Spain, the World Cup was being contested. I watched the final between Italy and West Germany at my grandmother's apartment in Naples. Italy won the game 3–1, and the city's empty streets were soon filled with thousands of people. An explosion of joy soon erupted along those cobblestoned piazzas. I still remember my father's tears—the first time I'd ever seen him cry—and people waving Italian flags from their balconies and on street corners.

My family joined in on those street celebrations that night. It was a source of great pride that renews itself every four years with the arrival of another World Cup. Every four years, people throughout the planet partake in this ritual. Their ultimate hope is that their nation can lift the

World Cup trophy. For many, this is a game tied to their cultural heritage. It's the one sport that has given Brazilians, Argentines, and Germans, among many other nations, a sense of national pride where politics has often made it taboo. It is a passion that permeates from every part of society and a love that's passed down from one generation to the next.

In general, sports have an ability to awaken passion in people—and soccer is no different. The globe's marquee sporting event, the FIFA World Cup, features the best national teams and players. The month-long tournament has had an ability to paralyze entire countries. Never underestimate the power of national pride—in this case a positive version of it—to excite a people. Only eight nations have ever won the World Cup—Brazil, Italy, Germany, Argentina, Uruguay, France, England, and Spain—making it one of the most exclusive clubs on the planet. There isn't anything some people wouldn't give to see their country make this list.

Soccer is relatively inexpensive and simple to play. As a result, it has been adopted as the sport of choice by the masses in both poor nations as well as wealthy ones. FIFA, the game's world governing body, estimates that 270 million people regularly play the sport in more than 200 countries. The chances are good that you could be hit by a stray soccer ball on your next vacation.

The game has been part of my life since childhood. Writing about the game has allowed me to travel around the world and visit places I'd likely never otherwise visit, like Johannesburg, Rio de Janeiro, and Moscow. It has allowed me to get into discussions—and sometimes disagreements—with taxi drivers in my native New York, throughout Europe in cities like Rome, and in South America, especially in a place like Buenos Aires. Indeed, never underestimate the soccer IQ of a taxi driver!

I've eaten alligator in Durban (tastes a lot like boiled chicken), a city on the east coach of South Africa, while overlooking the Indian Ocean; walked the sandy beaches of Rio's famed Ipanema; and marveled at the breathtaking and colorful onion-shaped domes of Saint Basel in Moscow's Red Square. I could only do those things because of the World Cup and journalism. I had an excuse to visit those places and engage in the local culture. They remain unforgettable experiences.

On the field, I witnessed Spain win its first World Cup in 2010, although the highlight from that night remains seeing a frail Nelson Mandela riding around the field in a car before Shakira swung her hips during the pregame show. Mandela smiled from ear to ear, delighted to see his nation host the planet's biggest sporting event following decades of state-sanctioned racism known as apartheid.

Four years later, I watched Brazilians cry as their team lost to Germany, 7–1, in the semifinals. That took place just days before I caught a glimpse of the great Pelé exiting Subway—the sandwich chain, not the train—in Rio, where he was making a stop to promote the eatery as their brand ambassador. My biggest takeaway from my Brazilian sojourn was that every World Cup should be held near a beach.

In 2018, I was far from water and sand in Russia. Moscow was great, but the train ride to St. Petersburg to watch the France-Belgium semifinal was truly amazing. The high-speed, four-hour ride north was incredible and a reminder of how bad American trains are.

I cried when Italy won the World Cup in 2006. I cried in 2020 when the legendary Diego Maradona died. Come to think of it, there is often a lot of crying in soccer. That's another big difference with other sports. Tom Hanks warned us that "there's no crying in baseball," but someone never told that to soccer players or their fans.

Soccer, like most team sports with a long tradition, brings out the tribalism in us. The game can also be very parochial, despite being a global phenomenon. Just ask anyone in Buenos Aires if they root for Boca Juniors or River Plate or in Manchester for either United or City. Location, when it comes to club soccer, makes for a great rivalry.

The World Cup, on the other hand, is different. It's a global tournament. Sure, national pride is on display, but the World Cup belongs to everyone. Even a country that isn't yours can move you. Maybe you became a Croatia fan at the 2018 World Cup, a Central European nation of just four million. Maybe you cheer for Brazil because you like Pelé or the country's iconic canary-yellow jerseys. Whatever nation you adopt (often once yours is eliminated) is what makes the World Cup such an inclusive event with something for everyone. As former president Bill Clinton said to kick off the 1994 World Cup in the United States: "The love of soccer is a universal language that binds us all together."

No politician has ever spoken truer words. The World Cup is an emotional experience. While soccer brings with it tears, both in victory and defeat, it also elicits lots of singing and dancing. I am not someone who is good at either, although that hasn't stopped me from singing "New York, New York" with South African fans or Italian songs with Russians (yes, Russians love '80s Italian pop music) during past World Cup trips.

This competition is not just a sensory experience. It's also a tournament with a rich history. This book is a chance for fans to learn about the game's past, specifically the World Cup's ability to popularize soccer globally in the last nine decades. No continent has been left untouched by this tournament (the 2022 edition will be hosted by Qatar, the first time ever it will be held in the Middle East) since its very humble origins in 1930.

This game has been a constant companion in my life. At age 19, the World Cup came to me when the United States was given the right to host the 1994 tournament. The party I had watched on TV had come to me. The Italians weren't so fortunate that summer, reaching the final but losing to mighty Brazil on a penalty-kick shootout at a sun-drenched Rose Bowl.

The goal of this book is to recount the history of the World Cup—with a mix of research and interviews I have conducted over the years—to younger audiences aware of Lionel Messi but not around to have seen Diego Maradona. For older readers, this book will help revive memories or fill the gaps left by the passing of time. Overall, this book is here to provide a resource for your bookshelf whenever the World Cup rolls around.

This book was written at a particularly difficult time. I began researching and writing it just nine months into a pandemic that paralyzed much of the planet. COVID-19 also had the ability to create political and cultural divisions, maybe exacerbating already-existing ones, across many nations.

My hope is that this book can unite us around the single love that is soccer. Even non-soccer fans get caught up in World Cup mania. It's the promise of another World Cup that will be a welcome respite from our societal ills and a chance for the globe to again come together around the game they love.

CHAPTER ONE

Crossing the Ocean

THE MUSEO DEL CALCIO IS A SMALL PLACE. THE MUSEUM, DIVIDED INTO just six rooms, is located in Coverciano, a neighborhood in Florence that is also home to the training center that houses Italy's national soccer team. For a country that features nearly 500 museums spanning art that dates back some 3,000 years, this place can be easily overlooked.

The complex, a quiet location lined with cypress trees, features two training fields on either side of the beige-colored building with terra-cotta roof. Inside, the place is loaded with relics of the sport's past, among them replicas of the two World Cups Italy won in 1934 and 1938.

Considering how loud sporting events can typically be, whether it's the fans in the stadium or players in the dressing room following a victory, Coverciano was a very quiet place when I visited in June 2018. It is a place of reverence, almost like a church, in which current players, coaches, and fans pass through as a place of pilgrimage.

"When I decided to start up this museum," Fino Fini recalled, "it was obvious that I decided to have it opened here."

Obvious because Fini was involved with the Italian national team, in one form or another, since 1958. Also obvious because the place had been Italy's main training center since that same year. During his tenure, Fini served as national team doctor and was the long-standing director of the Italian Football Association's technical center. A soft-spoken man with a grandfatherly appearance, Fini's emotional connection to his country's soccer heritage came through with the affection with which he spoke about the place.

"This museum, an idea that came about in 1990 when Italy hosted the World Cup, is a constant reminder of our success," he said. "The wealth with which these objects displayed here in Coverciano for the world to see is second to none."

It's that same emotional connection that prompted Fini to go to great lengths throughout his lifetime to accumulate and house memorabilia that highlighted the nation's glorious soccer past.

"For me, this place represents passion," Fini added. "It's where I started my career. I saw this place from birth, from its very foundations. I know every bit of this place—both as its former director and national team doctor—so for me this place is my first home."

Fini's passion reflects the same love that millions upon millions of people around the globe have for their national teams, something that would not have been possible if not for the power of a sporting tournament like the World Cup.

1930 World Cup

The very first World Cup began with a two-week journey across the Atlantic Ocean to Montevideo. The SS *Conte Verde* left the Italian port city of Genoa on June 21, 1930, headed to South America with Romania's national soccer team. The Italian steamboat stopped at Villefranche-sur-Mer, where they picked up the French team, three referees, and a group of dignitaries, including FIFA president Jules Rimet, who packed the shiny, gold World Cup trophy in his suitcase. The creation of French sculptor Abel Lafleur, Rimet noted in his journal that "the gold of the trophy is symbolic for the World Cup becoming the world's greatest sports event."

The ship made stops in Barcelona, where they were joined by the Belgians, and then picked up the Brazilian team in Rio do Janeiro on June 29 before arriving for its final stop in the Uruguayan capital five days later. Rimet noted that there was no shortage of distractions on board during the transatlantic voyage. "One can use the swimming pool, the fitness room, and the library," Rimet recalled in his diary. "In the evening after dinner—that is by itself a distraction—passengers have to choose between the ballroom, cinema, and live comedy shows."

Only Yugoslavia failed to join them because the *Conte Verde* was fully booked. Instead, they took a three-day train trip to Marseille in order to board the cruise liner *Florida*. Egypt, the only African team at the World Cup, had been scheduled to join them, but their boat from Africa was delayed by a storm. As a result, the *Florida* left without them. Instead, they sent a cable apologizing for their absence. At the same time, the Mexicans sailed from Veracruz to Hoboken, near New York City, so they could join the Americans on the SS *Munargo*. Players on the three boats spent the journey training on the deck—jogging, stretching, lifting weights, and even running up and down the ship's narrow stairs to stay fit.

For Rimet, a Frenchman, the trip to the first-ever World Cup had been decades in the making. Rimet had been involved in the founding of the Fédération Internationale de Football Association (commonly known as FIFA) in 1904. Creating a competition open to professionals allowed the World Cup to be unique, distinguishing itself from the Olympics. It had not been an easy road, but Rimet was used to adversity. Born in the eastern French town of Haute-Saône in 1876, the first of five children, Rimet was the son of a grocer who moved the family to Paris when Jules was just 11. Rimet, a fencer and runner in his youth, was not a very good soccer player. He became a lawyer and at age 24 started a soccer team called Red Star. The club—now known as Red Star Saint-Ouen—is one of France's oldest. Although he had political ambitions, Rimet would never be elected to public office. Instead, he would prove to be a visionary leader for a sport that would become global within decades.

In 1910, Rimet was instrumental in the creation of France's Football Association League, the country's first national soccer competition, and was named its first president. By 1919, the league's foundation led to the formation of the French Football Federation, which exists to this day. Rimet's work in France led to his election as FIFA's president in 1921. Rimet had been shocked by the horrors of World War I. A global tournament for nations could be a uniting force, Rimet argued. When the war ended, FIFA's members proved they were not immune to conflict themselves when some members called for the expulsion of Germany and the nations from the Central Powers, though they were in the minority.

3

The major issue at the time, however, was the definition of what constituted an amateur athlete. This was crucial for determining who could or couldn't play at the Olympics. Could a player be financially compensated to play for his country in the World Cup and still be considered an amateur? Opinions ranged drastically before a temporary compromise was agreed upon: a player could be compensated for loss of earnings—known as "broken-time payments"—as a result of being called on international duty and still be considered an amateur. As a result, the British associations, which included England, left FIFA in 1920, returned three years later under this fragile compromise, and then left yet again in 1926.

An astute administrator, Rimet was in for an uphill fight when it came to creating the World Cup. Since the start, FIFA had been looking for a way to host an international tournament featuring national teams. Rimet always had plans for a global professional tournament. World War I had put those plans on hold. It was at the 1920 Summer Olympics in Antwerp that Rimet first made a strong push for the World Cup's creation. Rimet's plan for an international tournament featuring pros, while also unifying the world through sport, was met with opposition. Rimet and fellow soccer administrator Henri Delaunay persevered in their efforts. By 1926, both men were convinced a World Cup needed to happen. "International football can no longer be held within the confines of the Olympics, and many countries where professionalism is now recognized and organized cannot any longer be represented there by their best players," Delaunay told the FIFA Congress in 1926.

Four years later, FIFA—by a vote of 25 to 10—approved the creation of a World Cup tournament that would be held every four years. The vote would forever transform the sports world. At a time when boxing and horse racing had emerged as the biggest spectator sports of the Roaring '20s, soccer would forever change that thanks largely to the World Cup. "FIFA's claim to be the only corporation entitled to organize and control a championship is rather old indeed," according to Heidrun Homburg, a historian who teaches at the University of Freiburg in Germany. "It was already alleged and written into its first statutes of 1904, and it was closely related to its sporting engagement and financial interests."

The choice of Uruguay—and in the case of the inaugural World Cup, limited to the city of Montevideo in a style similar to the Olympics—as host was ultimately an easy one. Uruguay had won the gold medal at the 1924 Summer Games in Paris and again four years later at the Amsterdam Games and were the best team in the world at the time. The team was led by José Leandro Andrade, a defensive midfielder known as *la maravilla negra* ("The Black Marvel" in Spanish). Behind Andrade on the right was José Nasazzi, a center back who also served as team captain, while Lorenzo Fernández, who had been born in Spain but represented Uruguay at the international level, was the team's midfield lynchpin. La Celeste employed a 2–3–5 formation—a tactic widely used at the time—with striker Pedro Cea as a key cog in attack.

Following Uruguay's success in 1924, Enrique Buero, who was an Uruguayan diplomat, persuaded Rimet that the very first World Cup should be held in the small South American nation. Like Rimet, he had witnessed the crowd's delight at the sight of Uruguay winning the gold medal, and he wanted to replicate that enthusiasm back in Montevideo.

The first World Cup had no qualification process, meaning the tournament was open to all of FIFA's members. European nations refused to embark on the long trip and boycotted the tournament. In response, Uruguay offered to cover the travel and lodging costs of all the participants. Nonetheless, European nations refused to commit by the February 1 deadline. Argentina, Brazil, Bolivia, Chile, Mexico, Paraguay, Peru, and the United States all entered.

"Despite the host country's financial provisions and an extension of the registration deadlines, the European football nations were putting forward various pretexts not to go to Montevideo," noted Lorenzo Jalabert D'Amado in his research article "Montevideo 1930: Reassessing the Selection of the First World Cup Host." "It was only when the South American nations, led by Argentina, decided to take the European absence as a personal insult and threatened that if no European teams showed up in Montevideo, they would break off from FIFA and create an independent Pan American football federation that the World Cup project was ultimately saved by the last-minute registrations of Belgium, France, Romania, and Yugoslavia."

Rimet knew that the competition—underwritten by the Uruguayan government—needed European representation in order to truly be considered a global event. When Rimet intervened, four European teams eventually agreed to the trip. The French decided to take the trip as a favor to Rimet. FIFA's vice president at the time, a Belgian named Rodolphe Seeldrayers, insisted that his country participate. The Romanians entered the competition after newly crowned King Carol II was persuaded to send a team, and he leveraged his relationship with the Yugoslavs to convince them to also send a team. "The restrained enthusiasm that manifested itself on the European continent disappointed the Cup's organizers and was criticized both by FIFA officials and South Americans alike," Homburg said.

Carol II was one soccer-mad king. Just 37 years old when he was crowned king, Carol II joined the team on Romania's trip to Uruguay and even took part in daily training sessions. To this day, Carol II, whose father and mother were born in Germany and England, respectively, remains a legend among Romanians for his deep interest in promoting his country's national team. Soccer, he believed, was a way to connect with the Romanian people. It would not be the last time that the World Cup would be used as a political tool among leaders throughout the world looking to promote nationalism.

Rimet's vision, meanwhile, had finally come together. In the end, only 13 teams decided to make the trip. Italy, Sweden, the Netherlands, Spain, and Hungary had all previously been interested in hosting the competition. All of them decided to boycott once Uruguay had been chosen as host nation. All the games would be played in three stadiums—the Estadio Centenario, Estadio Pocitos, and Estadio Gran Parque Central—all of them in Montevideo. All these venues, with the exception of Estadio Pocitos, exist to this day.

The Centenario, with a capacity of 95,000 (but limited to 80,000 for the World Cup), had been built both for the tournament and as a celebration of the centenary of the country's first constitution. Designed by the noted architect and urban planner Juan Scasso, Rimet called the stadium the "temple of football," and it would host 10 of the tournament's 18 matches, including both semifinals and the final. The Centenario, whose construction was funded by the government, was built in the neighborhood of Parque Batlle, an area known for its green space. "The Centenario is a large circular amphitheater built entirely of concrete," Rimet said. "The stadium's dimensions are approximately those of the Colosseum in Rome, and it can hold 80,000 spectators. Located in the center of town, in the middle of a park, it is easily accessible from all neighborhoods, and numerous entrances allow for the fast flow of crowds after a game." Scasso had been more than happy to be involved in the very first World Cup project given his lifelong affection for Peñarol, one of the country's most-storied clubs.

In a letter to Brazil's soccer federation, Rimet reiterated the promise made to all participating nations:

> The Uruguayan Association will give to each Federation, before the match against the respective team, 17 train tickets, from the player's reunion spot to the boarding point, with seats when traveling during the day, and beds for trips at night. The Association (Uruguayan) will give in Montevideo, before the match, the necessary number of train tickets to the return trip. The Association (Uruguayan) will also give round trip first-class train tickets to the participant teams. Only luxurious train rides will be considered. To cover the expenses during the stay in Montevideo, the Uruguayan Association will give to each Federation a daily amount of 75 American dollars. Also, the amount of $0.50 a day to each player during their traveling time. The Uruguayan Association will pay all the teams' transportation expenses, from their hotel to the match location, until the end of the championship.

Money wasn't an issue for Montevideo at the time. It was a bustling port with goods coming and going out of the city. The 1929 stock market crash had yet to have its reverberations in Uruguay. While the effects would be felt a year later, the country had become a major South

American economic center. Uruguay had also not suffered the fallout of World War I, which had ravaged much of Europe. On the contrary, Montevideo was a bustling city and saw an increase in exports and capital investments. Scasso, famous for designing the city's public school buildings, added to Montevideo's Art Deco splendor. His touch was exactly what the World Cup's centerpiece venue needed—both simple and practical in its purpose, but also aesthetically pleasing through its representation of technological advancement and a demonstration of the nation's economic stability. The tournament's official poster was designed by Uruguayan painter and sculptor Guillermo Laborde.

While Laborde's black-and-white design was plastered across Montevideo once the tournament got underway, Scasso's work encountered some problems. A rainy year meant construction on the venue had to endure some delays, and its completion took place a few days into the tournament. Nonetheless, the project took a total of just nine months to complete. The stadium had four grandstands, a press box, and a VIP section that could hold Rimet and nearly 2,000 spectators.

The inaugural World Cup would be the only one in history without a qualifying tournament. The teams, all invited to participate, were drawn into four groups. Group 1 contained four teams, while the remaining three groups were made up of just three apiece. The opening round featured a round-robin format. The winners of each group would progress to the semifinals. Uruguay, Argentina, Brazil, and the United States were seeded, meaning they could not meet in the group stage.

Group 1: Argentina, Chile, France, and Mexico

Group 2: Brazil, Bolivia, and Yugoslavia

Group 3: Uruguay, Peru, and Romania

Group 4: United States, Paraguay, and Belgium

The very first World Cup remains the stuff of sepia-toned photography. While it would only feature 18 matches, it was the start of a tournament that would eventually go on to surpass the Olympics in terms of global popularity.

Group Stage

The construction delay at the Centenario forced the schedule to be hastily rearranged, and Uruguay would not open the tournament. The World Cup instead began with France taking on Mexico on July 13 at the Estadio Pocitos. It took place at the same time as the United States–Belgium match. It was winter in South America, and it snowed on the day of the game. The opening match lacked the glamour of the home side and only drew some 4,000 spectators. Lucien Laurent scored the tournament's first goal after 19 minutes, paving the way for a 4–1 French victory.

Soccer footage prior to 1950 is rare. Newspaper accounts of the time, however, are able to tell us about the many talented players and colorful characters that dominated the sport in those years. Interviews with many of the players from the 1930s, often conducted decades later, remain the only witness accounts of that bygone era.

"[Striker Ernest Liberati] beat the full back and sent over a cross which I managed to volley from about 12 yards into the corner," Laurent recalled in an interview with the *Independent* in 1998. "Of course, back then I couldn't have imagined the significance the goal would have. We didn't even know the World Cup would last. I remember when I got home, there was just a tiny mention in one of the papers. [Soccer] was in its infancy."

Two days later, France took to the field against Argentina at Parque Central. Laurent was unable to get on the score sheet after a tough challenge from Argentina's Luis Monti left him limping for much of the contest. Monti was nicknamed Doble Ancho (Spanish for "double wide") due to his often-aggressive man-to-man coverage. Alex Thépot was the hero for much of the match, but Monti's free kick nine minutes from time was too much for the French goalkeeper to handle. The fireworks wouldn't end there. Brazilian referee Gilberto de Almeida Rêgo whistled the end of the game six minutes early, just as France was mounting an offensive play. The French players protested, and only after a 10-minute dispute did the match resume. The game ended 1–0 in favor of Argentina. It would be the South Americans who would ultimately win the group, thanks largely to center forward Guillermo Stábile. His five goals in two games—including a hat trick in a 6–3 rout of Mexico on July 19—in

9

his international debut would make him a regular in the lineup for the remainder of the tournament.

Three days later, a Stábile brace in a 3–1 victory versus Chile gave the Argentines six points after three games and passage to the semifinals. Argentina had proven the tough opponent many had predicted on the eve of the tournament. In turn, Stábile turned out to be a leader both on the field and in the dressing room. "In 1930 there were no nutritionists or anything like that. In that World Cup we had a typical Argentine diet: meat and more meat. Before playing, we asked for a double portion. It helped me score goals," forward Francisco Varallo recalled in a 2010 interview with the Spanish daily *El País*. "There was one condition: Guillermo Stábile told us no salami sandwiches. We also didn't eat pasta like now, but we took good care of ourselves."

In Group 2, underdogs Yugoslavia got the best of Brazil on July 14, recording a 2–1 win at Parque Central. The outcome, an upset, was sealed in the first half thanks to goals by winger Aleksandar Tirnanić in the 21st minute and forward Ivan Bek just nine minutes later. For Brazil, who at the time played in an all-white uniform, World Cup glory would have to wait. Three days later in the same stadium, Yugoslavia trounced Bolivia 4–0 thanks to three goals in a span of seven minutes midway through the second half. Bek, who netted a brace, spearheaded the scoring that day to help the Yugoslavs win the group. They would be the only European nation to advance out of the group stage.

Brazil's João Coelho Neto, known more commonly by his nickname Preguinho, scored two goals for his country in Brazil's three games. He scored Brazil's first goal in World Cup history in a defeat to Yugoslavia, then added two in a 4–0 win against Bolivia on July 20 at the Centenario. A forward on the soccer field, Preguinho was a multisport athlete after having also played volleyball, basketball, roller hockey, table tennis, and water polo. In addition, he competed as a diver and swimmer, and in track-and-field events. Although he played for famed Brazilian club Fluminense, he maintained his status as an amateur by refusing payment his entire career, which ended in 1939.

Group 3 opened with Romania's emphatic 3–1 win on July 14 against Peru at Estadio Pocitos. The game remains noteworthy for being the first ever at a World Cup to see a player ejected: midfielder Plácido Galindo of Peru in the 70th minute. Galindo was involved in a series of fights throughout the emotional match, even breaking the leg of Romanian defender Adalbert Steiner. As a result, Chilean referee Alberto Warnken demanded Galindo leave the field, officially marking the first ejection in World Cup history.

The group's most anticipated game would be played four days later at the Centenario, featuring Uruguay and Peru. With nearly 58,000 spectators in attendance and scaffolding still visible in some parts of the venue, the game was preceded by a ceremony honoring the country's centennial celebrations. The team had spent two months in training camp, going into complete isolation at the Prado Park Hotel in Montevideo. Goalkeeper Andrés Mazali, who had helped Uruguay win two gold medals, was dropped from the roster for breaking a strict curfew one night to visit his wife. Alberto Suppici, Uruguay's head coach, was a disciplinarian and did not tolerate dissension among his players.

Uruguay was on a mission to win the tournament at home and prove that their success at the Olympic level had been no fluke. On the day of the match, Enrique Ballestrero started in goal, recording the shutout after Uruguay could only muster a 1–0 win. The narrow victory, via a goal from Héctor Castro in the 60th minute, was a result of Peru's defense putting on an extraordinary performance that afternoon. But Peru gained lots of attention. A dispatch from the Associated Press noted the following: "Among the Peruvian players stood out: the center half, Galindo, and the goalkeeper, [Jorge] Padrón, especially the latter, who, after a somewhat indecisive first half, stopped formidably countless shots. Of the forwards highlighted [José María] Lavalle, who led the line admirably and shot good shots."

It was a determined Uruguay that took to the field on July 21 at the Centenario against Romania. The 70,000 in attendance witnessed a masterful performance by the hosts, cruising to a 4–0 win. Suppici's move to start Héctor Scarone, who scored a goal, proved key as he helped propel the Uruguayan attack. The win gave Uruguay top spot in the group and passage to the semifinals. The team's performance confirmed that La Celeste were still the heavy favorites to win it all.

Group 4 opened on July 13, with the United States taking on Belgium at Parque Central. The Americans, which featured six British-born players, won 3–0 following two goals by Bart McGhee. One salient footnote to this game involved the third U.S. goal, scored by Bert Patenaude. The 69th-minute strike marked the first time a header had resulted in a goal at a World Cup. Jimmy Douglas, who started the game, was the first goalkeeper in World Cup history to record a shutout. The result was unexpected, prompting the Uruguayan daily newspaper *Imparcial* to declare that "the large score of the American victory has really surprised the experts."

Nicknamed the "shot-putters" by the press because of their size, the United States won the group four days later after another 3–0 victory, this time in a win against Paraguay. Patenaude scored a hat trick in the game, although it took FIFA 76 years before crediting him with one. The amended statistic made Patenaude the player to record the World Cup's first-ever hat trick. The box score published in several newspapers at the time, including Argentina's *La Prensa*, credited Patenaude with three goals. The discrepancy—the goal had originally been credited to Tim Florie—is likely to have been a result of players not wearing numbers on the back of their jerseys at the time. "The choice of the seeded teams was justified, with the exception of Brazil," Rimet noted, "who was beaten out in their group by Yugoslavia."

Semifinals

The Centenario hosted the last three games. The first semifinal, between Argentina and the United States, was contested on July 26. The teams were evenly matched in the early going, but Monti's physical play made the difference. Monti's goal in the 20th minute put the South Americans ahead, while his rough play—typical at the time—put Ralph Tracey out of the game by the second half with a knee injury. Down a player (there were no substitutes in those days), Argentina steamrolled the Americans. Stábile scored two goals as Argentina won 6–1. *El Heraldo de Madrid*, a Spanish newspaper published from 1890 to 1939, summed up the game this way: "In the second half, the American defense was powerless to contain the impetuous attacks of the Argentine strikers, who acted more blended than in the first 45 minutes. . . . In this second half, the Americans gave the impression of being completely confused by the technique used by the Argentines."

The Argentines were a tough side, and they physically overpowered the Americans that day. London's *Telegraph* noted that the South Americans "proved too strong—literally—even for the fit and fast American 'shot-putters,' who found themselves only one down at halftime but with one player missing, another suffering from a kick in the jaw, and their 'keeper also badly injured. It was not surprising that Argentina put five goals past them in the second half."

The following day, Uruguay won their semifinal against Yugoslavia by the same score. Yugoslavia took the lead after just four minutes with forward Dorde Vujadinović, to the dismay of the 80,000 fans jammed into the Centenario. Goals from Cea in the 18th minute and two from forward Peregrino Anselmo in the 20th and 31st minutes gave Uruguay a 3–1 lead. The most controversial moment of the match came as a result of Anselmo's first goal. Rêgo, the match official for the game, failed to see that a police officer along the sidelines had kicked the ball back in play, a move that resulted in Anselmo's goal. Yugoslavia's Milorad Arsenijević confronted the officer, even grabbing him by the throat, and authorities even threatened to arrest him after the final whistle.

Despite the three goals, Yugoslav goalkeeper Milovan Jakšić—nicknamed "El Grande Milovan" by journalists for his saves at this tournament—kept the score respectable with a series of stops. After World War II, he helped establish Red Star Belgrade, one of the best clubs in Serbian soccer history, and served as the club's technical director. *El Sol*, a Spanish newspaper in operation between 1917 and 1939, published the following dispatch of the game: "The first half ended with three goals to one in favor of Uruguay. From the first moment, the superiority of the local players over their opponents was evident. However, the Yugoslavs produced a good impression because they made excellent plays made up of short passes. The game during this time recalled the characteristics seen by Argentine teams. In general, the game was animated and at times quite abrupt. The goalkeeper stood out remarkably for the Yugoslav team."

Three more goals in the second half, two from Cea in the 67th and 72nd minutes, allowed him to complete the hat trick. The article in *El Sol* described the game's final 45 minutes this way: "In the second half, the superiority of the Uruguayan team became even more evident. As they made forays against the enemy goal, the enthusiasm of the public overflowed. The match ended 6–1 in favor of Uruguay. The superiority of the local team was so obvious that most of the match was played near the Yugoslavian goal. Thanks to the magnificent performance of the Yugoslav goalkeeper, who played brilliantly, the Uruguayan triumph was prevented from reaching truly exceptional proportions."

Uruguay had reached the all–South American final against Argentina in a battle between teams with formidable offenses. Accounts differ as to whether a third-place match was originally scheduled. A FIFA technical committee report following the 1986 World Cup included full retrospective rankings of all teams at previous finals, ranking the United States third and Yugoslavia fourth due to better goal differential. In 2010, the son of Kosta Hadži, the then-head of the Yugoslav delegation at the 1930 World Cup and vice president of the country's FA, claimed that Yugoslavia had been awarded a bronze medal by virtue of their defeat to Uruguay.

Final: Uruguay vs. Argentina

The buzz in Montevideo and throughout Uruguay and in neighboring Argentina was palpable in the days leading up to the July 30 final at the Centenario. The creation of the World Cup was meant to undercut the Olympics, and this game would go a long way in doing just that. The first World Cup final, as it turned out, was a rematch of the gold medal game at the Olympics just two years earlier. In his book *The Mammoth Book of the World Cup*, author Nick Holt noted that "this match may not have had much impact in Europe, but the atmosphere during the build-up in Montevideo and Buenos Aires was near rabid."

In the three days between Uruguay's semifinal demolition of Yugoslavia and the final, interest throughout the country indeed reached a fever pitch. While Argentina was confident of a victory, Uruguay saw this game as an opportunity to get one over on their larger neighbor. With tensions simmering, extra police were deployed outside the Centenario. As fans packed into the stadium, Uruguay's coach Alberto Suppici opted for a more defensive formation.

The referee for the game was John Langenus of Belgium. Langenus had already officiated three games at the tournament as the main match official, and two others as a linesman. He had also officiated at the 1928 Olympics, although this game would turn out to be the biggest of his career. Langenus had been on the receiving end of criticism, most notably in the semifinal between Argentina and the United States when he whistled a foul against the Americans. English journalist Brian Glanville described the incident this way in his book *The Story of the World Cup*: "At this the team's medical attendant raced, bellicose, on to the field, to berate Langenus. Having had his say, he flung his box of medicines to the ground, the box burst open, various bottles smashed, including one full of chloroform, and its fumes rose to overpower the American. He was helped from the field."

A peculiar disagreement before kickoff on which team should provide the match ball forced FIFA to intervene. Langenus ultimately decreed that the Argentines could provide the ball for the first half, the Uruguayans for the second. Before 69,000 spectators (20,000 of them Argentines who had made the trip), Uruguay again confirmed its global supremacy. Tactically, both teams lined up in a similar formation—a 2–3–5 with a multiskilled, two-way player in the middle of the park—although they featured contrasting styles within that same framework. The emphasis in those days was on attack, and the final, in that regard, did not disappoint. Both teams featured inside forwards who tracked back, essentially turning the formation into a 2–3–2–3. While Argentina relied on the individual flair of Monti in midfield, Uruguay used passing to effectively break down the opposing defense and outmaneuver any Argentine attempt at an offside trap.

The Argentina-Uruguay rivalry, a derby given the geographic proximity of the two nations, continues to this day. Argentina led 2–1 at halftime. After just 12 minutes, Pablo Dorado put Uruguay ahead, before Argentine winger Carlos Peucelle equalized eight minutes later. In the 37th minute, Stábile, who would finish as the tournament's top scorer

15

with eight goals, gave Argentina the lead as the sides headed into the dressing room.

Uruguay's offensive might would shine through in the second half, scoring three unanswered goals for the 4–2 win. Uruguay tied the game 12 minutes into the second half thanks to Cea's fifth goal of the tournament, before Santos Iriarte scored in the 68th minute to make it 3–2 off a 25-yard shot. With a minute left in the match, Castro scored a fourth to seal the win for Uruguay. The final whistle brought with it hugs on the field and loud cheers from the flag-waving crowd.

The Uruguayan belief of *garra charrúa*, a spirit that highlights the importance of tenacity alongside skill, had come into play for Uruguay. Literally meaning "the claw," this characteristic brings to the forefront the mentality Uruguay would employ in 1930 and at future World Cups when players believed they had greater fury and intensity compared to their opponents. The notion of *garra* isn't new. It dates back centuries and has come to mean different things in different eras. The phrase comes from the Charrúa Indians, a tribe of indigenous warriors. Overshadowed by their South American neighbors, La Celeste have always had to fight harder to maintain their status as a soccer nation.

"We used to be known for our violent play—whether it was a legitimate accusation or not—and not being known for our fair play. We have responded to that by creating great footballers," said Óscar Washington Tabárez, who went on to coach Uruguay at the 1990 and 2018 World Cups. "We have worked hard at youth level and we only have a little over three million inhabitants. When you produce one great player in Uruguay, that's equal to 20 in Brazil and 10 in Argentina. Therefore, we have had to approach the game differently compared to everyone else."

Rimet, writing in his journal, noted the enthusiasm of that day. "In truth, I have rarely seen a storm of enthusiasm, of released emotion, comparable to the one that arose from the stadium bleachers at the end of this match," he wrote. "Maybe the Uruguayans attached to their triumph excessive significance, but they shouted their joy with such conviction that it almost seems, in this minute, shared by the whole mass of spectators. The squall grew again when the [Uruguayan] national flag was hoisted atop the stadium."

Uruguay's triumph wasn't without controversy. Monti, it turns out, had been on the receiving end of death threats on the eve of the game. Holt writes that, "in keeping with the gangster age . . . Monti was told by Buenos Aires mobsters that unpleasant things might happen to his family if Argentina lost." Uruguayan gangsters had also gotten to Monti in the days leading up to the match. Following those threats, Langenus demanded (and received) a police escort so he could safely depart the stadium once the game was over. Curiously, Langenus was also tasked with working as a journalist, writing up dispatches and sending them back to Europe via ship. The German soccer magazine *Kicker*, which did not send a correspondent to the tournament, ran Langenus's reports of the first-round matches near the end of July. The report regarding the World Cup final appeared a month after it had been contested. Not surprisingly, there wasn't a negative word said regarding the refereeing that had taken place.

In Buenos Aires, upset Argentines threw rocks at the Uruguayan consulate. In Montevideo, the government declared the following day a national holiday. Rimet presented Nasazzi with the trophy that would eventually come to bear his name and would be awarded to the world champions for the next 40 years. Uruguay, undefeated at the tournament, could not have given its citizens a better gift in the year of its centenary.

For FIFA, the tournament had been a big success. As a result of holding the competition, FIFA "earned a net profit," and its proceeds "showed a remarkable propensity for growth," Homburg said. "Moreover, they [the three war World Cups] were understood and read as a message that FIFA was on the right track; there was a market for the product it offered." FIFA, founded as a nonprofit organization (it maintains that dubious status to this day), had created a new revenue stream, one that would increase substantially in the coming decades with the advent of television and increased marketing and commercial opportunities.

"The World Cup is solid gold. It's a symbol," Rimet noted. "The World Cup must be the first among sporting events and gold is the symbol of primacy."

1934 WORLD CUP

The second edition of the World Cup was held in Italy at a time of sweeping political unrest throughout Europe. The tournament would be one of the first during that decade in which dictatorial regimes used sports for political gain. Benito Mussolini and the fascist regime meddled with the Italian team before and throughout the tournament. As Adolf Hitler would do at the Berlin Olympics two years later, Mussolini used the event to extol the virtues of his fascist state. For Mussolini, victory for his nation at the tournament would help with the propaganda machine he had unleashed.

This World Cup was the first to feature a qualifying tournament. Thirty-six countries applied to take part in the 16-team competition. Defending champions Uruguay declined to take part, a retaliation for the many European nations that had refused to travel to South America four years earlier. The four British Home Nations also refused to participate, even though FIFA had offered England and Scotland automatic berths. Football Association committee member Charles Sutcliffe called the tournament "a joke," according to the book *The Leaguers: The Making of Professional Football in England, 1900–1939.*

"The national associations of England, Scotland, Wales, and Ireland have quite enough to do in their own International Championship which seems to me a far better World Championship than the one to be staged in Rome," Sutcliffe said.

After a lengthy decision-making process, Italy was chosen as the host nation in 1932 at a meeting in Stockholm, with the bid beating out Sweden. Despite being the host nation, Italy was still required to qualify—the only time in tournament history a nation had to do so—by defeating Greece 4–0 in Milan. Qualifying matches were based on geography. Twelve of the 16 spots were allocated to Europe, three to the Americas, and one to Africa or Asia. Withdrawals by Chile and Peru meant Argentina and Brazil qualified without playing a game. The United States, the last team to qualify, defeated Mexico 4–2 in Rome on the eve of the World Cup. For Mexico, they had taken the long journey to Italy just to go home without ever playing in the finals.

Instead of a single city—Olympic-style tournament as had taken place in Montevideo—the Italians decided to host matches in eight cities. The final was slated for the capital, Rome. Italy had been a sensible host. The Stadio Nazionale PNF, built in 1927, was a modern multipurpose venue that was one of the best in Europe at the time. Italy's fascist party was formed in 1922 but didn't exert dictatorial rule under Mussolini until 1925. In 1926, soccer became a fascist game. Italy's first division, divided up into regions, was made into a national league and renamed Serie A. The aim was to create a sense of national identity among Italians and form a tournament that was more competitive in order to develop the best players for the national team. The Italians would also play with the *fascio littorio* on their left chests, a symbol depicting a bundle of sticks and an axe. Carried by the Romans as a sign of law and order, it had been used by Mussolini's regime once he came to power. The World Cup would be a great way to show the world Italy's domination, both on and off the field, in the span of just a few weeks.

Italy's nationalistic furor spilled over to the team. The Italians featured three naturalized Argentine-born players—known as *oriundi*—that included Monti, Raimundo Orsi, and Enrique Guaita. The term is used to describe people of Italian descent living in a country other than the one of their birth. After Italy's unification in 1861, a mass emigration of Italians had commenced. Buenos Aires was a favored destination for many immigrants, second only to New York. As a result, Italian culture and language took hold in Argentina. By the 1930s, political instability in Argentina caused by a coup d'état prompted many to seek other places to live. For talented soccer players at the time, Serie A offered both cultural familiarity and high salaries. Under Mussolini, these players were automatically considered citizens. Italy manager Vittorio Pozzo, who also worked as a journalist for the Italian daily *La Stampa*, took advantage of this law to call up Monti, a veteran of the 1930 World Cup, and several others. Pozzo himself referred to their eligibility for military service as a reason why they could play for the Azzurri, saying, "If they can die for Italy, they can play for Italy."

The group stage used in the first World Cup was discarded in favor of a knockout tournament. If a game was tied after 90 minutes, 30 minutes of extra time was employed to determine a winner. If the score was still tied after extra time, the match was to be replayed the following day. The tournament's eight seeded teams—Argentina, Brazil, Germany, Italy, the Netherlands, Austria, Czechoslovakia, and Hungary—were kept apart in the first round of the bracket-style competition.

Round of 16

The tournament began on May 27, with all eight games played on the same day at 4 p.m. A superior Italy squashed the United States 7–1 before 30,000 fans at the Stadio Nazionale PNF, spearheaded by an Angelo Schiavo hat trick and Orsi's brace. The Italians opened the match with the outstretched-arm fascist salute to the cheering crowd, which included Mussolini. Italy dominated the match, with most of the action taking place in the American half of the field. Footage from Italy's Istituto Luce, founded in 1924 and used as a propaganda tool under Mussolini, glorified the team's victory to the masses.

The gray-haired Pozzo, known for being a great motivator of players, composed his team around a 2–3–2–3 formation that saw Schiavo in the center forward position, with Giuseppe Meazza on the right and Giovanni Ferrari on the left. The trio made for a powerful attack, aided by Orsi on the left flank and Monti in midfield responsible for doing lots of the dirty work needed to clear balls and transition into attack.

At the Stadio Luigi Ferraris in Genoa, Italy's quarterfinal opponent Spain defeated Brazil 3–1 thanks to a José Iraragorri brace. The Brazilians, who fielded a second-string side for this tournament, had only kept Carvalho Leite from the previous World Cup. Nonetheless, the team featured a budding star named Leônidas da Silva—known simply as Leônidas, his nickname translating from Portuguese to "The Black Diamond"—who would go on to be one of the most important players of the pre–World War II era. It had become a custom among Brazilian players to use a nickname starting at the turn of the century, a tradition that continues to this day. Credited with inventing the bicycle kick, Leônidas would score his team's only goal at this World Cup, a glimpse of what would come four years later.

1930s Innovation: Balls

A leather soccer ball like this one was used throughout the 1930s.

The nationalism of Benito Mussolini's fascist regime called for the balls used at the 1934 World Cup to be produced in Italy. The majority of soccer balls at the time were manufactured in Great Britain. The leather ball used at the 1934 tournament, known as the Federale 102, was made up of 13 polygonal panels sewn together at 90-degree angles. For the very first time, the laces were placed on a separate panel to facilitate the inflating of the ball. The cotton laces—the first time they were made of such material—made the ball easier to head.

By comparison, five different types of balls had been used at the 1930 tournament. The most famous, known as the T-Model, featured 12 panels and thick leather laces. It was the ball Uruguay chose to play with against Argentina in the second half of the World Cup final. The thicker leather of those balls often absorbed water, making them heavier and harder to kick and head.

The Federale 102, named after its Italian manufacturer, was an improvement and opened the door to ball innovation. In 1872, it was agreed that the ball "must be spherical with a circumference of 27 to 28 inches" and weigh 13 to 15 ounces. The rules were revised in 1937, when the official weight was slightly increased to range between 14 and 16 ounces. It would take another four decades before the look and feel of a soccer ball would dramatically change.

Austria, one of the pre-tournament favorites, edged out France 3–2 in extra time after the match at the Stadio Benito Mussolini in Turin ended tied at one. The greatest period in Austrian soccer came in the 1930s when they enjoyed a 14-game unbeaten streak. Under manager Hugo Meisl, a World War I veteran and hailing from a Jewish family, the Austrians became the envy of Europe. The extra session, the first in World Cup history, saw three goals—although it was a Josef Bican strike in the 109th minute that made the difference in the end. Known as the "Wunderteam," the Austrians featured superstar Matthias Sindelar. The slender center forward, who scored his team's opening goal, had become famous throughout the continent as a fantastic dribbler and creative player.

In Naples, meanwhile, Hungary overcame Egypt, the first African nation to participate at a World Cup finals, 4–2, at the Stadio Giorgio Ascarelli, with Géza Toldi tallying a brace. Oldřich Nejedlý's goal in the 67th minute at the Stadio Littorio in Trieste allowed Czechoslovakia to defeat Romania 2–1. At Milan's Stadio San Siro, Switzerland outlasted the Netherlands 3–2, while Germany breezed past Belgium 5–2 at the Stadio Giovanni Berta in Florence via an Edmund Conen hat trick. Down 2–1 at halftime, the Germans reversed the score, proving that they too could contend for the trophy. In the last match of the round, Sweden defeated Argentina, runners-up four years earlier, 3–2, as Knut Kroon's goal ensured that no South American nation would reach the quarterfinals.

Quarterfinals

The remaining eight teams played for a chance to advance to the semifinals on May 31. All four matches kicked off at 4:30 p.m. The round would go on to feature some of the tournament's best, and most vicious, matches. Millions huddled around radios listening to Italy play Spain in Florence before 35,000 spectators. The Azzurri's attack had a much tougher defense to face. Spain's goalkeeper and captain, Ricardo Zamora, was one of the best in the world. Getting past him would prove difficult, although not impossible.

Spain jumped into the lead in the 30th minute when Luis Regueiro's shot got past goalkeeper Giampiero Combi. Italy leveled the score in the 44th minute through a Ferrari goal. The Spanish players protested the goal—video footage today shows that Schiavo had impeded Zamora from getting to the ball—but the goal was allowed to stand. The bruising encounter ended in a 1–1 draw after extra time failed to produce a goal. The sides would have to play each other again 24 hours later.

The replay, played on June 1 in unbearably humid weather, featured plenty of fresh legs: seven changes for Spain and five for the Italians. A larger crowd of 43,000 in Florence was eager to see an Italian win. Spain, on the other hand, was considerably weakened after being forced to go without Zamora in the lineup. Meazza's header off a corner kick after just 12 minutes propelled the Italians to the semifinals, to the delight of Mussolini. Two Spanish goals were disallowed by Swiss referee Rene Mercet; his poor officiating met with criticism and eventually a suspension by his country's football association.

In the round's other matches: Austria outlasted Hungary 2–1 in Bologna, reaching the semifinals following a 51st-minute goal by Karl Zischek. In Milan, two goals in a span of a mere three minutes from Karl Hohmann midway through the second half got Germany through with a 2–1 victory versus Sweden. In Turin, Czechoslovakia edged Switzerland 3–2, earning passage to the semifinals via a Nejedlý goal, his second of the tournament, eight minutes from time.

Semifinals

The Italians faced Austria on just two days' rest following the two-game battle against Spain. Nonetheless, the game had all the talent of a final, and 60,000 fans squeezed into the San Siro under a torrential rain. The Austrians, who relied on possession and intricate passing, found themselves bogged down by the muddy field. As a result, the Italians managed to take the lead after 19 minutes, with Guaita putting the ball past Peter Platzer after the goalkeeper had collided with Meazza. The Italians took that 1–0 lead into the dressing room. The Austrians came out rejuvenated in the second half as the attack—spearheaded by Sindelar—found itself in desperate search of a tying goal. Sindelar, nicknamed Der Papierene (German for "the Paper Man") because of his thin build and ability to get past defenders, was neutralized by Monti. The

Italo-Argentine had once again come through for Pozzo. The Italians prevailed and were off to the final.

In the other semifinal, played in Rome, Czechoslovakia, one of the most entertaining teams at this tournament, would ultimately defeat Germany. A Nejedlý hat trick, two of those goals coming in the second half, was too much for the German backline to handle. There would be no German comeback this time around. Nejedlý's five goals would be good enough to make him the tournament's top scorer. Mussolini's dream of an Italy–Germany final, where he would have had a chance to show his domination over Adolf Hitler, was not to be. Instead, Italy now had to tangle with Czechoslovakia for the World Cup title.

Third-Place Game

The very first third-place match ever played at a World Cup took place on June 7 in Naples. The semifinal losers, Austria and Germany, would initiate a tradition—that of playing a meaningless game after having failed to reach the final—which lives on to this day. The notion of a bronze medal in soccer competition never took on the cachet experienced at the Olympics. As a result, this game—and the many that would follow in the ensuing decades—most often featured second-string players and no more intensity than a friendly.

In the inaugural edition of the third-place match, Germany defeated Austria 3–2 before just 7,000 spectators. Ernst Lehner's goal for the Germans just 25 seconds into the match set the tone. A Conen goal in the 27th minute, his fourth of the competition, doubled the German lead, but Austria pulled one back a minute later with Johann Horvath. A second Lehner goal three minutes before halftime paved the way for Germany's win. The soccer rivalry between the two nations that would continue in the ensuing decades would take a dark turn. Meisl died of a heart attack in 1937. A year later, the Anschluss Österreichs marked the annexation of Austria (where Hitler had been born) into Nazi Germany. War was on the horizon. Sindelar, however, refused to play for Germany. On January 23, 1939, both Sindelar and his girlfriend, Camilla Castagnola, were found dead inside their Vienna apartment. The official cause was carbon monoxide poisoning. It marked a tragic end to the glorious Wunderteam.

Final: Italy vs. Czechoslovakia

The night before the final, Mussolini met with Pozzo and the Italian players. He gave them an impassioned speech before the Italians faced off against Czechoslovakia in Rome. "If the Czechs play fair, we'll play fair. That's the most important thing," Mussolini told the players. "But if they want to play dirty, then we Italians have to play dirtier." For both the Italian team and Mussolini, winning the final would cap off a memorable tournament.

The Italians, favored to win, had the power and stamina of Monti and Meazza, but the Czechoslovakians featured the artistry and skill of Nejedlý. The match—played before 50,000 fans (2,000 of them traveling from Czechoslovakia)—was an even affair in the first half and for much of the second. Goalkeepers on both sides, Combi and František Plánička, kept the game scoreless. While both also captained their sides that day, it would be Antonín Puć to show the most leadership on the field. Puc's attempt on goal in the 71st minute beat Combi to put Czechoslovakia ahead. They could have put the game away, but Jiří Sobotka and Nejedlý were both thwarted by the post and crossbar, respectively. Italy had been spared.

Just when it appeared that Italy would lose, Orsi tied the score nine minutes from time. The game ended 1–1, the players now forced to play an additional 30 minutes in the intense heat. The thermometer read 104 degrees, and it certainly impacted the quality of play that afternoon. The Italians didn't play the most entertaining form of soccer, often resorting to brute force to outmuscle opponents. The scorching heat turned out to have hurt Czechoslovakia more, while the Italians were able to power through aided by the crowd's support.

The tense match was settled five minutes into extra time when a limping Meazza pushed the ball up the right wing for Guaita in a central position. Guaita passed the ball forward to Schiavo who put the winning shot into the left side of the goal past Plánička for his fourth goal of the competition. The Italians had put together a remarkable comeback to win the World Cup. A beaming Mussolini presented Combi with the trophy. The Italian players lifted Pozzo on their shoulders to the delight of the cheering crowd. Monti had added a World Cup to the runners-up medal earned four years earlier with Argentina.

The following day, the Italian sports daily *La Gazzetta dello Sport*, famous for its pink news pages, featured the headline "The Azzurri Conquer the World Cup in the Presence of Mussolini." The regime granted each player a cash prize of $17,000. In a tournament marred by violent games and poor refereeing (something that would unfortunately take place at future World Cups as well), Italy became the second straight host nation to capture the title to mark the start of a decade of soccer domination.

1938 WORLD CUP

Four years after the World Cup in Italy, the third edition of the tournament would be the last to be staged before World War II. Europe was on the brink of war. Hitler and Mussolini wielded power, and fascism had also taken its grip on Spain, which did not take part in the World Cup after having to deal with a civil war that eventually brought Francisco Franco to power. By the summer of 1938, the Third Reich had already established absolute power in Germany, annexed Austria, and established concentration camps. Within a few years, Hitler would invade Poland. In 1939, both France and Britain would declare war on Germany, which would eventually plunge the continent—and later the world—into war.

France, Rimet's birthplace, was chosen to host the competition, picked ahead of Argentina and Germany. FIFA's decision caused outrage in South America, who unsuccessfully argued that the host nation should alternate between the two continents. As a result, Uruguay again boycotted the 16-nation tournament, joined this time by Argentina. It was the first time the hosts, France, as well as the defending champions automatically qualified for the finals. For the remaining 14 spots, 11 were allocated to Europe, two to the Americas, and one to Asia. In the end, only three non-European nations—Brazil, Cuba, and the Dutch East Indies (now known as Indonesia)—made the trip to France.

The hosts, along with Italy, Germany, Czechoslovakia, Hungary, Cuba, Brazil, and Austria, were seeded ahead of the draw held in Paris. Austria, swallowed up by Germany, did not participate, and their round-of-16 opponents, Sweden, were given a bye to the next round as a result. The format remained the same as the one used in 1934: a single-elimination tournament with the winners advancing to the next round. Games that ended in a draw would be replayed. For the first time at a World Cup, numbers were required to appear on the backs of players' jerseys.

The Italians, who won a gold medal at the 1936 Berlin Olympics with a team made up of university students, came into the World Cup as favorites. The Germans, too, were put in that category after the Nazi regime ordered that Austria's best players join their national team. The Wunderteam was no more. England, arguably the best team at the time, was offered Austria's place in the competition but again refused to participate as a result of their ongoing dispute with FIFA. England were one of the best teams at the time, their 3–2 win in November 1934 against Italy—a match dubbed the "Battle of Highbury"—proving that theory. Nonetheless, the inventors of the modern game would have to wait until 1950 to make their first appearance at a World Cup finals.

Round of 16

The World Cup would be played in 10 venues in nine French cities. Lyon, however, never got the opportunity to host the Austria-Sweden match. The tournament officially kicked off on June 4 at the Parcs des Princes in Paris, with Germany squaring off against Switzerland on a hot afternoon. The Germans were surprised by the Parisians, some hurling rocks at the team bus as it approached the stadium. Once inside, they were greeted by jeers as the German players made the Nazi salute before kickoff. The crowd of nearly 30,000 then watched in awe as the sides traded goals in the first half in a game that ended 1–1 following extra time. The teams would be forced to replay the match five days later at the same venue. The Germans, not sharp in the first match, came out strong in the replay and jumped out to 2–0 in the game's opening 22 minutes.

Four unanswered Swiss goals—including a brace from André Abegglen—eliminated Germany. Switzerland's 4–2 upset win turned around a result that had previously appeared out of reach.

The round's other seven matches were played on June 5 and kicked off simultaneously at 5 p.m. In Reims, Hungary strolled past the Dutch East Indies 6–0 at the Vélodrome Municipal. Two goals apiece by György Sárosi and Gyula Zsengellér sealed the win. Sárosi, primarily used as a striker, had the ability to play a variety of positions, including as a midfielder and central defender. It was this versatility that made Sárosi one of the best players of his era and catapulted Hungary as one of the favorites for the trophy.

France, meanwhile, eliminated Belgium at Stade Olympique de Colombes in the Paris suburb of Colombes, a venue that had hosted the 1924 Summer Olympics. A Jean Nicolas brace delighted the 30,000 in attendance and put the hosts through to the quarterfinals with relative ease. At the same time in Marseilles, Italy barely got past Norway 2–1, as the match at the Stade Vélodrome turned out to be harder for Pozzo's men than first expected. It took an extra-time goal from Silvio Piola in the 94th minute to power the defending champions through to the next round. Piola, who was making his World Cup debut, formed a formidable attack alongside Meazza, who was named team captain ahead of the tournament. Piola's knack for goals would make him one of the best to ever suit up for Italy. He remains the third-highest scorer in national team history and holds the record for most career goals in Serie A with 290. Awaiting Piola and his teammates in the quarterfinals was France.

Cuba and Romania, meanwhile, locked horns at the Stade du T.O.E.C. in Toulouse. The game turned out to be a rollicking affair thanks to six goals. Extra time could not produce a winner, and the 3–3 final score forced a replay. The sides met again on June 9 at the same venue. Despite being down 1–0 at the half, the underdog Cubans managed two goals—from Héctor Socorro in the 51st minute and what turned out to be the winning strike seven minutes later by Tomás Fernández—for the 2–1 upset.

The round of 16 continued with Brazil taking on Poland at the Stade de la Meinau in Strasbourg. The Brazilians put on a clinic. In the end, a Leônidas hat trick was enough to win the game, 6–5, his goal in the 104th minute clinching the victory for the Brazilians. Meanwhile, in the round's final matchup, Czechoslovakia overcame the Netherlands at Stade Municipal in Le Havre. The game was scoreless after 90 minutes, but the Czechoslovakians put on the pressure in extra time for a 3–0 win.

Quarterfinals

The tournament's eight remaining teams featured favorites Italy, hosts France, and Hungary. Cuba and Switzerland were the surprise sides of the round after pulling off upsets in the round of 16. Brazil, the round's lone South American representative, was also a formidable opponent, but not yet the powerhouse that would emerge in ensuing decades.

The matches were again played at the same time on June 12 at 5 p.m. Hungary proved too strong for Switzerland at Stade Victor Boucquey in Lille, and they were through to the semifinals thanks to a 2–0 win. Sweden, with their fresh legs after getting a bye, crushed Cuba 8–0 at Stade du Fort Carré in Antibes. A pair of hat tricks from Harry Andersson and Gustav Wetterström overwhelmed the Cubans.

In Colombes, the French crowd greeted the Italians with hostility. Anti-fascist Italians had moved to France and were in the crowd that baton-wielding police had to disperse outside the stadium. "In 2001 I interviewed Piero Rava, the only surviving member of that team. He was unable to remember the alleged protest," observed English journalist Simon Martin. "Whether his memory had been reduced by the years or was deliberately selective I was never able to ascertain. . . . Less doubt surrounds the intended recipient of the protests: the team. As the representative of the regime rather than the nation, it reaped what Fascism had sowed 12 years earlier with its politicization of football."

Both France and Italy traditionally wore blue shirts. The 58,000 in attendance did not appreciate when the Italians, deemed the road team, opted to play in an all-black uniform—the color of the ruling fascist party—on orders from Mussolini, rather than their usual white shirts. After the defending champions greeted the fans with a fascist salute (something they repeated on Pozzo's orders), the French crowd whistled during the playing of the Italian anthem. Pozzo, who had served in

World War I on Italy's northern border, was a patriotic man. His loyalty to the fascist regime would hurt his legacy in the postwar years, although he would continue to serve as national team manager until 1948. Pozzo treated his players like a military unit. Pozzo's training sessions involved long runs through the woods and plenty of physical conditioning using a medicine ball. That military-style fitness regimen would help the Italians persevere at this tournament.

Once the game got underway, the sides traded goals in the game's opening 10 minutes. Gino Colaussi put Italy ahead in the ninth minute, only to see France even the score with Oscar Heisserer a minute later. The French backline, however, struggled throughout much of the second half. Two Piola goals, in the 51st and 72nd minutes, silenced the crowd and ensured the Italians' passage to the semifinals. The fascist daily *Il Popolo d'Italia* basked in the win. "It is Italy—the blue shirt with the Savoy shield and the Fascio Littorio on its chest—that has won the right to contest the final in Paris," the newspaper reported.

Brazil's match at Bordeaux's Parc Lescure against Czechoslovakia proved to be a tense affair. The shambolic officiating of referee Pál von Hertzka of Hungary certainly didn't help. As a result, the game devolved into a brutal series of fouls. Brazilian Zezé Procópio was sent off after just 10 minutes for a vicious foul on Nejedlý. His teammate, Arthur Machado, and Jan Říha were also sent off just before halftime. It was the first time in World Cup history that three players were sent off in a single match.

In between, the sides managed to score some goals. The Brazilians opened the scoring after 30 minutes with Leônidas. The Czechoslovakians managed to draw level on a Nejedlý penalty kick in the 65th minute. The penalty came after Domingos da Guia played the ball with his hand in the box. Plánička suffered a broken right arm and Nejedlý a broken leg, which forced him to leave the match early, as a result of the brutality. On the Brazilian side, Leônidas and Perácio were also forced to abandon the match as the sides played to a 1–1 draw after extra time failed to yield a goal.

The game was replayed two days later at the same venue. The "Battle of Bourdeax"—as the game was later dubbed—left both sides with no choice but to field reserve players. Leônidas recovered in time for him to play the second match. It was his goal that put Brazil level. The South Americans won the game in the end, 2–1, thanks to a goal by Roberto in the 62nd minute. Brazil hobbled into the semifinals, where they would face Italy.

Semifinals

The tournament's final four teams—Italy, Brazil, Hungary, and Sweden—represented a clash of styles. Pozzo used *Il metodo*, a tactical formula that had worked well for the Italians. Brazil, their semifinal opponent, employed a 2–3–5 lineup at a time when most nations had adapted the "W-M" formation. It's true that the Italians were a better team, but the Brazilians had been hampered by injuries and an unbearable travel schedule. Aside from the long boat trip to Europe, the team was forced to travel great distances by train between games. On only two days' rest after the bruising Czechoslovakia match, the players and staff traveled 400 miles across the south of France from Bordeaux to the seaside city of Marseilles.

The June 16 game between Italy and Brazil—the first time these sides ever met at a World Cup—would be the start of a soccer rivalry that would come to highlight a series of great matches in the decades to come. The Brazilians were without the injured Leônidas, forcing coach Ademar Pimenta to again reshuffle his lineup with eight changes from their previous game. Despite some notable absences, Brazil played well, and the game was scoreless at halftime. The Italians would break the deadlock in the 51st minute with Colaussi. The Italians doubled the lead on a penalty kick after Domingos da Guia kicked Piola in the box. The Brazilian defender argued with the match officials that his actions had been in retaliation for Piola having kicked him first. Referee Hans Wüthrich of Switzerland whistled a penalty kick for Italy. Meazza, a player who had reached his prime at this tournament, slotted home the ensuing kick in the 60th minute. The Italians would win the game, 2–1, to reach their second straight final. Brazil would later take third place.

At the same time, Hungary cruised to another win in Paris. The Hungarians got off to a bad start when Sweden's Arne Nyberg put them ahead in the first minute. Sweden remained a largely unknown entity in terms of soccer pedigree and had reached the semifinals almost by default after getting a bye and defeating Cuba. Hungary, unfazed by conceding an early goal, would score five—Zsengellér tallying a brace—for the 5–1 win. Hungary, an emerging soccer power, had reached the final in stunning fashion. Awaiting them would be the Italians. The final would feature two of the competition's best attacks and stingiest defenses.

Final: Italy vs. Hungary

Legend has it that Mussolini sent a telegram to the Italian team prior to the final with a message: "Win or die." That's the literal translation in English, but the phrase in the original Italian could also be considered a call to arms. When asked about it years later, Italian players insisted they never got such a telegram. "Not surprisingly it wasn't archived among government foreign dispatches and neither did Rava give it credence when I met him. No, no, no, that's not true," Simon Martin later relayed. "He sent a telegram wishing us well, but no never 'win or die.' Sometimes truth gets in the way of a good story."

Whether or not Mussolini ever sent such a warning remains irrelevant. The Azzurri were favorites to repeat against a Hungarian side that represented an Eastern European style of play that would impact the game in the coming decades. Both sides featured strong individual talent, but the Italians had the duo of Meazza and Piola in attack, who had a knack for breaking down opposing defenses with ease.

The largely French crowd of 45,000, which also featured Rimet in the stands, who attended the game in Colombes on June 19, were pulling for the Hungarians. The Italians, despised for political reasons, appeared unfazed by it. Meazza and his teammates had been able to shrug off previous protests. At the same time, Italy had looked better with each game at this tournament, a trait that would carry over at future World Cups. The slow start against Norway had been a wake-up call for Pozzo's men, and they came into the final prepared for victory.

When the Italians scored with just six minutes into the game with Colaussi, it appeared they would stroll to victory. Pál Titkos tied the score just two minutes later, but the goal proved to give the Hungarians the illusion that they could win. Ferrari and Meazza combined to set up Piola for a goal in the 15th minute to put Italy ahead, 2–1. Ten minutes before half-time, Ferrari and Meazza again broke down the Hungarian defense, this time finding the unmarked Colaussi who scored his second of the contest. Sárosi scored in the 70th minute, but Italy put the game away 10 minutes from the end when Amedeo Biavati backheeled a cheeky pass to Piola, who beat goalkeeper Antal Szabó with an unstoppable left-footed shot.

The Italians were crowned world champions for a second time. Pozzo went into the history books as the first manager to win two titles. Despite their success on the field, World War II was on the horizon. The secret of Italy's success? "There was no secret. All of it was dependent on the seriousness and depth with which we did things," Pozzo said in 1968 during an appearance on Italian state broadcaster RAI. "Every order I gave I also gave a reason. I knew everything about my players. I would read their mail and give them the letter opened. I told them I had read their mail and assured them that no one would know what had been in them. I did not allow them to read newspapers because I wanted the players to hear only one voice and that they would obey my orders. Previous national coaches would choose the players and then let them go off into a game. I formed the team and I assumed all the responsibility. It was up to me to take them into battle, like a good military official like I did when I had been a soldier for seven years."

Hitler would redraw the map of Europe, and the war would result in the destruction of much of Europe. Mussolini's regime collapsed in 1943 following the Allied invasion, and Italy was liberated two years later. Rimet would be forced to put the World Cup on hiatus. As a result, the editions scheduled for 1942 and 1946 were scrapped. For Rimet, the two World Cups won by Italy proved how successful an international soccer tournament could be. Nonetheless, the tournaments had been tarnished by their overt politicization. FIFA had been unable to stop Mussolini from turning the tournament into propaganda. One may even question why FIFA would award the 1934 tournament, for example, to a nation consumed by a dictatorial regime. Rimet's inability to limit the fascist symbolism would come to haunt him years later when he'd been nominated for a Nobel Peace Prize in 1956. The committee opted not to give out the prize that year.

Chapter Two

Brazil's Revenge

Take a stroll along the boardwalk of Copacabana, the famous waterfront that hugs the coastline of Rio de Janeiro, and you will see sandy beaches, women in flesh-revealing bikinis, and lots of boys juggling soccer balls. It's a place with plenty of good food, drinks, and smiling people.

It remains the best-known beach on the planet, but it's also the place where people showcase their impressive skills for all to see. In soccer-obsessed Brazil, the game has taken on greater significance than perhaps anywhere in the world. No other country can claim to have won five World Cups, a record, and no other place can say it is the birthplace of Pelé, arguably the best player the game has ever seen.

"Brazilians always think there is a critical situation with the national team," former defender Carlos Alberto told me while on a walk along Copacabana in 2014 just days after their 7–1 humiliation to Germany in the semifinals. "Individually, Brazilians are always the best. As a team, that is not always the case."

No longer the lean figure he was when he helped Brazil capture the World Cup in 1970, Carlos Alberto knew the pressures players have to shoulder as a result of representing a country where everyone likes to think they are national team manager. Working as a commentator for Brazilian TV network SporTV during the 2014 World Cup, Carlos Alberto relished reminiscing about his time as a player.

"The pressure the people put on the players is never good psychologically," he noted. "Only someone who has lived with that experience can understand."

The iconic black-and-white mosaic pattern that runs along the Avenida Atlântica is where Zizinho had mastered his craft. The attacking midfielder, who was a member of Brazil's 1950 World Cup squad, was the best player Pelé said he had ever seen. The Italian sports daily *La Gazzetta dello Sport* had likened Zizinho to Leonardo da Vinci, "creating works of art with his feet on the immense canvas of the Maracanã field."

"Brazil always has the chance to be the champions of the world," Carlos Alberto said. "That doesn't always mean they will win."

The Brazilians would not prevail in 1950. The defeat was a national trauma. Despite winning so many World Cups, the country never really got over losing that tournament. Pelé, just nine at the time, would later recall his father's tears following the shock defeat.

Pelé promised his father all would be better because he would some-day win a World Cup for Brazil. He recalled years later, according to the book *Passion of the People? Football in Latin America*, that the unexpected defeat produced "a sadness so great, so profound that it seemed like the end of a war, with Brazil the loser and many people dead." Within eight years, Pelé would emerge as one of world's best talents, setting Brazil on a quest that would include three World Cup titles.

1950 WORLD CUP

Europe lay in ruins in the aftermath of World War II. FIFA's vice president, Ottorino Barassi, had stashed the trophy away in a shoebox under his bed for safekeeping in his Rome apartment located near the Vatican. With the war over, FIFA was keen on bringing the World Cup back in 1950. The tournament was awarded to Brazil after the South Americans—along with Germany—had put in bids for the 1942 edition that had been scrapped. As a result, the tournament returned to the Southern Hemisphere in connection with the 25th anniversary of Rimet's presidency. To honor the Frenchman, the trophy was referred to as the "Jules Rimet Cup."

The 16-nation tournament featured the automatic qualification of hosts Brazil and defending champions Italy, leaving 14 more spots available via qualification. Germany and Japan did not participate, while the United Kingdom's four national teams—England, Scotland, Wales, and Northern Ireland—had rejoined FIFA four years earlier following

17 years of self-imposed exile. England would win the "Home Championship" and qualify for its first World Cup, an experience that would turn out to be memorable for some and forgettable for others. The Soviet Union, along with Czechoslovakia and Hungary, refused to take part, as did Argentina, following a disagreement with the Brazilian FA.

Brazil, untouched by the horrors of the war, embarked on a massive effort to host the tournament. Organizers decided six cities would host matches—Rio de Janeiro, São Paolo, Belo Horizonte, Porto Alegre, Recife, and Curitiba—with the newly built Maracanã Stadium the crown jewel of all the venues. Owned by the Rio state government, the stadium, located in Rio's Maracanã section, is now used by clubs Botafogo, Flamengo, Fluminense, and Vasco da Gama. The stadium's construction at the time was criticized by several Brazilian lawmakers—something that would repeat itself when Brazil hosted the tournament for a second time in 2014—given its large expense. After a design contest and contract awarded to engineer Humberto Menescal, work on the stadium began in August 1948, giving organizers just two years to complete it before the start of the World Cup. The work quickly fell behind schedule, prompting FIFA to send Barassi, who had also helped organize the 1934 World Cup, to help. Logistics eventually improved—as did the number of men needed to complete the work—with nearly 2,000 workers feverishly trying to finish the project in the months leading up to the tournament. The stadium, officially named Estádio Jornalista Mário Filho after the Brazilian sportswriter and editor, would be used at the World Cup, but construction would not officially come to an end until 1965.

Once again, FIFA had to deal with withdrawals and disputes with several nations in the months leading up to the competition. India decided against going to the tournament, citing travel costs and valuing the Olympics over the World Cup. The Indian team had played barefoot at the 1948 London Games, a practice FIFA had banned. France also withdrew, citing the amount of travel that would be required. Given the lack of time before the start of the World Cup, the tournament would only feature 13 teams. Of those finalists, several South American teams were returning to the World Cup for the first time since 1930: Uruguay, Chile, Paraguay, and Bolivia.

FIFA decided to abandon the single-elimination format and replaced it with a first round featuring four groups of four. The winner of each group advanced to a final group stage, which would decide a champion by playing a round-robin format. It would be the first—and last—time this format was used. The draw resulted in the following groups:

Group 1: Brazil, Mexico, Yugoslavia, and Switzerland

Group 2: England, Spain, Chile, and the United States

Group 3: Sweden, Italy, and Paraguay

Group 4: Uruguay and Bolivia

Teams were awarded two points for a win and one for a draw. Had there been a tie on points for first place, a playoff would have been held to determine the group winner—although it turned out this tiebreaker was never needed. The tournament was also not arranged by geography, meaning teams were forced to travel great distances within Brazil. The hosts, however, were allowed to play two of their three group matches at the Maracanã, while the other was held in São Paulo.

Brazil entered the tournament as favorites, while Italy looked like a long shot to defend its crown following the Superga air disaster that killed the Torino team that had formed the backbone of the national squad. England, Sweden, and Uruguay were also among the pre-tournament favorites.

Group Stage

Brazil opened the tournament on June 24 at the Maracanã with a resounding 4–0 victory against Mexico. Ademir was the hero that day, tallying two goals, as the home side was cheered on by 82,000 fans. The Brazilians, who featured plenty of attacking flair, had gotten off to a very good start. It was fitting that Ademir, a center forward, had spearheaded the attack. He had emerged as one of the best strikers in the country in the 1940s. A tall and lean man, Ademir, famous for having a very large overbite and a thin mustache, was also able to take on defenders with the

1940s and 1950s Innovation: Sambas

A German cobbler-turned-entrepreneur named Adi Dassler started Adidas in 1946 with the aim of improving the performance of athletes through the creation of better shoe designs. Dassler's family had been making shoes since the 1920s, and many athletes, including U.S. sprinter Jesse Owens, had worn them at the 1936 Berlin Games.

The family decided to go their separate ways, prompting Adi to create Adidas. His brother, Rudolf, would go on to start Puma. The Adidas logo—featuring three white stripes on its black shoes—would become synonymous with soccer following the creation of the Samba, a shoe the company makes to this day. The shoe was first produced in 1949—and named after the iconic Brazilian dance—to help players train on icy surfaces. The shoes featured an innovative rubber sole that made it better to grip hard surfaces compared to previous boots.

Adidas wanted to unveil the revolutionary shoe at the 1950 World Cup, but the company hit a snag. The Samba had been designed to be used in harsh European weather, while Brazilian winters aren't known for their extremely cold temperatures. That's when the company decided to name the shoe Samba, a moment of sheer marketing brilliance, so that it would capture the attention of the South American nation.

The shoe was used at the tournament at a time when player endorsements were not yet a thing. As the years progressed, the leather shoe evolved (mostly used today to play indoor soccer and as part of the company's casual-wear line), laying the groundwork for companies like Nike and Reebok to create their own cleats decades later.

The national teams of East and West Germany, all wearing Adidas cleats, line up before the start of their 1974 World Cup game.
DPA PICTURE-ALLIANCE/ALAMY STOCK PHOTO

skill and agility that would come to define generations of his countrymen in the ensuing decades. Under coach Flávio Costa, Ademir became the focal point of his attack, along with Zizinho, and the Brazilians truly looked like the side to beat early on in the tournament.

The following day, Yugoslavia defeated Switzerland 3–0 at the Estádio Independência in Belo Horizonte. The Yugoslavs represented the only real obstacle to Brazil winning the group, and the win solidified its position as a potential spoiler. The group's next two games—Brazil versus Switzerland and Yugoslavia taking on Mexico—were played on June 28, the outcome determining who would be in the best position to finish first in the group heading into the final match day. Yugoslavia eliminated Mexico following a 4–1 win at Estádio dos Eucaliptos in Porto Alegre. Brazil, meanwhile, could only muster a 2–2 draw at Estádio do Pacaembu in São Paulo. The Brazilians needed two points against Yugoslavia in the final group game to take the group.

The July 1 encounter between Brazil and Yugoslavia had it all. The Maracanã, teeming with 142,000 fans, created an intimidating setting for the visiting team. The Brazilians would have a great afternoon after Ademir put them ahead in just four minutes. Zizinho doubled the lead in the 69th minute to seal the 2–0 win and advance to the final group stage. The Brazilian offense had lived up to the hype, outscoring opponents 8–2 in their first three matches.

England entered the tournament as favorites to win Group 2. Bookmakers were offering 3–1 odds that England would win the tournament. The English, who invented the game, played their first-ever World Cup game on June 25, defeating Chile 2–0 at the Maracanã in the group's opening match. Four days later, England traveled to Belo Horizonte to take on the United States, a hastily assembled squad made up of semi-pros. The Americans, who had a 500–1 chance of winning the World Cup, had come off a 3–1 defeat to Spain and were the underdogs against an English side widely known as the "Kings of Football."

England had a postwar record of 23 wins, 4 losses, and 3 draws. The *Daily Express* newspaper wrote, "It would be fair to give the U.S. three goals of a start." The residents of Belo Horizonte were excited about the chance to see the English team, and nearly 11,000 tickets were sold

(3,000 of them distributed to members of Sete de Setembro Futebol Clube, owners of the newly inaugurated Estádio Independência) for the eagerly anticipated match. England's best player, Stanley Matthews, had not played with the team in the three international matches before the World Cup. Matthews had joined the team late, something that would come to haunt England, after taking part in a tour of North America with a group of English all-stars. Matthews was not included in the starting lineup against the United States, the decision being made to save him for later in the tournament against more difficult opposition.

England dominated early on in the match and managed six shots on goal—two of them hitting the post—in the opening 12 minutes. In the 37th minute, the unexpected took place. American Walter Bahr took a shot from 25 yards out, a pass that connected with a diving Joe Gaetjens. He grazed the ball just enough with his head, allowing the ball to beat goalkeeper Bert Williams to his left. It would be the only goal of the game. The upset was complete. "The crowd ran onto the field and lifted Joe on their shoulders and paraded him around the field," Bahr recalled. "The crowd had really been behind us for most of the game. The English players were really good sports. They shook our hands and were respectful. In the locker room, no one said a thing. There wasn't any champagne or anything like that." The victory would do little to propel the sport back home. The Americans would not qualify for another World Cup for another 40 years, plunging the sport into obscurity in the United States for decades to come.

In the end, it was Spain that had the most to celebrate. The team took the group after winning all their games, including a 1–0 victory against England on July 2 at the Maracanã. Telmo Zarra, one of the best players at the tournament, netted the winning goal after 48 minutes. Zarra had been a scoring machine for club side Athletic Bilbao, something he brought with him to the national team. Spain dominated the group with relative ease following England's sudden implosion. For Spain, qualification to the final four represented their best finish at a World Cup until they lifted the trophy 60 years later.

Sweden opened Group 3 on June 25 with a 3–2 win against Italy in São Paolo. The world champions traveled to Brazil by sea after the

Superga air crash. Players arrived in São Paolo unfit—despite a layover to practice in Las Palmas—while others had even gained weight. As a result, the Swedes, powered by Hans Jeppson's brace, got off to a strong start.

The group only featured three teams after India's decision to drop out. Sweden, needing at minimum a draw four days later in Curitiba against Paraguay, gave up a late goal. In the end, Sweden pulled off a 2–2 draw. The Swedes won the group and advanced to the final round following Italy's 2–0 victory against Paraguay on July 2 in São Paolo. The dejected Italians left Brazil—a majority of them by plane—as Sweden, comprised entirely of amateur players, looked to add a World Cup to the gold medal they had conquered at the 1948 London Games.

Group 4, the oddest in tournament history, featured just two teams after France's withdrawal. As a result, Uruguay had to play a single game against Bolivia to ensure passage to the final round. Uruguay, the champion just two decades earlier, featured a new generation of players. Juan Alberto Schiaffino and Alcides Ghiggia, teammates at Peñarol, were two of the country's best offensive players of this era. In the end, Uruguay cruised to victory on July 2 in Belo Horizonte, routing Bolivia 8–0. An Óscar Míguez hat trick, aided by two goals by Schiaffino and one by Ghiggia, sent the message that Uruguay could be a factor in the final round.

Final Round

A week after that big win, the final round began with Uruguay, Brazil, Spain, and Sweden. The round opened on July 9 with Uruguay taking on Spain in São Paolo, while Brazil faced Sweden in Rio. For Brazil, the tactics that would come to define their national identity—a style that has come to be known as *jogo bonito*—was still a ways away. The 1950 Brazil team showed for the first time something known as *ginga*. The term comes from capoeira—the Afro-Brazilian martial art that features elaborate maneuvers and acrobatics—and is used to describe someone who can go with the flow, with a dose of street smarts sprinkled in.

This team had *ginga*, and it could be seen in its offensive prowess. The Brazilians opened the final round with a 7–1 thumping of Sweden. Ademir's four goals cemented his position as tournament top scorer. Four days later, Spain was on the receiving end of another Brazilian shooting gallery. Brazil's 6–1 victory (with Ademir scoring only once this time) set up the encounter with Uruguay as a de facto final. Uruguay, meanwhile, had tied Spain 2–2 and beat Sweden 3–2. As a result, they needed to defeat Brazil to win it all.

Final: Uruguay vs. Brazil

The Maracanã was packed to the rafters on July 16 with 200,000 spectators—about one-tenth of the city's population at the time. Waving white handkerchiefs, they made their way into the concrete grandstands. A band stood along the sidelines—prepared to play a song called "Brasil Os Vencedores" (Brazil the Victors)—once the final whistle sounded. It was a scene of happiness and national pride. By the end of the game, it would become one of despair and sadness.

In *Passion of the People? Football in Latin America*, author Tony Mason noted that Brazilian radio and newspapers had spent weeks hyping the tournament. The trophy had been placed on display in the window of a shoe store along the Avenida Rio Branco in Rio, and "thousands of Brazilians filed past it as if it was a religious experience," Mason noted.

Rio, the then–Brazilian capital, was awash in festivities. The nation's press and public, based on Brazil's wonderful form at the tournament, were so confident of victory at this point that they had already declared Brazil the new world champions days before the game. *O Globo*, one of the nation's leading newspapers, took part in the hype, reflecting the country's mood going into the game. "The draw will bring the title, there is no doubt, but the whole country expects the repetition of the big wins that elevated Brazil's soccer reputation to an international level. A big win would not mean an expressive final score," the newspaper noted. "But a big win in terms of playing with the impressive class and clearness presented in the first two games of the knockout stage. The entire Brazilian crowd, possibly around 200 thousand spectators and the rest millions in spirit, will be at the game to support the national cracks to the accomplishment of the world championship. And hopefully, the players will match the supporters' enthusiasm."

In its pre-match coverage, *O Globo* also lauded Brazil's opponents: "The Uruguayans come as typical dangerous opponents and who demand caution from the Brazilian national team. Any mistake, any underestimation can be fatal to our aspirations. The Brazilian team will have to fight with similar determination exhibited against Yugoslavia, Sweden, and Spain because the opponent is tough and aggressive."

The government made 22 gold medals, one for each player, with the intent of awarding them to the team after the game. At the Copa America held in Brazil the previous year, the hosts won after scoring an astounding 46 goals over eight games. Brazil defeated Uruguay 5–1 at that tournament. Despite all that, Paulo Machado de Carvalho, a noted lawyer and businessman, was among the few who doubted a Brazilian victory. During a visit to the training session at the Estádio São Januário on the eve of the game, he stumbled on several politicians making impassioned speeches to the players. After warning the coaching staff about the risk of upsetting the players' concentration, he was ignored. Frustrated, he told his son, "We are going to lose."

Rio's streets bustled with activity on the morning of July 16 when an improvised carnival was organized. Thousands of fans—holding up signs and chanting "Brazil must win!"—made their voices heard all the way up to kickoff. Newspapers had already printed special editions proclaiming the hosts "Champions of the World." This appeared to be a done deal, at least as far as the press was concerned, and the Uruguayan delegation didn't let it get to them. "It was a fantastic atmosphere," Ghiggia recalled in a 2014 BBC interview. "Their supports were jumping with joy as if they'd already won the World Cup."

The teams played a tactically similar 2–3–5 formation, with Brazil known for scoring goals, Uruguay for their smart midfield play. The game itself was tense, but the Brazilians broke the deadlock when striker Friaça scored in the 47th minute. The goal only fueled the inevitability of a final victory. While the country basked in what they thought was an impending win, Uruguay tied the score in the 66th minute via a Juan Alberto Schiaffino goal after connecting with a Ghiggia cross. In the 79th minute, Ghiggia scored to make it 2–1, beating goalkeeper Moacir Barbosa. Radio Globo's Luiz Mendes, whose call was heard by millions throughout Brazil, exclaimed, "Gol do Uruguay!" He then, incredulously, asked himself aloud, "Gol do Uruguay?" His words reflected those of a nation. Indeed, those in the stadium couldn't believe it.

The final whistle brought with it jubilation from the Uruguayan players, prompting some to even hug and kiss English referee George Reader. Uruguay had done the impossible to win a second World Cup. Brazilians throughout the city openly wept. The nation had been so invested in the success of its team that it was not emotionally prepared for defeat. FIFA presented the trophy to Uruguay without a ceremony. "I had a split second to decide what to do," Ghiggia recalled. "I shot and it went off the post. . . . It was the best goal I ever scored."

Outside the stadium, fans knocked over a bust of Angelo Mendes de Moraes, the mayor of Rio, who was reviled due to his premature congratulations. The Uruguayan players, some in a state of disbelief, did a lap of honor with the trophy. The Maracanã fell silent. "Three people have silenced the Maracanã: Frank Sinatra, the pope, and me," Ghiggia later said.

The game came to be known as "the Maracanazo," which translates into the "great Maracanã blow." A young Pelé was home at the time listening to the game on the radio, recalling that it was the first time he'd ever seen his father cry. Barbosa was largely blamed for the defeat, something he was forced to deal with for the rest of his life. For half a century, he would take his phone off the hook on July 16. "Otherwise it rings all day," he recalled, "from people all over Brazil, asking why we lost the World Cup."

The Brazilian team did not play in another game for two years or play at the Maracanã for nearly four following the defeat. The most visible consequence came when the team adopted the now iconic yellow shirts instead of the white ones the players had worn during the match. It had been a blow to the national psyche—despite future World Cup glory—that even superstars like Pelé would be unable to totally erase from their memories.

1954 WORLD CUP

Four years after Uruguay's shock victory, the World Cup was held in Switzerland. It would be a tournament dominated by European teams and one noteworthy, even all these decades later, for its high-scoring games. The hosts, awarded the tournament in 1946 to coincide with FIFA's 50th anniversary, and the defending champions qualified automatically. Of the remaining 14 places, 11 were allocated to Europe (which at the time included Egypt, Turkey, and Israel), two to the Americas, and one to Asia.

Before qualification was even completed, FIFA determined the eight seeded teams for the finals: Austria, Brazil, England, France, Hungary, Italy, Spain, and Uruguay. That process was thrown into disarray when Turkey eliminated Spain. FIFA resolved the situation by handing Turkey the seeded spot previously allotted to Spain. Here's what the final draw yielded:

Group 1: Brazil, France, Yugoslavia, and Mexico

Group 2: Turkey, Hungary, West Germany, and South Korea

Group 3: Austria, Uruguay, Czechoslovakia, and Scotland

Group 4: Italy, England, Switzerland, and Belgium

FIFA, once again, tinkered with the tournament's format. Rimet gave his blessing to combining an opening-pool format with the knockout system. Rimet's successor, a sports journalist-turned-administrator named Rodolphe Seeldrayers, took over the presidency on the eve of the tournament, officially ending Rimet's 33-year reign. The tournament's 16 finalists were divided into four groups of four teams. Oddly, each group contained two seeded teams and two unseeded teams. Instead of a round-robin format, only four matches were scheduled per group, each pitting a seeded team against an unseeded one. Another oddity that was introduced included the use of extra time—used in most tournaments only in the knockout rounds—during the group stage if games were tied after 90 minutes. The draw would be recorded as such if another 30 minutes of play failed to yield a winner.

Two points were awarded for a win and one for a draw. The top two teams with the most points from each group qualified to the knockout round. If the first- and second-placed teams were level on points, lots were drawn to decide which one would top the group instead of using goal differential as is used today. Complicating the formula even further, if the second- and third-placed teams were level on points, there was a playoff game to decide which team would progress.

Another unusual feature was that the four group-winning teams were to be drawn against each other in the knockout stages to produce one finalist, while the four second-placed teams played against each other to produce the second finalist. In subsequent tournaments it would become customary to draw group winners against second-placed teams in the first knockout round. If knockout games ended in a draw after regulation, 30 minutes of extra time would be played. If the game ended in a draw after that, lots would be drawn to decide who advanced. The final was the only exception. A draw after extra time meant the game would need to be replayed the following day. If that game also ended in a draw, then lots would be drawn to determine the champion. Thankfully, it never came to that. Instead, the tournament would produce an avalanche of goals.

Six venues across six Swiss cities hosted the tournament's 26 games. The most used facility, St. Jakob Stadium in Basel, hosted six matches. The venues in Bern, Zurich, and Lausanne each hosted the second most with five. Wankdorf Stadium in Bern hosted the final. This World Cup was also a prelude to the modern era since the tournament received televised coverage. Though limited to Europe, it was the first sign that the World Cup would someday grow into a global commercial event. The Swiss, in turn, showed early signs of marketing savvy by issuing the first-ever World Cup coins—the type of trinkets that would come to dominate the tournament in the coming decades.

Group Stage

Brazil and France, Group 1's two seeded teams, took on Mexico and Yugoslavia, respectively, on June 16 to open the tournament. Brazil returned to World Cup action at Charmilles Stadium in Geneva with an emphatic 5–0 win. The Mexican backline could not contain the Brazilian onslaught led by Pinga's brace. A lively midfielder, Pinga and his team-mates sent a message that the Brazilians were trophy contenders. At the same time, Yugoslavia managed a 1–0 win against France, an upset of sorts, as a result of Miloš Milutinović's goal after just 15 minutes at the Stade Olympique de la Pontaise in Lausanne.

Three days later, Brazil would need only a draw against Yugoslavia to advance to the knockout round. In fact, the result would help both sides advance and avoid a threat by either France or Mexico, who were playing at the same time, to sneak into second place. In the end, Brazil and Yugoslavia tied 1–1 after extra time in Lausanne. France managed to defeat Mexico 3–2 in Geneva, the result having no impact on the group standings that saw Brazil finish first over Yugoslavia after lots were drawn.

Turkey and Hungary were the teams that were seeded in Group 2, but West Germany, playing at a World Cup for the first time as a divided nation following its separation from East Germany, were also a threat to advance. West Germany lived up to those expectations, sweeping Turkey aside in the group opener on June 17 at Wankdorf Stadium in Bern. West Germany's 4–1 victory was spectacular, but Hungary outdid them. At the same time at Hardturm Stadium in Zurich, the Hungarians routed South Korea 9–0. Hungary's attack was formidable, poor South Korean defending notwithstanding, as Sándor Kocsis opened the World Cup with a hat trick. His teammate, Ferenc Puskás, added a brace.

The June 20 encounter between Hungary and West Germany pitted two of the best attacking sides thus far at the tournament. The Hungarians, who used an offensive 3–2–1–4 formation, were the best team in the world at the time. Nicknamed the "Mighty Magyars," the team featured Puskás, who possessed the most lethal left foot in Europe at the time. Team manager Gusztáv Sebes, inspired by Austria's Wunderteam and Pozzo's Italy, stacked his team with players hailing from primarily Honved, the Budapest-based army club. The side, playing a style some referred to as "socialist football," was a prelude to the "total football" that would come to be identified with the Netherlands in the 1970s. Under Sebes, the team operated as individual talents who were interchangeable, all possessing their own skill sets. Put these pieces together and Hungary would function as an orchestra.

For all his skills, Puskás was an unusual-looking player. Squat and even sporting a bit of a belly, Puskás had a strong and accurate shot that could beat goalkeepers with unerring precision. Hungary, which became a communist nation in 1949, looked to sports as a propaganda tool, a prelude to what the Soviet Union would do at the World Cup and Olympics in the ensuing decades. As a result, Puskás, considered a soldier by the government, picked up the nickname the "Galloping Major." It was Puskás that made Hungary favorites to win the group and even the tournament, although an injury (a hairline fracture to his ankle) in the second half of the West Germany game was concerning after center back Werner Liebrich had spent the game kicking him in the shins.

The game did not disappoint. Basel was the setting for what would be another Hungarian scoring spree, despite a West German team that played a defensive-minded 4–3–3 that loved to clog the midfield. Kocsis put on a clinic, tallying four times, for an 8–3 win. In doing so, he became the first player to record two World Cup hat tricks. Puskás added a goal that afternoon before the 53,000 fans in attendance, only one of three matches to break the 50,000 mark. In Geneva, meanwhile, Turkey defeated South Korea 7–0 to set up a playoff game against the West Germans. The June 23 game would determine who advanced to the quarterfinals.

Zurich was the site for West Germany versus Turkey. What many had hoped would be a competitive match turned out to be anything but one. The West Germans, buoyed by the 17,000 fans in attendance largely rooting for them, put on an impressive show. They took the lead after just seven minutes thanks to an Ottmar Walter goal, and they never looked back. Max Morlock's hat trick was just one of the offensive displays of greatness that evening as West Germany went on to win the game 7–2.

Group 3 opened on June 16 in Bern as defending champion Uruguay outlasted Czechoslovakia 2–0. The game seemed destined to end in a scoreless draw, but two goals late in the match gave Uruguay the points. In Zurich, meanwhile, Austria also recorded a narrow victory by posting a 1–0 win against Scotland. Three days later, Uruguay, led once again by Schiaffino, turned on the offense in Basel. Powered by a Carlos Borges hat trick, Uruguay blanked Scotland 7–0 to advance to the knockout stage. La Celeste, playing in their first World Cup outside of South America, came to Switzerland with a roster largely unchanged from four years earlier, including 1950 World Cup–winning captain Obdulio Varela, who had turned 37 on the eve of the tournament.

The win against Scotland helped them win the group. The Scots were without their manager after Andy Beattie resigned following the opening defeat and a fallout with the Scottish FA. The team faced Uruguay with practically no coach and few choices for lineup changes after electing to take just 13 players (two of them goalkeepers) instead of the maximum of 18 allowed by FIFA at the time. "The heat was incredible and we were drenched in sweat," Scotland midfielder Tommy Docherty recalled in a 2014 BBC interview. "At halftime we had to get into a lukewarm bath to cool down. We just weren't prepared."

Austria, who would finish second, had come close to topping the group following their 5–0 victory in Zurich—thanks to an Erich Probst hat trick—against the Czechoslovakians. This was no Wunderteam, but they'd done enough to advance to the knockout round.

Italy, still in rebuilding mode after the failures of four years earlier, had the tough task of taking on the host nation on June 17 at the Stade Olympique de la Pontaise in Lausanne in Group 4. Nearly 41,000 fans showed up to cheer on the Swiss. The Swiss got on the board after just 18 minutes after striker Robert Ballaman found the back of the net. The Azzurri leveled the score a minute before halftime with striker Giampiero Boniperti, slamming the ball into the goal from just a few yards out after a scramble in front of the net. The Swiss, however, were determined to win the game. They did so thanks to a Josef Hügi goal 12 minutes from the end. The game became more physical at that point as the frustrated Italians tried to generate some offense. The final whistle ushered cheers and jubilation as dozens of fans stormed the field to celebrate the Swiss. The Italian players, meanwhile, irate at the result, crowded around referee Mário Vianna of Brazil. The referee needed a police escort to the dressing room to avoid the confrontation getting more heated.

England and Belgium did battle at the same time in Basel. The match—the first at this tournament to need extra time—resulted in a bevy of goals, like so many other games throughout the opening round. England held on to a 3–2 lead when Belgium mounted a late comeback. The *Times of London*, in its coverage the following day, reported that

England had "dominated the central hour with some pure cultured football to take a lead that should have given them a worthy victory." Instead, the newspaper noted, the team fell prone to "too much artistry at the time of their domination." A goal by striker Léopold Anoul in the 71st minute pushed the game into extra time. In the 30-minute session, the teams traded goals—Nat Lofthouse gave England the lead in the 91st minute, but Belgium made it 4–4 three minutes later thanks to a Jimmy Dickinson own goal.

On June 20, at Cornaredo Stadium in Lugano, the Italians, in need of a win, got just that against a tired Belgium side. While Italy's 4–1 win kept their hopes of advancing alive, England defeated Switzerland 2–0 in Bern to win the group. The win set up a tiebreaker match between Switzerland and Italy. Three days later in Basel, the Swiss and Italians engaged in a rematch. The Swiss won again, this time by a larger margin after the Italian defense fell apart early. Hügi scored in the 14th minute, the striker taking advantage of bad defending to put the ball past goalkeeper Giovanni Viola. Ballaman added a second in the 48th minute, but midfielder Fulvio Nesti's goal kept Italian hopes alive. The Swiss put the game away with Hügi in the 85th minute and Jacques Fatton in the game's final minute. The hosts were through to the next round in spectacular fashion. The Italians, thoroughly embarrassed by the defeat, were no longer the soccer power of the fascist era. It would take nearly another decade for them to become competitive again on the global stage.

Quarterfinals

The knockout stage opened on June 26 with 31,000 fans showing up to cheer on the Swiss side against Austria. The match featured the most goals ever recorded at a World Cup and one of the biggest comebacks in tournament history. Switzerland scored three times after just 19 minutes. The Austrians countered with three goals of their own—in a span of just three minutes—to make it 3–3. Ernst Ocwirk's goal in the 32nd minute put Austria ahead, a lead they would not relinquish. In the end, Austria managed to record a 7–5 win and advance to the semifinals.

At the same time in Basel, Uruguay got the best of England. Borges put Uruguay ahead after just five minutes with Borges. England leveled the score with Lofthouse in the 16th minute. Varela put Uruguay ahead in the 39th minute and never looked back. The game was contentious as both sides battled for the ball. In the end, the South Americans prevailed 4–2.

The following day, West Germany blanked Yugoslavia 2–0 in Geneva. The day's bigger game, between Hungary and Brazil in Berne, would turn out to be one of the most controversial matches of the tournament. The Brazilians had a growing reputation for playing a beautiful brand of soccer, but the Hungarians, who had scored 17 goals in the first round as a result of their all-out attacking style, were the offensive machine the 40,000 in attendance were waiting to see. Hungary had also won the gold medal two years earlier at the Helsinki Games. It was then, Puskás noted in the book *Puskas on Puskas*, that "our football first started to flow with real power." But Puskás had to miss the game due to injury, opening the possibility that Brazil could pull off an upset.

A torrential rain greeted both sides, causing slippery and adverse conditions. Even Mother Nature and a muddy field could do little to stop Hungary. The team took the lead after just three minutes with Nándor Hidegkuti. Just four minutes later, Kocsis doubled Hungary's lead. It was in the 18th minute that a glimpse of what would happen in the second half took place. A flying tackle by Mihály Lantos on Índio drew indignation from the Brazilians. After being awarded a penalty as a result of the play, Djalma Santos slotted in the kick past goalkeeper Gyula Grosics to make it 2–1.

The second half started off just as competitive as the first—but in no time at all, both sides would trade beauty for brutality. The game took a turn for the worse when referee Arthur Ellis of England whistled a penalty kick for Hungary. Lantos scored to make the score 3–1 in the 60th minute, setting off a pitch invasion by Brazilian officials. Police had to escort them off the field for the game to resume. From that point forward, the game devolved into a series of fouls and violent tackles. Brazilian striker Julinho scored in the 65th minute to bring the score to 3–2. Ellis struggled to maintain control of the game.

After József Bozsik was fouled by Nílton Santos, the two started fighting. Ellis promptly ejected both players. Hungary scored a fourth goal in the 88th minute with Kocsis to put Hungary up 4–2. Tempers frayed further, and the game's finale featured one last eruption of violence after Brazilian striker Humberto Tozzi kicked Gyula Lóránt, which resulted in his being sent off. Tozzi dropped to his knees, begging not to be sent off. The final whistle ended the game, but not the hostilities. Pinheiro was smacked in the head with a bottle hurled from the Hungarian bench, allegedly by Puskás. Pinheiro was left with a big gash and blood flowing down his face. The Hungarian delegation denied Puskás had thrown the bottle.

The anger spilled off the field when the Brazilian players invaded the Hungarian dressing room. Despite the game being dubbed the "Battle of Berne" by the *Times of London*, an inquiry yielded nothing. In fact, FIFA doled out no further suspensions or fines as a result of the fracas. Instead, like Pontius Pilate, it washed its hands of the whole thing. Sebes, speaking with reporters afterward, said, "This was a battle and a brutal, savage match."

Sebes, who received four stitches to his face as a result of the fighting, said the battle in the tunnel was the most dangerous. Three police officers were injured as the hostilities spilled over into the tunnel, a fight that took 20 minutes to put under control.

"Brazilian photographers and fans flooded on to the pitch and police were called to clear it. Players clashed in the tunnel and a small war broke out in the corridor to the dressing rooms," he said. "Everyone was having a go—fans, players, and officials."

"I thought it was going to be the greatest game I'd ever see. I was on top of the world. Whether politics and religion had something to do with it I don't know, but they behaved like animals," Ellis recounted in an interview with the *Independent* in 1998. "It was a disgrace."

Ellis said it was "a horrible match" and that he was keen the entire time to bring the game to its conclusion. "In today's climate so many players would have been sent off the game would have been abandoned," he added. "My only thought was that I was determined to finish it."

The Brazilian press had it in for Ellis for a series of what they considered bad calls. *O Globo* made the following observation: "Hours passed by, but the hurtful impression of the Brazilian team elimination on the fifth World Cup by the direct influence of the referee Mr. Ellis remains. We insist, once more, that this is not about losers crying, but about the confirmation of an outrageous reality. Throughout this entire unfortunate situation, there is only one comfort situation that leaves us in peace with our conscience: it is the fact that we are not the only ones disapproving of the performance of the English referee. Respected opinions, because of their technical experience and even more sincere because they are neutral spectators, also condemned Ellis's performance."

While the Brazilians had lost the chance at winning their first World Cup, *O Globo* noted that fans sent the players telegraphs featuring messages of support. "The messages have been comforting to the players and staff," the newspaper account noted.

Despite the Brazilian press blaming Ellis (and he did have his faults for failing to contain the violence), this is a game so significant and emotional that academics have even studied it. An analysis published in 2008 called "Brawling in Berne: Mediated Transnational Moral Panics in the 1954 Football World Cup," based on newspaper accounts of the time, highlighted the following: "We cannot know with any certainty, but it is not unreasonable to assume in the context of a major international sports tournament, that Hungarian pride in their success and Brazilian desire to giant-kill may be seen as combining to produce a heightened emotional atmosphere that was intensified by frustrations linked to the effects of the bad weather. Both teams were reported as taking part in the violence, which contributed to its intensification."

Semifinals

The semifinals, contested on June 30, featured two high-stakes games: West Germany versus Austria and Hungary versus Uruguay. This second game, the favorites against the holders, was the most anticipated of the two. Hungary, still without Puskás, was still recovering from the violent and emotionally charged quarterfinal clash against Brazil.

Uruguay, the only South American nation still alive in the competition, had yet to ever lose a World Cup match. The Hungarians jumped out to a 2–0 lead in Lausanne, but Uruguay pulled level thanks to two goals by striker Juan Hohberg. His second goal—just four minutes from time—pushed the match into extra time. Uruguay came close to taking the lead in the 107th minute with Hohberg, whose shot slammed against the post. Against the run of play, Kocsis scored two minutes later on a towering header. In the 116th minute, Kocsis added a second goal, and Hungary were through to the final following a 4–2 victory.

In the other semifinal in Basel, West Germany forged a spectacular path to the final, leaving Austria in its wake following a 6–1 win. A brace from team captain Fritz Walter and his brother Ottmar put the pre-tournament underdogs through. The West Germans, who gained confidence with each passing game, found themselves with a shot at the biggest prize in world soccer.

Hungary, the pre-tournament favorites, went up against upstart West Germany in Zurich. The game, a rematch of the first round, would go on to be one of the most memorable final games in World Cup history.

Final: West Germany vs. Hungary

The championship game would be one for the ages and another upset on the heels of the Maracanazo. Beyond the playing field, the game had a lasting impact on both German and Hungarian societies. The West Germans, still in a postwar rebuilding process, were allowed to express their love of country without the menace of Nazism. After all, this World Cup was the first time the German national anthem had been played for a global audience since World War II. For the Hungarians, in the grips of a totalitarian regime that would stay in power until 1989, the result would include a student-led revolt in 1956 that challenged Soviet control.

On the field, West Germany would begin a period of dominance that continues to this day—even after reunification with the east in 1990. Hungary, on the other hand, went from revolutionizing the game in the 1950s to soccer anonymity. Never before in the history of the game did the result of a final so impact two nations in the decades to come.

A heavy rain on July 4 at Wankdorf Stadium greeted fans and players alike. Despite the weather, a crowd of 62,500 showed up for the game. Vendors sold food outside the venue as a crowd of fedora-wearing men in long raincoats streamed into the stadium. Once inside, they were greeted by officials who made sure the field was in good enough shape for the game to be contested just as the rain stopped. Once the field was deemed good enough, the players exited the underground tunnel to loud cheers. Bill Ling of England was chosen to referee the match. By game's end, the decisions of an English official cast a cloud over the result.

True to form at this tournament, the game featured goals galore. The opening 10 minutes featured three. Puskás, latching onto a loose ball deflected in his direction in the penalty box, slammed the ball past goalkeeper Toni Turek in the sixth minute to put Hungary up 1–0. Puskás, with his hair slicked back, stuck out his chest and raised his arms in elation as teammates rushed to hug him. The Hungarians scored again just two minutes later with Zoltán Czibor. West Germany, not to be outdone, pulled one back in the 10th minute. After the Hungarian backline failed to swat away the offense threat, the ball clumsily fell to Morlock. The West German slid into the ball, pushing it past Grosics to the delight of the crowd. Hundreds of West Germans had crossed the border to watch the game, many of them unable to get inside when the $8 tickets were selling for more than $100 on the secondary market.

Fans inside and outside the stadium cheered once again in the 18th minute when West Germany tied the score. Grosics attempted to clear a corner kick by Fritz Walter in the air, but collided in the six-yard box with Hans Schäfer, a foul that Ling failed to whistle. As a result, the ball fell to Helmut Rahn, who scored. The Hungarians, with their fluid passing and offensive flair, pushed for the win. The West Germans, defensively solid thanks to center back Werner Liebrich, kept pace with their opponents for much of the first half and into the second. Fritz Walter, meanwhile, was the main reason West Germany was able to create chances. Six minutes from time, Rahn latched onto a ball from just outside the penalty area, following a poor clearance, and drilled a left-footed shot that just beat Grosics to his right.

Four minutes from the end, West Germany, hanging on to the upset, gave up a goal after Puskás appeared to tie the score. But Ling disallowed it, changing his mind after conferring with the linesman who had deemed Puskás offside. Witness accounts differ on whether Puskás was offside. Television footage allows no clarity since it fails to show Puskás's position at the time he received the pass. The dramatic finale was befitting a tournament that had featured plenty of goals. United Press International reported that 300 police officers and soldiers were needed to keep the "spectators from breaking through the fence and pushing on to the field."

The surprise win brought with it a wave of pride throughout West Germany. Public displays of patriotism were still taboo in the post-Nazi period, but the victory did go a long way in restoring the nation's standing in the world. It was an example of the power of the World Cup—whether a nation hosted the tournament or won it—in the post–World War II period. Rimet, following a brief speech, presented Fritz Walter with the trophy, telling the West German captain: "You have won well. Guard this trophy carefully for the spiritual value it represents."

1958

Sweden had been named host in 1950, following some initial interest from Argentina, Chile, and Mexico, putting the Scandinavian nation and the 12 cities that hosted matches at the center of the soccer world. Once again, the tournament went through a format change. The competing nations, still numbering 16, were placed in four groups of four. Only this time, each team played one another once, without extra time being used in the event of a draw. If the first two teams finished equal on points, then goals scored would be used as the first tiebreaker—the first time it would be used at a World Cup.

The top two teams advanced to the quarterfinals. FIFA wanted a playoff game to be used if the second- and third-placed teams finished even on points, but teams complained that it could mean three games in a span of just five days. The debate raged on once the tournament began. FIFA reversed itself and informed teams that goal average would be used before resorting to a playoff. The decision, however, was overturned when Sweden's FA complained, arguing that it was wrong to change the rules once the first round had begun. The FA also wanted the extra ticket revenue from these matches. In the end, three of the four groups would require a playoff game.

It marked the first World Cup without Rimet, who died in 1956 at age 83. It was also the first tournament since the creation of the Union of

European Football Associations, commonly known as UEFA. The organization would become very powerful in the ensuing decades after the creation in 1955 of the European Champions Cup, an annual continental tournament opened to clubs. The tournament would be renamed the Champions League in 1992. It is today the most coveted championship in all of club soccer and rivals the World Cup in prestige. UEFA would inaugurate its own quadrennial tournament for nations in 1960, something spearheaded by Delaunay, known as the European Championship. He died five years before the first edition was contested, but the trophy was named in his honor. The creation of both these tournaments would make Europe the focal point of the international game.

Sweden and defending champions West Germany qualified automatically, while the remaining 14 places were allocated this way: nine to Europe, three to South America, one to North/Central America, and one to Asia/Africa. This World Cup saw the entry and qualification of the Soviet Union for the first time, while Argentina reached the finals for the first time since 1934. Italy failed to qualify, joining two-time champions and 1954 semifinalists Uruguay, as well as Spain and Belgium, on the list of nations not to travel to Sweden. The draw, with teams separated, yielded the following four groups:

Group 1: West Germany, Czechoslovakia, Northern Ireland, and Argentina

Group 2: France, Yugoslavia, Scotland, and Paraguay

Group 3: Sweden, Hungary, Wales, and Mexico

Group 4: Austria, England, the Soviet Union, and Brazil

The draw's emphasis on geographical diversity, rather than ranking teams by recent success or reputation, resulted in four very even groups. West Germany was on the list of favorites to repeat. Other pre-tournament contenders included Brazil and Argentina, while Sweden had the benefit of playing at home, thereby giving it a chance at the title.

Group Stage

The West Germans were an even better team than four years earlier and featured a budding star in striker Uwe Seeler. On June 8, West Germany, thanks to a brace by Rahn and a goal by Seeler, defeated Argentina 3–1 in Group 1 at Malmö Stadion in Malmö. At the same time, Northern Ireland, who had eliminated Italy and Portugal in the qualifiers, edged Czechoslovakia 1–0 at Örjans Vall in Halmstad. The game's only goal by Wilbur Cush in the 21st minute decided the encounter.

Three days later at the Olympiastadion in Helsingborg, West Germany struggled against Czechoslovakia, one of Europe's best teams at the time with a rich soccer tradition. Falling behind 2–0, the defending champions mounted a second-half comeback. A Hans Schäfer goal in the 60th minute and the tying strike 11 minutes later by Rahn salvaged a 2–2 draw. Argentina, not to be outdone, defeated Northern Ireland 3–1 in Halmstad.

The group closed out on June 15 as West Germany played to another 2–2 draw, this time against Northern Ireland. The thrilling match in Malmö saw West Germany go down after just 18 minutes thanks to Peter McParland. Rahn tied the score just two minutes later, but McParland put Northern Ireland ahead in the 60th minute. West Germany, in need of a draw to win the group, launched attack after attack. In the end, they scored with 12 minutes left to go with Seeler. The German striker, appearing off balance, connected with the ball from 35 yards out with a missile of a shot. A hapless Harry Gregg could do nothing to stop the ball from getting past him. Czechoslovakia, meanwhile, trounced Argentina 6–1 in Helsingborg to push a playoff game against Northern Ireland.

The playoff was contested on June 17 in Malmö before just 6,200 spectators. Northern Ireland, hobbled by exhaustion and injuries, would reach the quarterfinals, pulling off what had been considered an improbable feat on the eve of the tournament, as McParland tallied twice, including the winning goal in extra time, to reach the quarterfinals. Although they were considered rank outsiders, Northern Ireland featured a roster rife with players who were members of English clubs. McParland played for Aston Villa, while other key players such as team captain Danny Blanchflower (Tottenham), Jimmy McIlroy (Burnley), Billy Bingham

(Sunderland), and Harry Gregg (Manchester United) had all traveled to Sweden. In a span of just nine days, Northern Ireland had turned the soccer world on its head. At the other end of the spectrum, Argentina, which finished last in the group, were greeted at Ezeiza Airport in Buenos Aires by a few thousand angry fans who hurled insults at them after such a poor showing. It would take another two decades for the South Americans to leave their mark on the tournament.

In Group 2, the weakest of the tournament's four groups, France, Yugoslavia, Scotland, and Paraguay all had an equal shot at advancing. As a result, the games produced wide-open play and little defense. The result was games loaded with goals. The group opener on June 8 at Idrottsparken in Norrköping saw France steamroll past Paraguay 7–3 thanks to a Just Fontaine hat trick. The French striker, who was born in Morocco to a French father and Spanish mother, would emerge as one of the tournament's most prolific scorers ever. In the group's other match on the same day in Arosvallen in Västerås, Yugoslavia and Scotland split the points following a 1–1 draw.

France, searching for a win in an effort to win the group, benefited from two Fontaine goals, but that wasn't enough to overcome Yugoslavia. In the end, the Yugoslavs managed a 3–2 win thanks to a Todor Veselinović goal with just two minutes left to play. In Norrköping, Paraguay defeated Scotland 3–2, dooming them to a last-place finish. France had the benefit of facing the already-eliminated Scots in the final group match on June 15 at Eyravallen in Örebro. Fontaine, once again, came through for the French with the winning goal in the 44th minute. The victory won them the group, while Yugoslavia finished second after a thrilling 3–3 draw with Paraguay at Tunavallen in Eskilstuna.

Sweden was lucky to have been drawn in a relatively easy group. That, coupled with playing at home, made qualifying out of Group 3 an attainable feat. Sweden featured several players who played professionally in Italy. Five players—Nils Liedholm (AC Milan), Kurt Hamrin (Padova), Arne Selmosson (Lazio), Lennart Skoglund (Inter Milan), and Bengt Gustavsson (Atalanta)—played for Serie A teams.

It was in the 1950s that the Scandinavian nation and Italy, countries separated by both distance and culture, embarked on a shared soccer tradition. Many Swedish players found a home playing in Italy, and some even stayed behind to spend the rest of their lives there. Swedish players hold a special place in the hearts of many Italians. The love affair between them and Serie A dates back to postwar Europe, specifically January 1948, when AC Milan signed the physically imposing Gunnar Nordahl. It was something of a gamble, despite his knack for scoring goals, given that he was one of the very first Swedish-born players to ever sign for an Italian club, but the gamble more than paid off.

In just half a season, Nordahl, then 27, blasted home 16 goals in 15 games. Standing six foot one, he was a menace in the penalty area, and was unstoppable once the ball landed at his feet. Nordahl gave nightmares to some of the best goalkeepers and defenders in the world with his volleys and simple ball movements. AC Milan had found their star player.

Nordahl's move to Italy in the 1940s turned him into an ambassador for talented Swedish players, as the club bought two of his former Swedish teammates, Gunnar Gren and Nils Liedholm, forming the "Gre-No-Li" attacking trio that would pile on goals for years. Liedholm would spend the rest of his life in Italy involved with the game. He coached Fiorentina from 1971 to 1973 and AS Roma from 1973 to 1977, before taking control of AC Milan in 1977, when he led them to their 10th league title before returning to the capital.

In the group opener on June 8, Sweden steamrolled Mexico 3–0 at Råsunda Stadium in Solna, near the capital Stockholm. A brace by striker Agne Simonsson and a Liedholm penalty kick powered the home side to the win. At the same time at Jernvallen in Sandviken, Hungary, who were expected to advance, could only muster a 1–1 draw against Wales. Political turmoil at home hadn't helped the team, and it had revealed itself on the field just four years after finishing runners-up. Kocsis, Czibor, and Puskás were no longer on the team after fleeing their homeland.

On June 11, Wales recorded another point after tying Mexico 1–1 in Solna, a game they should have won if not for a Jaime Belmonte goal in the 89th minute. The following day, Sweden defeated Hungary 2–1 in the same venue before nearly 39,000 supporters. Hamrin's two goals, in the 34th and 55th minutes, powered the Swedes to the knockout stage.

On June 15, Sweden, with nothing to play for, played Wales to a scoreless draw in Solna. For Wales, their third straight draw—coupled with Hungary's 4–0 win against Mexico in Sandviken—forced a playoff game for who would finish second.

Like Northern Ireland, Wales had overachieved in the opening round. The Welsh found success thanks to their frontline of Ivor Allchurch, Trevor Ford, and John Charles, the latter nicknamed the "Gentle Giant" by fans in Italy. Charles, who played for Juventus, was a hulking six foot two, but he'd never been thrown out of a game. On June 17, Wales defeated Hungary in what would go down as the greatest win in Welsh soccer history. Despite Lajos Tichy's 33rd-minute goal to open the scoring, Wales tied the score with Ivor Allchurch in the 55th minute, before Terry Medwin scored the winning goal 17 minutes from time to complete the shock defeat in Solna.

Despite the outcome of the two previous World Cups, Brazil remained a very strong team. The USSR, the defending Olympic gold winners from the 1956 Melbourne Games, and Austria, third-place finishers at the World Cup four years earlier, made Group 4 formidable. Even England—weakened by the loss of several Manchester United players in the Munich air disaster of February 1958—remained a competitive side, although not the team they had been before the crash. Players such as Roger Byrne, Tommy Taylor, Duncan Edwards, and Eddie Colman would have made the squad. Instead, they were dead, and England entered the tournament with relatively low spirits.

With only Tom Finney and Billy Wright on the roster from the team that went out at the 1954 finals, coach Walter Winterbottom had to rely on his best younger players like Don Howe, Ronnie Clayton, and Johnny Haynes. Winterbottom did reach out to Bobby Charlton, a Munich survivor. He traveled with the team but never played. "It was a hell of a job [trying to put together a roster]," assistant coach Bill Nicholson told the *Independent* in 1998, "because there weren't that many international class players around and one or two who looked up to it weren't quite ready."

Ticket sales for Group 4 games were swift and the highest of any first-round group, recording an average of 31,320 fans per game. That was higher than even Group 3, which featured the host nation. The group opened on June 8 before nearly 50,000 fans at Ullevi in Gothenburg between the Soviet Union and England. The sides split the points after a Tom Finney penalty kick five minutes from the end made the final score 2–2. At the same time at Rimnersvallen in Uddevalla, Brazil, after getting over an initial bout of nervousness, defeated Austria 3–0 thanks to a José Altafini brace. The Brazilians followed that up three days later with a scoreless draw against England in Gothenburg (the first World Cup match in tournament history to end 0–0), while the USSR blanked Austria 2–0 at Ryavallen in Borås.

All four teams remained in contention heading into the final match day scheduled for June 15. The Brazilians punched their ticket to the next round with a 2–0 win against the Soviet Union in Gothenburg after a Vavá brace. At the same time in Borås, England, in need of a win to advance, could only muster a 2–2 draw against Austria. The Brazil-USSR game also marked the debut of Edson Arantes do Nascimento, a then-17-year-old player known primarily by his nickname Pelé. He had arrived in Sweden sidelined by a knee injury, although that had not been his only hurdle. Team doctors had warned the coaching staff that Pelé was too immature to play at such a high level. Head coach Vincente Feola shrugged off the diagnosis and called him up anyway. After sitting on the bench for the Seleção's first two games, Pelé finally made his World Cup debut against the Soviet Union, providing an assist on Vavá's second goal. As a result, Brazil won the group, while England was forced into a one-game playoff against the USSR.

Pelé had grown up like many Brazilian boys of his generation, playing soccer on dusty streets with a ball made of rags. It was this impoverished upbringing that motivated Pelé to excel at the game. His skill was a ticket out of his family's economic situation. He signed his first pro contract in 1956 with Santos, a team he would play for his entire life until signing with the New York Cosmos in 1975. Pelé's career was coming full bloom now that he had been called up to the national team for the 1958 World Cup.

On June 17, in Gothenburg, the Soviet Union defeated England 1–0 to advance to the quarterfinals. In the midst of the Cold War, at a time when the Soviet communist state put a lot of emphasis on sporting success, the West looked at the USSR as a political threat more than a strong soccer team. In defeating England, the USSR sent a message to the world that they were interested in threatening the world soccer order. The game's only goal, scored by striker Anatoli Ilyin in the 69th minute, put the Soviet Union through. England played better in this game than their previous match against the USSR that had ended in a draw. Nonetheless, the Soviets had finished second and advanced to the knockout stage.

Quarterfinals

The four games of this round were played simultaneously on June 19 in four different venues. Brazil against upstart Wales in Gothenburg proved to be a delicious affair. Pelé, now fully fit, dazzled the crowd of nearly 26,000 with his footwork and skill. It would be Pelé who would slam in the winning goal in the 66th minute. After controlling the ball off his chest, Pelé flicked the ball into the air and rifled through a right-footed shot that rocketed past a few Welsh defenders and past goalkeeper Jack Kelsey. Despite being dwarfed by his more muscular and taller opponents, Pelé's assertive style and dribbling skills made up for it.

"I have no idea how many times I ran and jumped, ran and jumped, all the while screaming, Goooooooaaaaaaalllll! like a maniac," Pelé recalled to Harry Harris for his book *Pelé: His Life and Times*. "I had to get rid of that tremendous pressure of relief and joy. I don't know what was inside me. I was crying like a baby, babbling, while the rest of the team pummeled me, almost suffocating me."

For Wales, their fairy-tale World Cup run had come to an end. For Brazil, this would be just the start of a great run that would go a long way in making up for the World Cup final defeat just eight years earlier. "All of us are living a dream, but none more so than me," Pelé said. "I try not to waste time trying to analyze this strange feeling. I know this is no time to be distracted."

In Norrköping, France swept past Northern Ireland 4–0, thanks to two second-half goals by Fontaine, to reach the semifinals. Sweden, meanwhile, hosted the Soviet Union in Solna before 31,900 fans. All the energy and discipline demonstrated by the Soviets was nowhere to be seen as Sweden swept past them 2–0. Second-half goals from Hamrin and Simonsson were enough to get through to the semifinals. In the round's fourth match, West Germany advanced with a 1–0 win against Yugoslavia via a Rahn goal after just 12 minutes that proved to be the winner.

Semifinals

Brazil faced France in Solna on June 24, while Sweden traveled to Gothenburg to meet West Germany in the other semifinal. Brazil, increasingly the favorites to reach the final at this point, put on an offensive show against the French. Vavá put Brazil up after just two minutes, but Fontaine equalized seven minutes later. What looked to be a close game became anything but. Pelé, who had become one of the tournament's most popular players, netted a hat trick to power Brazil to a 5–2 victory. The game, largely lauded as the tournament's best match, showcased just how strong the Brazilians had become during the course of the decade. Indeed, under Feola, Brazil had been transformed into a creative attacking force. Brazil's 4–2–4 system favored the attack, and Pelé was just the right player given his exuberance and ability to score from practically anywhere in the penalty area.

While the French had proven to be offensive masters, it was a teenager named Pelé who showed them and the world that Brazil would forever be a World Cup favorite. Sweden, meanwhile, also reached the final—buoyed by the home crowd of nearly 50,000—to defeat West Germany 3–1. "When I saw Pelé play, it made me feel I should hang up my boots," Fontaine told reporters.

The final between Sweden and Brazil would prove to be a fantastic encounter between two teams who shrugged off defensive tactics in favor of attacking soccer. In the third-place match, Fontaine would score four goals in France's 6–3 win against West Germany to finish as tournament top scorer with 13 goals. Nonetheless, all eyes were on Pelé as Brazil prepared for the final.

Final: Brazil vs. Sweden

Following a day of heavy rain, Råsunda Stadium in Solna played host to the World Cup final on June 29 between Brazil and Sweden. Nearly 52,000 fans packed into the venue to cheer on the home side, while the Brazilians, looking to shake off the ghosts of 1950, came into the match as the favorites. It was the first time in World Cup history that a final featured a European nation pitted against a South American one.

The Brazilians, playing in their secondary blue shirts to avoid a clash with the home team, had insisted on playing in their canary-yellow shirts. A draw was arranged in order to decide which team would use its regular jerseys. When Brazil boycotted the draw, Sweden was announced as the winner, and Brazil was forced to find an alternate jersey color. Initially, Brazil considered wearing white, but the idea was rejected when the players were frightened by the notion that it recalled their defeat in 1950. Instead, the team purchased 22 blue jerseys and sewed the official national team crest on the chests on the eve of the game.

Both Sweden and Brazil played with defensive recklessness—although Feola made one key change that would prove crucial in the end. Out was defender Newton de Sordi, and in his place Feola inserted for the first time in the tournament Djalma Santos, a member of the 1954 team. Both Djalma and Nílton Santos combined to defuse the dynamic Swedish scoring duo of Skoglund and Hamrin.

Sweden, coached by the Englishman George Raynor and playing a 4–1–4–1 formation, took the lead after just four minutes, following an excellent finish by Liedholm after beating out two defenders. The Swedish tactic of scoring early had worked, but the effect of putting the Brazilians on their heels would not. It was the first time Brazil had been down a goal at this tournament, but the lead evaporated. Vavá equalized just five minutes later, poking the ball into the net right in front of goalkeeper Kalle Svensson after a pass from Garrincha, whose nickname translates into "Little Bird," after he flew down the wing. In the 32nd minute, Vavá scored a second goal, very similar to his first, to give Brazil a lead 2–1 at the break.

Ten minutes into the second half, Brazil put the match out of reach when Pelé scored in the 55th minute. The goal was born after Pelé took control of the ball inside the penalty area, chipped the ball over a defender, then brilliantly shot it past a helpless Svensson. The Brazilians totally dominated the Swedes from that point forward. Mário Zagallo, one of the team's most adept wingers, scored a fourth in the 68th minute, and Sweden responded with a goal by Simonsson in the 80th minute. With Sweden's backline in disarray, Pelé scored a second in the final minute, a goal that came after outjumping his marker to head the ball into the goal, completing the 5–2 win.

The crowd cheered at the sound of the final whistle. The Brazilian players, who had won the hearts of the home nation with their off-field friendliness just weeks prior, returned the favor by parading a Swedish flag around the field for the crowd to see. The players then received the congratulations of King Gustav IV as Pelé sobbed from overwhelming emotion. For a player who would come to be known as *O Rei* (The King), the finale was a fitting tribute to the game's new royalty. Pelé had left his hometown by train to embark on a pro career. He returned from Sweden just two years later by plane as a world champion.

In fact, Pelé and his teammates were treated like kings upon their arrival in Rio de Janeiro. The players were feted like heroes in the streets with carnival-like ecstasy. Scores of Brazilians jumped and screamed with joy, some passing out from the emotion. Confetti rained down from buildings, and Pelé needed dozens of police officers to protect him from the enthusiastic crowds as the players rode a bus hoisting aloft the trophy for the masses to see. The ghosts of 1950 had, in large measure, been exorcised.

CHAPTER THREE

Swinging Sixties

PORTUGUESE SCORING LEGEND EUSÉBIO WAS STILL HASSLED FOR AUTO-graphs at the World Cup, even though he hadn't played in one for more than 40 years. That was what he experienced wherever he went during the 2010 World Cup in South Africa.

Like Pelé, he was one of the greatest to ever play the game. And also like the Brazilian legend, Eusébio (whose full name was Eusébio da Silva Ferreira, nicknamed the "Black Panther") came to the United States to play in the North American Soccer League (NASL) as part of a wave of international stars-turned-ambassadors of the game in the 1970s.

Eusébio spent most of his career with Portuguese club Benfica, scoring 317 goals in 301 games in a 15-year career that included two European Cups. After a season with the Boston Minutemen, he added an NASL championship for Toronto Metros-Croatia as the club went on to win the 1976 Soccer Bowl. Eusébio would spend the following season with the Las Vegas Quicksilver before dropping down a division to finish his North American sojourn with the American Soccer League's New Jersey Americans in 1978.

A native of the African country of Mozambique, a former Portu-guese colony that gained its independence in 1975, Eusébio played for Portugal, scoring 41 times in 64 appearances. Eusébio's athleticism and ferocious right foot helped him score nine goals at the 1966 World Cup to end as tournament top scorer.

"That was a long time ago, but I do have a lot of memories," he told me ahead of the 2010 World Cup semifinal in Cape Town when asked about his past exploits.

Decades before African superstars George Weah, Didier Drogba, and Samuel Eto'o dominated the international game, there was Eusébio. He did it during an era that included Pelé, Bobby Charlton, and Johan Cruyff. Portugal's imperialism in Africa, which can be traced to explorer Vasco da Gama who made landfall there in the 15th century on his way to India, made it so that Eusébio would represent the European nation in international competitions. Nonetheless, he held two passports after his homeland gained independence.

Eusébio, who died four years later at age 71 from heart failure, was at that World Cup working for FIFA's 1GOAL project, a campaign aimed at helping to educate underserved children in African nations. A humanitarian during his retirement years, Eusébio was one of the game's best scorers in his playing days. One of his best memories was Portugal's win against North Korea at the 1966 World Cup. The game is remembered for being frenetic, frequently brilliant, and tremendously fun.

"The quarterfinal game against North Korea because they were a good team and it was 3–0 against us. I knew we could score and that is what we did," he said, a smile taking over his face after completing the sentence. "I also knew that if they scored another goal, we would lose. Then we won."

I remember cutting him off. "The final score was 5–3 for Portugal," I said. "Your team was really a great side. You regret not playing in more World Cups?"

Eusébio smiled again. This is a man who didn't have any regrets.

"That is the past. I enjoyed the World Cup in 1966," he replied. "The other times we did not qualify. I became famous with Benfica and the people still remember me. Now I enjoy going to the World Cup and watching these young players."

1962 WORLD CUP
The 1960s was a decade of changes. The game's response to the complex cultural and political revolution that took place around the globe during

this era wasn't limited to bushy mop tops. It was the decade that FIFA became the money-making machine it remains to this day. The World Cup, for the first time, became a global marketing success thanks largely to the advent of television.

The 1954 and 1958 editions were important for FIFA in terms of widening their global reach through television, but the 1966 edition was a turning point in regard to the link between television and the game. For the first time, organizers took into account the importance of TV. Improved camera locations and more dedicated space for TV and radio commentators all took place that year. In response, television makers used the World Cup as a publicity tool for sales, especially throughout Western Europe. The 1968 Summer Games in Mexico City, followed by the 1970 World Cup, also held in Mexico, became the first sporting events to be seen live across most of the planet.

"The technological platform for soccer to 'take off' in the second half of the 20th century was provided by two wartime developments: the jet engine and high-powered floodlighting. This permitted faster, easier midweek international travel and night-time football. The significance was first evidenced in the European club competitions and was magnified many times over by the advent of international television technology which opened the way for mass viewing and then sponsorship," said Keir Radnedge, a British journalist and author who covered his first World Cup in 1966. "The exclusivity value for TV and sponsors was developed for FIFA by the London PR firm West Nally, initially in 1978 but formally from 1982 onward. I would not pick out one single technology but the matrix of several."

Stanley Rous, an English-born former referee, took over the FIFA presidency in 1961. Rous had made a major contribution to the sport by rewriting the Laws of the Game in 1938, making them easier to understand. As a referee, he was also the first to employ the diagonal system of on-field positioning for referees as a standard practice, something used to this day. As president, Rous would end up alienating FIFA's non-European members by resisting efforts to expand the World Cup and by supporting apartheid South Africa's right to compete at the international level. The corruption FIFA would become known for wouldn't happen for another decade as television rights to the World Cup became increasingly more valuable.

The seventh edition of the World Cup was held in Chile. After Europe hosted two straight tournaments, the South American federations argued that the 1962 edition must be held in the Americas or they threatened a boycott. Argentina and Chile put forth candidacies. The Chilean bid, led by the officials from the country's FA Carlos Dittborn and Juan Pinto Durán, toured many nations trying to persuade FIFA members to vote in their favor. The FIFA Congress met in Lisbon, Portugal, in 1956, voting 31 to 12 (with 13 members abstaining) in favor of Chile. Dittborn, however, died a month before the start of the competition after succumbing to a heart attack.

Chile's bid had originally called for eight venues to host the games across eight cities up and down the geographically narrow nation: Santiago, Viña del Mar, Rancagua, Arica, Talca, Concepción, Talcahuano, and Valdivia. It was on May 22, 1960, two years before the World Cup was to be played, that a 9.5 magnitude earthquake struck southern Chile. The massive quake, which triggered tsunamis and landslides, claimed 50,000 lives and impacted an area that housed some two million people.

The earthquake forced the organizing committee to completely modify the World Cup. Talca, Concepción, Talcahuano, and Valdivia were severely impacted and removed from the list of host cities. Antofagasta and Valparaíso declined to host games. Viña del Mar and Arica, meanwhile, managed to rebuild their stadiums, while the U.S.-based Braden Copper Company, which controlled the El Teniente copper mine, allowed the use of its stadium in Rancagua. The setbacks resulted in the use of just four cities, including the northern city of Arica near the Peruvian border. The Estadio Nacional in the capital city of Santiago served as the centerpiece and would be the most used venue by hosting 10 games, including the final.

The 1962 tournament will be remembered as the last World Cup that bears no real resemblance to the supercharged soccer tournament of the modern era with its slick marketing and public relations campaigns. On the field, the tournament format went unchanged from 1958 and again featured 16 teams divided into four groups. In one major change, goal average was used to separate teams with equal points following the opening round, abandoning the need for a playoff game. In the knockout round, draws would be decided by playing 30 minutes of extra time. For any match other than the final, if the teams were still even, then lots would be drawn to determine who advanced. The final, however, would have to be replayed if still tied after extra time. Thankfully, no drawing of lots or replays were needed in the end.

Four teams were seeded in the draw—Brazil, England, Italy, and Uruguay—and the top two teams in each group advanced to the quarter-finals. The draw yielded the following groups:

Group 1: Uruguay, the Soviet Union, Yugoslavia, and Colombia

Group 2: Italy, Chile, West Germany, and Switzerland

Group 3: Brazil, Mexico, Czechoslovakia, and Spain

Group 4: England, Hungary, Argentina, and Bulgaria

A month before the start of the tournament, two Italian journalists, Antonio Ghirelli and Corrado Pizzinelli, arrived in Chile for pre–World Cup coverage. The dispatches that ran in the Italian press, comparing Santiago to a slum, angered the Chileans. Pizzinelli, writing for *La Nazione*, reported that Chileans were malnourished and illiterate. Ghirelli, writing for *Corriere della Sera*, questioned whether the host nation was up to the task: "Chile is a small, proud and poor country. It has agreed to organize this World Cup in the same way as Mussolini agreed to send our air force to bomb London (they didn't arrive). The capital city has 700 hotel beds. The phones don't work. Taxis are as rare as faithful husbands."

The journalists claimed that editors back home had embellished their reporting to sell newspapers. Nonetheless, the Chilean press responded by accusing the Italian players of being fascists and mobsters. It would be this animus that would spill over onto the field once the tournament got underway.

Group Stage

Group 1 opened on May 30—one of four matches at the tournament that kicked off simultaneously that day—when Uruguay met Colombia at Estadio Carlos Dittborn in Arica, a venue named in honor of the recently deceased administrator who had worked so hard to bring the World Cup to his country. The entire group would play their games in this northern outpost to avoid travel.

Uruguay had a tricky time against their South American counterparts. The Colombians, making their World Cup debut, were managed by the Argentina legend Adolfo Pedernera but were made up entirely of no-name domestic league-based players. Two goals in the second half, including the game winner from striker José Sasía, helped Uruguay grab the win. It also didn't hurt that the Uruguayans employed a rough style of play that resulted in an injury to Francisco Zuluaga. The Colombian captain and central defender had put his side ahead via a penalty kick after just 19 minutes.

The following day, the Soviet Union, building on their success after capturing the inaugural edition of the European Championship just two years prior, were in command for much of their match versus Yugoslavia. After a scoreless first half, striker Valentin Ivanov put the USSR ahead in the 51st minute, tallying the go-ahead goal after a Soviet free kick initially slammed across the crossbar. The Soviet Union sealed their 2–0 win with striker Viktor Ponedelnik's goal.

On June 2, Yugoslavia defeated Uruguay 3–1, while the following day saw the USSR and Colombia play a rollicking 4–4 draw. The Colombians knew they needed to pull off an upset to keep their chances alive, and they almost did in the end. The Soviets had jumped out to a 3–0 in the game's opening 11 minutes thanks to two goals by Ivanov and one by Igor Chislenko. In goal for the Soviets, Lev Yashin's skills weren't enough to keep Colombia off the score sheet. The usually reliable goalkeeper would have a bad day. The South Americans pulled one back for a 3–1 USSR lead going into the dressing rooms. In the second half, the USSR made it 4–1, but Colombia scored three unanswered goals in a span of four minutes to make it 4–4. The highlight of the match came in the 68th minute when midfielder Marcos Coll scored directly from a corner kick—known as an "Olympic goal"—the first time that had ever happened at a World Cup. The goal off a corner, when scored without any contact by another player, is named after Argentine striker Cesáreo Onzari's corner kick that spun directly into the goal for the then–defending Olympic champions Argentina in a 1924 friendly against Uruguay.

Coll, knowing that his teammates couldn't compete in the air against their taller opponents, aimed for the near post and put the ball into the net. The 8,000 in attendance loudly cheered the goal and for Colombia at the final whistle. "There was a huge roar because I scored a goal against the man who was the best goalkeeper in the world at that time," Coll recalled in an interview with FIFA's website in 2014. "Everyone was excited because I scored an Olympic goal direct from the corner. It really was madness."

On June 6, the Soviets needed a win to advance and got it with a 2–1 win against Uruguay on an 89th-minute goal by Ivanov, his fourth in three games. Yashin's confidence, still shaken after the Colombia game, would never truly recover at this tournament. The following day, a much-improved Yugoslavia defeated Colombia 5–0 to finish second and join the USSR in the knockout stage.

Group 2, one of the toughest at this tournament, saw Chile take to the field on May 30 against Switzerland before 65,000 fans at Santiago's Estadio Nacional. The excitement over the start of the tournament and the host nation's involvement reached a boiling point with this match. The nation's president, Jorge Alessandri, failed to meet the moment. He delivered an uninspiring inaugural speech before the game and left before it ended.

Alessandri and the crowd watched as Chile fell early to the Swiss. Rolf Wüthrich scored after unleashing a long-range shot, taking advantage of a bad throw by goalkeeper Misael Escuti. The Chileans responded by increasing their offensive pressure. The hosts hit the woodwork twice with defender Carlos Contreras and striker Leonel Sánchez. In the 44th minute, Sánchez scored to tie the game. Chile stormed back better in the second half, scoring with Jaime Ramirez in the 51st minute and again four minutes later with Sánchez. The following day at the same venue, Italy and West Germany played to a scoreless draw. Despite a series of vicious fouling—a trend that would grow at this competition—backlines on both sides of the ball helped to preserve the tie.

The June 2 encounter between Chile and Italy was tense from the start. The Italian players, fearing retaliation from the fans after the journalism snafu, greeted the 66,000 upon entering the stadium by tossing flowers into the stands. Many were tossed back. Referee Ken Aston was put in charge of the game. The Englishman would have a long afternoon ahead of him. Making matters worse for the Italians was that the team featured a new group of *oriundi*. South Americans largely saw these players as traitors willing to sell out to wealthy Italian clubs and masquerade as Italians. Indeed, the players—José Altafini, Omar Sívori, and Humberto Maschio—did have Italian blood and were more than happy to don the Azzurri's shirt as an homage to their heritage.

The match started with the Italians creating a few chances, but the situation changed just five minutes into the game when Maschio struck Sánchez while Aston had his back turned. Italian midfielder Giorgio Ferrini was sent off two minutes later—with help of a police escort—because he refused to leave the field after overreacting to a foul by Honorino Landa. The match was halted for eight minutes. Sánchez, in an attempt to try and put Chile ahead, was fouled by Mario David. Sánchez responded by punching David in the nose near the linesman. Aston, however, took no action despite the infraction. David tried to get his revenge in the 41st minute, kicking Sánchez in the head. Aston expelled the Italian defender, and the Azzurri were down to nine players.

The Italians walked off the field at halftime with the game scoreless and considered abandoning the game, but Aston feared a riot by the home crowd. Instead, the sides returned for the second half, and the animosity exhibited in the opening 45 minutes subsided a bit. The Italians hung on, hoping for a draw, but Chile had other plans. Ramirez headed in a free kick that Italian goalkeeper Carlo Mattrel failed to clear in the 73rd minute.

Midfielder Jorge Toro doubled the lead from 25 yards out three minutes from the end to make it 2–0. The players almost came to fisticuffs one more time, but Aston ended the game without having to punish any of the players. Some angry Chileans threw stones at the bus carrying the Italian players as it departed the stadium. FIFA handed Ferrini a one-game ban, meaning he would miss the following match against Switzerland. The game—dubbed the "Battle of Santiago"—had been a disgusting affair. When highlights were shown on British television, the game was described by BBC commentator David Coleman as "the most stupid, appalling, disgusting and disgraceful exhibition of football, possibly in the history of the game." Some questioned Aston's abilities. The Englishman would not referee at the tournament again, citing an Achilles' tendon strain as the reason. Nonetheless, Aston would go on to work for FIFA and invent the yellow and red card system used to this day to discipline players.

On June 3, West Germany defeated Switzerland 2–1 in Santiago. The Swiss had dominated the game, but it was Uwe Seeler's goal in the 59th minute that made the difference in the end. Three days later, West Germany won the group, beating Chile 2–0 in Santiago. As a result, Chile, who had already qualified for the knockout stage, finished second. The Italians, playing on June 7 in Santiago, blanked Switzerland 3–0, but the victory was unable to stave off early elimination for the Azzurri.

Defending champion Brazil, who had nine players on their roster who had helped the team win the trophy in 1958, headlined Group 3 as games got underway on May 30 at Estadio Sausalito in Viña del Mar. The Brazilians came into the tournament as favorites, and they did not disappoint in their opening match. Second-half goals by Zagallo and Pelé were enough to down Mexico. Pelé's left-footed goal in the box, after he aptly dribbled past four defenders, proved to be a highlight-reel masterpiece. It was exactly what the world had expected from the flashy Brazilians. The following day, the all-European contest between Czechoslovakia and Spain degenerated into a testy affair. Amid all the fouling and sloppy play, Czechoslovakia grabbed the win 10 minutes from the end after striker Jozef Štibrányi took advantage of a defensive error.

The Brazilians, favored to grab all the points against Czechoslovakia, could only manage a draw in Viña del Mar. Brazil, forced to play with 10 players after Pelé tore a thigh muscle in the first half, were now forced to play the remainder of the tournament without their star player. The following day, Spain, despite having the great Real Madrid side as its backbone, looked lackluster and did just enough to beat Mexico, recording a 1–0 win with a Joaquín Peiró goal in the final minute to keep the team's hopes of advancing alive. Despite being coached by Helenio Herrera, soon to conquer Europe with Inter Milan, and Puskás in the lineup after he was made a Spanish citizen, they entered their final fixture in need of a positive result.

With Pelé out for the June 6 encounter with Spain, Brazil manager Aymoré Moreira called on Amarildo to start alongside Zagallo and Vavá in the team's three-pronged attack. Spain, playing their best soccer to date, controlled the match early on and took the lead 10 minutes before the half when Adelardo Rodríguez's shot found the back of the net. Brazil, thanks to a series of refereeing errors in their favor, kept the score close. A Nílton Santos foul inside the box was not whistled as a penalty kick for Spain by Chilean referee Sergio Bustamante. Instead, Spain was given a free kick.

The 18,000 in attendance, enthralled by the Brazilians and the wonderful skills of Garrincha, would cheer the South Americans to victory. Amarildo, despite the weight of having to replace Pelé in the starting lineup, tallied twice, in the 72nd and 86th minutes, to carry Brazil to a 2–1 comeback. The win also gave the Brazilians a spot in the knockout round at Spain's expense. Joining them was Czechoslovakia, who lost to Mexico 3–1 the following day.

Hungary, not the team they used to be, and England, the team many wanted to see succeed, shared Group 4 with Argentina and Bulgaria. The entire group played their games at Braden Copper Stadium in Rancagua. Argentina and Bulgaria got the group going on May 30 before just 7,000 fans. The South Americans got on the board after just four minutes when Héctor Facundo scored off a cross. Argentina then retreated into its own half in a bid to preserve the win. When not playing defensive soccer, the Argentines engaged in a series of fouls that constantly broke up play and frustrated the Bulgarians. The fouling was so brutal that two Bulgarian players, midfielder Todor Diev and striker Hristo Iliev, were sidelined for the remainder of the tournament. Argentina walked away with the 1–0 win.

Hungary, wearing their iconic cherry-red jerseys, versus England, in their classic white ones, attracted almost 10,000 fans. Those in attendance saw a better game than the one played the previous day. The match—marred by a slippery field after a heavy downpour the night before—pitted Hungary's wonderful passing and deft defending against England's offense and long-ball play. Grosics, the lone survivor of Hungary's 1954 team that lost in the final, started in net. The game, knotted 1–1 into the second half, was resolved in the 71st minute with a Flórián Albert goal that resulted after he out-dribbled goalkeeper Ron Springett. Hungary prevailed 2–1, putting England in a precarious position and in need of a win in their next match against Argentina.

On June 2, England, playing a more defensive game, took on Argentina in a match that would become a rivalry decades later. The Three Lions jumped out to a 1–0 lead with Ron Flowers via a penalty kick after 17 minutes. The English doubled their lead three minutes before halftime when Bobby Charlton's shot beat goalkeeper Antonio Roma at the far post. Jimmy Greaves put the game away in the 67th minute before Argentina pulled one back nine minutes from time with José Sanfilippo in what turned out to be a hard-fought 3–1 England victory. The following day, Hungary trounced Bulgaria 6–1 thanks to an Albert hat trick, to remain undefeated and in first place in the group heading into the final match day.

The June 6 Hungary-Argentina match ended scoreless, as did England versus Bulgaria the following day, which allowed the Hungarians to win the group and advance to the knockout stage. England, tied on points for second place with Argentina, had only needed a draw heading into their last group game. They ultimately advanced thanks to a better goals scored average than Argentina over the three group games.

Quarterfinals

The knockout round got underway on June 10 in Viña del Mar, with Brazil's game against England the highlight of the day. Brazil, a team with a deep talent pool, came into the knockout stage needing Garrincha to have a big game. His inventiveness with the ball did not always translate to numbers on the stat sheet, but his play would be a determining factor for the Brazilians. Garrincha had been born with his right leg two inches shorter than his left and both legs slightly bent inward, so it looked "as if a gust of wind had blown his legs sideways," according to Alex Bellos in *Futebol: The Brazilian Way of Life*. His bent legs were a genetic trait—passed down from the Fulnio, the Indian tribe of his grandparents—and it allowed him to move in dangerous ways.

Garrincha, like so many Brazilians who would come after him, delighted in toying with defenders by dribbling around them. Garrincha possessed amazing dribbling skills and could also unleash deft passes and crosses at will. Garrincha, however, had to deal with demons of his own off the field. Those demons, which included alcoholism, resulted in his death in 1983 at the age of just 49.

"While Brazilians put Pelé on a pedestal, they do not love him the way they love Garrincha," observed Bellos. "It is more than the fact that tragic figures are naturally more appealing, since they are more human, although this probably helped. It is because Pelé does not reflect national desires. Pelé, above everything else, symbolizes winning. Garrincha symbolizes playing for playing's sake. Brazil is not a country of winners. It is a country of a people who like to have fun."

The game against England, played in Viña del Mar, featured an energetic Brazil side hell-bent on winning. Garrincha had menaced opposing defenses with his ability to unleash assists on the right flank; this time, he showed a different part of his game by scoring with his head in the 31st minute off a Zagallo corner. England equalized just seven minutes later when Greaves's header hit the bar, only for Gerry Hitchens to slam the ball into the net off the rebound. Soon after halftime, Brazil regained its advantage in the 53rd minute after Vavá headed in Garrincha's perfectly executed free kick.

"Garrincha was a very individualistic player, everyone knows, but that was great for the team," Pelé recalled in a 2014 interview conducted with Brazil's World Cup Organizing Committee to help promote the tournament. "Every team that would play against Brazil would play defensively, and they would need two or three [players] to take care of Garrincha."

Garrincha's ability to get past defenders and create chances caused problems for the English defense throughout much of the second half. It would be Garrincha's second goal, to the delight of the 18,000 in attendance, with an unstoppable curling shot that got past Springett into the top corner, that sealed the 3–1 victory. It would be one of the best goals of the tournament. Even without Pelé, the Seleção had found a way to win in flashy style. The only thing that could upstage Garrincha was when a dog ran onto the field during the match, forcing Greaves to take matters into his own hands.

"No one could get a hold of him. Suddenly, I got on my hands and knees, being that I'm a dog lover, and called the dog over," Greaves recalled during a 2014 panel discussion held in London sponsored by the English FA. "And he came over. I picked the dog up and cuddled him. As I cuddled him, he peed all down my shirt."

Greaves recalled that Garrincha adopted the pup, taking it with him to Brazil once the tournament came to an end. He even noted that Brazilian photographers hounded him because, as Greaves put it, "they wanted a picture of the man who got Garrincha his dog."

"I'm known in Brazil as Garrincha's dog catcher," he joked.

At the same time, Chile took the field against the Soviet Union in Arica. The home crowd of 18,000 cheered on the hosts from the opening whistle. Eleven minutes into the game, Leonel Sánchez opened the score with a free kick from the right side of the penalty area that stunned Yashin at the near post. Igor Chislenko equalized for the USSR just 14 minutes later after picking up a deflected shot by Viktor Ponedelnik.

Not to be outdone, Chile regained the lead with Eladio Rojas who scored off a low shot from 30 yards away to beat Yashin. The goal unleashed wild celebrations in the stands, and a few dozen fans even stormed the field to exult. Order was eventually restored, and the game resumed without incident. The Soviet goalkeeper, still reeling from his poor performance in the opening round, was not playing like he was one of the world's best shot stoppers. Chile then deftly took control of the match to hang on for a 2–1 win and a date with Brazil in an all–South American semifinal.

The other two quarterfinals both ended by identical scores of 1–0. Czechoslovakia got past Hungary in Rancagua thanks to an Adolf Scherer goal. Yugoslavia, meanwhile, defeated West Germany in Santiago with a Petar Radaković goal five minutes from the end. The win set up an all-European contest between Czechoslovakia and Yugoslavia, putting the nations in the semifinals for the first time since the 1930s.

Semifinals

Chile, still reeling from the earthquake that rocked their nation, found itself a step away from the final. The June 13 encounter against Brazil in Santiago attracted a capacity crowd of 67,000. The Brazilians, forced into a more defensive mode than they were used to, still had the tournament's most talented players. Chile's dream run would end in Santiago. As for Brazil, they would be flying high thanks to Garrincha's wizardry. It was his explosive pace that made Brazil a strong contender to repeat as world champions.

By game's end, the French sports newspaper *L'Equipe* would proclaim Garrincha to be "the most extraordinary right winger football has known." Brazil's 4–2 win was highlighted by Garrincha and Vavá, who both recorded a brace each, to power their side to a second consecutive final. Again, Garrincha was the man of the match, even scoring another goal via a header off a Zagallo corner kick in a replay of his strike against England. Garrincha's abilities proved once again to be out of this world. After the win, a headline in the Chilean newspaper *El Mercurio* read: "What Planet Is Garrincha From?"

Despite the achievement, Brazil's shot at winning the World Cup hit a snag when Rojas fouled Garrincha seven minutes from time. Garrincha retaliated, resulting in the Brazilian being sent off. To Brazil's delight, FIFA did not impose any further punishment, and Garrincha was green-lighted to play in the final. Chile had put together a wonderful effort, both in terms of their play and as tournament organizers. Chile's third-place finish was better than anyone could have predicted on the eve of the competition. Thanks to Dittborn's vision, Chile had achieved the impossible.

In the other semifinal played at the same time in Viña del Mar, Czechoslovakia got the best of Yugoslavia 3–1 after a scoreless opening half. Czechoslovakia's 4–3–3 was played to great effect, and their domination of the midfield paid off in the end. Adolf Scherer's exceptional play—including a goal in the 80th minute, followed by a second on a penalty kick four minutes later—put the Czechoslovakians in the final, for the first time in 24 years.

Final: Brazil vs. Czechoslovakia

Brazil came into the final as the heavy favorites. Czechoslovakia, 24–1 odds to win the title at the start of the tournament, played the role of underdog. Nonetheless, the Brazilians knew not to take any opponent lightly, especially in a deciding match. Both teams had played one another during the group stage, which ended in a goalless draw. This was the second World Cup final match featuring teams who had already played against each other during the group stage after Hungary and West Germany in 1954.

"Everybody thinks that Brazil are red-hot favorites, but we're ready to spring a surprise," Czechoslovakia manager Rudolf Vytlačil told reporters on the eve of the game. "I've got faith in my players. They're fit, they're skillful and they're in a better frame of mind than they were in the first game against Brazil. We can win."

The final, held at the Estadio Nacional in Santiago, saw Czechoslovakia take the lead in the opening 15 minutes with midfielder Josef Masopust. His exploits at this World Cup would earn him European Player of the Year honors by year's end. It was a long pass from Adolf Scherer that split the Brazilian defense and found Masopust one-on-one with Gilmar. Masopust's low shot got right past the Brazilian goalkeeper.

The Czechoslovaks, hoping their defense could make up for the gap in attacking talent, weren't able to hang on to the lead. Two minutes later, Amarildo, who had filled in admirably for Pelé, tied the score. Pelé, who was watching the game from the stands, erupted with joy along with the 69,000 in attendance. The goal, born from a throw-in, saw Amarildo blow past two defenders and score from an impossible angle on the left side of the area past goalkeeper Viliam Schrojf. The crowd approved by enthusiastically waving handkerchiefs.

The Brazilians, playing a 4–2–4 with Garrincha powering the offensive efforts from both wings, embarked on a series of raids that had the Czechoslovakians in convulsions. The defense, along with Schrojf, thwarted several scoring attempts during the course of the first half. After the first half ended tied at one, the Seleção continued to apply the offensive pressure that had characterized much of the opening 45 minutes. In the 69th minute, Amarildo, after running straight at the goal, put up a delightful ball that found Zito. The Brazilian midfielder headed the ball into the net for the 2–1 lead. Nine minutes later, Brazil put the game away when Vavá pounced on the ball following a blunder by Schrojf, who wasn't able to latch onto the ball. As a result, the ball rolled into the net. Again, the crowd celebrated.

Back in Brazil, the streets of Rio and other major cities erupted into carnival-like celebrations. Brazil won the match 3–1, becoming just the second team after Italy in 1938 to successfully defend its World Cup title. The Brazilians finally proved to be the soccer heavyweight that we know them to be to this day. They also proved that with or without Pelé, this was a nation capable of producing a plethora of talents, like Garrincha's genius and Zagallo's guile. Pelé, meanwhile, had contemplated leaving the squad once injured. The coaching staff and team officials begged him to stay, saying his presence would help morale. Pelé reconsidered. In the end, his presence had helped to inspire his teammates to victory.

1966 WORLD CUP

England was chosen as host of the 1966 World Cup in 1960, ahead of rival bids from Spain and West Germany. For FIFA, it marked a return to a nation directly affected by World War II. The four previous postwar tournaments were held in countries not involved in the war or that had been neutral during the conflict.

The tournament was highlighted by the absence of 1962 semifinalists Czechoslovakia and Yugoslavia. Portugal and North Korea, meanwhile, qualified for the 16-team tournament for the first time. The finals also featured no African teams after the 31 nations from that continent boycotted the qualifiers. The protest came after a 1964 FIFA ruling that required the three second-round winners from the African zone to enter into a playoff round against the winners of the Asian zone in order to qualify for the finals. The Confederation of African Football, arguing that winning their zone should have resulted in automatic qualification, demanded that FIFA guarantee at least one African nation a spot in the finals. They also argued that South Africa's readmission to FIFA—after the CAF had booted them out due to apartheid in 1958—sent the wrong message. Rous ignored these pleas, and South Africa was initially assigned to the Asia and Oceania qualifying group. South Africa was eventually disqualified following pressure from other African nations in 1964. It would take another decade, and a new FIFA presidency under the stewardship of a Brazilian official named João Havelange, for FIFA to shake off its Eurocentricity.

The tournament, held for the first time in an English-speaking country, was expected to be a marketing bonanza for FIFA and the World Cup. Television, and its global popularity, would play a large role. The tournament would prove to be a key moment for the game's globalization and "a turning point in the bond between TV and the FIFA World Cup," according to sports historian Fabio Chisari.

"There were two reasons for this: firstly, because of the growth of the worldwide television audience and secondly, because England was the country that, USA apart, had the best TV organization and facilities, and it was very likely that there would be a real chance to offer a really well made broadcast," he wrote in a 2006 study that examined the power of television and the World Cup.

Television was changing culture in the West. The mores that had dominated for much of the century were losing out in influence to pop culture. The game's best players, like Pelé, became pitchmen for a variety of products. The sale of television rights would fill FIFA's coffers starting in the late 1960s, a trend that would transform it into a multibillion-dollar organization.

World Cup organizers settled on eight venues, many of which are familiar to those who are regular viewers of the Premier League. The largest was Wembley Stadium in London, which would host a total of nine games. That included both the final and third-place match. Group 1 games were all played in London: five at Wembley, which was England's national stadium and was considered to be one of the most important venues in the world, and one at White City Stadium. Group 2 called Hillsborough Stadium in Sheffield and Villa Park in Birmingham home, while Group 3 games took place at Old Trafford in Manchester and

Goodison Park in Liverpool. Group 4's matches were played at Ayresome Park in Middlesbrough and Roker Park in Sunderland.

Chisari noted that even the choice of venues had to do with television and accommodating the growing medium. The final would be the last ever broadcast in black and white. By the 1968 Summer Olympics in Mexico City, color would become the norm.

For the first time, World Cup broadcasts would feature slow-motion replays, an innovation used to this day, to 75 countries and be watched by a cumulative audience of 400 million. Chisari noted that BBC executives feared that English homemakers would object to the blanket coverage because it would interfere with their normal daytime programming. Instead, the coverage was welcomed, Chisari found, as noted by British sports broadcaster Peter Dimmock: "Housewives have begun to appreciate that football is not just 22 chaps kicking a ball about, but something involving a great deal of skill. A woman in front of me at Wembley on Tuesday was screaming 'Hold it! Hold it!' when she thought one of our players was going to pass too early. She told me afterwards she had never been to a match before. She'd learned it all from the telly."

For the first time, the tournament featured a mascot. "World Cup Willie," a cartoon lion wearing a Union Jack jersey, became the tournament's symbol. The mascot, designed by British children's book illustrator Reg Hoye, was an instant success. Willie ignited a merchandising boom that accompanies major sports tournaments to this day. The lion was based on Hoye's son Leo. Hoye, who also did illustrations for shows like *Dr. Who*, died in 1987.

Hoye's son, Leo Francis Hoye, recalled that Willie drew instant international interest. "There was a lot of interest from West Germany and the Soviet Union, which was quite extraordinary, everyone entered into the spirit of celebrating sport without the nationalism you see today," he told the BBC in 2012.

Hoye said Willie "was used on everything from tea towels to bedspreads and mugs."

"All those things are very common [as merchandise] now, but at the time it was very new," he added. "My father was very patriotic so he was very happy about the excitement that surrounded the mascot."

The lead-up to the tournament featured another unusual hero alongside Willie—a dog named Pickles. On March 20, about two months to go before the start of the tournament, the Jules Rimet Trophy was stolen from an exhibition display in Westminster's Central Hall. A nationwide hunt ensued.

"The idea there were people by the display case all the time is just not true," said Dr. Martin Atherton, author of the 2008 book *The Theft of the Jules Rimet Trophy: The Hidden History of the 1966 World Cup*. "The whole thing was amateurish. The fact the FA let the trophy out, the security arrangements and the whole recovery of the trophy."

Atherton, speaking to the BBC in 2016 on the 50th anniversary of the theft, noted, "The security was quite inadequate. We think two people broke in through an emergency exit, took the trophy and walked out again."

Scotland Yard investigators took control of the probe, but they had very few leads to go on. One of the only clues emerged later when a ransom note for the trophy was received by then–English FA chairman Joe Mears signed by someone called "Jackson." With help from the police, Mears pretended to agree to the deal. An undercover police officer met "Jackson"—later revealed to be a former soldier named Edward Betchley—in a London park. Betchley was arrested on the spot. With the trophy still missing, the crucial moment happened seven days after its theft.

A man named Dave Corbett took his dog Pickles, a black-and-white collie, for a walk. It was the dog that made the amazing discovery behind some bushes. "Pickles was running around over by my neighbor's car," Corbett told the BBC. "As I was putting the lead on I noticed this package laying there, wrapped just in newspaper but very tightly bound with string. I tore a bit off the bottom and there was a blank shield, then there were the words Brazil, West Germany and Uruguay printed. I tore off the other end and it was a lady holding a very shallow dish above her head."

Corbett said he quickly realized he was holding the Rimet trophy. "I'd seen the pictures of the World Cup in the papers and on TV so my heart started thumping," he recalled.

The English FA, fearing the trophy would not be found, immediately commissioned a replica. Pickles gained a cult following and was feted throughout the country. The replica, along with Pickles's collar, are on display at the National Football Museum in Manchester. The actual Rimet trophy would be stolen for a second time in 1983 from Brazilian FA headquarters in Rio. This time the trophy was not recovered. It is believed that it was melted down for gold.

The draw, the first ever to be televised, featured the host nation, West Germany, Brazil, and Italy as the top seeds. These were the four randomly drawn groups:

Group 1: England, Uruguay, France, and Mexico

Group 2: West Germany, Switzerland, Argentina, and Spain

Group 3: Brazil, Bulgaria, Hungary, and Portugal

Group 4: Italy, Chile, the Soviet Union, and North Korea

The tournament format remained the same as in 1962: 16 finalists divided into four groups of four. Each group played a round-robin format with the top two teams advancing to the knockout stage. Goal average was again used to separate teams that finished tied on points. In the knockout phase, if the teams were tied after 90 minutes, 30 minutes of extra time was played. For any match other than the final, if the teams were still tied after extra time, lots would be drawn to determine who advanced. The final, the only exception to this rule, would have been replayed if tied after 120 minutes failed to yield a winner.

Group Stage

The tournament's first group opened on July 11, with England unable to get past Uruguay. The scoreless draw, before 87,000 at Wembley, was an inauspicious start for the hosts. The Three Lions, captained by Bobby Moore, had yet to excite the nation. That would come over the span of the next three weeks.

"You could walk up to Wembley and buy a ticket on the night," BBC soccer commentator John Motson recalled. "So that's how long it took for the World Cup to grip people's imagination."

Two days later, France and Mexico played to a 1–1 draw at Wembley, leaving the group wide open with two match days left to play. On July 15, Uruguay defeated France 2–1 at White City Stadium, a win matched by England the following day at Wembley. England's 2–0 victory against Mexico, via goals from Bobby Charlton and Roger Hunt, put them first in the group.

On July 19, Uruguay advanced out of Group 1 following a scoreless draw against Mexico at Wembley. The following day at the same venue, England managed to post a 2–0 victory against France thanks to a Hunt brace. The French, in need of a win, abandoned their defensive tactics and made forays into the English half. The Three Lions were a superior squad, both tactically and physically, and by winning, the group kept their hopes of winning the trophy at home very much alive.

The West Germans were the team to beat in Group 2 when it opened on July 12 in Sheffield. The West Germans, led by innovative sweeper Franz Beckenbauer and striker Uwe Seeler, trounced Switzerland 5–0 thanks to a Beckenbauer brace. Striker Helmut Haller also scored twice in a win that would also help their goals average should it come down to it. Argentina, playing the following day in Birmingham, got past Spain 2–1 thanks to two goals from Luis Artime. The striker's goal in the 77th minute broke the tie and allowed the South Americans to collect two points.

On July 15, in Sheffield, Spain and Switzerland squared off, both in need of a win, in a do-or-die game. In a tightly contested match, Spain stormed back by scoring two unanswered goals—including the winner from Amancio Amaro 15 minutes from time—for the 2–1 win. The defeat eliminated the Swiss. In Birmingham the following day, West Germany and Argentina could only muster a scoreless draw to share the spoils before a crowd of 46,500, the largest a game in this group would draw.

The West Germans failed to take advantage of Argentina having to finish the game a player short after defender Rafael Albrecht was ejected in the 65th minute after a collision with midfielder Wolfgang Weber. Argentina's overly aggressive play marred much of the match, a tactic that would hurt them over the long arc of the tournament. The West

Germans, meanwhile, were thwarted once by the crossbar and Roma in goal in the game's dying minutes. Both teams, along with Spain, entered the final match day for a shot at two spots in the knockout stage.

Argentina had the easier game, having to take on the Swiss, on July 19 in Sheffield. The Argentines dominated from the start, putting together a 2–0 win with second-half goals by Luis Artime and Ermindo Onega. The win put Argentina through to the quarterfinals. They were joined the next day by West Germany, 2–1 winners versus Spain. Seeler's goal six minutes from the end proved to be the winning goal against a very lively Spain side. The win also helped West Germany finish first in the group by virtue of having scored more goals over three matches.

Brazil came into the opening round as favorites to win Group 3. Despite that, a trio of European sides—Portugal, Hungary, and Bulgaria—would be tough opponents. Sure, the Brazilians had the offensive-minded, free-flowing *jogo bonito*, but the physicality of this tournament, especially the kind employed by European sides, meant that Pelé and his teammates had a tough task ahead. Nonetheless, Pelé, who entered the tournament at the age of 25 and in the prime of his career, would need to avoid injury this time should Brazil want to contend for the trophy again.

The group opened on July 12 in Liverpool before 47,000 fans with the Brazilians defeating Bulgaria thanks to a goal by Pelé after just 15 minutes. Garrincha added a second in the 63rd minute, proving again that the Brazilians were for real and that the connection between Pelé and Garrincha would prove unstoppable. Indeed, Brazil never lost a game whenever these two were in the starting lineup together. It would also be the last time the two would ever again play together for Brazil. The following day, Portugal steamrolled Hungary 3–1 thanks to a José Augusto brace.

While London was treated as the tournament's epicenter because it featured the host nation, there was little sign of the mass hysteria that would be evident later in the tournament once England began its march to the final.

"This is the football city of England—not stiff and serious London where you can hardly tell there is a World Cup competition going on," reported Swedish newspaper *Dagens Nyheter*. "I don't think I have ever heard a football crowd enjoy themselves as they did in last night's game between Brazil and Bulgaria."

Once again, Pelé had been manhandled at the World Cup. A mix of fouling and bad officiating conspired against the Brazilians. Pelé had been on the receiving end of some rough fouling against Bulgaria and, in the process, suffered an injury to his right knee that forced him to miss the second group match against Hungary. Tostão was used in his place, but it wouldn't be enough. Led by Flórián Albert and Ferenc Bene, the well-drilled Hungarians defeated Brazil 3–1 on July 15 in Liverpool to the shock of many in the crowd of 51,000. The following day, Portugal defeated Bulgaria 3–0 to remain undefeated and go atop the group.

Brazil's task in their last group match was to grab a win against a tough Portugal side. Ahead of what was a make-or-break game, Feola chose to make nine changes to the starting lineup. He dropped Garrincha and brought back Pelé, who was still struggling from the injury. Portugal's João Morais made sure Pelé was limited to just a few touches after spending most of the game following him. At the same time, Brazil could not match the power and finesse of a Portugal side that featured Eusébio. The striker, who scored twice, ended Brazil's tournament. The 3–1 win helped Portugal win the group, joined by Hungary who defeated Bulgaria by the same score the following day.

By the 1960s, Italian soccer was a game unto its own. After its heyday in the 1930s, the game evolved in the postwar years as did Europe's power. Nations throughout the continent had dominated the game at the club level in the European Champions Cup, led by Real Madrid in Spain and Benfica in Portugal. In the middle of the decade, for three straight seasons between 1963 and 1965, Italian sides AC Milan and Inter Milan dominated the competition.

The success of the Milan sides, which would continue on and off for decades, infused Italy with confidence entering the World Cup. The Azzurri, featuring towering sweeper Giacinto Facchetti and strikers Sandro Mazzola and Gianni Rivera, formed the backbone of a team that could go far. Both Facchetti and Mazzola played for Inter, while Rivera was the attacking engine for their rivals AC Milan. Together, they

91

formed a dynamic side. In their way stood a trio of formidable opponents in the Soviet Union and Chile, while North Korea was seen by everyone in the group as an easy two points.

The Soviet Union opened Group 4 on July 12 in Middlesbrough, blanking North Korea 3–0 via a brace from striker Eduard Malofeyev. The following day in Sunderland, the Italians took on Chile, a rematch of the "Battle of Santiago" from four years earlier, under a much calmer climate. Italy, as expected, dominated the match for long stretches for the 2–0 win on a rain-soaked field. Mazzola's opening goal, after just eight minutes, set the tone for the game. Even a constant drizzle couldn't stop the Italians from mounting attack upon attack. It was a wonderful start.

On July 15, in Middlesbrough, Chile and North Korea played to a 1–1 draw, splitting the points in a shock result that eliminated the South Americans. The draw kept the North Koreans alive in the competition following the USSR's 1–0 victory against Italy in Sunderland. It was another stunning result, aided by Chislenko's lone goal in the 58th minute and Yashin's amazing goalkeeping. The Azzurri now needed a win in their final group match against North Korea.

The North Koreans had become the tournament's darling, a Cinderella team in the making. Nonetheless, it was difficult for many Britons to cheer for them just a few short years after the Korean War. The communist nation were underdogs, something residents of blue-collar Middlesbrough could not resist. It also helped that the North Koreans wore red jerseys, the same color as the local team Middlesbrough FC, a team in the third division at the time. Italy, in bad form against the Soviets, were still favorites to advance on July 19 when they faced North Korea. Italian captain Giacomo Bulgarelli had been doubtful for the game thanks to a lingering knee injury sustained in the Chile game, but coach Edmondo Fabbri deemed the forward too important and gambled on his fitness after he was cleared by the medical team.

Early in the match, Bulgarelli tried a challenge on Pak Seung-zin and aggravated the injury. With no substitutions allowed at the time, Bulgarelli hobbled around the field. The Italians were essentially playing a man short. Unable to generate much offense, the Italians tried to keep things tight. Three minutes before halftime, North Korea did the impossible. A poor Italian clearance allowed Pak Doo-ik, a little-known 24-year-old midfielder, to put the ball past goalkeeper Enrico Albertosi. The Italians went into the dressing room feeling disheartened and desperate. The second half was highlighted by two squandered chances by striker Marino Perani, and North Korea, by virtue of a 1–0 win, eliminated the Italians and pulled off one of the greatest upsets in the competition's history. Fans greeted the Italian players upon their arrival home with a frenzy of rotten tomatoes.

"When you lose, you can't say anything to those who criticize," noted Fabbri in a 1985 interview on Italian state TV station RAI. "The attack, featuring Mazzola and Bulgarelli, featured the best of that time. Some talk about bad luck, but I don't believe in it. I don't believe in bad luck because they are always a base of factors that determine such situations."

For Fabbri, the injury to Bulgarelli in hindsight proved to be one of those determining factors. He added, "Unfortunately, after his impact with the North Korean player in midfield, it was clear that he wasn't able to play. It's not bad luck. At its foundation, there had been a big error, whether by me or the medical team, but knowing what I know now I would not have let him play."

North Korea's fairy-tale run would see them through to the quarterfinals, joined the following day by the USSR who won the group after a 2–1 victory against Chile in Sunderland.

Quarterfinals

The knockout round kicked off on July 23 with four games. England versus Argentina at Wembley, the biggest game of the round, captivated the nation. The excitement England had generated in the first round grew to a crescendo as 90,000 spectators packed into the venue. By game's end, England would advance to the semifinals in what would become known as one of the most controversial encounters in tournament history.

The English made two changes to the starting lineup from the previous match: Alan Ball replaced Ian Callaghan, and Geoff Hurst took the place of the injured Jimmy Greaves. The subs would make the difference in the end. The game got off to a tense start, both sides employing fouls to break up play. Nobby Stiles took down defender Roberto Ferreiro and escaped with no punishment from referee Rudolf Kreitlein of West Germany.

The fouling dominated the first half as neither side was able to create many scoring chances. The Argentines, who had barricaded themselves in their own half, played a defensive style. The English, on the other hand, abandoned wing play in favor of trying to score through the middle of the field. In the 36th minute, the referee ejected Antonio Rattín for dissent by pointing to the dressing rooms. Rattín initially refused to leave the game, arguing furiously with Kreitlein, and play was delayed for several minutes. Oddly, it was also the same game that Jack Charlton was given a warning by the referee, only to discover the fact the next day from newspaper reports. As a result, Ken Aston developed the idea of yellow and red cards to aid on-field communication regarding warning and ejections.

Down a player, the stalemate continued. Argentina's cynical tactics continued. The crowd, loud and cheering on the home side, grew more impatient as the second half wore on. The goal that decided the match came 13 minutes from the end when Hurst put in a long cross from the left by Martin Peters to give England a 1–0 victory and a place in the semifinals for the first time in their history.

England manager Alf Ramsey, furious after the game for how the Argentines had played, told reporters, "We have still to produce our best football. It will come against the right type of opposition, the team who come out to play football, not act as animals."

The English press followed suit the following day. *News of the World* labeled them as "Argentinian butchers," while the coverage in general focused on Kreitlein's poor officiating. Frank Butler, writing in the London-based newspaper, noted, "I blame much criticism on the shoulders of the referee. . . . Kreitlein was too fussy, too dictatorial, and notebook-happy."

In the other quarterfinal clashes, West Germany trounced Uruguay 4–0 in Sheffield thanks to a brace from Helmut Haller. The Soviet Union edged Hungary 2–1 in Sunderland with Valeriy Porkujan tallying the decisive goal. The victors of these two games would meet in the semifinals. But the most exciting match of the round—even more than England versus Argentina—took place in Liverpool when Portugal took on upstart North Korea.

North Korea, with 1,000-to-1 odds to win the tournament, were the surprise side of the tournament—even to the team itself. So much so that the players had expected to pack their bags after three games, leaving no plan to have to book hotels and travel for the quarterfinals. Instead, North Korea continued their English sojourn, traveling to Liverpool to play plucky Portugal. They stayed in a Jesuit retreat center. After arriving there, defender Shin Yung-kyoo told reporters the players were both "tired" but still "tremendously fit." The North Koreans made up for their lack of soccer prowess with peak physical fitness. Their stamina had helped propel them to victory against Italy.

Nonetheless, North Korea jumped out to an early 3–0 lead. Pak Seung-zin scored in the opener just after the starting kickoff. Two more goals in a span of three minutes, from Li Dong-woon in the 23rd minute, followed by Yang Sung-kook, put Portugal in a deep hole.

Portugal coach Otto Gloria, speaking to reporters after the game, said, "We do not like defense. Attack is our best defense. We do not like to play on defense. We do not know how to play on defense."

Going down three goals midway through the first half was clearly a sign of a side where defense wasn't a priority. What happened next was one of the greatest comebacks in World Cup history. North Korea's stamina was no match for Portugal's offensive prowess and sheer offensive power. The 40,000 spectators were in for a treat as Portugal scored five unanswered goals—four of them by the ebullient Eusébio—to win the game 5–3.

Semifinals

The first semifinal was played on July 25 in Liverpool between the Soviet Union and West Germany. In a tournament highlighted by rough play, this game followed that trend. Whether it was for fear of losing or inability to generate offense, both sides waged battle, and that resulted in Chislenko's expulsion. The crowd of 38,000 grew increasingly restless as the dour affair wore on. The game could have gotten a better attendance

1960s Innovation: Yellow and Red Cards

Today's soccer fans can't imagine a world where yellow and red cards don't exist. In fact, these cards weren't always part of the game. They came into use in the 1960s and made their debut at the World Cup only in 1970.

Steven Defour of Belgium is shown a red card during the 2014 World Cup against South Korea.
SHUTTERSTOCK

Referee Ken Aston, an English schoolteacher, was tasked with officiating the 1962 World Cup match between Chile and Italy, a game so brutal that it was later nicknamed the "Battle of Santiago." The following year, after refereeing the FA Cup final, Aston retired. In 1966, FIFA invited him to join their Referees' Committee, which he later chaired from 1970 to 1972. It was during this time that Aston, who died in 2001 at age 86, devised the system.

Aston was responsible for referees at the 1966 World Cup. In the quarterfinals, England played Argentina at Wembley Stadium. After the game, newspaper accounts reported that West German referee Rudolf Kreitlein had cautioned English players Bobby and Jack Charlton, as well as sending off Argentina's Antonio Rattín. The referee had not made his decision clear during the game, so England manager Alf Ramsey approached FIFA for clarification afterward. This incident started Aston thinking about ways to make a ref's decisions clearer to everyone during games.

In an effort to make it easier for players, coaches, and the public to know which players had been issued a warning, Aston, inspired by a traffic light, came up with a color-coded solution while driving in London: yellow for caution and red for a sending-off. A yellow card is used to caution players for fouls and other infractions, while a red results in the player's immediate expulsion.

had England played there, as had been previously scheduled, but the hosts' match against Portugal was moved to the final day at Wembley. Fans had purchased tickets in advance figuring England would win their group and advance to the semifinals. Instead, as the *Liverpool Daily Post* noted, FIFA's decision was "the greatest betrayal in sporting history."

At the same time, many South American soccer officials grew suspicious that the tournament was being fixed to help England. To support this claim, they pointed to the choice of referees for the four quarterfinal matches—three hailed from Europe and one from Israel—and the outcome resulted in an all-European semifinal. The change of venue was also seen as damaging to Portugal, who now had to travel from Liverpool to London. João Havelange, speaking to reporters in Lisbon after the Brazilian team made an impromptu stopover on their way home after being eliminated, lamented the decision. "I saw maneuvers with the intent to change the spirit of our sport," he complained.

English fans in the stands unfurled a series of controversial banners, including one that read, "Down with FIFA, England for the Cup," that was taken down by authorities. As for the game, Haller gave the West Germans the lead at the 43rd-minute mark. Shortly afterward, Chislenko was sent off. The second half continued much like the first, although the Soviets were reduced to nine players after Iosif Sabo injured himself in a clumsy challenge on Beckenbauer.

The game was over when Beckenbauer blasted the ball from 25 yards in the 67th minute past Yashin to give West Germany the 2–0 lead. Valeriy Porkujan scored a consolation goal two minutes from the end, but the match ended with the victorious West Germans walking off the field to chants of "England, England, England" from the crowd. West Germany reached the final for the second time, having won the tournament in 1954, with their opponents to be decided at Wembley the following evening.

England's semifinal clash against Portugal featured two of the strongest teams this tournament had to offer. More than 94,000 fans watched as the sides squared off in a game that was free of the malicious fouling that had typified so many games at this World Cup. Stiles was given the task of marking Eusébio, and he did so in superb fashion. The vivacious

Eusébio's ability to latch onto passes and unleash shots was hampered, and Portugal struggled to possess the ball.

At the same time, the English took advantage of a clean game to pass the ball and make regular forays into the Portuguese half. Moore was instrumental in the back, as was Jack Charlton's aggressive play in breaking up Portugal's midfield play for stretches of the match. Nonetheless, it was Jack's younger brother Bobby Charlton who made the difference, scoring a goal in the 30th minute and a second 10 minutes from the end, to help England land in the final. Eusébio finally got on the board with a consolation goal in the 82nd minute, but there was no Portugal comeback this time. Who knows if there would have been one had the game been played at Goodison Park as originally scheduled. Eusébio left the field, reduced to tears for his country's failed effort. Portugal's consolation would be a third-place finish, and Eusébio's nine goals would be good enough to be the tournament's top scorer.

Final: England vs. West Germany

Just 16 years after making their World Cup debut, England had reached the final. The inventors of the sport were a step away from achieving the ultimate in the sport. Standing in their way were West Germany, a team that had started to dominate the world's game starting in the 1950s and a legacy that persists to this day. In a span of 19 days, the notion that England could win it all became a reality.

England played the role of gracious host after deciding to play in their away red jerseys, while West Germany was allowed to compete in their home white shirts. Queen Elizabeth, who would award the winners the trophy at game's end, made her way to the Royal Box as 97,000 spectators filled the Wembley Stadium terraces.

England had a mix of strong defending and competent attacking. West Germany countered with its own blend of skill and tenacity that would make this game a tight affair. After just 12 minutes, the English backline collapsed. Striker Sigi Held put in a diagonal pass from the left in Helmut Haller's direction. When defender Ray Wilson failed to properly clear the ball with a poorly timed header, Haller got off a shot that beat Gordon Banks to his left for the West German lead. Eight minutes later, Geoff Hurst, unmarked in the box, struck the equalizer off a Moore set piece, and the sides went into halftime tied at one.

Both sides came into the second half in aggressive search for a goal. Martin Peters tallied the go-ahead goal in the 78th minute. The goal originated from Hurst, whose weak attempt on goal resulted in a poor Horst-Dieter Höttges clearance. Peters, in the correct place at the right time, rushed in and slammed the ball into the net, putting England just 12 minutes away from the title. West Germany, however, had other plans. England squandered a few chances to put the game away. In the 89th minute, defender Wolfgang Weber scored the biggest goal of his career to draw the sides level and push the game into extra time.

The 30 minutes of extra time featured exhausted players pushing themselves in a bid for ultimate glory. In the 94th minute, a Bobby Charlton effort resulted in the ball hitting the post. Seven minutes later, one of the most controversial goals in tournament history took place. Off an Allan Ball cross, Hurst—just 10 yards from the West German goal—unleashed a powerful shot toward Hans Tilkowski. The ball rocketed over the goalkeeper's head and off the underside of the crossbar before bouncing straight down on the line and back out. Hunt immediately turned to celebrate as the crowd erupted.

The West Germans, after Weber cleared the ball, expected referee Gottfried Dienst of Switzerland to whistle a corner kick. Instead, after consulting the referee's assistant Tofiq Bahramov of the USSR, Dienst declared the goal valid. To this day, Germans refer to such an officiating blunder as "ein Wembley tor" (a Wembley goal). It would not be the last controversial goal to ever be erroneously awarded at a World Cup. It wouldn't be until the start of the 21st century, and an increase in the use of better technology, that soccer would catch up with American sports and the use of instant replay.

Several studies using film analysis and computer simulation have failed to conclusively find whether the ball ever crossed the line for a goal. Nonetheless, Seeler and his teammates insisted for decades that it should not have been awarded. "I was standing at the back of the box and saw exactly that the ball didn't cross the line," Seeler told Agence France-Presse in 2016.

"We were all in a state of commotion, none of us knew what was going on," Seeler added. "No one [in the West Germany team] could understand why the goal was given."

The English sealed the 4–2 win in the 121st minute, with Hurst completing the hat trick. "That's it," declared ITV commentator Hugh Johns. "That. Is. It." Sure, a series of dodgy calls and home advantage aided England. It's also true they were the better team.

Moore led the team up the steps to the queen, who presented the England captain with the Rimet trophy amid loud cheers. Large crowds gathered in London's Trafalgar Square and Piccadilly Circus to celebrate, unleashing the biggest public displays of patriotism since the end of World War II just 21 years earlier. England had conquered the world at a time when it was coping with no longer being the colonial power it had once been. The tournament also capped off a three-week love affair between its people and their national team that endures in the nation's collective memory.

CHAPTER FOUR

The Beautiful Game

THE GAME'S LEGENDS CAN SOMETIMES BE FOUND IN STRANGE PLACES. One of those legends is Teófilo Cubillas. Take a drive along the South Florida coastline and make a stop at Pompano Beach, and that's where you'll find him.

There are many players who have played and succeeded at the World Cup. The club gets smaller when you look at players who did so at multiple World Cups. A member of that short list is the former Peru playmaker.

Nicknamed "Nene" (the Spanish word for baby) because of his boyish looks, which extended well into his 60s, Cubillas was one of the best attacking midfielders in the game. He made his World Cup debut with Peru in 1970 and helped that South American nation qualify again in 1978 and 1982. In all, he scored 10 World Cup goals.

"I would have to say that there are two of them," he said when asked about his favorite goals. "The first is when we were losing 2–0 to Bulgaria in the 1970 World Cup and we came back and tied the game 2–2. I then scored to put us up 3–2, and it turned out to be the winning goal of the match. This goal gave back hope to our country as two days before an earthquake hit Peru, killing 50,000 people.

"The second would have to be the free kick I scored in the 1978 World Cup against Scotland. The final score was 3–1 and I scored the second and third goal, but it was the final one where I set up for a free kick and bent it around the wall with the outside of my foot."

Cubillas, who runs soccer camps, has also worked for FIFA and as an ambassador for the Special Olympics. Cubillas dreamed of a pro career as a child and got his chance at 16 in 1966 with Alianza Lima. In 1972, Cubillas had his best year at club level, finishing as top scorer in the Copa Libertadores and taking South American Player of the Year honors. His goals eventually got him attention in Europe, and Cubillas went on to play with Swiss club FC Basel and Portuguese side Porto. He also played in the United States with the Fort Lauderdale Strikers and Los Angeles Aztecs.

All these decades later, Cubillas said people still recognize him thanks, in large part, to those memorable goals. It could also be his inability to age like the rest of us.

"It's a great feeling when people recognize me on the streets, especially in Peru," he said. "But since I have stayed involved in the soccer world over the years, even the youth of today that didn't even see me play know who I am thanks to their parents and videos or internet clips of goals. People will always ask to take a picture and I will always take the time to sign an autograph because these are and will be forever my fans and I am grateful for the opportunity I was given."

1970 World Cup

Two decades after the Maracanazo, Brazil had established itself as the football power we all know it to be today. Winners of the 1958 and 1962 World Cups, the Seleção set its sights on a third at Mexico '70. Pelé, out to prove that he wasn't made of glass at a World Cup, was coaxed into playing another tournament after the brutal fouling he'd been subjected to four years earlier in England.

"Getting knocked out of the World Cup in England was the saddest moment of my life," he said in a 2021 Netflix documentary.

Only 25 years old at the time, Pelé added that he didn't "intend to play in any more World Cups, because I'm not lucky in them."

"This is the second World Cup where I have been injured after only two games," he said of the 1966 tournament.

The late 1960s was a time of turmoil for Brazil. In 1964, the Brazilian military staged a coup, which led to a dictatorship that lasted until 1985. Widespread torture followed, and the national team became a tool to show the country and the world that Brazil was a soccer power. Before the World Cup, Juca Kfouri, a journalist and friend of Pelé's, recalled how important it became for the regime's international image that Brazil win the World Cup again—and that meant Pelé had to play.

"Winning the World Cup became a governmental matter," Kfouri said. "The team staff were almost entirely made up of military personnel."

The team manager, João Saldanha, ran the team like a dictator himself and worked behind the scenes to get Pelé off the team. Saldanha claimed that an eye exam revealed that Pelé suffered from diminished vision as an excuse to have him removed from the team.

"He wanted to be the big man in charge," Pelé said.

On the eve of the tournament, the federation booted Saldanha and replaced him with Zagallo. It was a risky move, but one that would help the team immensely once they arrived in Mexico for the tournament.

Mexico had been chosen to host the World Cup in 1964, becoming the first tournament to be held outside of Europe or South America. Mexico automatically qualified as host nation, as did England for being the defending champions. The remaining 14 teams featured eight from Europe, three from South America, and one from North/Central America and Asia/Oceania. Africa, too, was guaranteed one automatic spot in response to the 1966 boycott.

The tournament's 16 finalists were placed in four groups based on geography. This is how they were drawn:

Group 1: Mexico, the Soviet Union, Belgium, and El Salvador

Group 2: Italy, Sweden, Israel, and Uruguay

Group 3: Brazil, England, Romania, and Czechoslovakia

Group 4: West Germany, Bulgaria, Peru, and Morocco

Group 3 was dubbed the "Group of Death" by Mexican journalists because it featured England, Brazil, and Czechoslovakia—three teams who all had an equal shot at finishing first. It is a term used to this day to describe the most difficult group at a soccer tournament.

Despite issues like playing at altitude and high temperatures (played under a scorching midday sun to accommodate TV audiences in Europe), the finals would produce plenty of attacking soccer. Advancements in satellite communication meant that the finals could be broadcast live, and in color, around the world. Five venues, all located in the middle of the country, hosted matches: Mexico City, León, Guadalajara, Puebla, and Toluca. Of the five stadiums to host the 32 matches, the largest and most used was the Estadio Azteca in Mexico City, which would host 10 games, including the final and all of Group 1's matches (which included host Mexico). The Estadio Jalisco in Guadalajara hosted eight, and the Estadio Nou Camp in León hosted seven. The Estadio Luis Dosal in Toluca hosted four matches, and Estadio Cuauhtémoc in Puebla hosted just three.

It was the Azteca, however, that would be the tournament's centerpiece. The massive stadium, completed in 1966 to accommodate both the 1968 Olympics and the World Cup, would join the Maracanã and Wembley as one of the game's temples. The World Cup games it would host in 1970, and again 16 years at the 1986 tournament, helped forge a mystique that remains to the present day. The Azteca's imposing vertical architecture—combined with a capacity to hold 120,000 spectators—had taken five years to build. Now it was ready to take its place as one of the world's premier soccer venues.

The 1970 World Cup is regarded by many as one of the best and a tournament that gave birth to the modern game. Artistry with the ball, as showcased by Brazil and Peru, was a marvel to watch. Although this burst of offensive soccer would be squashed by a more cynical and defensive approach to the game, predominantly by the Europeans, as the decade wore on, the 1970s provided something for everyone as the game continued to evolve.

Group Stage

Following the opening ceremony on May 31 at the Azteca, Mexico faced the Soviet Union in Group 1, marking the last time (until the 2006 World Cup) that the host nation's first match, rather than the World Cup holders, opened the tournament. Kickoff took place at noon, and the sides struggled to generate offense. The 100,000 fans in attendance and the 104-degree temperature certainly intimidated the Soviets.

The players kicked around the Telstar, a leather ball made by Adidas that featured a 32-panel black-and-white design. It has become the standard design now used to portray a soccer ball. The ball got its name from the 1962 Telstar communications satellite, which was roughly spherical and dotted with solar panels. Only 20 Telstars were provided for the World Cup (forcing many matches to be played with a simple leather ball), although an estimated 600,000 replicas were sold subsequently around the world.

The game ended scoreless, although it would feature a series of firsts. The biggest footnote to the game was the introduction of yellow and red cards along with substitutions. The first yellow card in World Cup history was shown by referee Kurt Tschenscher of West Germany to Soviet midfielder Kakhi Asatiani in the 40th minute. The very first substitution ever at a World Cup took place when the USSR's Anatoliy Puzach came in for Viktor Serebryanikov in the 46th minute.

On June 3, Belgium took on El Salvador at the Azteca, where midfielder Wilfried Van Moer's brace powered Belgium to a 3–0 win. The Belgians were unable to conjure up that type of offensive magic three days later against the Soviet Union. After a lackluster opening match, the USSR put on a beautiful display and dispatched Belgium 4–1 thanks to an Anatoliy Byshovets brace. The four-goal day was also useful should qualifying hinge on goal differential. On June 7, the Mexicans had their way against El Salvador 4–0 to stay in contention for one of two quarterfinal spots with one match day to play.

It was on June 10 that the USSR went through to the next round by blanking El Salvador 2–0. The following day, with the Azteca teeming with 108,000 Mexicans, the hosts took on Belgium. The Mexicans would be through with a draw, while Belgium needed the win. In the end, a penalty kick by defender and team captain Gustavo Peña after just 14 minutes made the difference, and the Mexicans were through to the knockout round. The goal wasn't without controversy. After referee Ángel Norberto Coerezza of Argentina made the decision following a foul in the box, the Belgian players mobbed him. More protests followed after the kick was converted. Belgium tried to get an equalizer, but the Mexican backline, who had yet to concede a goal, successfully held them off. Mexico finished tied on points and goal differential with the Soviet Union. FIFA decided the group winner by drawing lots and awarded the USSR first place.

The Italians were favorites to win Group 2 after capturing the European Championship two years earlier. Uruguay, the other heavy favorite to advance, opened things up on June 2 at the Estadio Cuauhtémoc in Puebla against Israel. A 2–0 win put them atop the group, where they were joined the following day by Italy by virtue of their 1–0 win against Sweden at the Estadio Luis Dosal in Toluca. The Italians had taken the lead after 11 minutes when a shot by striker Angelo Domenghini was misplayed by goalkeeper Ronnie Hellström with the ball getting past him, resulting in a goal. The Azzurri would go on to dominate long stretches of play and squandered a number of chances.

The match between Italy and Uruguay on June 6 in Puebla was one of the most anticipated of the opening round. But the game was dominated by defensive tactics, resulting in a goalless draw. Indeed, the game provided few scoring chances, and the sides were happy to split the points heading into the final match day. The following day in Toluca, Sweden and Israel played to a 1–1 draw, a lively affair that mathematically eliminated the Israelis from the tournament.

The final match day saw the Azzurri win the group following another 0–0 draw, this time against Israel on June 11 in Toluca. Joining them in the knockout stage was Uruguay, who, despite a 1–0 defeat to Sweden the previous day in Puebla, managed to get through thanks to better goal differential. The Italians had needed just a draw to advance, although it was worrying that their attack had failed for a second straight game to record a goal. The Italians had scored twice, but both goals were ruled offside by referee Ayrton Vieira de Moraes of Brazil.

All eyes were fixated on Group 3. Zagallo, who had retired as a player just five years earlier, had the World Cup in his blood. As a member of the military, he had served as a security officer at the ill-fated 1950 final. Zagallo won it twice as a player and now, just 75 days before the start of the World Cup, was tasked with coaching the national team. The country's repressive regime, led by General Emílio Garrastazu Médici, wanted the government to be seen as being in tandem with the national team. Success on the soccer field, after all, would mean political success. It was a means of controlling the discontent mob, but Médici's involvement with the team was more forced than welcomed. The final straw for Saldanha was when the regime tried to dictate which players would get called up for the World Cup. "I do not mess with his cabinet, he will not mess with my team," he said.

Médici fired Saldanha, and Zagallo, who coached Brazilian club Botafogo at the time, was hastily brought in. As a blueprint, Zagallo used the 4–2–4 that helped Brazil win the World Cup in 1962.

"When I was with Botafogo, the CBF officials turned up at training and I was told by our physical trainer, 'Go over to that car. You're being called to lead the Seleção.' The squad was already at a training camp. They took me home, I grabbed some clothes and off we went," Zagallo told FIFA.com in 2020. "It was what I wanted the most in my life. It was funny because when [João] Saldanha took over the Seleção the previous year, I took over his radio show, and when he left the Seleção, I replaced him there."

Zagallo had a task not many national team managers struggle with— an overabundance of talent. He had five playmakers at his disposal in a lineup that needed just one. Pelé, Gerson, Rivellino, Tostão, and Jairzinho could all fulfill that role. That meant Zagallo had to use his genius to come up with a lineup that could include all these players—something Saldanha had been unable to do—and make them gel with just weeks to play. Off the field, the political climate in Brazil was repressive. On the field, Brazil was free.

Zagallo had been a standout midfielder during his playing days, and he brought that knowledge to the finals. Tim Vickery, writing for ESPN, noted that the Brazil side of 1970 not only had talented players, but also focused on physical preparation ahead of the tournament.

"At a time when many teams were happy to run a couple of laps round the field and then adjourn to the golf course, Brazil were attempting something more specialized," he noted. "In the post-mortem after their failure in the 1966 World Cup—Brazil were eliminated after losing two of their group games—one of the many errors identified was that the physical training man came from a background of martial arts rather than football. In 1970 they would not be so careless."

Brazil's stamina and ability by the players to keep their work rate up in the second half helped them to dominate the group. England, the defending champions, would prove to be Brazil's toughest opponents in the opening round, while Romania and Czechoslovakia only had an outside chance of advancing.

England opened the group on June 2 at the Estadio Jalisco in Guadalajara, where all the group's matches would be contested. The English struggled, but a goal by Hurst in the 65th minute gave the holders a 1–0 win against Romania. Brazil, playing the following day, sent a message by tallying four times—with Jairzinho netting a brace—for the 4–1 victory against Czechoslovakia. Zagallo's bet to use the 4–2–4 with Pelé as the playmaker, aided by Jairzinho, Tostão, and Rivellino, had paid off. The players dazzled with their fast passing and trickery.

Romania kept their dreams of advancing alive by defeating Czechoslovakia 2–1 on June 6, but it was the clash between Brazil and England scheduled for the following day that had been the most awaited match of the first round when the draw was set. The English had never defeated Brazil in their own hemisphere, a troubling statistic as the defending champions stepped onto the field that afternoon. The Brazilians had the offensive talent and stamina, but their backline looked suspect (despite the talent of team captain Carlos Alberto), as did starting goalkeeper Félix.

The match turned out to be a battle between England's methodical defending led by Bobby Moore and Brazilian skill spearheaded by Pelé and the Brazilian offense. The game was just 10 minutes old when Jairzinho beat defender Terry Cooper, floating a cross in for Pelé. In typical fashion, he rose into the air with the grace of a ballerina and headed the ball downward for what certainly appeared to be a goal.

Instead, Banks came up with a huge save, using his catlike reflexes to parry the ball away. "For many people, their memory of Gordon Banks is defined by the save he made against me in 1970. I understand why," Pelé said in a Facebook post in 2019 after Banks's death. "The save was one of the best I have ever seen—in real life and in all the thousands of games I have watched since.

"When you are a footballer, you know straight away how well you have hit the ball. I hit that header exactly as I had hoped. Exactly where I wanted it to go. And I was ready to celebrate. But then this man, Banks, appeared in my sight, like a kind of blue phantom, is how I described him. He came from nowhere and he did something I didn't feel was possible. He pushed my header, somehow, up and over. And I couldn't believe what I saw. Even now when I watch it, I can't believe it. I can't believe how he moved so far, so fast."

It remains arguably the best save ever made at a World Cup. In recalling that moment for the BBC in 2019, Banks said, "The ball actually hit the top of my hand and looked as though it was going into the top of the net. As I hit the floor I saw that the ball had missed the goal. At first I thought, 'You lucky so-and-so,' but then I realized it has been a bit special. I've met Pelé many times since. He thought he'd scored."

Overall, the English did a wonderful job keeping the Brazilians from scoring, but all that changed in the 59th minute to the delight of the 66,000 in attendance. Rivellino, effective on the wing for much of the match because of his slick dribbling, linked with Tostão, who beat three players before passing the ball to Pelé. From there, Pelé sent a pass to Jairzinho, who beat Banks. "The move was so simple," the *Guardian* noted in its game story, "but simplicity is often devastating." Indeed, both the pass and goal were sparks of genius that seemingly only the Brazilians were able to conjure up to devastating effect.

The goal, with only 30 minutes left to play, brought more offensive urgency for the English. A tying goal was still possible, but the Brazilians played with both a swagger and a confidence of few teams. England, it should be underscored, did squander some chances, but Brazil emerged victorious. They were a step away from advancing, although England and Romania still had a shot at getting to the quarterfinals with one final match day to play.

Brazil won the group and earned passage to the quarterfinals on June 10, defeating Romania 3–2 thanks to two Pelé goals and a *jogo bonito* style that typified the zest for attacking soccer. Brazil, who rested

Rivellino, jumped out to a 2–0 lead early on, but poor defending did make the game interesting in the second half. But the emphasis on attack is what scared opponents. Romanian goalkeeper Stere Adamache was even subbed off after 27 minutes. England, meanwhile, joined them in the knockout round the following day after a 1–0 win against Czechoslovakia. Allan Clarke's penalty kick after 50 minutes proved to be the game's only goal.

West Germany may have been the favorites to win Group 4, but it would be Peru that would showcase some of the best soccer. The group, contested entirely at the Estadio Camp Nou in León, opened on June 2 with Peru overcoming a two-goal deficit to defeat Bulgaria 3–2. The goal by Cubillas, a spectacular solo effort, in the 73rd minute won them the match. Peru, playing in their iconic white shirts featuring a diagonal red sash, had played at the World Cup in 1930, a decade that saw them capture the Copa America in 1939. For decades, Peruvian soccer played second fiddle to the powerhouses that were Brazil and Uruguay. The tournament in Mexico put Peru, coached by Brazilian World Cup veteran Didi, in the limelight for the first time in four decades. They were no longer South American underachievers.

Within just a few short hours after the first ball was kicked on May 31 to open the tournament, news came through to the Peru camp that an earthquake had struck their nation, specifically along the coastal area of Chimbote. The effects of the devastating quake had been felt in the capital Lima, some 400 miles away from the epicenter. At a time when electronic communication was still largely in its nascent stage, the players—unsure whether their loved ones had been injured or killed—agonized over whether they should have even played against Bulgaria, a game scheduled just 48 hours after the quake had struck. The players took the field that afternoon as the death toll rose to 70,000. Against the backdrop of a national tragedy, Peru proved they could compete for the title.

"Knowing that we'd brought a little bit of happiness to the country was a feeling that is impossible to put into words," Cubillas recalled.

West Germany, taking on Morocco the following day, also needed a comeback win to grab the points. Down 1–0 at halftime, the West Germans scored two unanswered goals in the second half. It was Gerd Müller's goal 10 minutes from the end that won West Germany the match. Crisis had been averted. Peru, out to prove they were for real, managed to defeat Morocco 3–0 on June 6 with a mix of skill and flair. This time, Cubillas scored twice to put Peru temporarily in first place. The skill demonstrated on the field, and a sense of duty and national pride off of it, made Peru favorites among neutral spectators.

The following day, West Germany had another troublesome show-ing—but one they were able to convert into victory. Down 1–0, West Germany scored five goals, which included a Müller hat trick, to grab the 5–2 win against Bulgaria. The victory put West Germany and Peru through to the quarterfinals with a game to spare. Their meeting on June 10 would determine who would finish first and avoid Group 3 winner Brazil. Peru put on a valiant effort, but the West Germans had finally shown that they could play as a unit. Another Müller hat trick in the first half led West Germany to a 3–1 win. Peru's lone goal by Cubillas, meanwhile, kept him alive in the race for the tournament's top scorer. Peru, who had conquered adversity on and off the field, would face Brazil in the knockout stage.

Quarterfinals

The vivid multicolor carnival that was Mexico '70 came down to just eight teams. Mexico was looking to make a deep run, while Brazil and Uruguay remained favorites from South America to win the title. Italy, England, and West Germany were also in the mix as title contenders with the tournament going down to the elimination phase.

All four matches were contested on June 14 at noon. The hot tem-peratures would make for a very uncomfortable afternoon, especially given the altitude that so many teams had slowly started to get used to during the last two weeks. Uruguay took to the field in Mexico City and needed extra time to defeat the Soviet Union. The goal by midfielder Víctor Espárrago in the 117th minute, who had been subbed into the match just 14 minutes earlier to provide the South Americans with some fresh legs, made the difference in the end.

Brazil, meanwhile, outmatched Peru in Guadalajara before 54,000 fans, the largest crowd to watch a quarterfinal match. Brazil lit up the scoreboard once again, scoring four times—two of them coming from

Tostão—to defeat Peru 4–2. Cubillas managed to score another goal, his fifth of the tournament, to emerge as one of the best players of his generation. Many in Peru still believe their national team could have lifted the trophy if not for the mighty Seleção. The Brazil win set up an all–South American semifinal.

In Toluca, Italy managed to breeze by Mexico, much to the chagrin of the 27,000 in the stands to root on the home team. The Italians overcame the crowd and an early 1–0 disadvantage to score four unanswered goals—two of them by Gigi Riva—to reach the semifinals. The Azzurri would face West Germany, 3–2 winners against England in León. The game, which ended 2–2 after 90 minutes, was decided in the 108th minute by Müller. England had been without Banks in goal after he suddenly fell ill a few days earlier. In his place was backup goalie Peter Bonetti. Despite taking a 2–0 lead, England fell apart. What had been a one-sided affair for most of the match changed during the course of the final 22 minutes when Beckenbauer's shot and Seeler's header each found the back of the net. The goals came off of two Bonetti blunders, while Banks continued to nurse his case of Montezuma's revenge. The West German win set up the all-European semifinal against Italy.

Semifinals

The semifinals did not disappoint as high-stakes games often can at this level. The games were played at the same time on June 17. The unstoppable Brazilian juggernaut dispatched Uruguay 3–1 in Guadalajara, but not without some early trepidation. Uruguay took an early 1–0 lead—again the Brazilian defense was suspect—but it was the offense that would make the difference. Three unanswered goals, starting with midfielder Clodoaldo in the 44th minute, paved the way for the win. Jairzinho and Rivellino added goals in the second half, and Pelé put on another fantastic display to put Brazil in yet another final.

Over at the Estadio Azteca, Italy and West Germany did battle in what is still remembered as an epic encounter. It is with good reason that it is still widely referred to as the "Game of the Century." The Italians won 4–3 after five goals were scored in extra time, a record for any two 15-minute sessions at a World Cup. The record endures to this day.

The defending European champions led 1–0 for the majority of the match after Roberto Boninsegna scored in the eighth minute. In typical Italian fashion, their defense barricaded the backline and frustrated the Germans for much of the second half. The *catenaccio*, the dreaded door-bolt defensive tactic that prioritized the backline over offense, was in full effect by Italy manager Ferruccio Valcareggi. This Machiavellian style, a mix of cynicism and pragmatism, was a carryover from the 1960s and was popularized by the Inter Milan sides managed by Helenio Herrera. It saw the Azzurri line up in what would today be considered a 3–4–3 formation, with sweeper and captain Giacinto Facchetti the defensive anchor in this system. The Azzurri would employ these tactics, with mixed results, for the next four decades. Favoring defense over offense, Valcareggi refused to field two creative strikers at the same time, meaning Mazzola and Rivera would not take the field simultaneously.

With a growing sense of urgency to score weighing on them, the Italians seemed to have the psychological edge with each passing minute. Making matters worse for the West Germans was when Beckenbauer dislocated his shoulder following a foul. The famed *libero* stayed on the field, his arm in a sling, after his side had already used their two substitutions. Defender Karl-Heinz Schnellinger equalized for West Germany in stoppage time, putting the ball past goalkeeper Enrico Albertosi to push the game into extra time. The psychological edge appeared to be on the side of West Germany as commentator Ernst Huberty famously exclaimed, "Schnellinger—of all people!" Schnellinger, a defender, played in Serie A for AC Milan, a team he would never score a goal with. It would also be his first—and only—goal in a career total of 47 matches for West Germany.

With temperatures soaring to past 92 degrees and the crowd of nearly 103,000 growing louder, the players went into extra time exhausted. The blistering midday sun and the altitude made for a lethal combination that afternoon. Little did they know it then, but the sides would produce 30 minutes of heart-pounding soccer. Müller put West Germany ahead in the 94th minute after a rare defensive error by substitute Fabrizio Poletti. His fresh legs had done nothing to help the Italians.

113

Another defender, Tarcisio Burgnich, tied it back up only four minutes later. With the game level at two, the Italians, not afraid to push forward, took the lead in the 104th minute thanks to Riva. Not to be outdone, Müller scored yet again, this time on a header that slipped past Rivera standing near the far post, and the game was tied 3–3 in the 110th minute. Rivera, who had come in as a second-half substitute for Mazzola, scored what ended up being the game winner just a minute later. Left unmarked near the penalty area, Rivera connected perfectly with a Boninsegna cross, grabbing the 4–3 win for the Italians and landing them in the final.

"I felt a weight taken off of me after I scored the goal," Rivera recalled in a 2013 interview with Italian state broadcaster RAI. "Mostly because I felt responsible for the goal the Germans had scored. I could have done nothing in that situation but extended my hand."

The game—forever remembered with a plaque outside the Azteca—opened the way for the Italy–Germany rivalry that persists to this day. Brazil, and its offensive 4-2-4 that also featured Rivellino and Jairzinho, may have been the best team at the tournament—and among the best of all time—but it was the Italians and West Germans who delighted fans with their persistence, guile, and tenacity. West Germany had to console itself with a third-place finish.

Final: Brazil vs. Italy

The championship game at the Azteca on June 21 featured 107,000 spectators and pleasantly cool temperatures that afternoon in Mexico City after a night of rain. The final would be a contrast in styles—Brazil's flamboyant attack against Italy's tight defending—between two of the planet's best teams. The game also pitted nations that had each previously won two World Cups.

Although Brazil were favorites, the Italians had scored eight goals in the knockout phase, so exactly which Italian team would show up that day was anyone's guess. The Italian camp remained divided over whether Mazzola or Rivera should get the start. The Azzurri would end up going with Mazzola. Both teams had won two World Cups apiece entering the game.

After 19 minutes, Pelé leaped high over Burgnich and headed in a Tostão cross off a Rivellino throw-in to give Brazil a 1–0 lead following a desperate Albertosi dive. Pelé's dolphin-like ability to jump through the air and score a goal of that caliber forever cemented his legacy as one of the greatest athletes in history.

"We jumped together, then I came down and he stayed up," Burgnich told Harry Harris for his book *Pelé: His Life and Times*.

For Brazil, it marked the 100th goal for the South Americans at a World Cup. Fittingly, it had been Pelé to mark the milestone. Eight minutes before halftime, the Italians, composed in midfield, strung together a series of passes after a defensive Brazilian mishap, and Boninsegna fired home the equalizer.

With the sides tied 1–1 at the half, Carlos Alberto said Pelé remained keen that the Brazilians could win the World Cup. "When you have a player like him on your team," he said, "then you're halfway to achieving such a goal. It was a great time to be playing the game."

In the second half, Brazil turned on the pressure, like they had so many times at this tournament, and the Italians succumbed. Brazil's artistry and technique was able to cover much of the field thanks to pinpoint passes that helped them create plays as well as conserve energy. The Italians, exhausted from the marathon match against West Germany, could not keep up.

Gerson fired off a marvelous shot in the 65th minute, putting Brazil ahead 2–1. Mazzola struggled to create offense as the Brazilians continued to dictate the tempo. In the 71st minute, Gerson's long ball found Pelé, who instead of going for the goal passed it to Jairzinho. The Brazilian striker scored his seventh goal of the competition, becoming the first player to tally in every World Cup match at a single tournament.

Not done yet, Brazil scored a fourth goal with Carlos Alberto four minutes from the end. His ferocious shot, off a Pelé assist, zoomed past Albertosi. The 4–1 victory allowed Brazil to retire the Rimet trophy as three-time champions. In the process, Zagallo had won the World Cup as both a player and a manager, the first in a line of coaches who would achieve such a feat in the decades to come.

The win allowed Pelé to gain his redemption four years after Brazil had been dumped out of the tournament. He'd gone back on his word never to play again at the World Cup, and the game was grateful for it. The final whistle ushered an invasion by hundreds of Mexican fans, some of them gathering to hoist a shirtless Pelé in celebration. In Brazil, millions flooded into the streets. In Italy, fans greeted the players at the airport in Rome with jeers, some even tossing tomatoes at them in protest. It was an ugly display following a three-week festival of joyful soccer.

"Pelé's personal contribution was, of course, accidental and coincidental," Radnedge said. "He happened to be the great player, and there have been many great players, in the right place at the right time."

Brazil's beautiful game had won out. Many consider the 1970 Brazil team to be the greatest in the history of the game. Pelé, writing in 2006 in his book *Pelé: An Autobiography*, reminisced about his time as a World Cup superstar: "Our time was a pure one, innocent, almost rough-and-ready, in the sense of the simplicity, which was within our reach, before technology invaded our lives."

1974 WORLD CUP

The early part of the 1970s ushered in an era where FIFA not only ran the sport globally, but also enriched itself, starting with the election of Brazilian sports official João Havelange as its new president. His election took the power away from Europe and put it in the hands of even fewer members independent of geography. Rous, the incumbent, lost after Havelange campaigned to spread the power of international soccer to South America. He also campaigned promising African and Asian nations better infrastructure to help grow the game. After his election in 1974, Havelange wanted to bring unity to the game. Instead, it was the start of a decades-long era of greed, scandal, and wrongdoing. Most of it revolved around the World Cup, which nations would get the right to host it, corporate sponsorships, and the selling of television rights for the tournament. At a June 2010 conference in Miami, investigative journalist Andrew Jennings discussed at length the scams that, years later, would form the basis of indictments. He said FIFA's actions qualified it as "a global organized crime syndicate."

Co-Player of the Century: Pelé

Considered one of the best players in the game's history, Pelé became a superstar with his performances at the 1958 World Cup. A three-time World Cup champion, the Brazilian played with an unmatched flair and joy. He remains a global sports icon.

National team career: The world was introduced to Pelé at the 1958 World Cup as a shy 17-year-old. He had made his Brazil senior team debut the prior year in a 2–1 win against Argentina at the Maracanã. He scored in that game. At age 16 years and nine months, he remains the youngest player ever to score for Brazil. He would go on to play at four World Cups, winning three of them: 1958, 1962, and 1970. In all, he scored 77 goals in 92 appearances for Brazil.

Club career: Pelé played professionally in Brazil for two decades with Santos from 1956 to 1974. He won the Campeonato Brasileiro six times and the Campeonato Paulista 10 times. He was twice winner of the Copa Libertadores in 1962 and 1963. He led Santos to the Intercontinental Cup. After being lured to the North American Soccer League, he joined the New York Cosmos in 1975 and won the 1977 Soccer Bowl before retiring.

The great Pelé, pictured here in a Santos jersey, won three World Cup titles with Brazil.

MINISTÉRIO DA JUSTIÇA E SEGURANÇA PÚBLICA/ ARQUIVO NACIONAL

Honors: Pelé retired from playing in 1977. Named FIFA Co-Player of the Century in 1999 (alongside Diego Maradona), he worked for decades as a global ambassador for the game and other humanitarian causes such as UNICEF. Pelé was voted World Player of the Century by the International Federation of Football History & Statistics. He was also named Athlete of the Century by the International Olympic Committee and included in *Time* magazine's list of the 100 most important people of the 20th century.

The 1974 World Cup was awarded to West Germany and was the first time that the current trophy, created by the Italian sculptor Silvio Gazzaniga, was awarded. Some of the game's most successful nations failed to qualify, including 1966 champions England, France, Mexico, Spain, Portugal, Peru, Belgium, Czechoslovakia, Hungary, and Romania. The Soviet Union was also disqualified after refusing to travel for the second leg of their playoff match against Chile as a result of the 1973 Chilean coup d'état. The Netherlands and Poland qualified for the first time since 1938, while Scotland was back in the finals after a 16-year absence. Argentina and Chile were also back after missing the 1970 tournament, and Yugoslavia also qualified after missing both the 1966 and 1970 tournaments. First-time qualifiers included East Germany (who made their only World Cup or European Championship appearance as a separate team), Australia, Haiti, and Zaire.

The tournament featured a new format and a new trophy. After Brazil retired the Rimet Trophy with their third win in 1970, FIFA commissioned a new one. Made of 18-carat gold with malachite at its base, the trophy is 14.5 inches tall and weighs 13 pounds. The trophy depicts two human figures holding up the planet. FIFA had received 53 submissions, but the design by Silvio Gazzaniga won in the end. After the 1994 World Cup, a plate was added to the bottom of the trophy's base with the engraved names of the winning countries. The names are not visible when the trophy is standing upright. Although Germany was the first to win this version of the trophy three times, FIFA has said the trophy would not be retired given its iconic status and association with the tournament. "If I ever have to re-create it, I would not make any changes to the original," Gazzaniga told FIFA.com. "The fact that the trophy still endures today in this changing world of fashions is a testament to the fact that I was inspired by beautiful symbols and universal principles that became part of my creation."

While the competition once again began with 16 teams divided into four groups of four teams, the eight teams that advanced did not enter a knockout stage as in the previous five tournaments. Instead, they would be funneled into a second group stage.

The draw resulted in the following four groups:

Group 1: West Germany, East Germany, Chile, and Australia

Group 2: Brazil, Yugoslavia, Scotland, and Zaire

Group 3: The Netherlands, Sweden, Bulgaria, and Uruguay

Group 4: Italy, Poland, Argentina, and Haiti

The winners of the two groups of the second stage then played each other in the final. The runners-up from each group would meet in the third-place match. The matches would be played in nine German cities: Dortmund, Düsseldorf, Frankfurt, Gelsenkirchen, Hanover, Hamburg, Stuttgart, West Berlin, and Munich.

Group Stage

West Germany was favored to win Group 1, and having to play East Germany in the opening round was both a curiosity and a potential political problem. The geopolitics as it pertained to the Iron Curtain never did become a major factor, and the sides would meet without many off-field distractions. Nonetheless, the contest would be, at least on the eve of the game, one of the most politically charged in World Cup history. West Germany, winners of the European Championship in 1972, opened the group on June 14 against Chile at the Olympiastadion in West Berlin. Defender Paul Breitner scored in the 18th minute, a goal that won West Germany the match 1–0. The other noteworthy event from the game came in the 67th minute when Chilean striker Carlos Caszely received a red card. While players had been ejected from World Cup games before, Caszely became the first player to be sent off at a World Cup with a red card, an innovation that had been introduced four years earlier at Mexico '70.

On the same day at the Volksparkstadion in Hamburg, East Germany, who had taken bronze at the Munich Olympics in 1972, got the best of Australia 2–0, although their fans weren't among the 17,000 in the stands because they weren't allowed to leave the Eastern bloc nation. At the same venue on June 18, West Germany triumphed over Australia

3–0 to put them one step closer to qualifying for the second round. Over in West Berlin, East Germany and Chile played to a 1–1 draw, keeping both of those nations' hopes alive of trying to qualify out of the first round.

The final match day was contested on June 22. Australia and Chile could only manage a scoreless draw, a result that eliminated the South Americans. Nearly four hours later, in Hamburg, a derby of sorts was played when the hosts faced off against their brethren. Both sides were through. On the line was first place and pride. It would be the first, and the last, time the nations ever took the field against one another at a World Cup. It was also the first time the Federal Republic and the GDR met at the senior international level, past squabbles taking place in Olympic qualifiers or at the Olympic soccer tournament.

Friendlies between West and East German clubs had been staged throughout the 1950s, but those became infrequent as the Cold War dragged on. In what resembled an all-Germany playoff match that took place in 1956, Kaiserslautern—West German champions in 1951 and 1953 and one of the country's best clubs from that era—played against Wismut Karl-Marx-Stadt, at the time the defending East German champions. The game, played at the Zentralstadion in Leipzig, drew massive interest as Kaiserslautern won 5–3.

In the 1970s and 1980s, these encounters became more intermittent and were limited to European Cup games. Their respective national teams even played one another at the 1972 Olympic Games, where they met for a spot in the bronze medal match. East Germany won 3–2. Overall, West Germany and their clubs dominated the scene, as evidenced by Bayern Munich's success during much of the 1970s and beyond. But at the World Cup, as a result of the draw, the teams would meet before 60,000 fans—of which only 1,500 selected guests from East Germany would be allowed to travel from across the border to watch. Many of those guests were East German state security policemen, known as the Stasi.

Enthusiasm was high in the West German camp ahead of the game. Veteran manager Helmut Schön, himself a former World Cup star, had been born in the city of Dresden, located in East Germany once World War II had ended. Schön's family had fled the city to escape the Soviet regime, and Beckenbauer used that as a pre-match talking point to motivate his teammates.

A tense match after months of anticipation and debate on both sides of the wall, the West Germans dominated as chants of "Deutschland, Deutschland" rang out from the stands. In the 39th minute, Müller had a clear chance to put West Germany ahead, but his attempt struck the upright. In the second half, with the East Germans barely able to create any scoring chances but also using their well-drilled backline to thwart their opponents, West Germany looked happy to settle for a draw. Instead, East Germany, which had played as its own national team at the international level since 1952, managed a 1–0 victory via a goal by midfielder Jürgen Sparwasser, 13 minutes from the final whistle, following a rare West German defensive lapse. The result helped East Germany win the group, while West Germany were also through after finishing second.

"Of course it was glorified by the politicians," East German goalkeeper Jürgen Croy told the German magazine *Der Spiegel* in 2006, "but that happens everywhere. All countries try to take political advantage of sports success."

Sparwasser and Breitner, out of respect for each other, exchanged jerseys while they were in the tunnel and away from the cameras. While Croy had been more cynical regarding what the win meant, Sparwasser basked in the glory in defeating his capitalist cousins. "If one day my gravestone simply says 'Hamburg '74,' everybody will still know who is lying below," he said.

Müller, speaking to FIFA.com in 2007, said the stinging defeat did have its benefits. "It was a good thing we lost. Otherwise, we'd have been in the other group," he said. "If we'd won, we'd have been in the same group as Holland and Brazil."

Brazil, having to compete in a post-Pelé landscape, remained favored to defend the title. The Seleção, again coached by Zagallo, had some holdovers from the 1970 squad, like Rivellino and Jairzinho, but overall the team lacked the offensive power of past editions. That fact became evident in Brazil's opener on June 13 against Yugoslavia at the Waldstadion in Frankfurt. The Group 2 match ended scoreless, as did Brazil's second match at the same venue five days later against Scotland.

Scotland, meanwhile, managed a 2–0 win versus Zaire on June 14 at the Westfalenstadion in Dortmund. Scotland's scoreless draw versus Brazil put them in position to advance, but that was thwarted in the final match day. It was on June 22 in Frankfurt where Scotland could only muster a 1–1 draw against Yugoslavia. The draw got the Yugoslavs through to the second round. Scotland, undefeated in group play, had fielded arguably their best team in World Cup history, and they had nothing to show for it.

"There was serious pressure on us because we were the favorites," midfielder David Hay told the BBC in 2020, reflecting on the Yugoslavia game. "I remember it was exceptionally warm and, being 2–0 up at halftime, I think we took the foot off the gas."

"Over the three games, we only conceded one goal," recalled striker Joe Jordan. "You go back to the Zaire game, there's a lot of disappointment. We should have done a lot more damage."

Goal differential got Yugoslavia through as the second-place team, a 9–0 victory over Zaire on June 18 in Gelsenkirchen getting the job done for them. Over at the Parkstadion, it would be Brazil that would finally show glimpses of that flashy offense they've come to be known for in a 3–0 victory on June 22 over Zaire. Goals from Jairzinho, Rivellino and winger Valdomiro, who had made his national team debut the previous year, put Brazil atop the group and in the next round.

The Netherlands were the big favorite to win Group 3, which also featured Sweden, Bulgaria, and Uruguay. If the 1600s reflected the height of Dutch painters, headlined by Rembrandt, the 1960s saw a different breed of Dutch masters emerge on the soccer scene. The nation's culture at the time, as in many parts of the West, encouraged a free-thinking attitude. Hippie culture prospered. After all, Amsterdam is the city where John Lennon and Yoko Ono held the "Bed-In" in 1969 to bring attention to the cause of world peace. It was a world that was changing rapidly, and a lot of this thinking spilled over to the sport.

Before 1974, the Dutch were not major players on the international soccer scene. The team had previously competed at the 1934 and 1938 World Cups but had failed to qualify for the finals for another four decades. The Dutch soccer revolution began at club level with Ajax, first under manager Rinus Michels and then Stefan Kovács. The team dominated the European Cup with a style known as "total football," which led to three consecutive continental titles from 1971 to 1973. Michels and midfield wizard Johan Cruyff arrived at Barcelona, quickly injecting newfound enthusiasm into the Spanish club after winning the league title in 1974.

It was this club success that made the Netherlands, once soccer nobodies, into outside contenders. After barely qualifying for the finals under Czechoslovakian-born coach František Fadrhonc, the Dutch FA brought in Michels. The managerial move drastically altered the national team's playing style. He used friendlies leading up to the tournament to test players and tactics. Michels built his team around Cruyff. Players like goalkeeper Jan Jongbloed, defenders Arie Haan and Ruud Krol, midfielder Johan Neeskens, and striker Johnny Rep would turn out to be key.

"People talk of total football as if it is a system, something to replace 4–2–4 or 4–3–3. It is not a system. As it is at any moment, so you play," Haan told the *Guardian* in 2018. "That is how we understand. Not one or two players make a situation, but five or six. The best is that with every situation all 11 players are involved, but this is difficult."

The Oranje opened the group on June 15 at Hanover's Niedersachsenstadion against Uruguay. Under the system of total football, Michels expected all his players to be able to play every position. That meant the slender Cruyff, an attacking player, could be converted into a defender. The same went for Haan and Krol, who could dash forward depending on the situation. This tactical innovation was too much for opponents to handle. The Dutch, using that style, overcame Uruguay 2–0. Rep tallied twice, the opening goal after just seven minutes and a second in the 86th. On the same day at the Rheinstadion in Düsseldorf, Sweden and Bulgaria played to a scoreless draw.

The Dutch, temporarily in first place, could only manage a 0–0 draw versus Sweden on June 19 at the Westfalenstadion in Dortmund. The Dutch offense didn't look as sharp as expected, but Cruyff showed off his individual skill with a move that made him famous. The move, known as the "Cruyff turn," is an evasive piece of dribbling. It was in the 24th minute that, while Cruyff had control of the ball in an attacking position but was facing his own goal and being guarded tightly by Swedish defender Jan Olsson, he feigned a pass before dragging the ball behind his standing leg, turning 180 degrees, and accelerating away. The move, so simple yet so unpredictable, remains one of the most commonly used dribbling moves in the modern game.

In Hanover, the outcome of the Bulgaria-Uruguay match, which ended 1–1, helped the Netherlands stay in first place. Michels's focus on the individual, and how that could help the collective, was working to plan. "Michels was for me one of the first guys who was talking not just about individual great players, but the team; for him, everyone was the same," defender Wim Rijsbergen told the *New York Times* in 2005.

The players, Rijsbergen said, called Michels "the General" for the manager's many war analogies. "He was a guy who told people that football is war; he created very aggressive teams," Rijsbergen added.

The Netherlands reached the second round in Dortmund, defeating Bulgaria 4–1 on June 23. Neeskens tallied twice, both via penalty kicks, with Rep and midfielder Theo de Jong also adding goals. Michels's tactics had worked, and the Oranje won the group, joined by Sweden, 3–0 winners against Uruguay the same day in Düsseldorf.

"Sometimes it looked like we had no tactics," Rijsbergen said. "Sometimes it looked like we had an extra man on the field. Sometimes we looked disorganized. But the greatest thing about Michels is that he always gave the players the credit and he never criticized his players outside the locker room. For me, he was the best coach."

Runners-up four years earlier, the Italians were drawn into a manageable group, alongside Argentina, Poland, and minnows Haiti. After the defeat to North Korea in 1966, the Italians feared their opening match on June 15 versus Haiti at Munich's Olympiastadion. Instead, the Azzurri came through with an emphatic 3–1 win. Although the Italians had fallen behind after goalkeeper Dino Zoff was caught by surprise, a three-goal second half gave Italy all the points. The Azzurri's temperamental striker Giorgio Chinaglia, subbed out by Valcareggi in the 76th minute, did not take the decision well. Chinaglia's response was to storm off the field and into the dressing room, where he proceeded to smash eight mineral water bottles against a wall.

"That was the moment where I told everyone to screw off, not just the manager," Chinaglia recalled. "The players on the bench were applauding. Didn't these people understand who I was? I'm Giorgio Chinaglia, Lazio's biggest star. The people loved me!"

The volcanic Chinaglia, an arrogant as well as talented scorer, was clearly upset by the move. Valcareggi and Chinaglia tried to make amends with a hug in the days that followed, but the damage had been done. After the substitution, Chinaglia disappeared, spending a few hours strolling in a park near the team hotel and eventually falling asleep under a tree.

Not caught napping was Poland. Gold medalists at the Summer Games just two years earlier, the Poles had ousted England during World Cup qualifying. While critics gave Poland mixed reviews, the team featured a wonderful mix of talent. Like many Eastern bloc nations at the time, the teams from this part of the world featured an air of mystery to them. In defense, Poland was anchored by Jerzy Gorgoń, a giant center back who could also score goals. In the midfield, the team featured Kazimierz Deyna, a talented passer with lots of vision. The Polish offense, made up of Grzegorz Lato, Andrzej Szarmach, and Robert Gadocha, was one of the finest at the time. The balding Lato looked older than his 24 years, but his speed and nose for goal would make him one of the players of the year. It was Lato's brace at the Neckarstadion in Stuttgart on June 15 that helped down Argentina. Lato's winning goal in the 62nd minute helped Poland grab the 3–2 victory.

Four days later, Italy and Argentina played to a 1–1 draw in Stuttgart, a result that kept the group wide open. In Munich, meanwhile, Poland blitzed Haiti 7–0. The Polish offense had an easy time. Szarmach tallied a hat trick, and Lato scored another brace to put Poland first place in the group and a step closer to qualifying for the second round.

The final match day on June 23 saw Argentina get the best of Haiti 4–1 in Munich. At the same time, Italy and Poland did battle in Stuttgart. The Italians needed a victory, especially as Argentina was running up the score and getting the best of them on goal differential. Poland, however, jumped out to a 2–0 lead in the first half. Goals by Szarmach in the 38th minute and a second from Kazimierz Deyna six minutes later put the Azzurri in a tailspin. Poland won the game, 2–1, and the group after winning all three of their first-round matches. Argentina joined them as the second-place team, displacing the Italians on goal differential.

"For me, the World Cup was a big deal," Chinaglia said. "We had been in a very good position to win it. It was a total disaster. But I wouldn't change anything I did. I did nothing wrong."

Second Round

The knockout round was replaced with two round-robin groups. The top teams from Group A and Group B would advance to the final, while the second-place sides would play for third place. Group A featured a fearsome foursome in the Netherlands, Brazil, East Germany, and Argentina. The Dutch and Brazilians were favored to advance, but East Germany and Argentina had proven to be pesky opponents.

In Group B, West Germany, despite their first-round hiccups, still appeared formidable alongside Sweden and Yugoslavia. The well-drilled Poles, the surprise side from the opening round, were out to prove they were no fluke.

Group A opened on June 26 when the Dutch squared off against Argentina in Gelsenkirchen. Total football won out again as Cruyff and his teammates demolished the South Americans 4–0. Cruyff scored twice, his side's opening goal in the 11th minute and the team's final strike in the 90th, to successfully send the message that they were for real. At the same time in Hanover, Brazil could only score once against East Germany via a Rivellino goal in the 60th minute. The 1–0 was enough, but it didn't fill many Brazilians with confidence that the side could challenge for the trophy.

The Netherlands and Brazil were both on the brink of qualifying for the final. The Dutch, by virtue of their 2–0 victory against East Germany on June 30 in Gelsenkirchen, remained in contention. The Brazilians, meanwhile, edged their South American rivals Argentina 2–1 in Hanover after Jairzinho tallied the winner in the 49th minute. On July 3 in Dortmund, the Netherlands and Brazil faced off with the victor making the final.

"The Brazilian defense will be the toughest for us," Cruyff told reporters. "We are going on attack and I hope they do the same."

After a scoreless first half, the Dutch masters turned on the pressure. The Brazilians, unable to stay focused, gave up two goals: one by Neeskens in the 50th minute and a second from Cruyff 15 minutes later. The Dutch had eliminated the defending world champions before 57,000 fans. Brazil had resorted to roughhouse tactics in an effort to thwart the Dutch. Three yellow cards later and a red card to defender Luís Pereira in the 84th minute told the story of just how badly the Brazilians had played.

Michels avoided talking about the rough play when asked by reporters. "The Brazilians tried to hold the ball and make it difficult for our men," he said. "We were lucky when they missed two chances. But our game improved in the second half."

The Dutch players, however, were outspoken about Brazil's negative tactics. "What the Brazilians did was a shame," Theo De Jong said. "When they cannot succeed with ordinary means, they employ brutality."

In Group B, West Germany defeated Yugoslavia 2–0 in Düsseldorf in front of a home crowd of 68,000. Breitner opened the scoring after 32 minutes, and a second from Müller eight minutes from time were examples of West Germany's superior play. In Stuttgart, Poland kept on winning, this time a 1–0 result against Sweden. Lato's close-range header in the 43rd minute was enough to grab the points.

In Frankfurt, the Polish juggernaut continued on June 30 following a 2–1 victory that eliminated Yugoslavia. Lato's goal in the 62nd minute, his sixth goal of the tournament, gave his side another win. West Germany, playing in Düsseldorf, overpowered Sweden 4–2. West Germany's last group match against Poland would determine which of the two would advance to the final. As expected, the July 3 encounter between the hosts and Poland was a tight affair. The 62,000 spectators under stormy skies in Frankfurt cheered in unison for long stretches following a 30-minute weather delay.

Poland manager Kazimierz Górski put Jan Tomaszewski, Deyna, and Szarmach—all suffering from injuries—in the starting lineup. "They will play in the most important game our country has ever played," Górski told reporters. "The event itself, the thought of playing in the final of the World Cup, is all the incentive our players need."

The Polish defense, unfazed by it all, kept the West Germans off the scoreboard. The first half ended scoreless. The game was largely foul free as both sides tried to use their brilliant passing and amazing midfield play to move the ball.

"What distinguishes this team is spirit," Schön told reporters the day before the game. "The 1972 side was more elegant, but the present team has stronger fighters."

The wet field and excess water stopped both sides from playing their best soccer. The game was marred by the ball often being stuck in puddles and stopped from moving. Poland needed a win, while the West Germans could use a draw and advance on goal differential. West Germany's Uli Hoeness missed a penalty kick at the hour mark, but the fight Schoen had talked about came through.

West Germany won in the end when Rainer Bonhof's run into the muddy penalty area ended with the ball rolling loose to Gerd Müller, who scored with a low shot for the winning goal in the 76th minute. Poland had fallen short in their crucial game, but a 1–0 win against Brazil gave them third place and an amazing end to their World Cup. Lato's game-winning goal gave him seven for the tournament, where he finished as top scorer. Many heralded the Poles, including some West German players, as the tournament's top team.

In a 2007 interview with FIFA.com, Breitner observed, "I can remember one game where I've always maintained we beat a team which was fundamentally better than us. In fact, it was definitely the best team in the competition and still didn't win the World Cup."

Final: West Germany vs. the Netherlands

The all-European final between West Germany and the Netherlands took place on July 7 at Munich's Olympiastadion. The game, featuring 75,000 fans, began in spectacular fashion. The Oranje, who had scored 14 goals and conceded just one in six previous games, scored even before a West German player could touch the ball. Cruyff set off on a solo run from the center circle but was tripped by Hoeness in the box. Neeskens took the penalty kick to make it 1–0 after just two minutes. It was the first penalty kick ever awarded—and converted—in a World Cup final.

West Germany, led by Beckenbauer, struggled to come from under the Dutch's ball possession. Beckenbauer had revolutionized the center back position. A hardworking player with a wonderful ability to win the ball, Beckenbauer was both forceful and elegant in his moves, attributes that earned him the nickname Der Kaiser (German for "the Emperor"). He was also a great distributor of the ball and was actively involved in his team's midfield. His great dribbling abilities gave West Germany both a strong defense as well as an extra offensive tool with his accurate, long-range passes. In the process, Beckenbauer recreated the sweeper position and would be a key contributor to West Germany's domination for much of the decade.

The hosts caught a break when in the 26th minute they were awarded a penalty after Bernd Hölzenbein fell in the Dutch box, causing English referee Jack Taylor to award another penalty. Breitner scored from the spot to tie the game. Breitner, recalling the pressure he and his teammates endured, said of that day: "I couldn't say I was under pressure to win the World Cup because it was what I expected of myself. In addition, I must say we didn't notice much pressure in 1974. There wasn't so much hysteria, football hadn't become what it is today, with global interest, a never-ending open air concert, a 24-hour happening of the type we experience in every stadium nowadays. We've seen a gigantic spectator boom during the past few years, not because the football being played is so good but because people have different expectations now."

West Germany, momentum on their side after tying the score, stretched the Dutch backline like no other opponent had at this tournament. Müller scored what turned out to be the winning goal, and the last of his career as he retired from the national team, in the 43rd minute. "The day before, I read in a newspaper that a clairvoyant had said Holland would win," Müller told FIFA.com in 2007. "I lost a lot of sleep that night, thinking about it and hoping it wouldn't come true. When we won 2–1, it was just the most wonderful feeling."

The West Germans took a 2–1 lead into the dressing room and hung on to win the game after the sides traded several chances each in the second half. "Perhaps the Dutch thought we would be easy after they scored that goal in the first minute," Schoen told reporters. "A soccer match lasts 90 minutes and the better fighters won it."

Adversity had worked in West Germany's favor. Even Müller admitted that going down early in the final helped motivate him and his teammates. "At the end of the day, it was a good thing the Dutch scored so early," he said. "I think they underestimated us, they started to spray the ball about and then they thought, 'Hang on, the Germans are getting back into it.' Then they started giving it everything again."

Michels, upset following the defeat, applauded the West Germans and his side's effort. Total football had not been a failure. Instead, they were defeated by a superior team. "It hurts, but I must congratulate the German team and all German fans," he said. "We did not underestimate the Germans—but we came a long way, too."

1978 WORLD CUP

The decade brought with it more political unrest for much of Latin America. In Argentina, chosen as the 1978 World Cup host in 1970, the years leading up to the finals were dominated by a military coup in 1976. The event, triggered by the death of President Juan Perón just two years earlier, sent the nation into turmoil. In charge now were Lieutenant General Jorge Rafael Videla, Admiral Emilio Eduardo Massera, and Brigadier General Orlando Ramón Agosti.

Although a right-wing military junta was now in charge of the nation, the World Cup logo was designed to resemble the populist Perón's signature gesture: a salute to the crowd with both arms extended above his head. The new military leadership, aware that the logo symbolized Perón's gesture, tried in vain to change it. The design had already been part of an international marketing campaign, and FIFA was not going to alter it.

The tournament was once again a chance for a dictatorial regime to broadcast its best self to the planet. The reality, however, was grimmer. The regime, through the creation of military death squads, was responsible for a series of human rights violations. During what was called the "Dirty War," more than 30,000 *desaparecidos* (Spanish for "disappeared persons," the name given to political dissidents) were tortured and killed—simply made to disappear—until democracy was restored in 1983.

Some of these prisoners were held in concentration camps located just a mile away from the Estadio Monumental in the capital Buenos Aires, one of six venues that would host matches. La Escuela Superior de Mecánica de la Armada (also known by its acronym ESMA) was a clandestine detention center located only a few city blocks away from the stadium.

Graciela Daleo, one of 5,000 people who were tortured inside the facility, said detainees could hear the celebrations at the stadium during the World Cup matches.

"So close, and light years away from ESMA," she recalled during one of the many trials held after it was uncovered that military and police officials had committed such heinous acts.

Her captors, she recalled, even took her out in a car to see the euphoric celebrations following one of Argentina's victories. Daleo realized that "if I had attempted to shout out that I was a desaparecida, nobody would pay attention because this is part of what I was saying about us not belonging to the world of the living."

Ana María Soffiantini, another prisoner held at ESMA, said she was "surprised by the fact that they had brought a television set for us" so they could watch the games.

"I do not know if it was meant to make [the detained] feel worse or to distract them," she said. "So, while we listened to the screams of those being tortured, we could also hear the cheers for the goals."

This state-sponsored torture and murder was the backdrop for the 1978 World Cup. Sports and politics make for a bad mix, and the World Cup had not been immune from this in the past. FIFA, no stranger to deal making, found itself in the middle of a public relations mess. Amnesty International led a global protest under the slogan, "Yes to football, no to torture!"

It turned out that Videla was not a soccer fan, but he understood that millions of his countrymen were obsessed with the game. The junta knew that hosting the World Cup wouldn't only serve as a distraction, but could be used as an effective propaganda tool to solidify their power.

A year before the tournament was scheduled to be played, a group of French journalists formed the Organizing Committee for the Boycott of the Argentina World Cup, known by its French acronym COBA. They planned an organized campaign designed to persuade the French national team, led by Michel Platini, to skip the tournament. They also urged other teams, such as Italy, Sweden, and the Netherlands, to skip the competition.

"We should not play soccer amid the concentration camps and torture chambers," the organization's manifesto read.

Players such as Breitner threatened to boycott the tournament, while Cruyff actually did. Thirty years later, however, Cruyff told Catalunya Radio that the real reason was not in protest to the Argentine regime, but because he and his wife had been tied up at gunpoint inside their Barcelona home during a kidnapping attempt.

"It was the moment to leave football and I couldn't play in the World Cup after this," he said.

Through it all, FIFA remained unmoved. Talk of moving the tournament was ignored by Havelange. Instead, he praised the government for all it had done. Adidas unveiled a new ball for the tournament, called the Tango, in homage to the nation's favorite dance.

"I am among those that most depended on the hard work that your country undertook and I haven't been disappointed," he told reporters when he arrived in Buenos Aires on the eve of the tournament. "It fills me with pride, first from knowing that Argentina responded to the challenge and second because I am also South American. We have achieved everything we proposed."

The format remained the same as in 1974: 16 teams qualified and divided into four groups of four. All the major teams qualified, including Brazil and the Netherlands. Notable absences included Czechoslovakia, winners of the 1976 European Championship, England, Uruguay, and the Soviet Union. Here's how the four groups of qualified nations were composed:

Group 1: Argentina, Italy, France, and Hungary

Group 2: West Germany, Poland, Tunisia, and Mexico

Group 3: Brazil, Spain, Austria, and Sweden

Group 4: Netherlands, Scotland, Peru, and Iran

Each group played a round-robin format with goal differential used to separate teams tied on points after three matches. The top two in each group advanced to the second round, where they would be split into two groups of four. The winners of each group would play each other in the final, the second-place finishers in the third-place match. FIFA introduced the penalty-kick shootout as a way to determine a winner during the knockout stage should it end in a tie after 30 minutes of extra time, an innovation first used at the Euros two years prior.

Group Stage

Under the cloud of a totalitarian regime, Argentina counted itself among the favorites for the title. Playing at home certainly helped, as it had for other past hosts. The team was coached by César Luis Menotti, nicknamed "El Flaco" (The Thin One) because of his slender build. Menotti, ironically, was a proud socialist, famous for his chain-smoking on the sidelines. He sported long hair and open-collared shirts, unafraid to go against the soccer status quo that increasingly called for defensive tactics as a recipe for success.

"I want my team to play better than my opponent and to win the game," said Menotti. "I don't like to win by any means necessarily or by accident."

In fact, Menotti favored offensive soccer and was a risk taker, a style that highlighted the South American game. He had been appointed Argentina manager in 1974, although he submitted his resignation in the wake of the coup. The Argentine FA, led at the time by Alfredo Francisco Cantilo, refused, and Menotti was cajoled into returning to the job.

On February 15—106 days before the start of the World Cup—Menotti awaited the arrival of 24 players for an initial assessment that was to take place at Villa Marista in Mar del Plata. Daniel Passarella, who played for Argentine powerhouse River Plate, was named team captain after Jorge Carrascosa quit the national team for personal reasons. Not on the roster was a then-17-year-old budding playmaker named

Diego Maradona. Menotti had deemed him too young for the pressures of such a high-profile competition. Maradona would have to wait four years before he got his chance to play at a World Cup.

"Most of the players at the time played domestically," Menotti recalled. "We had great talents that played domestically."

Mario Kempes, the team's best striker, was the only foreign-based player on the roster. He played his club soccer at Valencia in Spain and was blessed with exquisite ball control. Kempes didn't like to orchestrate plays. Instead, he wanted to get that final pass that would help him score.

"The players knew each other well," Kempes said. "They would play with their clubs on the weekends and train with the national team during the week. I arrived late, only after the season was over in Spain, because I was with Valencia at the time."

Left back Alberto Tarantini had been dropped by the Boca Juniors following a contract dispute. Debate over whether a player had to be signed to a club to play in the World Cup meant Tarantini was originally left off the roster. Tarantini joined the players in Mar de Plata and was overjoyed when FIFA responded that he could be on the roster even as a free agent.

In the weeks leading up to the finals, Menotti put together a cohesive unit that was free to express itself on the field. It was, in a way, a contrast to the tyranny around him. Menotti demanded attacking skill and individual flair.

"His was an Aristotelian style that emphasized the realization of players' maximum creative potential, both to influence results on the field and society off it," Daniel Altman wrote of Menotti in a 2014 piece for *Foreign Policy*. "He called soccer 'a joyous fiesta in which human beings must participate, because it expresses their feelings and delivers the happiness of being alive.' He wanted to win, he said, 'because my team played better, not because I stopped the other team from playing.' For Menotti, soccer was a force for good and could only be played in a positive way."

It was that force for good that took the field against Hungary at the Monumental. Of course, there were constant reminders of the regime's power. "The thousands of men and women from the most diverse regions of the Earth honor us with their visit here, under the condition that it be in a climate of affection and mutual respect," Videla told the crowd. "It is the competition on the playing field and the bonds in the field of human relations that permit us to affirm that it is possible to harmonize unity and diversity, even today."

The sports authorities at the time didn't make things better. In his opening message to the fans and to an international TV audience, Cantilo said, "Welcome all to the land of peace, liberty and justice. We are honored by your presence."

Havelange, his dark-rimmed glasses slightly askew and Videla standing to his left, thanked the authorities for their "dedication and tenacity" for having organized the tournament and the "importance of football for its people."

After doves were released into the air, the match saw Hungary take the lead after just nine minutes. The offensive-minded Argentines got caught ball watching in the back, and Károly Csapó tapped the ball in from a few yards out after goalkeeper Ubaldo Fillol had failed to latch onto the ball. Csapó ran toward his teammates with his arms aloft as a chorus of jeers and whistles from the 72,000 in the stands greeted his celebration.

Menotti's attacking style was on full display that evening as Leopoldo Luque and Kempes showed a clear understanding of one another even though the Valencia striker had joined the team just a few weeks before the tournament began. Luque equalized five minutes later, putting the ball into the net off a rebound after goalkeeper Sándor Gujdár failed to hang on to a well-kicked Kempes free kick. The fans waved the country's sky-blue and white flags in delight.

As Menotti continued to puff on cigarettes from the Argentina dugout, the players continued to create chances. Tied at one after the opening 45 minutes, Argentina kept putting pressure on the Hungarians who appeared out of ideas. Nine minutes from time, Argentina were rewarded with a goal by second-half sub Daniel Bertoni. Hungary, frustrated and unable to create much offense, saw two of its players—strikers András Törőcsik and Tibor Nyilasi—red-carded in the finale after each had committed two brutal fouls. By game's end, ticker tape and confetti rained down from the stands, a custom of Argentine fans that would come to be one of the tournament's indelible images.

In the day's other group match, Italy and France, two of Europe's strongest teams, met at the Estadio José María Minella in Mar del Plata. The French took the lead after just a minute with striker Bernard Lacombe. The Italians, known for their great defending, used the counterattack to great effect. Paolo Rossi tied the game in the 29th minute. Rossi and Platini would become teammates at Juventus in the early 1980s, making the Italian club one of the best in the world. The Argentine press had dubbed the striker Pablito because of his diminutive size. In the second half, the Azzurri put the game away with a goal by midfielder Renato Zaccarelli in the 54th minute. Italy and Argentina were tied for first place.

The Monumental hosted Argentina's second group game on June 6 against France. Before a raucous crowd of 72,000 fans, the Albiceleste got on the board with a penalty kick at the end of the first half. Swiss referee Jean Dubach made a dubious call, whistling a hand ball on Marius Trésor. Passarella took the penalty shot and banged in the ball. In the second half, the French were forced to sub out goalkeeper Jean-Paul Bertrand-Demanes, who was stretchered off after injuring his back by crashing into the post while making a save. He was replaced by Dominique Baratelli in the 55th minute. Five minutes later, after a scramble in front of the Argentine goal, Platini scored the equalizer after the ball had ricocheted off the crossbar.

Argentina, at real risk of losing the match, doggedly chased the ball in an attempt to shut down the French attack. France, playing at a high tempo, could have put the game away, but a second goal didn't come. Instead, with the crowd roaring in support, the hosts scored the go-ahead goal. Luque, standing unmarked outside the box, drilled a shot that sailed past the French defense and into the goal for the 2–1 win.

A 2018 *Esquire* magazine piece looking back at the tournament reported the following: "A Luque 25-yarder settled the game at 2–1, but years later the fire was restoked when a caller on a radio phone-in—claiming to be a former French international footballer—made unsubstantiated claims that FIFA officials were turning a blind eye to Argentine amphetamine use."

It was also alleged that after urine samples were taken, a FIFA official discovered one of the Argentina players was pregnant. It wasn't the first allegation of wrongdoing against the Argentines. But the team, as well as the dictatorship, seemed to be getting stronger. The Italians, meanwhile, got off to another slow start against Hungary in Mar del Plata. Rossi finally broke the deadlock after 34 minutes, a goal that opened the floodgates. Roberto Bettega added a second just a minute later, and a third from Romeo Benetti were the highlights of a 3–1 victory.

The final group matches were played on June 10. Argentina and Italy were both through to the next round, but a win for either side would allow them to win the group. The sides played a tight match at the Monumental, but the stingy Italian backline did a solid job of thwarting Luque and Kempes. Luque played through emotional pain since his brother had been tragically killed in a traffic accident on the day of the game. The Italians, meanwhile, found the back of the net in the 67th minute with Bettega. The Italian striker put the ball past Fillol one-on-one for the win. For the Argentines, the defeat was a minor setback.

The Estadio Monumental played host to West Germany's Group 2 match against Poland on June 1 in an all-European clash and rematch of their second-round encounter at the World Cup just four years earlier. The match ended scoreless, a result that served as motivation for Tunisia and Mexico. The sides played one another the following day at Estadio Gigante de Arroyito in Rosario. The winner would temporarily take control of the group. While Tunisia and Mexico were underdogs to advance, the 3–1 win by the North Africans got them off to a great start. It also marked the first time that an African team had won a World Cup game.

The Carthage Eagles had been fortunate to be in the finals after having been suspended just months earlier for walking off the field during an Africa Cup of Nations match in Nigeria, which prompted a two-year ban for the team and a three-year sanction for their goalkeeper, Attouga Sadouk. The Confederation of African Football threatened to ask FIFA to extend the ban to worldwide competition, although it was decided that it would be too difficult to appoint a new African representative to travel to Argentina for the World Cup.

The defending World Cup champions, without Beckenbauer, who had retired, ended the scoring drought on June 6 at Estadio Chateau Carreras in Córdoba. West Germany's 6–0 thumping was highlighted by a brace from striker Karl-Heinz Rummenigge and another by midfielder Heinz Flohe, which exposed just how weak the Mexican backline was at the tournament. Poland, meanwhile, earned a win in Rosario, a 1–0 defeat of Tunisia. West Germany and Poland, favored to advance on the eve of the competition, had destiny on their side. The North Africans, however, needed to score an upset against West Germany in order to advance.

The final match day on June 10 saw Poland defeat Mexico 3–1 in Rosario thanks to two goals from striker Zbigniew Boniek. At the same time in Córdoba, West Germany could only muster a 0–0 draw against Tunisia. The draw put West Germany in second place, but just barely, and into the second round. Tunisia's performance helped make a successful case for Africa to have the number of slots at the World Cup finals doubled in 1982. Poland, by virtue of their two wins and a draw, won the group and now hoped to build on their third-place finish four years earlier.

Brazil, the uncrowned kings of the game, came into the tournament as the favorites to win Group 3. Austria, making their return to the World Cup for the first time since 1958, Spain, and Sweden rounded out the rest of the group. The three European nations would fight for second place.

Austria opened the group on June 3 against Spain with a 2–1 win at Estadio José Amalfitani in Buenos Aires. Striker Hans Krankl tallied the winning goal in the 76th minute. In Mar de Plata, Brazil made their tournament debuts—but couldn't do better than a 1–1 draw against Sweden. A new generation of players, including midfielder Toninho Cerezo and striker Zico, highlighted the squad, but the Brazilians didn't look as strong as their usual selves. Rivellino, the leading veteran left over from the Pelé era and only one of four players on the team with prior World Cup experience, was also on the tournament roster.

Rivellino, however, clashed with Brazil manager Cláudio Coutinho following the draw. The striker was dropped from the starting lineup for the remainder of the first round. Rivellino wouldn't see any more playing time until the second round. Coutinho, who had taken the team on a tour of Europe on the eve of the tournament, had attempted to blend total football with the skill and enthusiasm the Brazilians had traditionally brought to the game. Rivellino, the team captain, had been asked to play in midfield, as he had in 1970, and not as center forward. Rivellino refused, and Coutinho's tactical tinkering continued for the remainder of the tournament. At the same time, goalkeeper Émerson Leão was named team captain.

Four days later, Austria got closer to taking on the Cinderella side moniker at the tournament, defeating Sweden 1–0 at Estadio José Amalfitani. Once again, it was Krankl who scored the winner via a penalty kick three minutes before halftime. While big things were expected from Brazil in Mar de Plata against Spain, the game ended scoreless. The Brazilian attack appeared to be in chaos, although qualification to the second group phase was not. Nonetheless, there was turmoil in the Brazil camp. Coutinho had offered to resign following the Spain game, but the Brazilian FA refused to accept it. The rift with Rivellino spilled over to other squad members, including Zico. The "Europeanization" of the Brazilian game, a struggle that would persist for another two decades, had brought chaos to the team.

With Spain and Sweden eliminated, Brazil squared off against the plucky Austrians in Mar de Plata. Coutinho made some tweaks to the lineup, benching Zico and starting Roberto Dinamite at forward. The move proved prescient as the striker scored in the 40th minute for what turned out to be a 1–0 win. Dinamite would start for the remainder of the tournament. The victory, however, wasn't enough to capture the group, and the Brazilians had to settle for second place. Austria had stunned the field, taking first place on goal differential.

The Netherlands, the team to beat in Group 4, came into the tournament without Cruyff, who had retired from the national team. Even without Cruyff, the Dutch continued to possess a team strong enough to sustain a serious challenge.

The team's 22-man roster—minus defender Hugo Hovenkamp, who withdrew from the squad before the tournament began, but after the deadline for naming replacement players had passed—assembled by the Austrian-born Ernst Happel, looked very competitive. Happel had been named Dutch manager in 1977, replacing Jan Zwartkruis. In turn, Zwartkruis was demoted to assistant coach.

The group presented little difficulty for the Netherlands. Peru, Scotland, and debutants Iran did not pose a major threat. The altitude of Mendoza, in Argentina's Andean west, was certainly an obstacle, but the South American winter made it so that the heat players had experienced at Mexico '70 would not be an issue this time.

The Netherlands opened things up with a 3–0 win against Iran on June 3 at the Estadio Ciudad de Mendoza in Mendoza. A Rob Rensenbrink hat trick—two of those goals coming from penalty kicks—and the Dutch had gotten the campaign off on the right foot. Meanwhile, at Chateau Carreras in Córdoba, Peru marked their tournament opener with a 3–1 victory against Scotland. Two Cubillas goals was reminiscent of the Peru side that had captured so many hearts eight years earlier in Mexico.

Match day 2 on June 7 was highlighted by two draws: Scotland and Iran playing a 1–1 game in Córdoba; the Netherlands and Peru both unable to score in their clash in Mendoza. That set up the decisive final day four days later. While Peru won the group by defeating lowly Iran 4–1 in Córdoba via a Cubillas hat trick and were through to the next round, Scotland pulled off the upset and downed the Dutch 3–2 in Mendoza. That put both sides level on points, but the Netherlands—thanks to Johnny Rep's goal in the 71st minute—gave the Dutch better differential in the tiebreaker for second place.

Behind the scenes, the Dutch FA was ready to give control back to Zwartkruis, while Happel would continue on as a figurehead. While the players were fully aware of what had transpired, the public were not until the publication of Zwartkruis's book *Kapitein van Oranje* in 2008. The coup aside, what the Dutch were really lacking was the skill and creativity of Cruyff. His pace and power, coupled with his ability to play anywhere on the field, rendered the Netherlands akin to an orchestra without its conductor.

Second Round

The eight remaining teams were split into Groups A and B. Four European sides—Italy, West Germany, Austria, and the Netherlands were placed in Group A. Argentina, Brazil, Peru, and Poland made up Group B.

Buenos Aires and Córdoba would host Group A, where the West Germans and Dutch were reunited after having contested the final four years earlier. The Netherlands routed Austria 5–1 on June 14 in Córdoba, while West Germany couldn't do better than a 0–0 draw versus Italy at the Monumental.

Four days later, West Germany took on the Netherlands in the group's most anticipated game. The Netherlands fielded six players who had played in the 1974 final to West Germany's four. Coincidentally, the match official, Ramón Barreto of Uruguay, had served as one of the assistant referees at that final.

West Germany took the lead after just three minutes when Dutch goalkeeper Piet Schrijvers could only swat away Rainer Bonhof's free kick into the path of Rüdiger Abramczik, who headed the ball in for a goal. The Netherlands equalized in the 27th minute when Haan's bullet of a free kick from 35 yards hit the top corner. All the West German players could do is watch in amazement. The Dutch, who needed a draw to stay on course to win the group, retreated into their own half. West Germany, in need of a win, used the wings to score a goal in the 70th minute. Erich Beer crossed the ball for Dieter Müller to put in a header with three defenders around him. Six minutes from the end, René van de Kerkhof took a pass from his twin brother Willy, beat the offside trap, then cut inside past a defender and unleashed a shot to make it two-all.

The drama didn't end there. While there wouldn't be any more goals, second-half sub Dick Nanninga was given a yellow card for a foul in the 87th minute, then seconds later Barreto showed him a red one for laughing at him. It took several minutes to restore order as Nanninga was escorted into the dressing room for an early shower. Italy, meanwhile, defeated Austria 1–0 at the Monumental on a Rossi goal after just 13 minutes, meaning their final group match against the Netherlands would serve as practically a semifinal.

The winner of the Netherlands-Italy game on June 21 at the Monumental would be assured a place in the final. The Dutch could also win the group with a draw and a Germany draw or defeat against Austria. It was the Azzurri who got off to the better start, opening the scoring after just 19 minutes when Ernie Brandts, in an attempt to stop Bettega, put the ball into his own net for an own goal. The crowd of 67,000, made up largely of Italian immigrants, cheered on their countrymen. Schrijvers, however, was injured on the play after crashing into Brandts and had to be subbed out for Jan Jongbloed.

The match grew increasingly physical amid the jeers of the 67,000 in attendance. Referee Angel Franco Martínez of Spain warned the players, cautioning Rep for fouling Romeo Benetti, who later picked up a yellow card himself for fouling Rensenbrink. In the 49th minute, Brandts scored from outside the box with a thunderous blast to even the score. Fourteen minutes from time, the Dutch, once again using long-range shots to score, saw Haan hit a 30-yard shot that went off the left post and past Zoff. Haan was hugged by his teammates as the deflated Italians looked on. The Netherlands won the game 2–1 and were in the final once again. "The Netherlands were true winners," Happel told reporters after the match. "We have returned to our normal playing level."

Group B, meanwhile, was contested in Mendoza and Rosario. Although Brazil and Argentina had failed to win their opening-round group, these were the two teams most were excited to watch. Brazil, 3–0 winners against Peru on June 14 in Mendoza, faced Argentina, 2–0 winners versus Poland, in an all–South American battle. Failure to win the group had forced Argentina away from the Monumental, but the excitement around the national team only intensified when they took the field on June 18 in Rosario. A loud crowd of 37,000 cheered on the Albiceleste, but both offenses couldn't get the job done and the match ended scoreless.

That score set up a final match day on June 21. Brazil needed a win against Poland in Mendoza, as long as Argentina didn't win by four goals or more versus Peru. Both games were scheduled to kick off at 4:45 p.m. But the Argentines delayed the start of their game in Rosario after Brazil had already defeated Poland 3–1 in Mendoza thanks to two Roberto

Dinamite goals. Videla had a keen interest that his nation defeat Peru and reach the final. In fact, Videla even visited the Peruvian dressing room before the start of the match, an encounter that took on greater significance at the end of the match.

As 37,000 fans waved flags and cheered them on, Argentina recorded the most improbable of results, defeating Peru 6–0, with Kempes and Luque both netting a brace. The Brazilians, losers because of goal differential but overall undefeated at the tournament, cried foul and immediately accused Peruvian goalkeeper Ramón Quiroga, who had been born in Rosario, of throwing the match.

"We have confidence in Quiroga. He will play like a Peruvian," Peru manager Marcos Calderón had told reporters on the eve of the big game.

In the game's aftermath, many were left scratching their heads. Indeed, Argentina, after cruising past Peru with a suspicious degree of ease, were off to the final. Brazil, on the other hand, would finish third.

Raanan Rein, a professor of Latin American history, told a FIFA-hosted conference on World Cup history in 2010 that he was "100 percent persuaded" that the junta had been involved, along with "at least one foreign government," to fix the game.

Two years later, former Peruvian senator Genaro Ledesma admitted that the shock result had been agreed upon before the match by the dictatorships of the two nations. Ledesma made the accusation before an Argentine judge after an arrest order was issued against former Peruvian leader Francisco Bermudez. Ledesma, an opposition leader at the time, said Videla accepted political prisoners in return for Peru deliberately losing the game.

"Videla needed to win the World Cup to cleanse Argentina's bad image around the world," he said. "So he only accepted the group if Peru allowed the Argentine national team to triumph."

Final: Argentina vs. Netherlands

Argentine passion was ready to explode on June 25 at the Estadio Monumental. The 71,000 in the stands chanted "Ar-gen-ti-na, Ar-gen-ti-na" as the players walked onto the confetti-littered field five minutes after the Dutch already had. The move angered the Dutch, as had the

Argentines questioning whether the plaster cast on René van de Kerk-hof's wrist was allowed, despite him having worn it in earlier games without objections. Italian referee Sergio Gonella quelled the concerns and forced Van de Kerkhof to apply an extra bandage over the cast.

A dash of black paint was featured at the base of each goalpost, a symbol akin to black armbands worn by players. The reason was a subtle protest, a sign of mourning for those who had been kidnapped and tortured by the country's murderous regime at the time. The generals never knew that was the reason. Instead, Videla and his fellow military junta members, Admiral Emilio Massera and Air Force general Orlando Agosti, looked on proudly as Argentina were playing in their first final since 1930. Ticker tape cascaded from the stands in the 38th minute when Kempes, off a pass from Luque, opened the scoring, tucking the ball past Jongbloed from just 12 yards out.

A tense match, Argentina looked assured of the win until the Oranje equalized eight minutes from time when Van de Kerkhof's cross found Nanninga, who headed home the ball to make it 1–1. The Dutch could have even won the game in the final minutes after Rensenbrink's attempt went past Fillol, but the ball bounced off the post. The failed attempt meant the game was going to extra time.

The game had been marred by a series of fouls—especially tackles from behind at a time when FIFA didn't clamp down on such plays—that highlighted Gonella's ineptitude. By game's end, Gonella would hand out just five yellow cards—three against the Netherlands and just two for Argentina—in a game that certainly warranted many more even by 1978 standards. Passarella was by far the biggest offender, but he was never even booked.

As the Dutch swarmed Kempes each time he got the ball, Argentina maintained its attacking pace as the crowd continued to sustain them in a manifestation of nationalistic fervor. It was in the 105th minute that Kempes scored, marking the sixth time he'd found the back of the net and a goal that would ensure he'd finish as the tournament's top scorer. Jongbloed had tried in vain to keep the ball from getting past him, but a series of unfortunate bounces allowed Kempes, ever the opportunistic goal poacher, to score what would be the winning goal.

The Albiceleste didn't stop there. With Menotti continuing to bark orders from the bench between cigarettes, Argentina scored for a third time in the 115th minute, and the decibel level was off the charts as the crowd roared in ecstasy. With Jongbloed out of position and the Dutch backline left in tatters by Kempes's ball-control skills, Bertoni scored and raced off to celebrate the goal and the title. For the Dutch, it marked their second straight defeat in a World Cup final.

"Arrogance among their players, which has been an abiding problem for Dutch teams down the years. To be successful is not only a matter of skill and entertaining football—it also demands realism and a winning mentality," Radnedge observed. "The balance is essential. Talent alone is not enough. That said, the Dutch contribution to soccer development is remarkable for a nation of only 17 million. Perhaps the correct perspective should be to appreciate how much they have achieved—punching far beyond their weight, like Uruguay for example—rather than what they have not achieved."

Videla presented Passarella with the trophy. "When you're handed the cup, you feel numb," he told FIFA.com in 2020. "It's like a never-ending orgasm. That might sound vulgar but it's true. You have to experience it to understand."

A party broke out in the streets in Buenos Aires and throughout the country. Nonetheless, few around the world celebrated with them. The victory, unlikely if it hadn't occurred on home soil, would usher in a new era for Argentine soccer.

CHAPTER FIVE

Maradona's Ascent

THE 1986 WORLD CUP FEATURED MANY OUTSTANDING PLAYERS AND coaches. One of them was Velibor "Bora" Milutinović, the man who coached Mexico at that tournament. He would go on to coach at five consecutive editions of the World Cup with five different teams: Mexico (1986), Costa Rica (1990), the United States (1994), Nigeria (1998), and China (2002). In doing so, he became the first man to guide four teams beyond the opening round (all but China). It was under his leadership that China, the planet's most populous nation, qualified for the World Cup for the first time.

Talk with Milutinović and the stories pile up. He's been virtually everywhere—and in the process earned the nickname "miracle worker," first given to him by former U.S. Soccer Federation president Alan Rothenberg. I have run into Milutinović numerous times throughout the years. Always sporting a smile, the tanned Milutinović, who still has a 1960s-style haircut as if he were a member of the Beatles, greets anyone he meets like an old friend.

"I always try to be happy," he told me in 2018 during another chance encounter in Moscow ahead of the World Cup final. "This is a wonderful game and I continue to be a part of it."

He routinely shows up at games and tournaments, often with no credentials since everyone knows him. As former U.S. star Alexi Lalas has said, Milutinović is "part Yoda, part Yogi Berra." Although he retired from coaching years ago, Milutinović was in Russia as a member of

FIFA's Technical Study Group, a cabal of former players and coaches who come together every four years to look at tactical trends.

Milutinović was born in the former Yugoslavia (present-day Serbia) and moved to Mexico in 1972 to finish his playing career with UNAM. He later coached the club and Mexico. Milutinović claims that connecting with others and a mix of good fortune has been the secret to his success. "I like to make friends," he said. "Luck is also a big part. I have made my own luck."

He has made lots of friends throughout the decades, although he does hold some grudges despite his beaming smile. He coached the United States at the 1994 World Cup but was forced to resign a year later, much to his chagrin. When I asked him whether he missed seeing the United States play at the 2018 World Cup after failing to qualify for the first time since 1986, Milutinović replied, "Ask them if they miss me!"

1982 WORLD CUP

The 1980s were an era of greed, and soccer was no different. This was the decade where European clubs initiated massive transfer fees to get the players they wanted. It was the decade that saw Italy's Serie A rise to the top thanks to clubs there gobbling up the planet's best talents. It was the precursor of what we see in the sport today. The amount of money in the modern game has reached numbing new heights. In 1996, England's Alan Shearer became the most expensive player in the world after moving from the Blackburn Rovers to Newcastle United for $23 million ($39 million in today's money). Neymar, who is currently the world's most expensive player, cost French club Paris Saint-Germain 11 times that amount from Barcelona in 2017.

By the late 1970s and early 1980s, sponsors began popping up on the front of jerseys at the club level. The game was changing, and money had become a bigger part of it. While money made some of Europe's top leagues more predictable as a smaller and smaller group consolidated power, that phenomenon didn't naturally transfer over to national teams. Nonetheless, the 1980s saw traditional powers like Italy, West Germany, and Argentina emerge as three of the strongest. Perennial favorites Brazil also fielded some amazing teams, to much less success. Other European nations, most notably France, became very competitive during this time. It's no coincidence that their star player, Michel Platini, featured for Italian powerhouse Juventus.

This was a decade that would be the start of big business for FIFA. The television rights to the tournament in 1982 earned the governing body $42 million, an amount that would increase to $123 million, according to FIFA, in time for the 1994 edition. Marketing revenue also became a cash cow for FIFA during this time as nations clamored to host what had by now become the planet's biggest sporting event.

"Havelange, whatever the dark side of his reign, brought vision, ambition, professionalism, and commercial business acumen to FIFA," Radnedge said. "When he was elected, FIFA had a scruffy little office in Zurich and ten employees. Today's multi-national, multi-billion, international monolith is the direct result of his reign."

Spain had been chosen to host the 1982 World Cup. The tournament was expanded from 16 to 24, which allowed more nations from Africa and Asia to participate and made good on Havelange's electoral promise. At the conclusion of the tournament, Havelange, in a letter published in FIFA's official report following the 1982 tournament, made the following statement: "The facts proved we were right. The participation of six teams from developing countries—and I am only speaking in a footballing sense—has undeniably enriched this World Cup."

The expanded field didn't mean that all the game's heavyweights had qualified. The Netherlands, runners-up in 1974 and 1978, failed to reach the finals, along with Mexico and Sweden. On the other hand, Northern Ireland qualified for the first time since 1958, while Belgium, Czechoslovakia, El Salvador, England, and the Soviet Union were all back in the finals after 12-year absences. Algeria, Cameroon, Honduras, Kuwait, and New Zealand all qualified for the very first time.

The 24 teams were placed into six groups of four teams. The top two teams from each group advanced. In the second round, the 12 remaining teams were split into four groups of three teams each, the winner of each group advancing to the semifinals. Spain, as the host nation, along with Argentina, Brazil, Italy, England, and West Germany, were seeded and could not meet in the opening round. Here's how the groups were composed:

Group 1: Italy, Poland, Peru, and Cameroon

Group 2: West Germany, Austria, Chile, and Algeria

Group 3: Argentina, Belgium, Hungary, and El Salvador

Group 4: England, France, Czechoslovakia, and Kuwait

Group 5: Spain, Northern Ireland, Yugoslavia, and Honduras

Group 6: Brazil, Scotland, the Soviet Union, and New Zealand

England, instead of Belgium or Poland, were seeded so they could play in Bilbao for security reasons. Spanish officials feared that traveling English hooligans, known for rioting and other disruptive behavior in and around games, would cause problems at the World Cup. The phenomenon had grown in England throughout the 1970s but would create massive problems throughout Europe in the next decade at both club and national team matches.

Brazil, once again, came into the tournament as the heavy favorites. The team was coached by Telê Santana and came into the tournament riding a 19-game unbeaten streak, which had included wins against England, France, and West Germany. Santana fielded a very offensive-minded team that relied heavily on passing and set pieces to score goals. Santana was credited with reintroducing *jogo bonito* and was inspired by total football's ability to involve players on both offense and defense. Santana had several weapons at his disposal, including talented players like Paulo Roberto Falcão, Sócrates, and Zico. It would be on the strength of these players that Brazil embarked on the month-long journey to win the cup.

Seventeen stadiums in fourteen cities hosted matches. All six groups were assigned stadiums in cities near to each other in order to reduce travel for both players and fans. The Nou Camp in Barcelona hosted five matches, the most of any venue, while the final was set for the Estadio Santiago Bernabeu in the capital Madrid.

Group Stage

Italy were favorites to advance out of Group 1, but not all went according to plan. The Azzurri got off to a very slow start, opening the group on June 14 with a scoreless draw against Poland at Estadio Municipal de Balaídos in Vigo and a 1–1 result versus Peru four days later at the same venue. It was an inauspicious start, and with just two points it seemed Italy's chances of advancing had been severely diminished.

The Italians entered the tournament dogged by controversy. Italian journalists and fans had criticized manager Enzo Bearzot for their country's poor start and blamed much of it on his reliance on Paolo Rossi. The diminutive striker had managed 13 goals for Perugia during the 1979–80 Serie A season. It was during that season, however, that Rossi was implicated in the now infamous 1980 match-fixing scandal known in Italy as Totonero. As a result, Rossi was banned from playing for three years, although the punishment was later reduced to two. As a result, Rossi had missed the 1980 European Championship, where Italy finished fourth on home soil. Despite the ban, Rossi, who signed with Juventus once his ban ended, claimed to be innocent of any wrongdoing.

Bearzot, his trademark pipe clenched between his yellowed teeth, had gambled on a young Rossi at the '78 tournament in the center forward role, a move that had paid off. In Spain, Rossi was unable to score in his first two games—the lone goal after that pair of matches coming from Bruno Conti. Poland won 5–1 against Peru on June 22 at Estadio Riazor in La Coruña, putting them temporarily into first place. The Italians faced Cameroon in their final group game the following day, where a draw would put them through since they had a better goal differential than the Cameroonians. In other words, another draw would work, but the Italians were a much better side, and a win would certainly have staved off criticism.

"The tension and the fear were there," captain and goalkeeper Dino Zoff recalled. "There was the fear of not advancing."

The Azzurri, under the psychological weight of it all, continued their poor form. A scoreless first half left Italian fans disgusted, but a goal in the 60th minute from striker Francesco Graziani off a beautiful cross from Rossi temporarily quelled the criticism. The 20,000 in the stands cheered the goal, but even before they could take their seats, the Indomitable Lions equalized a minute later. Despite featuring Zoff in goal and a defense that had Claudio Gentile and Gaetano Scirea, midfielder Grégoire M'Bida, just a few yards in front of the goal, blasted the ball past Zoff.

The Italians hung on for a draw and were through after finishing second to group winners Poland, a team inspired by the brilliant play of Zibi Boniek. Their hopes remained alive, as did the criticism. After three lackluster draws, Bearzot announced a *silenzio stampa* (Italian for "press silence") in an effort to isolate himself and the players from the press. Cameroon, meanwhile, had gone undefeated, but they were going home early after doing Africa proud.

West Germany was the team everyone in Group 2 feared, although that didn't stop Algeria from pulling off a major upset on June 16 at Estadio El Molinón in Gijón. The Algerians prevailed over Die Mannschaft 2–1, twice taking the lead. The first goal, after 54 minutes, came via a Rabah Madjer goal. Rummenigge tied it up in the 67th minute for the European champions, only for Lakhdar Belloumi to tally what would be the winning goal a minute later in one of the biggest upsets in tournament history.

Four days later, West Germany regained their form—Rummenigge scoring a hat trick—in a 4–1 rout of Chile in Gijón. Austria beat Algeria 2–0 on June 21 at Estadio Carlos Tartiere in Oviedo. The North Africans tallied two points three days later, again in Oviedo, in a 3–2 win against Chile.

Algeria, at four points, had completed its three group-stage matches. They had to wait 24 hours to see whether they would go through upon completion of the West Germany–Austria match on June 25 in Gijón. What transpired was a farce, a game later dubbed the "Disgrace of Gijón." Austria knew that a West German win by a goal would qualify them both, while a German victory by a larger margin would qualify the

Algerians. Among the other permutations that would eliminate the West Germans was a draw or an Austria win.

After 10 minutes of all-out attack, West Germany scored through a goal by Horst Hrubesch. After the goal, the two proceeded to kick the ball around aimlessly. The crowd of 41,000 chanted "fuera, fuera" (Spanish for "out, out"). The game ended 1–0 for Die Mannschaft, allowing them to win the group. As a result, Austria finished second over Algeria with better goal differential. Algeria protested the outcome to FIFA, but there was nothing anyone could do to reverse the outcome.

After the game, West German coach Jupp Derwall told reporters, "We wanted to progress, not play football." The players also seemed oblivious to what they had done to damage the game. When protestors gathered in front of the West German team hotel demanding answers, several players threw water balloons at them. As a result, FIFA introduced a revised system at subsequent World Cups, used to this day, in which the final two games in each group are contested simultaneously.

In Group 3, the defending World Cup champions Argentina opened their title defense on June 13 at the Camp Nou in Barcelona. The team, stronger than four years earlier with the insertion of Maradona, suffered defeat at the hands of Belgium in their opener before 95,000 fans. Erwin Vandenbergh's goal after 62 minutes decided the match as Menotti's men were forced to regroup after a 1–0 defeat.

Like Italy and West Germany, Argentina was another powerhouse that had gotten off to a bad start. Maradona in the lineup promised something special. He had already become an icon back home, helping Argentina win the 1979 FIFA Youth World Cup, reserved for players under the age of 20, and signing with famed side Boca Juniors in 1981, where he led them to the league title. A year later, on the eve of the World Cup, Maradona was sold to Barcelona for a then–world record $7.6 million transfer fee. The Catalan fans were giddy to see their club's investment up close on the world's biggest stage.

What those fans saw was a subpar Argentina and Maradona repeatedly fouled by the Belgians. The tactic was clear—stop Maradona and you stop the whole team. Argentina's second game on June 18 at the Estadio José Rico Pérez in Alicante saw a better outcome against

Hungary, who had gotten the better of El Salvador in a 10–1 rout in their opener. Argentina's 4–1 win against the Hungarians was good for their standing and morale as Maradona netted a brace.

Belgium won the group following a 1–0 win on June 19 against El Salvador at the Estadio Martínez Valero in Elche. They followed that up with a 1–1 draw in Elche three days later against Hungary. Argentina finished second on June 23 following a 2–0 win against El Salvador in Alicante. Passarella scored on a penalty kick after 22 minutes, and Bertoni added a second in the 52nd minute in a game that conjured up some of the magic of four years earlier. Maradona was living up to the pre-tournament hype, although he'd been limited to a pass here and a free kick there against the Salvadorians given all the fouling he was forced to endure.

England and France headlined Group 4, and the sides met in the opener on June 16 at the Estadio San Mamés in Bilbao. Bryan Robson put the Three Lions ahead after just 27 seconds, but Gérard Soler tied the score for France in the 24th minute. Robson restored England's lead in the 67th minute, and Paul Mariner put the game out of reach seven minutes from time with an insurance goal for the 3–1 victory. Four days later, England blanked Czechoslovakia 2–0 in Bilbao. This time it took two second-half goals, a Trevor Francis strike in the 62nd minute and a Jozef Barmoš own goal four minutes later, to see England through to the second round. France, as expected, would join them after a 4–1 win against Kuwait on June 21 at the Estadio José Zorrilla in Valladolid and a 1–1 draw with Czechoslovakia at the same venue.

It was the clash against Kuwait that is most remembered for the actions of Sheikh Fahad Al-Ahmed Al-Jaber Al-Sabah, the prince of Kuwait, who also served as the president of the nation's FA. The prince was in the stands for the match when his team, down 3–1, endured another French goal. But the Kuwaiti players protested after freezing up to the buildup to the goal in reaction to a whistle from the crowd, which they thought had come from Soviet referee Miroslav Stupar. Prince Fahad rushed onto the field to argue the call. After Fahad threatened to have his team abandon the match, Stupar disallowed the goal and the game continued.

Les Bleus needed just a few more minutes to add that fourth goal as Maxime Bossis tallied in the 89th minute. France would finish second, while England won the group on the group's final day with a 1–0 victory against Kuwait before 40,000 in Bilbao. Francis scored the winner after 27 minutes, coming through again for his side, as England, absent from the World Cup since 1970, recorded a third successive win.

Group 5 may have been the easiest for the host nation to be drawn in, as Spain played all three of their opening-round matches in Valencia at the Estadio Luis Casanova, now known as the Mestalla. It was on June 16 that Spain opened the tournament against Honduras, but they couldn't do better than a hard-fought 1–1 draw against that team. Spain seemed destined for defeat until a Roberto López Ufarte penalty kick in the 65th minute earned them the draw.

The following day, Yugoslavia and Northern Ireland went scoreless at the Estadio La Romareda in Zaragoza, meaning the group remained wide open. Northern Ireland's Norman Whiteside broke Pelé's record as the youngest player to appear in a World Cup game at age 17 years and 41 days. When selected for the team by manager Billy Bingham, Whiteside had played just two competitive games for Manchester United. The game against Yugoslavia marked his international debut, and he received a yellow card for a rough tackle in the second half.

Spain managed to win their first game on June 20, outpacing Yugoslavia 2–1 and grabbing the winner when second-half sub Enrique Saura tallied in the 66th minute. A home crowd of 66,000 cheered them on, and Spain were now favorites to take the group. The following day in Zaragoza, Northern Ireland and Honduras drew 1–1. As a result, Spain's final group game against Northern Ireland would decide the group, while Yugoslavia still had a chance if they could defeat Honduras.

Yugoslavia did just that, recording a 1–0 win against Honduras on June 24 in Zaragoza. Spain would go through with a draw, while Northern Ireland had to win in order to advance. A hostile crowd of 50,000 in Valencia would ultimately leave disappointed after Gerry Armstrong's goal in the 47th minute downed Spain. It had been a blunder by Spanish goalkeeper Luis Arconada that resulted in the goal. Despite having Mal Donaghy sent off in the 60th minute and having to endure Spain's rough

155

play, Northern Ireland won the group, while Spain advanced as the second-place team on goal differential.

The samba drums were beating in Seville on June 14 at the Estadio Ramón Sánchez-Pizjuán for the start of Group 6. The 68,000 in attendance were rooting for a Brazil win against what turned out to be an unexpectedly strong Soviet Union. The Seleção did not disappoint. Their flashy attacking style failed to penetrate the Soviet backline in the first half, but a Sócrates goal in the 75th minute and a second from Éder 13 minutes later gave them the 2–1 win. The following day, Scotland hammered New Zealand 5–2 at the Estadio La Rosaleda in Malaga in a game where defending was not a priority, a trait that would hurt both teams against Brazil.

The Seleção's *jogo bonito* was both spellbinding and sublime, and the crowds in Seville, where the team would play all their first round matches, delighted in it. A 4–1 victory over Scotland on June 18 and a 4–0 win against New Zealand five days later helped Brazil top the group, outscoring their three opponents by a staggering 10–2. New Zealand's fairy-tale qualification to the finals quickly turned into a nightmare. Zico opened the scoring in the 29th minute with a memorable overhead kick, then added a second during Brazil's four-goal performance.

Brazil's 4-2-2-2 formation relied on the full backs to push forward, joining the two attacking midfielders and strikers in what looked like a seven-player attack that overwhelmed opposing defenses. It had worked, albeit with some frustration, versus the USSR and easily against weaker sides like New Zealand and Scotland. The team's midfield fulcrum was Falcão—nicknamed the "Eighth King of Rome," as he had been dubbed by Roma fans—a deep-lying playmaker with exceptional vision who could pass the ball with pinpoint accuracy. Along with Zico, considered the best player on the planet heading into the tournament, Brazil truly appeared hard to defeat.

Second place went to the Soviet Union by virtue of their 3–0 win against New Zealand in Malaga and a 2–2 draw at the same venue versus Scotland. Spearheaded offensively by Oleg Blokhin, the USSR managed to avoid dropping points in two crucial matches and scoring enough goals to edge out Scotland on goal differential. The Soviets, now expected to be one of the tournament's Cinderella teams, had momentum on their side.

Second Round

The 12 remaining teams were placed in four separate groups. Each group would be assigned a host city and serve as a three-game mini-tournament. The four winners of each round-robin group advanced to the semifinals. Total points would determine the semifinalists, with the first tiebreaker being goal differential.

Group C, which would be hosted at the Estadio de Sarrià in Barcelona, was the ultimate "Group of Death" with Brazil, Italy, and Argentina. The hosts ended up in Group B, which took place at the Santiago Bernabeu in Madrid, with West Germany and England. Meanwhile, Groups A (Poland, Belgium, and the Soviet Union at the Camp Nou in Barcelona) and D (France, Austria, and Northern Ireland at the Vicente Calderón in Madrid) guaranteed that at least three European teams would be represented in the semifinals. For all of FIFA's attempts to enlarge the tournament and provide spots to nations from outside Europe and South America, the game continued to be dominated by those two continents.

Poland opened things up in Group A on June 28 against Belgium. Boniek's hat trick helped Poland sail to a 3–0 victory. Three days later, the Soviet Union had their way against Belgium. The Soviets squeezed past Belgium 1–0 on a goal by midfielder Khoren Oganesian after 48 minutes. On July 4, Poland, in need of just a point against the Soviet Union, advanced to the semifinals following a scoreless draw.

West Germany and England opened Group B on June 29 with a 0–0 draw. Three days later, West Germany's offense was reawakened, putting two past Spain for a 2–1 win. It was striker Klaus Fischer's goal in the 75th minute that turned out to be the match winner. In the final group game, England needed to defeat Spain by two or more goals in order to reach the semifinals. Instead, the Three Lions could only get a scoreless draw. As a result, Die Mannschaft finished first to reach the semifinals.

Group C, the toughest of the four second-round groups, saw Italy open things up on June 29 versus Argentina. What ensued was a brutal contest as Gentile hacked away at Maradona's tree-trunk legs, putting him out of the game. The Azzurri, meanwhile, got goals from Marco Tardelli in the 57th minute and another from Antonio Cabrini 10 minutes later to win the game 2–1.

"Everyone remembers how Claudio Gentile marked me when we played against Italy in the second round, on 29 June in Barcelona. We lost 2–1 and he only got booked for it," Maradona recalled in his book *Maradona: The Autobiography of Soccer's Greatest and Most Controversial Star.* "But, of course, people only remember the result. In Italy, many years later, Gentile admitted to me that his game had been to stop me from playing: every time I tried to receive the ball he'd be snapping at my ankles. I could hardly move or turn around and he didn't even get sent off. It wasn't Gentile's fault, that's his job; it was the ref's."

Argentina's do-or-die game against Brazil on July 2 ended with a 3–1 win for the Seleção. Goals from Zico, Serginho, and Léo Júnior sealed a comfortable win for the Brazilians as Maradona's tournament ended in acrimony after he was given a red card with five minutes remaining in the game following a retaliatory kick against second-half sub Sergio Batista. Three days later, Italy and Brazil—in a rematch of the 1970 final—met for a spot in the semifinals. The much-maligned Rossi put on a master class that afternoon, netting a now memorable hat trick to lift the Italians to a 3–2 win. It had been an enthralling match, with the Italians taking the lead twice, only to see the Brazilians tie it up. But the Brazilians had no response to Rossi's goal in the 74th minute, and the Italians were through to the semifinals. This Brazilian team is still remembered as the best team to have never won the World Cup.

In Group D, France edged Austria 1–0 on June 28 via a goal by Bernard Genghini after 39 minutes. Les Bleus were the team to beat in this group, especially after Austria and Northern Ireland played to a 2–2 draw on July 1. It was three days later that France steamrolled Northern Ireland 4–1. Midfielder Alain Giresse and striker Dominique Rocheteau both tallied a brace to stamp France's ticket to the semifinals. Along with Italy, the French had scored five goals in the second round and looked like serious challengers to win their first World Cup title.

Semifinals

The Italians, transformed after their win against Brazil, came into their semifinal clash against Poland on July 8 energized. So, too, were the 50,000 inside the Camp Nou. Their constant cheering served as the soundtrack to a game that pitted two of the most in-form teams at the tournament. Boniek, who had received a yellow card in the second round, was suspended for this match. The Poles would be forced to reorganize their attack given the star striker's absence. The Italians, meanwhile, were without the suspended Gentile, meaning their backline would lack some aggressive defending.

The 93-degree heat favored no one, although the sides had previously met in Group 1. Unlike that match, this one could not end in a draw. Rossi, who was now in top form, made sure of that, putting Italy ahead after just 22 minutes. The Azzurri's ability to shut down their opponents defensively, then quickly attempting to score on a counterattack, had worked. Rossi had returned to the form seen at the 1978 World Cup. But Rossi wasn't about just scoring goals. He was seeking redemption and trying to get Italy to the final. Ever opportunistic in the box, Rossi doubled the score in the 73rd minute to put the Azzurri in the final.

The day's other semifinal between West Germany and France is considered a classic encounter between two of the game's better teams. Played at the Estadio Ramón Sánchez-Pizjuán, the game will forever be known as "A Night in Seville." The game's constant back-and-forth, and four goals in extra time, followed by a dramatic penalty-kick shootout has made it one of the best soccer matches ever contested.

Platini and the bearded Manny Kaltz, who replaced Rummenigge as team captain after he injured a hamstring, shook hands with the match official Charles Corver of the Netherlands to start the contest. The 70,000 in attendance were in for a treat, although the 99-degree heat and soaring humidity made for an unbearable evening.

In the 17th minute, Breitner, the only member of the team from their World Cup conquest in 1974, got things started in midfield, and the play resulted with Klaus Fischer charging in to challenge the French goalkeeper Jean-Luc Ettori from 12 yards out. But the ball rebounded to

Pierre Littbarski, who drilled a low shot into the net. In the 27th minute, Bernd Förster was penalized for holding Rocheteau. The French were awarded a penalty, which was converted by Platini to make it level at one.

In the 60th minute, French defender Patrick Battiston, taking a pass from Platini, ran toward the bushy-haired Toni Schumacher with a clear one-on-one chance at goal. Instead, Battiston and Schumacher collided violently, the West German goalie kicking the French defender as the ball rolled wide. "I saw him coming, but it was too late," Battiston recalled in a 2012 interview with FIFA's website. "I was desperate to score. That's why it was such a big collision. I don't remember much more about it."

The collision knocked Battiston unconscious, and he had to be stretchered off the field. For three frantic minutes, as the French team doctors worked on stabilizing Battiston, the Spanish police searched for Red Cross medics to come onto the field and remove the player. "I raced out of the goal," Schumacher said when recounting the incident. "I jumped toward him, but turned my body so the impact wouldn't be so great."

Replays show that Schumacher's hipbone hit Battiston's face at full force. The result for Battiston was two missing teeth and three cracked ribs. No foul was given after the referee deemed it a fair challenge. When Schumacher was told after the match that Battiston had lost two teeth, he told reporters, "If that's all that's wrong, tell him I'll pay for the crowns."

Despite several decent scoring chances for both teams, including Manuel Amoros hitting the crossbar in stoppage time, the adrenaline-packed game remained 1–1 as the teams headed into extra time. In the second minute of the first period of extra time, Marius Trésor struck an 11-yard volley to give France a 2–1 lead. The injured Rummenigge was subbed in soon after to reignite the attack. Instead, France made it 3–1 in the 98th minute with Alain Giresse firing a first-time shot that hit the post to the right of Schumacher and went into the net.

Four minutes later, West Germany scored. Rummenigge flicked the ball in from just six yards out. Three minutes into the second extra time period, Fischer scored on a magnificent bicycle kick from inside the box to make it 3–3. Just when it had appeared that the French would contest the final against Italy, West Germany's two goals forced a World Cup semifinal to be resolved via a shootout for the very first time in World Cup history.

On the excruciating spot kicks that followed, Giresse, Kaltz, Amoros, Breitner, and Rocheteau all scored. Uli Stielike shot weakly, and French goalkeeper Jean-Luc Ettori made the easy save. Then Didier Six shot softly to Schumacher's right for the save. On the next kick, Littbarski tied the score. Platini and Rummenigge both scored. Next up came Bossis. He struck his kick to Schumacher's right and watched as the goalkeeper dived to make another save. Hrubesch then scored the winning kick to land West Germany in the final. "You must give my players the credit they deserve," Derwall told reporters after the game. "They showed such strength of character."

Poland would go on to defeat France to take third place. Nonetheless, France would win the European Championship two years later and again contend for the World Cup in 1986. Despite the outcome of that semifinal, Platini said of the wild semifinal, "That was my most beautiful game. What happened in those two hours encapsulated all the sentiments of life itself. No film or play could ever recapture so many contradictions and emotions. It was complete. So strong. It was fabulous."

Final: Italy vs. West Germany

The 90,000 that packed into the Santiago Bernabeu on July 11 watched as Italy and West Germany contested the final. The first half ended scoreless, highlighted by Cabrini missing a penalty kick wide to the right of Schumacher's goal. It was the first time a player had missed a penalty kick in a World Cup final.

The missed kick would have caused weaker teams to wilt. Not the Italians. "Naturally, something like that can upset the player and also the team," Bearzot told reporters afterward. "But, if you notice, our players were very supportive of [Cabrini] and we pulled together."

In the second half, it was Rossi who put Italy ahead after 57 minutes. In fact, he scored his tournament-leading sixth goal, heading in from close range off a well-executed Gentile cross from the right to beat Schumacher. Bearzot's men, masters of the counterattack, ran West Germany ragged for much of the game.

It was that ability to create offense that led to Italy's second goal. Spanish fans began to chant "olé, olé" as the ball moved from one Italian player to another. It was during that sequence that Marco Tardelli scored from the edge of the box from about 30 yards out with a low, left-footed shot in the 69th minute to make it 2–0. The West Germans, out of steam and ideas, couldn't stop the onslaught as Alessandro Altobelli, at the end of a counterattack by the speedy Bruno Conti, made it 3–0 nine minutes from the end.

The Italians, after such a slow start at this tournament, had defeated Argentina, Brazil, and Poland to reach the final. Once there, it was with relative ease that they swept aside the West Germans, tired from their marathon semifinal against France. "Our team could not play our best because of that late game," Derwall told reporters. "I knew it was better Rummenigge play at the start, and I felt his injury would cause pain later and I would take him out."

Breitner scored a consolation goal for West Germany in the 83rd minute, firing a low shot into the net to Zoff's right. But Italy had been the superior side when it mattered most at this tournament. Rossi was named the tournament's best player, the first time such an award had been handed out. He became an international star in the process and a symbol of success for many Italians, especially the millions living abroad. Italy's win had ultimately been a team effort, and an unlikely one after such a poor start. King Juan Carlos of Spain presented the golden trophy to Zoff, and after 44 years the Azzurri were once again crowned world champions.

1986 WORLD CUP

The year was 1983, three years before the World Cup finals were scheduled to take place, and Maradona lay in a bed, convalescent after recovering from a bout with hepatitis. His recovery took place at his private home in Barcelona. More than a house, the place looked like a hotel. Maradona lay in a bed located in the garden; around him you could often find people eating and drinking.

It was on one of those days that Argentina's new manager Carlos Bilardo flew to Spain for an audience with Maradona. The man who had

1980s Innovation: VHS tapes

It was not until the 1980s that video technology started to make its way into our living rooms. That same technology also led to increased video analysis in sports. For a game as global as soccer, the ability to watch matches involving your opponent from the comfort of your office or living room was easier than sending a scout thousands of miles to watch them in person.

Coaches and players were able to watch their games over and over, picking them apart and seeing plays from a different perspective. This ability, through the use of Video Home System (VHS) tapes, completely changed the way the game was played. Tactically, managers became better prepared and sharper. At the same time, players could see exactly what had gone wrong and work in training to avoid such mistakes in the future.

VHS, first invented in 1976, dominated the market by the early '80s. By 1996, the VHS fell victim to the DVD format. The use of these systems also allowed fans to record games or buy them later. It spawned video libraries where fans could rewatch matches or highlights of their favorite players.

FIFA's official World Cup films dated back to 1954. Those same documentaries could be sold in VHS form for all to have. One of the most popular, called *Hero*, was released in 1987 and served as the official film of Mexico '86. Narrated by British actor Michael Caine, the cover featured a beaming Diego Maradona holding the World Cup trophy. You can watch the same film today on YouTube for free.

taken over for Menotti wanted to build his team around the budding star and asked Maradona to be Argentina's new team captain. Maradona was only 22 at the time, but Bilardo knew this was the man Argentina should rest their hopes on.

"I talked to him for five hours, about three in the morning in his house," Bilardo said.

Maradona and Bilardo would become close during the next three years, like father and son, as the duo remained focused on winning the World Cup after the disaster of 1982. Unbeknownst to Bilardo at the time, Maradona was embarking on a road that would take him to great heights, but at a bitter cost.

The same bed where Maradona held court day after day was no ideal place for a recovery. In fact, as journalist Josep María Casanovas recalls, it was where Maradona's abyss into cocaine use began. "Diego was in a bed in the garden, around him were more than ten people eating and drinking at six in the afternoon as if it were a party. It was the first time I saw white powder snorted, from the corner of the ping pong table. I confess that I didn't know what cocaine was then. His then representative, Jorge Cysterpiller, approached me and said: 'Only publish what Diego tells you. No photos.'"

In no time at all, the people around Maradona became his enablers. Casanovas said even Menotti had submitted to Maradona's penchant for the night life and partying into the wee hours of the morning. "Tired of Diego being late for training since he lived his life at night," Casanovas said, "the coach decided to train in the afternoon and like a good Argentine he invented a white lie, saying, 'We have decided to train at the same time as the games, in the afternoon, it is better for the metabolism of the footballers.'"

Bilardo would do the same. As long as the team was winning, why make a fuss? Passarella, who never got over having the captaincy taken from him, also had to submit to Maradona. After all, this was a team that featured a few veterans and a great many average players. Maradona would have to be the one to carry the side. He had grown accustomed to such a role. After his two-year stay at Barcelona went awry, Maradona became the first player to set the world record transfer fee twice: in 1984 he did it a second time when he moved to Italian club Napoli for a fee of $10.5 million.

At the same time, the 1986 World Cup finals were in peril. With European nations not allowed to host after the previous edition was held in Spain to maintain the tradition of alternating the competition between the two continents, Colombia had been originally chosen to host the finals. As a result of dire economic issues, the South American nation was not able to do so and withdrew as host. FIFA selected Mexico as the new host in May 1983. In doing so, Mexico became the first nation to host the World Cup twice. In September 1985, eight months before the start of the tournament, a massive earthquake rocked Mexico City, killing 20,000 people. Once again, there was concern about whether the finals would need to be moved again. But the financial interests at stake far exceeded any inability by Mexico to pull off the tournament.

The city's two main stadiums had suffered no structural damage. Some FIFA officials, led by Vice President Harry Cavan of Ireland, had proposed delaying the tournament, but Mexican officials argued that the venues had not been damaged and that news reports had exaggerated the extent of the quake. FIFA visited the venues, which included the Estadio Azteca. They deemed the situation safe, and the tournament went on as planned.

The World Cup remained a 24-team tournament, but the format changed from the previous edition. The teams were divided into six groups of four. The top two teams—along with the four best third-place finishers—advanced to a knockout round featuring 16 teams. Canada, Denmark, and Iraq qualified for the finals for the first time. Other nations absent from the finals for decades made their return: South Korea qualified for the first time since 1954, Paraguay since 1958, Portugal since 1966, and Bulgaria and Uruguay also returned following a 12-year absence. Mexico, as hosts, and Italy, the defending champions, were seeded, along with West Germany, Poland, France, and Brazil. The six groups were drawn as follows:

Group A: Italy, Argentina, Bulgaria, and South Korea

Group B: Mexico, Belgium, Paraguay, and Iraq

Group C: France, the Soviet Union, Hungary, and Canada

Group D: Brazil, Spain, Northern Ireland, and Algeria

Group E: West Germany, Uruguay, Scotland, and Denmark

Group F: Poland, England, Portugal, and Morocco

The result was a fairly balanced draw. Italy was once again in the same group as Argentina, hosts Mexico had a manageable group, and Brazil, with the exception of Spain, were favored to take their group. Eleven cities hosted matches. The Azteca, the largest stadium used for the tournament, would host nine matches, including the opener and final. The tropical weather, coupled with the high altitude of various venues and increased air pollution, made it extremely difficult for the players to maintain their stamina and endurance. Cities such as Toluca, located 8,730 above sea level, and Guadalajara, at 5,138 feet above sea level, made conditions particularly unbearable.

Most of the games were held in venues that were in close proximity to one another in order to reduce travel. Group A was contested at Estadio Olímpico Universitario in Mexico City and in Puebla at the Estadio Cuauhtémoc. Group B were at the Azteca and Toluca's Estadio Nemesio Díez. Group C's matches were held at the Estadio Nou Camp in León and the Estadio Sergio León Chávez in Irapuato. Group D, meanwhile, was played primarily in Guadalajara at the Estadio Jalisco and in the suburb of Zapopan at the Estadio Tres de Marzo. Group E was played in Querétaro at the Estadio La Corregidora and in Nezahualcóyotl at Estadio Neza 86. Group F was played in the northern city of Monterrey at the Estadio Tecnológico and in nearby San Nicolás de los Garza at the Estadio Universitario.

Group Stage

The Italians may have been the defending champions, but Group A was all about Argentina and Maradona. The playmaker had emerged as one of the best players of the decade, and this World Cup was his chance to show the globe he could win the sport's biggest prize. More than a player, Maradona was a composer. His job was to orchestrate goals, either by making that quick, clever pass to a teammate or by putting one in the net himself.

The Italians, meanwhile, appeared weaker than four years earlier. Players like Rossi, Cabrini, Tardelli, and Scirea had all excelled for Juventus at club level, and Bearzot hoped that bloc of players could help the Azzurri succeed once again. In the tournament opener at the Azteca before 96,000 fans, the Italians took on Bulgaria. Zoff, who had retired, was replaced in goal by Giovanni Galli. The starting lineup also featured Altobelli in attack. It was the striker, a member of the 1982 side and one of the most prolific scorers of those years, that put Italy ahead right before the stroke of halftime. It was off a free kick outside the penalty area where the ball—called the "Azteca" by Adidas in honor of the Mesoamerican civilization that ruled central Mexico for more than 200 years until the 16th century—went in Altobelli's direction, with the forward timing his run just right to avoid being offside and hitting it in for the goal.

The Italians tried to score in any way they could. Midfielder Fernando De Napoli, most notably, hit a shot from outside the box that sailed wide. With five minutes left to play, Bulgaria, against the run of play, created a chance in the Italian half that resulted in the tying goal by striker Nasko Sirakov. His header got past two defenders and Galli's left hand, and the game ended 1–1. It was a morale boost for the Bulgarians going forward, while Italy had gotten off to another inauspicious World Cup start.

Argentina, playing two days later at the Estadio Olímpico Universitario, gained two points by running over South Korea 3–1. Jorge Valdano, a striker who played his club soccer at Real Madrid, scored a brace. But it was Maradona who had made it all happen. Valdano's first goal after just six minutes had come as a result of a Maradona free kick that deflected off the wall and then returned to the Argentine star. Maradona's pass to Valdano helped put the Albiceleste ahead.

But Maradona's World Cup began much like the last one had ended. In Spain, players had gone unpunished for fouling him. In Mexico, he was offered some protection by referees. The fouling resulted in free kicks for Argentina, and Maradona made sure those chances weren't wasted. In the 18th minute, Maradona hoisted a free kick into the box. Once there, the ball was met by Oscar Ruggeri, who headed the ball in for goal number two. Maradona assisted on the third goal as well, crossing the ball for Valdano in the first minute of the second half.

Next up for Argentina was Italy. Maradona, well known to the Italians from his time in Serie A, was still in search of his first goal of the tournament. Despite that, it had become very apparent that Maradona made his teammates look a lot better than they would have been without him. The June 5 encounter in Puebla could decide who won the group, and the match didn't disappoint. Italy jumped out to a 1–0 lead after just six minutes when Altobelli slotted home a penalty kick. Argentina stormed back. Maradona got the tying goal in the 34th minute, beating Scirea along the left flank and putting in a volley that was too difficult for Galli to stop. The game ended 1–1, and Argentina maintained its top spot in the group after South Korea and Bulgaria also played to a 1–1 draw at the Estadio Olímpico Universitario.

South Korea–Italy at the Estadio Cuauhtémoc and Argentina-Bulgaria at the Estadio Olímpico Universitario were played simultaneously on June 10 in order to avoid teams making any pre-match calculations. The Italians managed to advance following a 3–2 victory, but it had been a hard-fought affair. No repeat of their shock defeat to North Korea took place this time, thanks to Altobelli's brace. The Italians would finish second, while Argentina's 2–0 victory, thanks to headers from Valdano and Jorge Burruchaga, against Bulgaria won them the group. Maradona assisted on the second goal, but he'd done so much more. He had put on a show for everyone. Argentina looked to be the team to beat. The best was yet to come.

There was plenty of buzz surrounding the Mexican team. The country, still reeling from the quake, was looking for a great performance from El Tri in Group B to lift the nation's spirits. The team, coached by Milutinović and led by Real Madrid striker Hugo Sánchez, were hoping the home support and strong emotions stemming from the tragedy would translate to success. Sánchez, known for his execution of overhead kicks after spending part of his childhood as a gymnast, had been very successful in Europe at the club level. His countrymen were expecting some of the same from him at the World Cup.

"We weren't affected by [the earthquake] personally but we saw it as our job to bring a little happiness to all those people who had suffered so much," Sánchez told *FourFourTwo* magazine in 2010. "As a team we made something positive out of it and helped speed up the recovery process. It inspired us to go out and get good results, the fans got behind us and we improved on our performance at Mexico 1970."

The Mexicans opened the group on June 3 at the Estadio Azteca against Belgium, a formidable opponent. The 110,000 fans in the stands were thrown into rapturous ecstasy when Sánchez's goal in the 39th minute proved to be the winning goal, as Mexico emerged victorious 2–1. The following day at the Estadio Nemesio Díez in Toluca, Paraguay beat Iraq 1–0 on a goal by attacking midfielder Julio César Romero in the 35th minute.

On June 7, Mexico and Paraguay squared off at the Azteca. It took just three minutes for El Tri to jump into the lead. Striker Luis Flores squeezed past defender Rogelio Delgado and blasted the ball past goalkeeper Roberto Fernández. Romero's goal five minutes from time leveled the score, and the match ended 1–1. It had been a wasted opportunity for Mexico after Sánchez missed a penalty kick in the game's final minute. "I have seen film of Sánchez and I have noticed that he always kicks to his right," Fernández, who saved the kick before the ball bounced off the post and back into play, told reporters after the game. "I was lucky."

The following day in Toluca, Belgium returned to the form everyone expected, edging Iraq 2–1 on goals from midfielder Enzo Scifo and a penalty kick by striker Nico Claesen. The Iraqis, reduced to 10 men in the 52nd minute after midfielder Basil Gorgis was red-carded, were officially eliminated from the tournament.

The Mexicans were playing unbelievable soccer and peaking at the right moment. Fans welcomed the wins as a respite from the horrors of the earthquake. Those in the stands made the "Mexican wave"—a tradition at sporting events in that country—known to the world. Indeed, the swaying arms of the spectators dazzled TV audiences globally and popularized the celebration, although the wave had been done before at college football games and at the 1984 Summer Olympics in Los Angeles. On the final match day, played on June 11, Mexico won the group following a 1–0 win against Iraq at the Azteca. The winning goal, tallied by defender Fernando Quirarte after 54 minutes, sent El Tri to the knockout stage. Sánchez had been forced to sit out the game after accumulating a second yellow card against Paraguay.

Paraguay, meanwhile, managed a 2–2 draw against Belgium. A Roberto Cabañas brace gave Paraguay second place. Belgium, who finished a disappointing third, were also through as one of the tournament's best third-place teams. "[Mexico] ended up winning the group anyway so it didn't affect me at all," Sánchez told *FourFourTwo* when asked about his missed penalty kick against Paraguay. "I didn't like missing penalties, of course, but it was good in one way because it showed everyone I was only human. I'd won all those titles with Madrid and top-scored in five seasons and people thought I was superhuman. I hated missing penalties, but in that way it was positive for me."

France and the Soviet Union were favorites to advance out of Group C. Platini had emerged as one of Europe's best players, and the draw looked favorable for them, especially with Canada and Hungary on the schedule. Les Bleus opened the group on June 1 against Canada at the Estadio Nou Camp in León. The French managed just a 1–0 win, taking the defending European champions 79 minutes before striker Jean-Pierre Papin scored. His goal was an oasis in a desert for the French. The following day, a strong Dynamo Kyiv–dominated USSR side took the field against Hungary at the Estadio Sergio León Chavez in Irapuato. The 6–0 victory would go a long way in helping the Soviets when it came to goal differential.

León hosted France and the USSR, one of the most anticipated matches of the group stage, and it did not disappoint. A crowd of 37,000 filled the stadium on June 5 as midfielder Vasyl Rats put the USSR ahead after 53 minutes. The French, who had struggled to ignite their attack once again, leveled the score nine minutes later with midfielder Luis Fernández for the 1–1 draw. The following day, Hungary eliminated Canada by beating them 2–0.

The final match day on June 9 saw France's attack go into overdrive, blanking Hungary 3–0 in León. Platini had yet to score a goal at the tournament, but the best was yet to come from the French. Meanwhile, in Irapuato, the USSR defeated Canada 2–0. The outcome of the two results allowed the Soviet Union to win the group, edging out France on goal differential, after both teams were tied with five points.

Brazil was back at another World Cup, this time trying to avenge their inability to win it all four years earlier. Brazil, coached again by Santana, had Careca on the team as their star striker, surrounded in the midfield by the veteran Sócrates, hell-bent on lifting the trophy. They retained their *jogo bonito* style and remained the team, aside from the host nation, that generated the most buzz among the Mexicans.

The Seleção opened Group D on June 1 against Spain at the Estadio Jalisco in Guadalajara. The 36,000 in attendance cheered as the Brazilians played to the beat of their samba drums. Spain, known at this juncture in history as perennial World Cup underachievers, featured a star-studded lineup with the likes of goalkeeper Andoni Zubizarreta, midfielder Míchel, and striker Emilio Butragueño, who had emerged as a budding star for Real Madrid, and Mexico '86 was expected to be his chance at having a breakout tournament. Instead, it was Brazil who won the game 1–0 thanks to a controversial Sócrates goal in the 62nd minute. The play began when Casagrande's right-footed kick from short range hit the crossbar with two Brazilians standing in front of Zubizarreta. The players looked to be offside, but no whistle came and the goal stood. Two days later, Algeria and Northern Ireland played to a 1–1 draw at the Estadio Tres de Marzo in Guadalajara. Whiteside's goal after six minutes put Northern Ireland ahead, only for Djamel Zidane to tie the score on a free kick in the 59th minute.

Brazil grabbed a second win on June 6 against Algeria at the Estadio Jalisco via a Careca goal after 66 minutes. The following day, Spain downed Northern Ireland 2–1 at the Estadio Tres de Marzo. Butragueño put La Roja ahead after just two minutes, beating veteran goalkeeper Pat Jennings. Spain doubled the score with center forward Julio Salinas in the 18th minute.

Brazil won the group on June 12 at the Estadio Jalisco, defeating Northern Ireland 3–0 thanks to a Careca brace. It was the Seleção's third win in as many games, while also marking the last time Jennings would play for Northern Ireland at the international level. The 41-year-old Jennings, who had made his senior team debut in 1964, ended his career at age 41 after making 119 appearances for his country. The Brazilians, meanwhile, had not conceded a goal, and their attack proved to be even more formidable than the one four years earlier. Spain would finish second by virtue of its 3–0 victory versus Algeria at the Estadio Tecnológico in Monterrey. Ramón Calderé, a Barcelona midfielder, netted a brace as Spain marched on to the knockout round. Calderé tested positive for ephedrine, a nervous system stimulant typically used to treat breathing problems, after the game. The Spanish FA claimed the drug had been administered to him at a local hospital following a stomachache. FIFA decided not to ban the player, a move that certainly would not happen today.

In a tournament with six balanced opening-round groups, Group E could be dubbed the "Group of Death" given that it featured two previous World Cup winners in Uruguay and West Germany, along with Denmark, an up-and-coming European power, and Scotland. It's no surprise that three teams would advance from this group, although the order would surprise many.

Denmark would storm through the group, defeating Scotland 1–0 on June 4 at the Estadio Neza 86 in Nezahualcóyotl. Striker Preben Elkjær, who played his club soccer for Verona in Serie A, scored the winning goal in the 57th minute. The Danes had a formidable roster with some of Europe's most exciting players who were earning a wage at some big clubs. The team's midfield was marshaled by Michael Laudrup, who played at Juventus, and their manager, the German-born Sepp Piontek, brought professionalism to the team. Their explosiveness in attack earned them the nickname "Danish Dynamite."

Earlier in the day, the group got off to a strong start when heavyweights West Germany and Uruguay met at the Estadio La Corregidora in Querétaro. The result was a 1–1 draw that made both sides happy in their respective quests to advance. On June 8, West Germany, coached by

Beckenbauer, got the better of Scotland 2–1 in Querétaro, with striker Klaus Allofs getting the winning goal four minutes into the second half. In Nezahualcóyotl, the 27,000 who came to watch Denmark play Uruguay were treated to a seven-goal bonanza. The Danes lived up to their nickname when Elkjær showed everyone why he would be one of the tournament's most clinical finishers. His hat trick powered Denmark to a 6–1 win as Uruguay's backline lay in tatters.

Uruguay would nonetheless get through to the knockout stage as one of the best third-place teams following a scoreless draw against Scotland on June 13 in Nezahualcóyotl. Uruguay manager Omar Borrás made four changes to his starting lineup. Borrás had been among the first to publicly proclaim his team as being part of the "Group of Death." He was also well aware that his side needed at least a point and that striker Enzo Francescoli, one of South America's classiest and most talented players, needed a big game. The attack, however, would fail to score a goal, but a draw got them through just the same. Scotland, who needed two points, were out once again at the group stage. The match, unfortunately, degenerated into a rough affair with fouls on both sides, something triggered by the ejection of Uruguay defender José Batista just 56 seconds after the opening whistle for a foul on Gordon Strachan.

At the same time, Denmark closed the group with another emphatic win, a 2–0 result over West Germany in a game that appeared to signal a passing of the baton in terms of which team from Europe was the strongest. Despite the defeat, Die Mannschaft finished second with plenty of time to regroup before the start of the knockout stage.

Group F could also have been a candidate for one of the tournament's toughest. England, always a contender but often unable to produce results when it counted, joined Poland, overachievers four years earlier, and Portugal. Morocco and Poland opened things up on June 2 at the Estadio Universitario in San Nicolás de los Garza with a scoreless draw. At a tournament where climate played a major factor, teams weren't always so quick to adapt, as Poland's inability to score demonstrated. The following day, Portugal pulled off a surprise, upsetting England 1–0 at the Estadio Tecnológico in Monterrey. Midfielder Carlos Manuel, unmarked in the box, came up with the game's lone goal 15 minutes from time. His close-range effort, off a cross from Diamantino Miranda, beat goalkeeper Peter Shilton, and the Three Lions were off to a bad start. Weather conditions aside, there was plenty of blame to go around the England camp.

England's futility spilled over into their second match at the Estadio Tecnológico against Morocco. On paper, this was an easy two points. On the field, it was to be a shock result. Frustration boiled over. England, unable to score, found itself down to 10 players after 42 minutes when midfielder Ray Wilkins was shown a red card for throwing the ball at referee Gabriel González of Paraguay. Wilkins, upset when an offside decision went against his team, became the first England player ever red-carded at a World Cup. The game ended 0–0.

Nearly 20,000 spectators came to the Estadio Universitario to witness Poland and Portugal lock horns. They would see a decent match that was solved by a single goal. Portugal's overly defensive approach didn't work this time as it had against England. Striker Włodzimierz Smolarek was able to pierce the backline in the 68th minute for the 1–0 Poland win. The group's first four games had yielded just two goals, with the *Daily Telegraph* reporting that locals dubbed it the "Group of Sleep."

England found itself in need of a win to stamp their ticket to the knockout round. A winnable group had now become a headache for the Three Lions. Finally, the English would get production out of their young striker Gary Lineker. His hat trick against Portugal on June 11 at the Estadio Universitario delighted the crowd of 23,000 eager to see goals. Lineker's first goal came after nine minutes, and a second just five minutes later. In the 34th minute, Lineker scored his third goal, and England locked up second place. Poland would finish third and advance as well. Surprise side Morocco won the group, sweeping aside Portugal 3–1 at the Estadio Tres de Marzo in Zapopan to become the first African nation to get past the group stage.

The searing Mexican heat hadn't affected the North Africans to the degree it had other teams. Morocco prepared for the tournament by spending 40 days training in Monterrey in order to get acclimated. "We played a lot of friendlies against clubs and got very familiar with our first round opponents," recalled midfielder Mustafa El Haddaoui in a 2018 interview with FIFA.com. "We were at an advantage, as we knew their players, while they did not know us very well. In those times, it was quite difficult to get information about other teams."

Known as the Lions of Atlas, Morocco was coached by the Brazilian-born José Faria, who had previously managed Fluminense's youth teams before being employed by Qatar to coach the country's under-19 team. It would be the start of a trend that saw Brazilians move to the Middle East to coach oil-rich nations high on soccer passion but low on talent and experience.

Round of 16

With television networks paying big money, especially in Europe, to broadcast matches in prime time, playing under the midday sun on the other side of the planet became a requirement. Players had to endure extreme conditions, with nothing but water bottles and a handful of salt pills before kickoff and at halftime. These were the days when teams didn't employ nutritionists and decades before FIFA would allow water breaks during games.

The knockout round would produce a few more surprises as well as reward the tournament's best individual efforts. Soaring temperatures be damned, some of the best soccer was yet to come. The 16 teams were placed in a bracket with Mexico pitted against Bulgaria, a favorable opponent, while Denmark took on Spain. Italy versus France, Argentina versus Uruguay, and Brazil versus Poland all promised to be competitive affairs as Morocco paid a price for winning its group by getting West Germany.

The round of 16 opened on June 15 with Mexico taking on Bulgaria at the Estadio Azteca before 115,000 boisterous fans. The offensive tandem of Manuel Negrete and Sánchez put the Bulgarians on the ropes soon after the noon kickoff. Under the black shadow cast by the stadium's ornate loudspeaker suspended above the center circle, Mexico took the lead with Negrete after 34 minutes. It was a lead El Tri would never relinquish. It was Negrete's karate-style volley from the edge of the box that beat goalkeeper Borislav Mikhailov. The Mexicans doubled the score in the 61st minute with defender Raul Servín heading the ball in off a corner kick. Mexico had made history by reaching the quarterfinals.

Milutinović was hailed a hero as the flag-waving crowd flooded into the streets of the capital and celebrated into the night.

Two hours later, Belgium played the Soviet Union in León. What ensued was a festival of goals and a match that needed extra time to find a winner. The back-and-forth affair saw the USSR take the lead twice, only to watch as the Belgians rallied. Striker Igor Belanov scored a hat trick that afternoon, but Belgium's offensive firepower won it for them in the end. Striker Nico Claesen's goal in the 110th minute proved to be the winning goal as Belgium eliminated the Soviet Union 4–3.

It was Brazil's chance to show that it could challenge for the World Cup title, taking the field on June 16 against a tricky Polish side at the Estadio Jalisco in Guadalajara. A four-goal performance—thanks to Sócrates, Josimar, Edinho, and Careca—sent a message that the Brazilians were for real. The 4–0 win also marked the end of Poland's short period of dominance. A golden generation that had stretched for more than a decade was over. It wouldn't be until 2012, when the country cohosted the European Championship with Ukraine, that Poland would be thrust into international soccer prominence once again.

Another clash later that day, the heated South American derby between Argentina and Uruguay, took center stage. The rivalry between the neighboring nations dates back to the early 20th century and grew in intensity at the first World Cup in 1930. In the ensuing decades, the countries battled many times in friendly matches, at the Copa America, and in World Cup qualifying. However, their round-of-16 encounter marked the first time they had met at a World Cup since that first final won by Uruguay.

The atmosphere inside the Estadio Cuauhtémoc in Puebla was tense as Maradona and his teammates faced a Uruguay side looking for an upset. Striker Pedro Pasculli, left unmarked in the box, put the ball past goalkeeper Fernando Álvez after the ball bounced off three defenders and to Pasculli's feet. Argentina had done just enough to get through to the quarterfinals.

Italy and France faced off on June 17 at the Estadio Olímpico Universitario in Mexico City. The Azzurri were not the force they had been four years earlier and succumbed to France's fast-paced offense. Platini powered France into the lead after just 15 minutes. The French doubled their lead in the 57th minute by Yannick Stopyra after being set up by Platini. With no Rossi to bail them out this time (he was an unused sub), the Italians were eliminated.

Later that day, West Germany ended Morocco's fairy-tale run with a 1–0 victory at Monterrey's Estadio Universitario. It was Lothar Matthäus who scored the winning goal off a 30-yard free kick with two minutes left to play that squeezed past the Moroccan wall. It was good enough to see West Germany through to the quarterfinals. The World Cup may not have been a Eurocentric game any longer, but teams from the Old Continent had found a way to win against the African upstarts. It was a trend that would manifest itself over and over again at future editions of the World Cup. Nonetheless, African soccer had left a mark, and the game had become truly global. "The defeat against West Germany was not easy to swallow as it was an avoidable goal, and we had the opportunity to win the match," El Haddaoui said. "The Germans suffered because of the heat. It was like they were boiling, but I think we were on par with them and it was a balanced game. Even though we lost, the Moroccan people were proud of us. When we came back, we had a parade in front of 100,000 people."

It was England's turn on June 18 against Paraguay to show that it could compete with the world's best teams. Paraguay were no world beaters, and a Lineker brace helped the Three Lions to a 3–0 win. English fortunes had changed, and on they went to the quarterfinals. Joining them was Spain. Denmark, their offense choosing the wrong moment to go on a drought, wilted at the Estadio La Corregidora in Querétaro. Spain, on the other hand, put on a memorable performance. Taking advantage of the counterattack, Butragueño tied the record for goals in a single match. His four-goal performance had the striker known by the nickname El Buitre (Spanish for "The Vulture") flying high.

Quarterfinals

The eight remaining teams featured pre-tournament favorites Brazil and France, who were pitted against one another in the quarterfinals. Maradona's Argentina faced surging England, and Mexico had a date with West Germany. Spain versus Belgium would close out the round. A European country had never won a World Cup in the Western Hemisphere, meaning Brazil and Argentina appeared to have an edge if history was any guide.

The quarterfinals opened on June 21 when Brazil took on France in Guadalajara. Careca opened the scoring for Brazil in the 17th minute after a series of passes broke down the French defense. Les Bleus responded in the 40th minute when Platini, who was challenging Maradona's role as the best player in the world, found the back of the net after the Brazilian backline failed to clear the ball. Just a few steps from the goal, Rocheteau's deflected cross was put in Platini's path for a goal. The French playmaker, despite a nagging groin injury, looked as lethal as ever on a day that also coincided with his 31st birthday.

Brazil continued to play its free-flowing style, despite the 120-degree temperatures at field level, and had a golden opportunity to take the lead once again 20 minutes from time. Brazil was awarded a penalty kick after goalkeeper Joël Bats brought down Branco in the box. Zico stepped up to take the spot kick—only for Bats to redeem himself and make the extraordinary save. Dejected, the Brazilians pressed on, but the game ended 1–1 and went into extra time.

The game, considered by many to be one of the most entertaining in World Cup history, ended in a draw after 120 minutes and would need a penalty-kick shootout to determine the winner. Bats pulled off another big move, denying Sócrates the ability to score Brazil's first kick with a left-handed save. Center back Julio César's fifth kick hit the post, and Fernández converted his kick for the 4–3 shootout win to send France into the semifinals. Brazil's efforts were thwarted once again as Platini and his teammates rejoiced. Brazil's early exit meant Argentina was now the lone nation from South America to still be alive at this World Cup. "I regret this game was a knockout match and someone had to lose," Santana told reporters after the game, announcing he was stepping down as Brazil manager. "To my mind, this was the true final."

The day's second quarterfinal between Mexico and West Germany at the Estadio Universitario in Monterrey also ended in a draw. El Tri nearly pushed West Germany to the brink, but their Cinderella tournament would come to an end in the shootout. The game, which had ended scoreless after 120 minutes, was decided when Mexico missed two of their penalty shots. West Germany prevailed 4–1 in the shootout. Milutinović had done the impossible, while the West Germans marched on to the semifinals where they would face France in a rematch of their unforgettable 1982 semifinal encounter.

In one of the most politically charged games in the tournament's history, Argentina and England met on June 22 at the Estadio Azteca. The game was the hottest ticket in Mexico City, and 115,000 fans piled into the grand stadium to see Maradona take on the English. The match was played four years after the Falklands War, referred to by Argentines by their Spanish name, Islas Malvinas. The 10-week conflict took place in 1982 between Argentina and the United Kingdom over two British territories in the South Atlantic Ocean. The conflict, which began on April 2, escalated when the British government dispatched a naval task force a few days later to engage the Argentine navy. In all, the war lasted 74 days and officially ended with Argentina's surrender on June 14. The islands were returned to British control, but not before 649 Argentine soldiers were killed.

While both sides restored diplomatic relations in 1989, the quarterfinal matchup at Mexico '86 exacerbated patriotic feelings on both sides. In Argentina, the political and cultural ramifications were felt for years. The outcome of the Argentina-England game, while not directly a part of the political conflict, went a long way in alleviating some of the national anguish in Argentina that had come with such a humiliating military defeat.

The days leading up to the match were tense—as any high-stakes quarterfinal would be—but it was compounded by talk of the conflict. Managers and players on both sides downplayed the military conflict. "Don't waste time on questions like that," England manager Bobby Robson told reporters on the eve of the match. "Don't ask me anything regarding the diplomatic situation or the political situation. We're here to play football. Don't confuse the two issues. So don't waste my time."

Maradona, who rarely disappointed journalists when they asked for his take on controversial topics, didn't play ball on this one. Asked whether the conflict was a motivating factor for Argentina heading into the game, Maradona replied, "It's only soccer—period!"

The truth is that the tense history between the nations had spilled over to the World Cup. The Mexican authorities, fearing the worst, assembled 20,000 police officers in and around the stadium to diffuse any trouble that might arise from this explosive match. Several skirmishes took place in the stands before kickoff after Argentine fans tried to tear down a Union Jack flag. Police confiscated any politically charged banners, although some were able to get into the massive stadium. One banner summed up the match as "The Malvinas II."

On the field, the midday sun was again too much for some of the players to handle. The Argentines appeared to fare better as a result of the noon kickoff, and Maradona maneuvered and dazzled in midfield as he had in previous matches. The Azteca was a cauldron, and the fans buzzed like bees, blowing horns, and chanting the entire game. Maradona was a marvel to watch. By the end of the game, Maradona would go down in history for two individual feats that are forever part of World Cup lore.

Maradona's first goal, scored six minutes into the second half, was vehemently disputed by the English players, especially Shilton, but referee Ali Bennaceur of Tunisia let it stand. Television replays showed that Maradona had not headed the ball past Shilton. Instead, he had punched it with his fist. Maradona and his teammates celebrated the goal as if nothing nefarious had happened. Bilardo had forbidden his players to waste energy running to join goal celebrations, but Maradona encouraged them to run toward him as to give the illusion that they also had no doubts about the goal.

"The first goal was handed," Robson told reporters after the game. "That cost us the result."

Maradona, asked to explain the goal after the game, caused even more controversy when he told reporters: "That goal was scored a little bit by the hand of God and another bit by Maradona's head."

As a result, the play is now forever known as the "Hand of God" goal. It still brings smiles to the faces of Argentines and disdain among the English. In 2006, Lineker, working as a broadcaster for the BBC, traveled to Buenos Aires to interview Maradona. When they first met, Lineker couldn't resist asking Maradona which hand he had used to score that first goal.

"Which hand was it? This one?" Lineker asked, pointing to Maradona's right hand.

Maradona, with a laugh, lifted up his left arm, telling him while shaking his wrist, "No, it was this one!"

Throughout the years, Maradona was not shy about discussing the controversial goal. In fact, he reveled in it. "I started to celebrate the goal," Maradona told Lineker, "then I looked back at the referee. Let's go, it's a goal."

Lineker followed up with another question. "Was it your hand or the hand of God?

"It was me," Maradona confessed.

If the first goal had been an act of cheating, the second in the 55th minute was pure genius. Maradona weaved the ball past England players as if it was attached to his left foot. His gliding run was too much for Robson's team to handle. Picking up the ball near the midfield line, Maradona ran the length of the English half. He dribbled past defenders Peter Reid, Terry Butcher, and Terry Fenwick like they were traffic cones. Maradona finished his brilliant run by eluding Shilton with a low shot to the far post. The crowd erupted with joy, and Maradona ran over to the sidelines to celebrate.

"The second goal was fantastic," Robson noted. "I didn't like it, but I admired it."

In Lineker's BBC interview with Maradona, the England star said, "Personally, I blame the referee and the linesman [for the first goal], not you. The second goal may be the one and only time in my career that I felt like applauding the opposition scoring a goal. Your best goal?"

"It's a dream goal," Maradona said. "All players dream about scoring the greatest goal of all time. We dream about it and think about it, but to score such a goal—and in a World Cup—was fantastic. It was incredible."

Maradona's second goal was scored with such beauty and finesse that it is considered the best goal ever scored at a World Cup, if not ever. Maradona had been born and raised in Villa Fiorito, a slum outside Buenos Aires. It was as a child playing for his youth team on a dirt field that Maradona had dreams of scoring such a goal. He now had. In his 2000 book, *Maradona: The Autobiography of Soccer's Greatest and Most Controversial Star*, he noted: "More than defeating a football team it was defeating a country. Of course, before the match, we said that football had nothing to do with the Malvinas War but we knew a lot of Argentinian kids had died there, shot down like little birds. This was revenge."

Maradona had always been a defender of the Global South. "Maradona's iconic match against England should remind us that, while there are always efforts to 'keep politics out of sports,' it is just a stubborn fact that sports is life and life is political," wrote Dave Zirin in a 2020 article for the *Nation* following Maradona's death. "Maradona was a political icon not only because he stood with the voiceless of the Global South. He was political because in 1986 he put a nation on his back and, with that devilish left hand, wrote his own chapter in a history with a reach well beyond the world of sports."

All England could do was pull a goal back in the 80th minute when Lineker's header, his sixth goal of the tournament, found the back of the net past goalkeeper Nery Pumpido. Argentina won the game 2–1. Maradona had single-handedly taken his team to the semifinals, and they were now the odds-on favorites to win it all. "I believe that he demonstrated that he is the best player in the world," Bilardo told reporters. "I think he is a true idol."

Next up for Argentina was a semifinal date with Belgium, winners against Spain on June 22 at the Estadio Cuauhtémoc in Puebla. The game had ended 1–1 as Spain snatched an equalizer five minutes from time with a goal by midfielder Juan Señor. Extra time yielded no goals. Belgium, on the ensuing shootout, scored all five of their kicks for the 5–4 shootout win to extend Spain's World Cup futility.

Semifinals

France and West Germany did battle in Guadalajara in a grudge match of their epic semifinal encounter four years earlier. It was also a reunion between Schumacher and Battiston, although no incident resembling the one that took place in 1982 took place the second time around. The game lacked the intensity of Seville. The Mexican heat could have been to blame, but it was largely due to West Germany's dominance. Andreas Brehme's free kick after nine minutes saw the ball streak under Bats's body for the 1–0 West Germany lead. Three minutes later, France had a chance to draw even when Platini's header turned into an assist for Giresse who volleyed the ball wide of Schumacher. Bossis had an even better chance to tie the score in the 15th minute, but he failed to deposit the ball into the empty net. The pressure-filled situation had gotten to the French, despite Platini continuing to provide balls for his teammates.

Platini had not been able to emulate Maradona. As the game progressed, he was limited to the role of spectator as defender Wolfgang Rolff's tight man-marking essentially took the playmaker out of the game. West Germany put the game away in the 89th minute when striker Rudi Völler scored on a breakaway for the 2–0 final score. History had repeated itself. West Germany reached a second straight final, while France would take third place as the Platini era at the World Cup had come to an end.

Argentina, meanwhile, were favorites to meet them in the title game. An intense heat was once again the setting at the Azteca. Belgium, in a bid to preserve their energy, were content with clearing balls and trying to keep Maradona from putting together one of those superhuman plays that would result in either a goal or a brilliant assist.

That tactic worked in the opening 45 minutes. The second half was a different story. Maradona broke free and scored Argentina's first goal in the 51st minute. After picking up a pass from midfielder Héctor Enrique, Maradona beat out two defenders with ease and deposited the ball past goalkeeper Jean-Marie Pfaff. In the 63rd minute, Maradona scored a second goal on a solo run, leaving three defenders in the dust, and Argentina won the game 2–0. Argentina was a very good team, but without Maradona they would have never reached the final. He made all the difference, and the West Germans had been put on notice.

Final: Argentina vs. West Germany

The final was a battle between continents. The game was played on June 29 before nearly 115,000 spectators amid the color and pageantry worthy of a coronation. Matthäus was given the responsibility of marking

Maradona, a double gamble on Beckenbauer's part. Matthäus remained the most creative player on a team known more for its efficiency than beauty, and now he had to fulfill two functions.

With Matthäus busy moving from the midfield to defense, the West Germans would be deprived of their most offensively gifted player. At the same time, Argentina wasted no time scoring first, taking a 1–0 lead thanks to a goal by Jose Luis Brown in the 22nd minute. Brown, who had shed tears during the playing of the national anthem, celebrated with his teammates as white confetti rained down from the stands. Although the West Germans were able to keep Maradona from finding the back of the net, it often meant that he was double-teamed, leaving his teammates wide open. The only way for West Germany to stop Maradona was to foul him. One of those fouls, which resulted in a free kick, gave Argentina the lead. Matthäus, who had earned a yellow card from Brazilian referee Romualdo Arppi Filho for his foul on Maradona from behind, could do nothing but watch as Burruchaga took the free kick and sent a cross in front of Schumacher, who was unable to catch the ball. That's when the ball reached Brown, who headed it into the net.

The crowd was back on its feet in the 56th minute when a Maradona pass found Enrique, who dished it off to Valdano. Schumacher came out of his goal to try and cut off the shot, and Valdano slipped the ball past him at the far post for a 2–0 lead. Brown hurt his right shoulder with 30 minutes left in the game, but Bilardo refused to take him out of the match. Brown played the rest of the contest with his arm strapped to his body. The game appeared over. Argentina was bracing itself for a massive celebration.

But Beckenbauer replaced Felix Magath with Dieter Hoeness five minutes after the second Argentine goal and picked up some momentum as a result of that substitution. Die Mannschaft rallied and got a goal from Rummenigge in the 74th minute off a Brehme corner kick that allowed the veteran striker to poke the ball in past Pumpido from a few yards out. The West Germans continued to attack and amazingly tied the score seven minutes later when an unmarked Völler headed it past Pumpido for the 2–2 tie. The Mexican crowd reacted with loud cheers.

"Nobody believed in us, everyone was knocking us, even our own government," Maradona wrote in his autobiography. "We felt insulted and criticized. Even the Mexicans turned against us, cheering the German goals. Solidarity among the South Americans? Solidarity my arse! Even right there in the Azteca, alongside our fellow Latin Americans, it felt like an away tie."

The West Germans had played their best stretch of the tournament in the second half, and it could not have come at a better time. Matthäus, whose job appeared done, deserted Maradona in the game's dying minutes. What a tactical error that would turn out to be. If the West Germans expected the Albiceleste to become complacent and gamble their hopes in extra time, they were mistaken. Instead, Bilardo's team stayed focused, and with six minutes remaining, Maradona, alone in the midfield, fed a perfect pass to Burruchaga. The striker, pressured by Hans-Peter Briegel, moved the ball into the penalty area and waited for the perfect moment to unleash a strong kick that beat Schumacher for a third time that afternoon. Argentina won 3–2 and had its hands on the World Cup trophy once again.

After the game, Bilardo, surrounded by microphones, called the triumph "a happy ending" for his team.

"This was a team," he added, "that comported itself properly throughout the tournament."

If Argentina was the best team in the world, then Maradona, a one-man highlight reel, was undoubtedly the best player the planet had seen since Pelé.

CHAPTER SIX

Magical Nights

ASKING AN ITALIAN WHO IS THE BEST PLAYER IN NATIONAL TEAM HIStory is a lot like asking for directions in Rome—there are plenty of possible answers, and no one can agree on them.

I found one possible answer to be Paolo Maldini. Twenty-four years after making his debut for AC Milan, the left back with piercing green eyes bid farewell to his adoring fans in 2009 at age 40. Since making his pro debut in 1985 at the tender age of 17, he racked up an impressive number of trophies—including the Champions League an astounding five times to go with his seven Serie A titles.

His reign as Milan captain defied all odds in the modern game during an era where pace and power have often rendered long careers a rarity. But the one thing Maldini, who's also known for his model good looks, never won was a World Cup.

Maldini played with aplomb for an Italy team that finished third at the 1990 World Cup and as runners-up to Brazil four years later at USA '94. By the time Italy won the World Cup in 2006—24 years after their last victory—Maldini was already in international retirement. He was as elegant on the field as he was off of it. Following every game, he would take off the captain's armband and place it in his locker. He would follow that up by thanking his teammates individually, taking the time to shake their hands. In other words, a real gentleman.

Humble and always interested in talking about the game, I noticed a lot of humility in him following our 2003 interview during an AC Milan preseason tour of the United States. While Maldini had an affinity for

Milan, it was the city of Naples where World Cup success escaped him. It was in the southern Italian city against Argentina in the semifinals of the 1990 tournament that the Azzurri were knocked out via a heartbreaking penalty-kick shootout.

"If we had played all our games in Rome, I don't think we would have ever lost," Maldini admitted to me. "We would have won the World Cup."

1990 WORLD CUP

The tournament returned to Italy for the first time since 1934, making Italy, after Mexico four years earlier, the second nation to host two World Cups. Serie A had come to represent the best of the club game in the late 1980s. Deep-pocketed Italian teams bought up some of the world's best players in those years. Aside from Maradona at Napoli, Inter Milan featured the West German trio of Andreas Brehme, Lothar Matthäus, and Jürgen Klinsmann, while AC Milan had the Dutchmen Ruud Gullit, Marco van Basten, and Frank Rijkaard. Those three had been instrumental in helping AC Milan win international dominance and translated that success for their national team, winners of the 1988 European Championship with the Netherlands. By the time the World Cup was over, even more international superstars would flood into Serie A.

The finals featured 24 teams. Europe was awarded 13 of those spots, with two each for South America, Africa, Asia, and North and Central America. The remaining place, a tiebreaker between a South American team and one from Oceania, ultimately resulted in Colombia's qualification to the finals for the first time since 1962.

Also making an overdue return was Egypt, who last appeared in 1934; the United States, competing for the first time since 1950; Romania, for the first time since 1970; along with both the Netherlands and Sweden for the first time since 1978. Three teams made their World Cup debuts: Ireland, Costa Rica, and the United Arab Emirates. Another World Cup first was the compulsory use of shin guards at the tournament, a mandate that had come down from FIFA two years earlier largely driven by the AIDS crisis. Soccer's world governing body feared that players were likely to contract the virus through the transference of blood as a result of hard tackles unless their legs were protected.

At the same time, FIFA disqualified both Mexico and Chile during the qualification process—the Mexicans for fielding an over-age player at a youth tournament and the Chileans after goalkeeper Roberto Rojas faked an injury after fireworks were thrown from the stands in their final qualifying match against Brazil, which caused the game to be abandoned. Chile was also banned from the 1994 World Cup. Among the notable teams who failed to qualify were France, Denmark, Hungary, Poland, and Portugal.

Italy and Argentina, the defending champions, were seeded, along with Brazil, West Germany, Belgium, and England. This was the draw for the six opening-round groups:

Group A: Italy, Austria, Czechoslovakia, and the United States

Group B: Argentina, Romania, the Soviet Union, and Cameroon

Group C: Brazil, Sweden, Scotland, and Costa Rica

Group D: West Germany, Yugoslavia, Colombia, and the United Arab Emirates

Group E: Belgium, Spain, Uruguay, and South Korea

Group F: England, the Netherlands, Ireland, and Egypt

Spain had made a strong case to be seeded, as had the Netherlands. In an effort to maintain some control over the hooligans and the potential for fan violence, FIFA made England the top seed in Group F. They were therefore forced to play the first round in Palermo in Sicily and in Cagliari on the island of Sardinia, both cities located off the Italian mainland. Group F also turned out to be the "Group of Death." Italy, meanwhile, was based in Rome and had the easiest group, Argentina placed in Naples to the delight of Maradona and the locals, while West Germany was in Milan, where Inter fans would make their heroes feel at home.

This World Cup also featured the last appearance for many nations. The Berlin Wall collapsed in December 1989, bringing down with it communism throughout Eastern Europe and eventually in the Soviet

Union. Following the World Cup, Germany was again unified; the Velvet Revolution saw the nonviolent transition back to two nations, Slovakia and the Czech Republic; while the USSR dissolved. Yugoslavia—at least one comprised of Serbs, Croatians, Bosnians, and Slovenians—made their last appearance ever at a World Cup.

The tournament was played in 12 cities: Rome, Naples, Bari, Palermo, Cagliari, Florence, Bologna, Genoa, Udine, Verona, Milan, and Turin. Two venues, the Stadio San Nicola in Bari and Turin's Stadio delle Alpi were new, while four others, the Stadio San Siro in Milan, the Stadio Luigi Ferraris in Genoa, the Stadio Comunale in Florence, and the Stadio Renato Dall'Ara in Bologna had been used at the 1934 World Cup. The final would be hosted at Rome's Stadio Olimpico, originally built for the 1960 Summer Olympics. Ten of the stadiums went through extensive renovations, some being virtually rebuilt, in order to conform to modern standards. Costs spiraled to almost $1 billion and years later became the focus of several major investigations that involved bribery and other financial mismanagement.

Group Stage

Italy were heavy favorites to win the tournament. The Azzurri had the home crowd behind them and could rely on their hard-nosed defense, anchored by AC Milan's Franco Baresi. The team's offense remained a work-in-progress, although Gianluca Vialli had developed into one of the country's strongest strikers despite questions about his fitness following a long season at Sampdoria. Italy manager Azeglio Vicini also had to contend with where to put rising star Roberto Baggio, while Juventus striker Salvatore "Toto" Schillaci, who had burst onto the national team scene late in his career, was relegated to the bench.

Italy opened Group A on June 9 against Austria at the Stadio Olimpico before 72,000 fans. Under tremendous pressure to win, Vicini's team fed off the enthusiasm generated by the crowd early on by creating a number of chances. The Italians were rewarded after 78 minutes when Schillaci, who had been subbed into the game four minutes earlier, headed in the game winner after connecting with a perfectly placed Vialli cross. The Italians won 1–0. Schillaci, relatively unknown outside of Italy, was on his way to becoming a global phenomenon.

A second 1–0 win against the United States, routed 5–1 by Czechoslovakia, helped Italy win the group. The Azzurri finished group play with a 2–0 win against Czechoslovakia and a perfect record. The Czechoslovakians ended runners-up, while the United States' first appearance in a World Cup finals since 1950 ended with three defeats.

Maradona was again the dominant figure going into this World Cup. He had led Napoli, a symbol of Italy's underprivileged south, to two Serie A titles and a UEFA Cup in the span of time since the last World Cup. At the same time, Argentina was not the same team from 1986. The defending champions were older, and Bilardo, like so many coaches before him, had failed to notice the cracks that were beginning to form around his roster. The defending champions opened the tournament on June 8 at the Stadio San Siro in Milan against Group B opponent Cameroon with a 1–0 defeat. The crowd of 74,000, filled largely with AC Milan and Inter fans, jeered the Argentine anthem, getting under Maradona's skin.

Cameroon's second match was highlighted by Roger Milla's brace in a 2–1 win against Romania. Milla's joyous goal celebration—swaying his hips near the corner kick flag—would become one of the memorable scenes from this tournament. "You couldn't describe it. There was a lot of joy obviously," Milla told FIFA.com in 2020. "We were so happy and it gave us a real confidence boost."

Cameroon would win the group, while Romania placed second. Argentina, meanwhile, lost veteran goalkeeper Nery Pumpido to a broken leg during a 2–0 win against the Soviet Union. Argentina qualified as one of the best third-placed teams.

In Group C, Brazil manager Sebastião Lazaroni opted to ditch the traditional style of *jogo bonito* and opted for a defensive-minded approach after the team's failed 1982 and 1986 tournaments. Brazil won the group, posting three straight wins against Sweden (2–1), Costa Rica (1–0), and Scotland (1–0). Debutants Costa Rica, coached by Mexico's miracle worker Milutinović, stunned Scotland 1–0 following Juan Cayasso's goal in the 49th minute. The Ticos would finish a surprise second to advance to the knockout stage.

West Germany, as expected, dominated from the start. Group D, contested in Milan and Bologna, produced few surprises. Playing in Milan allowed Matthäus, Brehme, and Klinsmann to enjoy crowd support. The West Germans wasted no time throttling opponents at the Stadio San Siro, defeating Yugoslavia 4–1 on June 10, then five days later trouncing the United Arab Emirates 5–1. West Germany won the group, joined in the knockout stage by second-place Yugoslavia.

Colombia, who finished third and also advanced, were led by the blond, bushy-headed midfielder Carlos "El Pipe" Valderrama. The result was proof of the growth of Colombian soccer in the years leading up to Italia '90, a boom fueled largely by narcotrafficking, which had pumped cash into the coffers of the country's club teams. As a result, teams like Atlético Nacional had won the 1989 Copa Libertadores, South America's premier club competition. Nine players from the Medellin-based team made up manager Francisco Maturana's 22-player World Cup roster. Before nearly 73,000 at the San Siro, West Germany, assured of a spot in the round of 16, played an entertaining, high-adrenaline contest. Nonetheless, it was the Colombians who displayed greater urgency. Other than making some great saves, goalkeeper Rene Higuita ventured outside his own penalty area, almost like an extra sweeper, in an effort to aid the midfield. It was the reason for his nickname "El Loco." West Germany took the lead with two minutes left when Pierre Littbarski thumped the ball past Higuita. Colombia's hopes appeared dashed. In the third minute of stoppage time, Colombia retook possession of the ball in its own half. Valderrama got the ball to Freddy Rincón, who unleashed a shot that went through goalkeeper Bodo Illgner's legs. Rincón ran toward the sideline with his fists clenched in celebration as the Colombian players cleared the bench in wild celebration. Colombia had reached the round of 16 in dramatic fashion. Simultaneously in Bologna, Yugoslavia defeated the United Arab Emirates 4–1 and would finish second.

Group E saw Spain edge Belgium for first place. La Roja defeated Belgium 2–1 on June 21 at Verona's Stadio Bentegodi. Spain took the lead after 27 minutes when Míchel converted a penalty kick. The Spanish lead was short-lived when Patrick Vervoort's free kick was redirected off the Spanish wall and into the goal. Spain clinched the win with a goal six minutes before halftime when defender Alberto Górriz headed the ball past Michel Preud'homme off a Míchel corner kick. Uruguay joined Spain and Belgium as one of the best third-place teams, securing its passage following a stoppage-time goal by striker Daniel Fonseca in a 1–0 victory against South Korea. "I think this Uruguay team plays best against the better teams," captain Enzo Francescoli told reporters. "This is a theory we will now put to the test."

Group F, the tournament's "Group of Death," was contested in Palermo and Cagliari. The English had been exiled there in an effort to limit fan violence. The move was controversial but deemed necessary by FIFA and the Italian authorities, who were expecting the worst. On the field, it was anyone's guess which teams would make the last 16.

The group opened on June 11 with the much-anticipated clash between England and Ireland at the Stadio Sant'Elia in Cagliari. Gary Lineker, top scorer at Mexico '86, found the back of the net in Italy, putting the Three Lions ahead after just eight minutes. Ireland, managed by former England international Jack Charlton, tied the game in the 73rd minute, and the game ended in a 1–1 draw. The draw against Ireland had been a poor one for England, although the players didn't take too kindly to that assessment. "There are people who don't want us to win the World Cup," midfielder Paul Gascoigne complained in a BBC interview following the press coverage the team had received. "And the public gets the wrong image. And, unfortunately for the players, we are trying to win a World Cup for the people back home."

The one thing in England's favor was the futility of the Netherlands, widely viewed as the other team favored to take the group. Egypt, meanwhile, had overachieved thus far, another sign the African game had grown on the international stage. The following day at the Stadio La Favorita in Palermo, the Netherlands and Egypt also played to a 1–1 draw. The outcome was a shock given how hyped the Dutch had been entering the tournament.

With all four teams tied in Group F at a point apiece and even on goal differential, the June 16 match in Cagliari between England and the

Netherlands had a feel that it could decide the group. Two hours before kickoff, police officers in riot gear and about 1,000 bottle-throwing English fans exchanged rocks and tear gas near the stadium after they had stormed a security barrier. There was seemingly more action outside the stadium than inside once the 35,000 fans got into their seats. Despite Lineker's attacking prowess and the ascension of Gascoigne as one of the tournament's best midfielders, England couldn't manage to score in Cagliari, and the match ended scoreless. The next day in Palermo, Egypt's scoreless draw versus Ireland left the group wide open with one match day to play.

The group's final two matches took place at the same time on the evening of June 21. Egypt had a real shot at becoming the second team from Africa at this tournament to advance out of the group stage. But England won the game 1–0 in Cagliari when Gascoigne's free kick set up a Mark Wright header after 58 minutes. It was good enough for the Three Lions to capture the group. In Palermo, the Netherlands and Ireland locked horns. Gullit had put the Oranje ahead in the 11th minute, his dreadlocks flowing behind him as he dashed into the box and scored with a diagonal shot to Packie Bonner's right. Ireland tied the score with a goal from Niall Quinn in the 72nd minute. The game ended 1–1.

"One thing I know for sure, teams hated playing against us," Bonner recalled in a 2020 interview with FIFA.com. "When you look back, we played against some great sides in those days—the likes of the Dutch, England, Spain and a really strong USSR side—and all of them found us horrible to play against. The pressing was non-stop."

Both Ireland and the Netherlands finished with identical records. FIFA ordered that lots be drawn to determine second and third place. The luck of the Irish allowed them to finish second (and play Romania in the round of 16), while the Netherlands were stuck playing West Germany.

Round of 16

The last 16 featured several great matchups. South American giants Brazil and Argentina squared off in Turin, followed by West Germany versus the Netherlands in Milan, a rematch of the 1974 World Cup final.

Uruguay's Héctor Castro (right) scores his team's fourth goal in the 1930 World Cup final.
PA IMAGES/ALAMY STOCK PHOTO

Italy manager Vittorio Pozzo (left) talks to his players before the start of extra time during the 1934 World Cup final against Czechoslovakia.
JONATHAN O'ROURKE/ALAMY STOCK PHOTO

Italy's Alfredo Foni kicks the ball during the 1938 World Cup final against Hungary.
KEYSTONE PRESS/ALAMY STOCK PHOTO

A boy holds up the official 1950 World Cup poster.
MINISTÉRIO DA JUSTIÇA E SEGURANÇA PÚBLICA/ARQUIVO NACIONAL

Hungary's goalkeeper, Gyula Grosics, remains vigilant as West Germany aims to score in the 1954 World Cup final.
COMET PHOTO AG

West Germany's Hans Schaefer (right) and Sweden's Nils Liedholm (left) exchange team pennants ahead of the 1958 World Cup semifinal.

DPA PICTURE-ALLIANCE/ALAMY STOCK PHOTO

Garrincha (center) dazzles as Czechoslovakia's Josef Masopust (left) and Jan Popluhar (right) look on during the 1962 World Cup final.

SUEDDEUTSCHE ZEITUNG PHOTO/ALAMY STOCK PHOTO

Pelé lies on the ground after suffering a foul during the match between Brazil and Bulgaria at the 1966 World Cup.

Brazil manager Mário Zagallo (right) and Pelé share a hug ahead of the 1970
World Cup.
MINISTÉRIO DA JUSTIÇA E SEGURANÇA PÚBLICA/ARQUIVO NACIONAL

Gerd Müller scores the winning goal for West Germany in a 2–1 win against the Netherlands in the 1974 World Cup final.

SUEDDEUTSCHE ZEITUNG PHOTO/ALAMY STOCK PHOTO

Mario Kempes (right) scores his second goal in the 1978 World Cup final for Argentina against the Netherlands as Daniel Bertoni (left) celebrates.

DOM SLIKE/ALAMY STOCK PHOTO

Italy's Paolo Rossi (left) dribbles away from Brazil's Léo Júnior at the 1982 World Cup.

TRINITY MIRROR/MIRRORPIX/ALAMY STOCK PHOTO

Diego Maradona (center) gets past England's defense on his way to scoring the greatest goal in World Cup history in 1986.
NIPPON NEWS/ALAMY STOCK PHOTO

Dutch midfielder Frank Rijkaard spits at West German striker Rudi Völler before both players are sent off at the 1990 World Cup.
DPA PICTURE-ALLIANCE ARCHIVE/ALAMY STOCK PHOTO

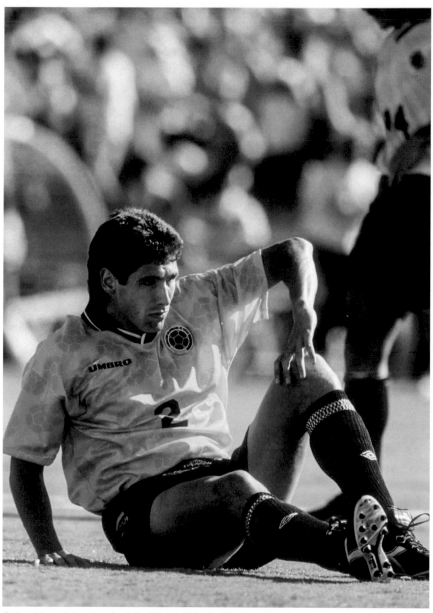

Colombian defender Andrés Escobar just after he scored an own goal against the United States at the 1994 World Cup.

England's David Beckham gets a red card after a foul on Argentina's Diego Simeone at the 1998 World Cup.

PA IMAGES/ALAMY STOCK PHOTO

South Korea manager Guus Hiddink is tossed in the air by his players at the end of their World Cup third-place game against Turkey in 2002.

REUTERS/ALAMY STOCK PHOTO

France's Zinedine Zidane jumps over Italy's Marco Materazzi during a fight for the ball in the 2006 World Cup final.
UPI/ALAMY STOCK PHOTO

Landon Donovan scores the winning goal for the United States against Algeria to advance to the knockout stage at the 2010 World Cup.
REUTERS/ALAMY STOCK PHOTO

Portugal's Cristiano Ronaldo tries to maneuver the ball past Germany's Mats Hummels at the 2014 World Cup.
WENN RIGHTS LTD/ALAMY STOCK PHOTO

Kylian Mbappe celebrates as France wins the 2018 World Cup in the final against Croatia.
SHUTTERSTOCK

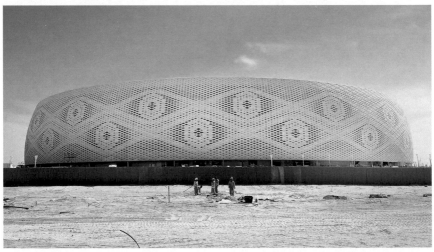

Al Thumama Stadium, one of eight venues that will be used at the 2022 World Cup in Qatar, highlights the fusion of Arab culture with modern architecture.
SHUTTERSTOCK

The round of 16 opened on June 23 when Colombia and Cameroon squared off in Naples. Both teams had unexpectedly qualified for this stage, and the 50,000 at the Stadio San Paolo would be treated to a wonderful game. Both teams employed a carefree, lively style—but the game ended scoreless. It was the super-sub Milla, who had entered the game in the 54th minute, who would once again make the difference in extra time.

After tallying the go-ahead goal in the 106th minute, Milla's individual prowess extended Cameroon's lead. Higuita, known for coming out of the penalty area, committed a blunder that cost his team when, just 10 yards from the goal, Milla dispossessed him of the ball. Milla ran toward the empty net and easily deposited the ball into the goal. Colombia scored with Bernardo Redín in the 115th minute, but it turned out to be nothing more than a consolation goal. The Indomitable Lions had made history as the first African nation to reach the World Cup quarterfinals.

The day's second match in Bari between Czechoslovakia and Costa Rica was another game between teams with an unlikely chance of advancing to this stage of the tournament. Tomáš Skuhravý's hat trick, after all three goals were scored on headers, elevated his stock on the transfer market. While Czechoslovakia advanced following the 4–1 win, Skuhravy's Italian stay would be extended after signing with Serie A side Genoa later that summer. The Ticos, meanwhile, had pulled off the impossible, and Milutinović cemented his legacy as a miracle worker.

The Stadio delle Alpi was the site of Argentina's clash against Brazil. Maradona's side didn't look as sharp during the group stage, but he had a history of always finding a way to win. The samba drums reverberated inside the stadium, but Brazil was playing to a different beat. The Brazilians had a perfect record in the group stage, although their style of play was nothing to brag about after Lazaroni's tactical tinkering to a more defensive approach that relied on dead balls and the counterattack. Absent from the game was the South American flair we had come to enjoy from these two sides throughout the decades. Brazil dominated possession for long stretches, but their talisman Careca was unable to beat Sergio Goychochea. Instead, with the game scoreless, it seemed as if extra time, and possibly even a penalty-kick shootout, would be needed to get a winner.

Maradona had been unable to do much after an ankle injury that required painkilling injections and dogged him throughout much of the tournament. Nonetheless, Maradona changed the outcome with a flick of the foot. With 10 minutes left in the game, Maradona sent a silky pass to Claudio Caniggia, who beat the offside trap, then calmly rounded the Brazilian goalkeeper Cláudio Taffarel and scored the winning goal. It was the only bright spot for Argentina. Even by playing badly, the Albiceleste advanced to the quarterfinals.

The match had an interesting footnote. Brazilian defender Branco told reporters two days after the game that he felt drowsy for much of the match. Branco had done a wonderful job canceling out Maradona in the first half, but he couldn't keep up with him as the match wore on and temperatures reached an unbearable 86 degrees.

Branco told reporters he had been "drugged" after drinking from a "spiked" water bottle given him in the 40th minute as Argentina's team doctors worked on Pedro Troglio after having suffered a hard tackle. Branco, who was also a free-kick specialist, said he had felt ill and even asked to be substituted, something Lazaroni refused to do. At the time, the story was dismissed, largely seen as an excuse for Brazil losing the game.

Two years later, Branco said he ran into Argentine defender Oscar Ruggeri at the airport in Rio de Janeiro. "That was a good trick we pulled on you back at Italia '90, wasn't it?" Ruggeri said to him, according to Branco. The comments appeared to confirm that there had been a laced bottle on the field.

The incident—known as the "holy water scandal"—was further confirmed in 2005 when Maradona, during an interview with Argentine channel Tyc Sports, confessed that Branco's accusation was true. Maradona said a bottle laced with the tranquillizer Rohypnol was offered to Branco on the sidelines that afternoon.

"Afterwards, Branco took the free-kicks and fell over," Maradona said.

Despite the incident, Branco said Maradona "was the best player he had ever seen play and the best he had ever faced. He had so much talent. He was a real phenomenon."

That evening, the all-European clash between West Germany and the Netherlands was played for a spot in the quarterfinals. There was bad blood between the sides. The match was barely 22 minutes old when a series of ugly events resulted in Rudi Völler and Rijkaard being ejected. The red cards came after Völler was tackled by Rijkaard. Referee Juan Loustau of Argentina whistled for the play to stop and to show Rijkaard a yellow card. Once the game resumed, Rijkaard spit at the back of Völler's head. The German, in response, shouted back at him. As a result, Völler was given a yellow card. Rijkaard's saliva sharing went unseen and unpunished by the referee.

The free kick bounced in front of the goal, where Hans van Breukelen picked it up just before a charging Völler could get to it. But the West German striker fell over, narrowly avoiding a collision with the goal-keeper. Before Van Breukelen and Völler could exchange words, Rijkaard joined the fray and got into the West German's face. Loustau sent him off. Also tired of Völler's antics, the referee also showed him a red card.

"Of course it wasn't nice what Frank Rijkaard did, but the match should have continued for me," Völler told *FourFourTwo* magazine two years after the tit-for-spit. "I still can't understand why the ref sent me off, and I guess he will take it to his grave. He wanted to make an example of both of us so that the situation would calm down—which did work."

As Rijkaard and Völler walked off the field, the Dutch defender spit on him for a second time, the saliva hanging off the West German's curly locks. Völler looked on in disbelief.

"There was some venom before between other players, but you know, it's always problematic between Germany and Holland," Völler added. "Frank apologized a few months later."

After a scoreless first half, Klinsmann put Die Mannschaft ahead in the 51st minute, and Brehme added a second with eight minutes left to avenge the defeat from two years earlier. A penalty kick by Ronald Koeman for the Oranje in the 89th minute narrowed the score to 2–1, but the West Germans clung on to the win as the 75,000 in attendance cheered.

On June 25, Ireland and Romania, two defensive teams, met in Genoa. The game was decided on penalties after a scoreless 90 minutes and no goals in 30 more of extra time. After both sides scored all four of their respective kicks, Ireland's Bonner stopped a shot by attacking midfielder Daniel Timofte to put his team in position to win the game. On Ireland's fifth kick, center back David O'Leary beat goalkeeper Silviu Lung with a high kick to his left for the 5–4 win. As a result, Ireland was in the quarterfinals without having won a game. That didn't matter to Charlton or Ireland fans.

"The pubs will sell more booze tonight than they have all year," Charlton joked at the postgame news conference. "I am delighted for the Irish people."

In Rome, Uruguay failed to show that it could challenge the better teams at this tournament. In fact, it was Italy who rolled on to the quarterfinals, where they would face Ireland, after downing the South Americans 2–0. Striker Aldo Serena assisted on Italy's opening goal in the 65th minute following a pass to Schillaci, who broke through two defenders and blasted a long, left-footed shot that dipped into the goal past Fernando Álvez. Serena added an assurance goal of his own off a header seven minutes from time, and Italians took to the streets in celebration.

The round of 16 concluded on June 26. In Verona, Yugoslavia stunned Spain 2–1 in extra time. A brace from midfielder Dragan Stojković was enough to decide who was the best team that afternoon. Stojković's winning goal, from a curling free kick that made its way around the five-man Spanish wall and into the net, put Yugoslavia through to the quarterfinals.

In the final game of the round, it was another piece of individual brilliance in extra time that allowed England to eliminate Belgium. Second half–sub David Platt scored a high-flying volley in the last minute of extra time—his first goal for England at the senior level—to send the Three Lions into the quarterfinals.

"The ball dropped over my shoulder and I just tried to get something on it," Platt told the *Guardian* in 2018. "There wasn't a great deal of power. It was all technique."

"I had an eye for getting on the end of that sort of ball and the technical ability to finish those chances off," he added. "I worked hard on practicing overhead kicks and volleys in training at Aston Villa but, even so, if I had re-enacted that chance against Belgium 10 times in training the next day, there's a very good chance I wouldn't have scored once from it. It was just one of life's rare, perfect moments."

Not rare was the fear of more fan violence now that England had progressed. Days earlier, confrontations between police and English fans in the coastal town of Rimini ended with 246 people expelled from the country. Fear spread throughout Italy that as England advanced, more troublemakers would follow.

Quarterfinals

The first match of the round saw Argentina play Yugoslavia on June 30 in Florence. The Yugoslavians were reduced to 10 men after only 30 minutes following the red card of midfielder Refik Šabanadžović. Argentina, unable to generate the offense needed to score, could not take advantage. Maradona was not much of a factor, being unable to create any scoring chances for himself or his teammates. The marathon game dragged on, and 120 minutes failed to produce any goals. A penalty-kick shootout would be needed to determine a winner.

Argentina's luck at this tournament reached a new level. Maradona, a penalty-kick specialist, failed his attempt when goalkeeper Tomislav Ivković saved the ball with a dive to his right. Argentina's hero that afternoon was not Maradona but Goycochea. The goalkeeper made two saves, and the Yugoslavs missed a third, to help Argentina advance following a 3–2 shootout win.

Once in Rome, the Ireland players and coaching staff made a trip to Vatican City for an audience with Pope John Paul II. But it was Italian prayers that were answered. The Azzurri defeated Ireland 1–0 before 75,000 flag-waving Italians at the Stadio Olimpico. Once again, it was Schillaci who continued to have an eye for the goal. His strike after 38 minutes won the Azzurri the game. The Azzurri had recorded their fifth straight shutout and now had to face Argentina in Naples.

West Germany, meanwhile, got the better of Czechoslovakia on July 1 in Milan. The West Germans advanced to the semifinals when Matthäus converted a penalty kick in the 25th minute. The result failed to tell the whole story. West Germany dominated the match and could have scored two more goals, but defender Guido Buchwald's attempt in the 20th minute was thwarted by goalkeeper Jan Stejskal. On the ensuing corner kick, Ivan Hašek cleared the ball off the line. After the penalty kick, Klinsmann came close in the waning seconds of the first half, but Hašek cleared the ball off his line.

The most exciting match of the quarterfinals took place that evening in Naples. The game between England and Cameroon was a clash of temperaments. The 55,000 at the Stadio San Paolo were clearly behind the underdog Africans as the crowd hoped to see another upset. Platt put England ahead after 25 minutes. Milla was brought in at halftime, and Cameroon's offense was reignited. In the second half, the match took a twist during a five-minute stretch starting in the 61st minute. Cameroon was awarded a penalty kick after Milla was taken down in the box. Defender Emmanuel Kundé scored the kick for the equalizer past Shilton.

Four minutes later, striker Eugène Ekéké put Cameroon ahead on a breakaway, blasting the ball past Shilton for the 2–1 lead. After defeating Argentina in the opener, the Indomitable Lions appeared close to a second big upset. However, England were awarded a penalty kick after Lineker was tripped in the box. The English striker then converted it seven minutes from time to bring England level 2–2.

In extra time, a beautiful pass from Gascoigne to Lineker could have resulted in a third England goal. Goalkeeper Thomas N'Kono, wearing his trademark black sweatpants, took Lineker down in the box, and another penalty kick was called in England's favor. Lineker converted in the 105th minute for a 3–2 win and an end of Cameroon's quixotic run.

England were through to the World Cup semifinals for the first time since 1966, where they faced rivals West Germany in Turin. As for Cameroon, the tournament's Cinderella team had made African soccer proud and won many hearts along the way. The Cameroonian players took a victory lap as the San Paolo crowd applauded them.

"We would have loved to have gone further because we really had what it took to do more," Milla told FIFA.com. "I don't want to get into a debate about the England match, but when I look back on it now there are a few regrets. I'm convinced we could have gone all the way. We were welcomed as heroes when we returned to Cameroon and that was when you realize that you've achieved something big."

Semifinals

The semifinals included two heavyweight clashes featuring four teams who had each won a World Cup at some point in their history. Authorities in Turin had asked FIFA to invert the semifinal venues and have England play West Germany in Naples, but FIFA chose not to alter the schedule. Instead, it offered a statement that said the English crowds had been "under control" and there was no need to fear any trouble.

The other semifinal between Italy and Argentina, meanwhile, also sparked controversy in its lead-up. Maradona tried to lobby the Neapolitan fans into cheering for Argentina, reminding them that northern Italians often regarded southerners as foreigners. Maradona had tried to take advantage of an ages-old rift within the country that had pitted the industrial north against the agrarian south. "The Neapolitans must remember one thing," Maradona told reporters. "Italy makes them feel important one day of the year, but forgets about them the other 364 days."

Schillaci took to the microphones to rebuke Maradona's comments. "Over the last month, I have become a bit of a symbol of the antiracist reunification of the country," he told reporters. "This is the part of the World Cup which I like best."

At the same time, Italy goalkeeper Walter Zenga was closing in on two records that on the eve of the tournament had appeared impossible even for a goalkeeper of his great talent. The Inter Milan goalie had played in all of Italy's 450 minutes. The record for consecutive scoreless minutes at a World Cup was 474 by West Germany's Sepp Maier.

Zenga, unfazed that he was on the verge of rewriting the World Cup record book, had his defense to thank. The Italian backline had not made any mistakes, although Argentina would be their biggest challenge to date. It's true that Maradona had appeared quite ordinary in Argentina's five previous matches. But the Argentine playmaker, like all great players, could change the outcome of a game with one play. That's what Vicini's squad feared most.

On July 3, the night of the game, a banner that hung from the San Paolo's upper deck appeared to sum up the city's mood: "Diego, you are always in our hearts—but we are Italian!" But something did appear and feel different. The 60,000 in attendance weren't nearly as noisy as the crowds in Rome. On the field, Argentina played with determination—the first time it had done so at the tournament—while Italy used its midfield to generate chances for Schillaci and Vialli. It was Schillaci—yes, him again—who scored his fifth goal of the tournament in the 17th minute.

The Azzurri tried to defend that lead, switching over to the *catenaccio*. This gritty tactic failed. Argentina equalized in the 67th minute when Maradona fed the ball to Julio Olarticoechea, who sent in a floating cross that allowed Caniggia to head the ball past the charging Zenga. The Italian goalie had finally been beaten after 517 minutes.

Zenga probably should have made the save, but Caniggia got to it first for the tying goal. Once again, the Albiceleste were hoping to get to a shootout. In extra time, Argentina was reduced to 10 players in the 105th minute after Ricardo Giusti hit Baggio, who had come on in the second half, in the head. The game, a three-hour marathon, failed to produce any more goals. In the shootout, Goycochea was once again the hero. It was his heroics—saving first Roberto Donadoni's kick, then Aldo Serena's attempt—that put Argentina on top 4–3 and in a second straight final.

Italy's World Cup dream was over. Those magical nights had come to an end. Many around the country had blamed the crowd, but Donadoni refuted such a theory. "We can't blame the fans. That's no excuse," he said. "We lost that game on the field and because Argentina was better than us in the shootout. We did everything we could to win the game."

During the post-match news conference, Vicini said, "It was an even game, a tough game, very difficult. I believe, overall, that the Italian team deserved much more. That's soccer. Argentina played well, but a few things in the shootout punished us."

Italy would finish third, defeating England 2–1. Schillaci's goal won the game, and he would finish as the tournament's top scorer with six goals. Argentina, meanwhile, had won just two games at this tournament and yet were in position to repeat as champion.

The following day, West Germany and England played before 63,000 at the Stadio delle Alpi. In one of the tournament's best games, West Germany powered into the lead after Brehme's free kick in the 60th minute deflected off Paul Parker and past Shilton. With 10 minutes left to play, Lineker equalized for England. Lineker's powerful left-footed shot, following a pass from Parker, beat Illgner to make it 1–1.

Like the other semifinal, extra time failed to yield a goal. The emotionally draining match took its toll on Gascoigne in the 98th minute. Following a rough tackle, Gascoigne received a yellow card, meaning he would have to miss the final if England won the game. There was no English stiff upper lip this time as Gascoigne began to tear up.

The 120 minutes failed to produce another goal. The winner of this one would also be decided on penalties. In the shootout, West Germany converted four of their attempts, while England's Stuart Pearce's shot was deflected by Illgner's leg. Chris Waddle's attempt went high over the crossbar, and West Germany advanced to the final with a 4–3 shootout win. Gascoigne was reduced to tears once again. "When things are good and I can see they're about to end, I get scared, really scared," he told FIFA.com in a 2017 interview. "I couldn't help but cry that night."

It had been a wonderful match, maybe the best at the tournament. It was also a memorable game and one befitting a final, especially after what would transpire in Rome days later. England had played a great tournament. The team's exploits allowed a nation to fall in love with them.

The team's success at Italia '90 also served as a springboard for English soccer as a whole. Clubs were readmitted to participate in European competition following the World Cup, and the Premier League was formed in 1992. That allowed English clubs to take advantage of lucrative TV deals and upgrade stadiums. As a result, it has today become the most-watched sports league in the world.

Final: West Germany vs. Argentina

The World Cup final was an afterthought for many Italians. The game at Rome's Stadio Olimpico featured a rematch of the 1986 final between Argentina and West Germany, and the 74,000 inside the venue didn't hide their support for the Europeans.

The crowd jeered the Argentine national anthem that July 8 evening, and a visibly upset Maradona could be seen cursing under his breath with a global TV audience of one billion watching. The competition's climax was a dour affair, highlighted by time-wasting tactics. The Argentines, without the suspended Caniggia due to yellow-card accumulation, employed negative tactics in the hopes of pushing another shootout. The West Germans, operating on 24 hours less rest, was livelier and tried in vain to get past the Albiceleste defense.

Midfielders Thomas Hässler and Matthäus controlled the ball, and Klinsmann and Völler were tasked with trying to score. Defensively, the plan was simple as Buchwald shadowed Maradona. The game reached a boiling point in the 68th minute when referee Edgardo Codesal of Mexico red-carded defender Pedro Monzón for a foul on Klinsmann, making Monzón the first player ever dismissed from a World Cup final.

This game was anything but champagne football. Instead, it could double as a cure for insomnia. West Germany won the game when Codesal awarded them a penalty kick after Völler was brought down in the box by defender Roberto Sensini. Brehme converted the kick in the 84th minute, drilling a low shot that went in between the right post and Goycochea's outstretched arm.

The goal brought newfound urgency on the part of Argentina to score. Frustrated, Gustavo Dezotti fouled center back Jürgen Kohler three minutes from time and was ejected. West Germany won the game and joined Italy and Brazil as the only nations to ever lift the trophy three times. West Germany were worthy winners. They had outshot Argentina 16–1 in the final and had played better throughout the entire competition.

"There were no doubts whatsoever who was going to win," Beckenbauer, the second man after Brazil's Zagallo to win the World Cup as both a player and a manager, told reporters. "For 90 minutes we attacked Argentina and there was no feeling of any danger that a goal would be scored against us. As I saw it, we outplayed them from beginning to end."

The outcome left Maradona in tears. He announced his retirement from the national team, although it was a year later that Maradona would test positive for cocaine and be banned from the sport for 15 months. He would play again at the 1994 World Cup, but a second suspension during that tournament would officially end his international career.

Maradona made headlines once the game was over. "I will have to tell my elder daughter Dalmita that the Mafia exists also in soccer. The penalty kick which defeated us did not exist and was given to award the victory to West Germany and punish Argentina," Maradona told reporters at Rome's airport before boarding a plane for Buenos Aires.

For West Germany, the victory marked the last time they would compete at a World Cup. German reunification, in the works on the eve of the competition, would allow East Germans to play for the team in the future. This infusion of talent would ensure the country's soccer competitiveness for years to come.

Inside the stadium, the scoreboard flashed the message: "Ciao Italia. Hello USA." A new era was dawning for the game, and a previously untapped market, in this case the United States, would bring commercial interests to the forefront like never before. It's true that Italia '90 had been a low-scoring tournament, but to this day it has a cult following among many Generation Xers who remember it fondly for its personalities, such as Schillaci, Gascoigne, and Milla, not to mention those magical nights.

1994 WORLD CUP

In Neil Diamond's song "America," Diamond portrays a positive interpretation of the history of immigration to the United States: "Everywhere around the world, they're coming to America," the words went.

They were again coming to America in the summer of '94 after FIFA awarded the United States the World Cup. Some of the same issues seen in the past regarding kickoff times that would accommodate prime-time viewership in Europe meant games played in extreme heat. The issues didn't end there. The question around whether the United States could generate enough interest in its own country worthy of such a massive event was asked by many in the lead-up to the competition.

FIFA saw the U.S. market as an opportunity to bring the game to an untapped audience. It was also a chance to make more money, as FIFA hoped to bring on new, big-brand sponsors like McDonald's, General Motors, and American Airlines. In the end, the tournament generated

Co-Player of the Century: Diego Maradona

Widely considered one of the greatest players in the history of the game, Maradona, along with Pelé, was named co-winner of the FIFA Player of the 20th Century award. Maradona's passing, dribbling, and free-kick abilities made him virtually unstoppable with the ball. Off the field, Maradona had a troubled life and spent years fighting drug addiction.

National team career: Nicknamed El Pipe de Oro (The Golden Boy), Maradona made his senior national team debut in 1977 at age 16 against Hungary. He was left off the squad for the 1978 World Cup by coach César Luis Menotti who felt he was too young. He helped Argentina win the World Cup in 1986 and finished runners-up four years later. Overall, he played at four World Cups, his last one in 1994. He scored 34 goals for Argentina in 91 appearances. Maradona later coached Argentina at the 2010 World Cup.

Club career: Maradona made his pro debut with the Argentinos Juniors at 16, before joining the Boca Juniors in 1981, where he led them to the domestic title. Maradona signed with Barcelona a year later, but once there he was riddled with injuries and unhappy. In 1984, he signed with Italian side Napoli and played there for seven seasons (helping them win two league titles, a UEFA Cup, a league cup, and the Italian SuperCup), but he failed a drug test in 1991 that ended his time in Serie A and resulted in a 15-month ban. He returned with Sevilla in 1992 before ending his career in his homeland with Newell's Old Boys and finally the Boca Juniors in 1998.

Argentina's Diego Maradona led Argentina to the World Cup title in 1986.
SHUTTERSTOCK

Honors: Aside from the FIFA Player of the 20th Century award, Maradona was named best player at the 1986 World Cup. In 1999, Maradona was placed second behind Pelé by *World Soccer* in the magazine's list of the "100 Greatest Players of the 20th Century." In a 2014 FIFA poll, Maradona was voted the second-greatest number 10 of all time, behind Pelé. Later that year, he was ranked second in the *Guardian*'s list of the 100 greatest World Cup players of all time, once again behind Pelé. Maradona died in 2020 at age 60 of acute pulmonary edema, a condition involving fluid buildup in the lungs. Following his death, the San Paolo Stadium in Naples was renamed in his honor.

$100 million in net revenue for FIFA, according to their financial reports, while Nike expanded into the soccer space after its longtime affiliation with basketball. The U.S. Soccer Federation made an additional $60 million, funds used to help grow the game. In fact, this World Cup, staged in the largest capitalist nation on the planet, introduced an era of slick marketing management to the game. Everything from commemorative coins to pennants to hats featuring the World Cup logo was for sale. It's true that this World Cup had the glitz only the United States could offer.

In an effort to generate more money from TV ad dollars, Havelange had even proposed four 25-minute quarters, instead of two 45-minute halves, during games—but the idea fell flat. The World Cup remained, despite ideas to improve the game, the planet's biggest sporting event, and its most lucrative.

The United States had only qualified for four World Cups (1930, 1934, 1950, and 1990). FIFA took notice of the 1984 Summer Olympics held in Los Angeles. The Olympic soccer tournament, held at the Rose Bowl, had been a rousing success. A crowd of 101,799 had attended the final. France defeated Brazil 2–0 for the gold medal, and FIFA officials were watching—and smiling. The USA's stock as an organizer, particularly of a soccer tournament, grew instantly.

Since 1962, the World Cup had alternated between the Americas and Europe. Although Brazil had a rich history of soccer and Africa remained a continent that had never hosted a World Cup, the United States—with its government support and NFL stadiums, many training facilities, and hotel accommodations—remained an untapped market. The United States' ability to market the game and lure advertisers would be a model FIFA would use for years to come.

The tournament would be contested in nine cities—Boston, New York, Washington, DC, Orlando, Chicago, Detroit, Dallas, San Francisco, and Los Angeles—and for the first time would be played across four time zones. The format remained the same, but the schedule was put together in a meticulous manner so as to cut down on teams having to crisscross the country, particularly during the group stage.

On the field, England, Uruguay, Portugal, France, Poland, and surprise European champions Denmark (a last-minute replacement for

Yugoslavia at that tournament) all failed to qualify. It would have no bearing on the level of play on display in the finals. England's failure to qualify meant that organizers did not have to deal with the threat of hooliganism. What they did fear was apathy from the American public, although tickets had sold out months before the start of the tournament. In the end, the United States staged a hugely successful World Cup, with an average attendance of nearly 70,000. To this day, the total attendance for a World Cup finals of nearly 3.6 million remains the highest in tournament history, despite the expansion of the competition from 24 to 32 teams at the 1998 World Cup in France.

The 1994 tournament was the last to employ a 24-team format. The World Cup draw featured six seeded teams—Germany, Italy, Brazil, Argentina, Belgium, and the United States—and three new entrants in Greece, Nigeria, and Saudi Arabia. Russia was also new to the World Cup, following the breakup of the Soviet Union, and for the first time since 1938, a unified Germany took part in the tournament. Here is a look at the six opening-round groups:

Group A: The United States, Romania, Switzerland, and Colombia

Group B: Brazil, Sweden, Russia, and Cameroon

Group C: Germany, Spain, Bolivia, and South Korea

Group D: Argentina, Bulgaria, Greece, and Nigeria

Group E: Italy, Ireland, Norway, and Mexico

Group F: Belgium, the Netherlands, Morocco, and Saudi Arabia

Group E was by far the toughest one of the opening round. In fact, Italy, Ireland, Norway, and Mexico were the tournament's "Group of Death." Meanwhile, the United States was attempting to avoid becoming the first host nation not to get past the first round. They were pitted against Romania, Switzerland, and Colombia, a team many had predicted could win the tournament. Brazil, Germany, and Argentina, the other three teams favored to capture the World Cup, all had been placed in manageable groups.

Group Stage

The United States entered the 1994 World Cup in an unusual position. The Americans were hosting the tournament for the first time but were in no way contenders. The United States opened Group A on June 18 against Switzerland at the Pontiac Silverdome in Detroit. The venue, retrofitted with natural grass, marked the first time in World Cup history that a match was played indoors. The 73,000 in attendance witnessed a tight game. The Americans, coached by Milutinović, had six players in the starting lineup who had played at Italia '90. In addition to those players, the Americans also added some naturalized players to the roster, including German-born defender Thomas Dooley, the Dutchman Earnie Stewart, and South African–born Roy Wegerle. All three had family ties to the United States and, more importantly to Milutinović, club experience in Europe. The Swiss, back at the World Cup for the first time since 1966, jumped in front after 39 minutes, firing home a free kick that flew past the wall and Tony Meola. The United States responded five minutes later. Eric Wynalda scored off a stellar free kick of his own to draw even. The match ended 1–1.

The Americans entered their second game needing at least a draw. The Americans were confident, but the odds appeared in favor of a Colombia rout. "We were nervous," recalled defender Marcelo Balboa. "The fact that we had never beaten Colombia leading up to the World Cup. They were also one of the favorites to win the World Cup that year."

On June 23 at a sun-kissed Rose Bowl, the Americans and Colombians squared off. Colombia was in a must-win situation after losing to Romania. To this day, American soccer fans can recount the sequence of events that led to the U.S. victory. The first goal for the United States was an own goal, mistakenly diverted into the net by defender Andrés Escobar. The second goal came in the 52nd minute when Stewart scored off a Tab Ramos assist. Down 2–0, the Colombians appeared lost. "I remember their faces as time passed by. The desperate look they got on their faces," said Balboa, who nearly scored a goal of his own when his perfect bicycle kick sailed wide of the post by a few inches.

The Colombians pulled one back in the 90th minute, but it was too little, too late. The Americans won 2–1, recording their biggest win at a

World Cup since the 1–0 victory against England in 1950. The Colombian coaching staff admitted afterward that a death threat against midfielder Gabriel Gómez sent via fax on the eve of the game to the team's hotel had shaken up his squad. Colombia coach Francisco Maturana said at the time that the people who sent the message threatened to blow up Gómez's home. Maturana, who said he had considered resigning before the game, replaced Gómez with Hernán Gaviria in the starting lineup. "Unfortunately, I have still not been able to find the explanation as to why we played this badly," Maturana told reporters. "The team wasn't up to the task when the time came."

As detailed in the ESPN documentary *The Two Escobars*, the game against the United States became a transitional moment for Colombia. Writing in the Colombian newspaper *El Tiempo*, Escobar reflected on his team's poor performance this way: "Life doesn't end here. We have to go on. Life cannot end here. No matter how difficult, we must stand back up. We only have two options: either allow anger to paralyze us and the violence continues, or we overcome and try our best to help others. It's our choice. Let us please maintain respect. My warmest regards to everyone. It's been a most amazing and rare experience. We'll see each other again soon because life does not end here."

Life, unfortunately, did end for Escobar. The 27-year-old defender was murdered outside a Medellin nightclub on July 2, reportedly killed because he'd scored the infamous own goal, angering gambling syndicates who had wagered heavily on a Colombia win. The killers had shouted "Goal!" right before pumping six bullets into Escobar's chest.

Romania would win the group (following a 2–1 win against the United States in the final group game), while Switzerland finished second after beating the Americans on goal differential. The United States went through as one of the first round's best third-place teams.

In Group B, Brazil dominated as it had at so many previous tournaments. Wins against Russia (2–0) and Cameroon (3–0) saw them top the group. "We arrived with a very big responsibility and an obligation to win. Brazil has not been world football champion since 1970," recalled Raí, one of the team's most talented attacking midfielders at the time. "Twenty-four years was too much for a place that's considered the 'country of football.' At the same time, we were very confident. And this came with a mixture on a team that was very cohesive, united, talented and pragmatic."

Pragmatic was the key difference between this team and the 1970 squad. Manager Carlos Alberto Parreira played an attack-minded 4–4–2 formation with Bebeto joining Romário in attack. Not always fun and dazzling, this Brazil team primarily chased results, often at the expense of beautiful play. The role of playmaker went to Raí, who had the extra burden of being team captain and wearing the iconic number 10 jersey. The younger brother of '80s great Sócrates, Raí would take on a leading role at the start of the tournament, only to end up on the bench. "The first time I wore the number ten shirt, I had been captain of the national team in 1991, three years before the World Cup," Raí said. "So, despite the pressure, I was already used to it by 1994."

Brazil tied Sweden, who would finish second and also advance to the knockout stage, 1–1 on June 28 at the Silverdome. Down a goal, Romário's strike in the 47th minute salvaged a draw. The Swedes had scored in the 24th minute after the cherub-faced striker Tomas Brolin avoided two tackles, then passed a perfect ball to striker Kennet Andersson on the left wing. Andersson placed a right-footed shot from a tight angle that got past Mauro Silva and goalkeeper Taffarel. It was the first goal Brazil had conceded at the tournament. "I was not surprised by the final score," Parreira told reporters. "I have said it all along that Sweden are a very strong team. I feel that what they tried to do was to get a tie."

The day's other game to close the group, between already-eliminated Russia and Cameroon, was highlighted by striker Oleg Salenko's goals. Russia's 6–1 rout also saw Cameroon make history when Milla tallied in the 46th minute after coming on as a sub at halftime, making him at age 42 the oldest player to ever score in a World Cup game.

Germany, the defending champions, played as a unified nation for the first time since the 1938 World Cup. It was on June 17 at Soldier Field in Chicago that Germany, managed by Beckenbauer's former assistant coach Berti Vogts, opened the tournament against fellow Group C side Bolivia, playing at its first World Cup since 1950. In the 61st minute, Matthäus, no longer a box-to-box midfielder and now a sweeper, sent a long pass that found Hässler who deflected the pass with his chest to Klinsmann. Bolivian goalkeeper Carlos Trucco came out and attempted to make a desperate save, but Klinsmann slipped the ball into the empty net for the game's lone goal. "Once I got the ball, there was almost nothing I could do wrong," Klinsmann said.

In a last-ditch effort to equalize, Bolivian striker Marco "El Diablo" Etcheverry came into the game with 11 minutes to play. Etcheverry, still recovering from a knee injury, never made an impact. He was ejected in the 83rd minute, four minutes after he had come into the match, for kicking Matthäus. He'd be the first of 15 players to receive a red card at this tournament after FIFA had ordered referees to crack down on violent play.

Germany, despite winning the group following a 1–1 draw against Spain and a 3–2 victory against South Korea, could have benefited from a generational shift. The team averaged 29 years in age, with some players in their 30s, like Völler, who was 34, and Brehme and Buchwald, both 33. West Germany was joined in the knockout phase by Spain, who defeated Bolivia 3–1 thanks to a two-goal performance from midfielder José Luis Caminero. "I believe we could have played better," Spain manager Javier Clemente admitted, "but to qualify was the main objective."

Meanwhile, Argentina featured the return of Maradona to the World Cup. The four years leading up to USA '94 had been tough on the Argentine. Following his 15-month suspension, Maradona signed to play for Sevilla in Spain, then returned home with Newells Old Boys. Maradona's fitness certainly came into question if you consider that he'd only played in 60 club games in the four years between World Cups. Maradona, now 33 but svelte and fit again in time for the tournament, would make headlines.

In Argentina's opener on June 21 at Foxboro Stadium outside Boston against Group D opponent Greece, striker Gabriel Batistuta lived up to his scoring hype, netting a hat trick in a 4–0 victory. The most memorable goal, however, was scored by Maradona in the 60th minute. A precise finish from outside the box was highlighted by Maradona's goal celebration. It was a mix of happiness and rage. It was hard to tell. It certainly was a release for an athlete everyone thought was forever out of the game.

He ran toward the sideline camera, eyes bulging, in celebration as his teammates embraced him. The 55,000 in attendance gave him a standing ovation when he was subbed out in the 83rd minute.

The goal would not turn out to be the most memorable thing from Maradona's U.S. sojourn. Nine days later, FIFA announced that Maradona had once again failed a drug test. His international career was over for real this time, and he left his teammates in disgrace. Maradona tested positive for ephedrine, an anti-asthma stimulant that was banned by FIFA.

Given Maradona's fitness and weight struggles, London's *Daily Mail* reported, few doubted the test's validity. Nonetheless, Maradona spent the ensuing years offering up crazy excuses for why he tested positive for what FIFA described as "a cocktail of drugs." FIFA handed Maradona another 15-month ban. In an interview with Argentina's *El Trece* soon after the announcement, Maradona said, "They have retired me from soccer. I don't think I want another revenge. My soul is broken." In his autobiography, Maradona claimed the failed test was a result of someone giving him an energy drink, which unbeknownst to him contained ephedrine.

Many Argentines saw in Maradona's positive test a secret FIFA plan that sought to undermine their nation's chances of winning the World Cup. In a poll, the Argentine newspaper *Página 12* found that nearly 60 percent believed Maradona and the Argentine team had been the victims of a plot. Only 10 percent said they were angry at Maradona. The support for Maradona and the credence given to the conspiracy theory came mostly because Maradona, a frequent FIFA critic, had spoken against the midday kickoff times and the extreme heat players had to endure at the tournament. Maradona had also said that the World Cup draw for this tournament had been rigged, an insinuation never proven but one tossed about with regularity at nearly every FIFA tournament. If Maradona had been the hero at Mexico '86 and the villain at Italia '90, then USA '94 highlighted his disgraced status. Either way, he remains immortal.

The Albiceleste managed to amass six points after a 2–1 win over Nigeria, putting them in a three-way tie for first place with the Africans and Bulgaria. Nigeria won the group on goal differential, a validation of what the African teams could do at a World Cup after Cameroon's heroics four years earlier. Bulgaria, featuring the barrel-chested striker Hristo Stoichkov, advanced as the group's second-place team. Argentina placed third and also advanced.

Italy was coached by former AC Milan manager Arrigo Sacchi, who triggered loads of controversy despite his success at the club level. The controversy centered on his tactics and commitment to a zonal marking 4–4–2 formation. Zonal play is a type of style where the players are assigned a position on the field rather than a player. While this plays to the strengths of some players, it can be constraining to others who are more creative and want to freely roam the field.

At the same time, Sacchi never fully abandoned the *catenaccio* style that had become such a staple of the national team's identity and added a midfield press to it all. Critics argued that Sacchi's tactics amounted to a basketball-style deployment of players, where the long ball reigned supreme and individual flair was squashed.

New York, home to many Italian and Irish immigrants, hosted the group's opening match between the Azzurri and Ireland. Giants Stadium played host to the Group E encounter on June 18, and 73,000, mostly Irish fans, packed the venue. Ray Houghton's chip shot got over goalkeeper Gianluca Pagliuca after 11 minutes, ensuring that Irish eyes were smiling. Ireland's 1–0 win was revenge for the previous World Cup, when the Italians had eliminated them in the quarterfinals. The following day at RFK Stadium in Washington, DC, Norway played its first World Cup game since 1938, and Kjetil Rekdal's goal five minutes from time defeated Mexico.

Italy needed a win in their second game against Norway to keep their hopes of advancing alive. Sacchi remained under pressure, but optimists pointed out that the Italians were no strangers to slow starts. What they needed was one player to become the breakout star and lead the team to victory. That star was likely to be Baggio, winner of the Ballon d'Or in 1993 as Europe's best player. Baggio, it was widely believed, would channel Paolo Rossi and the 1982 team that got off to a slow start and later won the World Cup.

The Azzurri took the field on June 23 at Giants Stadium, and Italian fans made their voices heard in support. Italy had three clear chances at goal early on, but optimism turned to gloom when Pagliuca was red-carded after 21 minutes. Sacchi subbed in backup goalie Luca Marchegiani and took off Baggio, sacrificing his best player as part of a tactical tweak. The move was controversial. Baggio did not take kindly to the substitution and as he walked off the field could be heard saying, "Who, me? This guy is crazy."

"I did it to save him and to save the team," Sacchi told reporters. "He has some injuries. We needed ten players on the field who could run all the time."

Baggio had been hampered by a sore Achilles' tendon, but the move was seen as reckless by Sacchi critics and gutsy by those few who supported him. Italy's problems were compounded as the tense game wore on. Baresi had to leave the match with an injury a few minutes into the second half, while Maldini, the left fullback who took over the captain's role after Baggio's exit, was kicked hard by Jostein Flo midway through the second half. Italy was forced to play two men short for four minutes while Maldini got the ankle taped. Maldini did return, but Baresi would have to undergo knee surgery after the game. His World Cup appeared to be over.

Norway resorted to fouling and long balls to try and break up Italy's attack. In the 69th minute, it was Dino Baggio, a lanky midfielder and no relation to Roberto, who produced a moment of individual brilliance following a free kick from Giuseppe Signori along the left flank. Baggio's diving header pierced the net, a reward for the Azzurri's commitment to attack, after he outjumped three Norwegian defenders around him. Sacchi looked at his watch while his players rejoiced on the sidelines. The goal salvaged a 1–0 win, and the Italians were still in this thing. "Playing 70 minutes with only 10 men is very hard," Sacchi said. "We left our hearts on the field."

Meanwhile, the Mexicans, unfazed by the tropical temperatures in Orlando, defeated Ireland the following day at the Citrus Bowl. The 2–1 win came thanks to a Luis García brace, in the 44th and 66th minutes, as the Mexicans were better able to manage the heat while Ireland wilted under the sun. Charlton, back for a second World Cup at the helm of Ireland, was blunt in his post-match assessment. "Unfortunately, we weren't playing in Europe today," he told reporters. "We were playing in 100-degree temperature, somewhere down in South America. And it wasn't easy for us. But we accept that we lost the game." After two match days, Ireland, Italy, Norway, and Mexico had each amassed three points and scored the same number of goals as they had allowed. Which two teams, and possibly even a third, to emerge from this group would be determined on June 28.

Ireland closed the group with a scoreless draw against Norway. Meanwhile, Italy and Mexico could only muster a 1–1 draw in Washington, DC. All four teams finished tied at four points. The results meant that Mexico would finish first by virtue of having scored three goals. Ireland qualified as the second-place team as a result of their win against the Italians, who placed third.

Belgium, meanwhile, had an easier time in Group F. Like Argentina, Belgium—despite winning its first two games—finished third after being upset by Saudi Arabia 1–0 on June 29 at RFK Stadium in Washington, DC. The heat didn't help the Europeans, and neither did the little-known Saaed Al-Owairian. The Saudi striker, wearing the number 10 jersey, pulled a Maradona. He ran with the ball from his own half through a maze of Belgian players before depositing the ball past Preud'homme. "It was the best goal I ever scored in my life," Owairan said after the game. "I scored it for every Saudi person in the world—for every Arab."

The defeat, coupled by the Netherlands beating Morocco 2–1 at the same time in the 104-degree heat of Orlando that afternoon, plunged Belgium into third place. Saudi Arabia, coached by the Argentine-born manager Jorge Solari and one of the tournament's biggest surprises, qualified for the last 16 after finishing second on goal differential. Their exploits and flashy play earned the Saudis the nickname "the Brazilians of the desert." The Netherlands, led by striker Denis Bergkamp, won the group.

Round of 16

Germany and Belgium got the knockout stage started on July 2 in Chicago, a clash of European heavyweights. The game began with a moment of silence following Escobar's death. The sadness permeated throughout the stadium and the soccer world that day.

Völler rolled back the years in this one, scoring twice as the Germans looked rejuvenated, temporarily anyway, in a 3–2 victory. The rainy and cooler afternoon—temperatures reached just 77 degrees that afternoon—certainly helped. So did Völler's skill. "I was hoping that if my hour would come, I would be able to help," he said.

The game was not without an officiating controversy. In the 69th minute, Belgian striker Josip Weber ran toward a long pass from Georges Grün in the German penalty area. Marked closely by Thomas Helmer, Weber was bumped from behind by the German defender and slid to the ground. Swiss referee Kurt Röthlisberger did not award a penalty kick, setting off boos among many of the 60,000 fans inside Soldier Field and protests from the players.

"Everybody saw it in the stadium and millions of people saw it on television around the world," Belgian manager Paul Van Himst said after the game. "Personally, I think this kind of call is scandalous. I don't know what goes through a referee's head."

In the round's second game, Spain advanced against Switzerland 3–0 to reach the quarterfinals. The Swiss were determined, and the score was not reflective of their efforts. But Spain did dominate for much of the game, and a Fernando Hierro goal in the 15th minute paved the way for victory. Luis Enrique added a second in the 74th minute, and Txiki Begiristain converted a penalty kick four minutes from time to cap off the win.

On July 3, Sweden took on surprise side Saudi Arabia in Dallas. Martin Dahlin put the Swedes ahead after just six minutes, marking his fourth goal of the tournament. The towering striker Kennet Andersson added two goals in the second half as Sweden put together a 3–1 win.

While the final score was emphatic, Sweden suffered throughout much of the 90-degree afternoon. The Saudis brought their flair and were more fun to watch, but in soccer the team that can score goals wins. Sweden manager Tommy Svensson admitted afterward that he and his players had taken Saudi Arabia seriously, the main reason why they won the match. "We knew before the match that it was going to be a difficult task for us," he told reporters.

Argentina, without Maradona, hobbled into the round of 16, and it showed against Romania. Two quick goals by striker Ilie Dumitrescu and one more by Gheorghe Hagi, known as the "Maradona of the Carpathians," sealed the win for the Romanians. Hagi's hypnotic runs, ability to provide pinpoint passes, and creativity powered his side to a 3–2 victory. "This is the greatest moment in Romanian soccer," manager Anghel Iordănescu told reporters.

Maradona watched from the Rose Bowl stands as tears streamed down his cheeks. Argentina was eliminated. It would take another 20 years before the Albiceleste, so dominant in the late '80s and early '90s, would reach a World Cup final.

Maradona was forbidden by FIFA from attending the mixed zone where reporters can interview players, but he still found his way into the press box. "There's nothing that can justify this," he said of his team's defeat. "This isn't the team I left, the happy team, the knowing team. They sawed off our legs, not just mine, but of all Argentines. I feel terrible for all the Argentines who had such high hopes and I feel bad for the world's soccer fans because we had trained with all our hearts."

The Netherlands and Ireland waged battle on July 4 in the steam bath known as the Citrus Bowl. Temperatures in Orlando had been some of the harshest of any venue at this tournament, and both teams did their best to get past it. The teams were pretty evenly matched, but a series of defensive blunders by the Ireland defense and Bonner in goal meant the Dutch emerged victorious. The Dutch goals came from Bergkamp in the 11th minute and midfielder Wim Jonk in the 41st minute to grab the win.

The day's second round-of-16 game featured the United States against Brazil. Independence Day was the backdrop for the match as patriotic fervor took over at Stanford Stadium. Indeed, in California and throughout the country, interest in soccer had grown. That afternoon, 84,000 covered in red, white, and blue were there to cheer on the Americans, although a healthy dose of yellow and green could be seen in the seats cheering on the Brazilians. On the eve of the match, Parreira tried to temper expectations, despite being heavy favorites in this match and to win the whole thing. "No, we are not the favorites. The favorites are the Italians, the Germans, the Argentinians, Holland," he told reporters. "We are not considered in this position. We were favorites in the last five World Cups. Where did we finish? Nowhere. So we are not favorites."

The Americans gained a one-man advantage in the 43rd minute in the worst possible way when Leonardo's bone-crunching elbow connected with Ramos's face. The U.S. midfielder went down like a prizefighter, knocked to the ground, while Leonardo was immediately shown a red card. Leonardo visited Ramos in the hospital two days later to apologize for what he said was an accident. "He was holding my arm and my natural reaction was to shake him off," the Brazilian told the *Washington Post* after the visit. "Unfortunately, he was falling and I hit him in the face. I know it looked bad on the television but it wasn't intentional."

Brazil pressured the U.S. goal the entire game until Bebeto, off a sensational pass from Romário, managed to score in the 72nd minute. Bebeto's goal, the only one of the game, ensured Brazil's passage to the quarterfinals. Milutinović and his players received loud cheers as they walked off the field. The Americans had put on too much of a defensive display against Brazil, but criticisms were largely muted by praise. Milutinović had pulled off another miracle. The team helped trigger the passion of American sports fans and, for the first time, the United States appeared to be a soccer-loving nation, too. American players won global respect. Lalas, for example, originally a long shot to make the U.S. team, signed with Padova in Serie A, becoming the first American in nearly 60 years to play in Italy. The team's legacy lives on to this day.

The following day, Italy, no room for error following a mediocre group stage, faced Nigeria in Boston. In attack, Baggio, Signori, and Daniele Massaro were tasked with spearheading what had been a poor attack. Italy stayed true to tradition, making their fans suffer while getting a goal in that decisive moment.

Before the Azzurri could do that, they went down after 27 minutes when Emmanuel Amunike scored. It looked as if that goal would get the Nigerians to the quarterfinals. Instead, Baggio spoiled it all for Nigeria. Channeling Rossi from 12 years earlier, the player nicknamed "the divine ponytail" found the back of the net two minutes from time. That last-gasp effort pushed the game into extra time, and the Nigerians were left deflated.

The Italians, down a player after second-half sub Gianfranco Zola was inexplicably sent off for what looked like a mundane foul, had spent much of the second half feverishly trying to tie the score. Baggio's talent and class—finally, some would have said—came through at the right time. He added a second goal, on a penalty kick in the 102nd minute, and the draining afternoon came to a glorious end for the Italians. "The World Cup begins now," Baggio told reporters after the game, "not just for me, but for Italy."

The Nigerians had given everyone some mesmerizing moments. Likewise, Bulgaria would do the same some three hours later and 215 miles south in New York. After a thrilling 1–1 draw that could not be broken after 120 minutes of action, Bulgaria and Mexico went to a penalty-kick shootout at Giants Stadium. It was the first match at this World Cup decided by spot kicks, and Mexican goalie Jorge Campos, famous for his fluorescent-colored shirts, and his Bulgarian counterpart Borislav Mikhailov, definitely felt the pressure of the moment on them. The 70,000 in the building rose to their feet. "It was actually our intention after the regular time ended 1–1 to play for a draw and then play for penalty kicks," Bulgaria's manager Dimitar Penev admitted to reporters after the game. "It worked out very well for us."

It did. Bulgaria buried three of their kicks past Campos, while Mexico failed three. Bulgaria won the shootout 3–1. Bulgaria, a first-time World Cup quarterfinalist, was still alive despite the victory not being a pretty win. The Bulgarians, who celebrated in the dressing room, didn't seem to mind. "I'm glad we won the game," Stoichkov told reporters. "It really doesn't matter how."

Quarterfinals

Italy and Spain opened the quarterfinal round on July 9 at Foxboro Stadium, two of seven European teams left in the tournament. The lone representative from outside Europe was Brazil, who would play the Netherlands in Dallas.

Italy got Pagliuca back after serving his two-game suspension, while Sacchi sat out Signori in favor of Antonio Conte, an extra midfielder. Six of Sacchi's starters were AC Milan players he had coached a few years earlier. The game marked the first time in 60 years that Italy and Spain would meet at a World Cup.

Spain fielded Caminero in the midfield and Luis Enrique up front. The mostly Italian crowd in Boston cheered as Dino Baggio opened the scoring, unleashing a shot from 25 yards out that found the back of the net. But the crowd awaited greatness from the other Baggio. A controversial figure among some Italians because of his lukewarm start to this tournament and for being a practicing Buddhist, love for Baggio had grown following his heroics against Nigeria.

The Italians used the wings to move the ball upfield for much of the first half, but Spain's well-organized defense and gritty midfield play broke up the Italian counterattack. In fact, it was Spain, not Baggio, who scored when Caminero tied it for Spain in the 59th minute. His shot from 15 yards away beat Pagliuca. The Italians, exhausted following the marathon match against Nigeria, closed themselves in defense as La Roja were on the front foot and continued to dominate possession.

The game was reminiscent of that 1934 encounter. Referee Sándor Puhl of Hungary, one of the most talented match officials at the time, missed one of the biggest plays when Italy defender Mauro Tassotti elbowed Luis Enrique in the face during the game's waning minutes. The foul busted the Spanish player's nose open, and blood was all over his white jersey. Tassotti was not punished for the foul during the game, but FIFA later handed him an eight-match suspension and he would miss the remainder of the tournament. Tassotti would never again play for Italy. "It's now been many years since that incident," the Spanish forward-turned-coach recalled. "I think my nose looks better as a result. I have spoken with Mauro Tassotti three or four times over the years. He is a good and honest person."

Spain could have won the game seven minutes from time after threatening the Italian goal several times when Julio Salinas found himself face-to-face with Pagliuca, but the Italian goalie blocked the shot with his legs. Baggio, often marked by as many as three defenders, struggled to get enough touches on the ball. With two minutes left to play, Signori got the ball on the left flank and put through a pass to Baggio. The Italian latched onto the ball, beat goalkeeper Andoni Zubizarreta, and unleashed a shot from the right side that went into the goal from an unbelievably tight angle.

Baggio blew kisses at the crowd, and the Italians advanced in dramatic fashion. "We were all exhausted physically. We had come off the Nigeria game and the temperature was unbearable," Baggio recalled in a 2021 interview with Netflix Italia. "Few can imagine how brutal it was."

The day's second match between Brazil and the Netherlands had fewer fireworks, but did feature more goals. After a scoreless first half, the game in Dallas featured the best second half at this tournament as five goals were scored in 45 minutes. The Brazilians, in full samba soccer mode, played with abandon. The Oranje kept up the best they could, but it was the Brazilians who ultimately reached the semifinals for the first time since 1978.

The Brazilians scored the winning goal in the 81st minute, breaking the 2–2 deadlock. The goal was scored when Branco's curving shot beat the Dutch wall and goalkeeper Ed de Goey to his right for the game winner. "It was without a doubt the best game of the World Cup and without a doubt one of the most dramatic," Brazil manager Parreira told reporters after the game.

The following day in New York, an equally dramatic, and more shocking, result transpired when Bulgaria scored two second-half goals—one from Stoichkov in the 75th minute and another by Yordan Letchkov three minutes later—to defeat Germany 2–1. The defending champions had been eliminated. Bulgaria, the Cinderella team at this tournament, had gained little notice at the start of USA '94. But Stoichkov's power and talent helped transform the team into a contender. "We've played other favorites before, and won," Letchkov told the *New York Times*. "We like the role of outsider."

The final quarterfinal between Sweden and Romania in Stanford later that afternoon also featured plenty of goals. The game, tied 2–2 following extra time, went to a shootout. So even were the teams that even the five-kick shootout went to sudden death. Tied at four, Henrik Larsson made it 5–4, putting the ball into the lower right corner. Miodrag Belodedici's subsequent kick was saved by Thomas Ravelli to send Sweden to the World Cup semifinals for the first time since 1958. "Ravelli was excellent during the game," Svensson observed afterward when asked by reporters for his impression of the game. "He was the key to our success during the penalty kicks."

Semifinals

Baggio, at the top of his game, came through again against Bulgaria in the first semifinal, played on July 13 at Giants Stadium. It turned out to be Italy's easiest game as Baggio effortlessly tore apart the Bulgarian defense with a pace not seen before at this tournament. The Italians were on the front foot from the start. Baggio powered Italy into the lead after 20 minutes, then added a second goal five minutes later. Stoichkov was able to pull one back on a penalty kick just at the stroke of halftime for his sixth goal of the competition. The Bulgarian and Salenko would finish tied for the honor of tournament top scorer.

The Italians clung on for the 2–1 win. Baggio hobbled off the field a hero.

Three hours later at the Rose Bowl, Brazil had a tougher time against Sweden in the second semifinal. The sides knew each other well after playing each other to a draw three weeks earlier during group play. The Swedes kept Romário and Bebeto from getting the ball for most of the game, but as the game wore on it was the Brazilians who remained relentless in their pursuit of a victory. Were the Brazilians nervous? Not a chance, according to Romário.

"You have to ignore it," he said of the fans. "The people of Brazil take football very, very seriously. They love the game and the Brazilian team."

In the 80th minute, it was Romário who was finally able to score to give Brazil the 1–0 win and a place in the final against Italy. Three days later, Sweden captured third place with a 4–0 win against Bulgaria.

Final: Brazil vs. Italy

The World Cup's finale was a dream matchup between soccer royalty. Brazil versus Italy, two nations that at that point in time had each won three World Cups apiece, was a rematch of the 1970 final. The winner of the July 17 contest at the Rose Bowl in Pasadena would make history and win the title for a fourth time.

The game also pitted Baggio against Romário in an all-out duel over who was the world's best player. The Azzurri, however, had an issue. Baggio had pulled a hamstring in his left leg in the Bulgaria match and was at risk of missing the game. "There is no status as to the certainty of whether I will play the final," a resigned Baggio told reporters at a news conference following the semifinal. "I am very happy for Italy. I hope I gave people plenty of joy."

Zola, who was coming off a red-card suspension, was set to replace Baggio after team doctors would only say that his chances of appearing in the final were 50 percent. In the end, Baggio would start and play the entire game. Sacchi had fielded six different lineups during the course of six games, forced to deal with injuries and red cards on a scale never before endured by a World Cup finalist. Injuries were not an issue for Brazil, but they did face in Italy their toughest opponent at this tournament.

The Rose Bowl was abuzz with 94,000 spectators. What they witnessed was a stalemate. The rhythm was bland for long stretches, and one had to wonder whether the fatigue of the month-long competition had gotten to the players. The Brazilians came closest to scoring in the 76th minute when Pagliuca nearly committed a blunder, bobbling a shot by Mauro Silva that bounced toward the goal. Instead, the ball softly rolled off the post. Pagliuca grabbed the rebound, kissed his hand, and then thanked the post by patting it.

Baresi had miraculously returned to the lineup, making a recovery three weeks after undergoing arthroscopic knee surgery. The AC Milan sweeper was everywhere on the field, foiling several Brazilian attempts. The game ended scoreless, and 30 minutes of extra time failed to produce a winner. Baggio had come close, rifling a shot that Taffarel tipped up and over the crossbar. Romário had a clear chance of his own, but his attempt just a few yards away from the goal barely missed finding its way into the net.

For the first time in World Cup history, a final would be decided via a shootout. Baresi went first, but his shot went high over the crossbar.

Pagliuca made up for the missed kick with a diving save on Brazil's Márcio Santos. Demetrio Albertini and Romário connected on their kicks, as did Alberico Evani and Branco. Then came the mistakes that allowed Brazil to win the cup. Massaro's kick was saved by Brazil's Taffarel. Dunga gave Brazil a 3–2 lead, meaning Baggio's attempt would be decisive. Score and take the shootout to sudden death. A miss would crown Brazil champions.

Baggio ran to the ball with the dreams of an entire nation resting on his shoulders. But his kick sailed high over the bar and into the bright blue sky. Taffarel dropped to the ground, pointing to the heavens in celebration. Baggio's late-game heroics had come to an end. Brazil claimed its fourth title to the delight of Brazilians everywhere.

Donadoni, a member of the team that had lost to Argentina four years earlier in a shootout, was stoic in defeat. "I don't look back at Italia '90 or USA '94 with any disappointment," he said. "You only get one, maybe two, chances in a lifetime to play for a World Cup."

Romário, cloaked in a Brazilian flag, was all smiles as he and his teammates posed with the World Cup trophy. "Winning the World Cup is everything for a player," he recalled. "It means you can say that you are the best in the world."

1998 WORLD CUP

The tournament returned to Europe in 1998. France was chosen over Morocco in 1992 to host the tournament. It would last 32 days, longer than any previous World Cup, and the field was expanded from 24 to 32 teams. It was also the second time in history that France would play host.

The 1998 World Cup would produce a worthy show for such a major event. Games were played in 10 cities, with the Stade de France in Saint-Denis, located outside Paris, as the tournament's centerpiece. The venue was met with controversy, but in the end—and $430 million later—it became the pride of France. The Stade de France would host nine matches—including the final—followed by the Parc des Princes in Paris, which hosted six games. The other cities to host matches were Marseille, Lyon, Lens, Nantes, Toulouse, Bordeaux, Montpellier, and Saint-Étienne.

The tournament also featured some innovations. For the first time, fourth officials on the sidelines used electronic boards, instead of plastic signs, to denote a substitution and stoppage time. On the field, teams could make three substitutions during a game, rather than two, and the introduction of the golden goal was put into place. Under the rule, extra time would end once a team scored a goal. The use of sudden-death over-time, which added a layer of excitement to the knockout rounds, would come to an end at the 2002 World Cup.

Croatia, Jamaica, Japan, and South Africa all made their first-ever appearances at the finals. England was back after missing out on USA '94, and it marked the first World Cup where Maradona did not suit up for Argentina since 1982. The draw featured eight seeded teams: France, defending champions Brazil, Argentina, Germany, Italy, Romania, Spain, and the Netherlands. The following eight groups emerged from the draw:

Group A: Brazil, Scotland, Norway, and Morocco

Group B: Italy, Austria, Chile, and Cameroon

Group C: France, Denmark, Saudi Arabia, and South Africa

Group D: Spain, Bulgaria, Paraguay, and Nigeria

Group E: The Netherlands, Belgium, Mexico, and South Korea

Group F: Germany, Yugoslavia, the United States, and Iran

Group G: Romania, England, Colombia, and Tunisia

Group H: Argentina, Croatia, Japan, and Jamaica

After expanding to 32 teams, each group could only send its top two teams to the knockout stage. That made Group D, led by Spain, that much more competitive. Nigeria and Bulgaria, the darlings four years earlier, were back, while Paraguay would end up being one of the most underestimated teams to ever enter a tournament. The South Americans were back at the World Cup for the first time since 1986.

Platini, the player-turned-executive who was also years later accused of corruption as a FIFA executive committee member, admitted to helping rig the draw in France's favor. In an interview with *France Bleu Sport*, Platini said they made sure Brazil and France would end up in Group A and C, respectively, so that if they both finished first, they wouldn't be able to meet until the final. "We did a bit of trickery when we were organizing the schedule," he said. "We did not spend six years organizing the World Cup to not do some little shenanigans. Do you think other World Cup hosts did not?"

Brazil came to France with its usual mix of veterans and rising stars. One of those youngsters was 21-year-old striker Ronaldo. The Inter Milan star, an unused sub at USA '94, finally got his chance to shine in front of billions. He had dazzled crowds in his native Brazil and subsequently in Italy, where he'd already earned the nickname O Fenômeno ("The Phenomenon"). While an injured Romário was forced to watch the tournament on TV back in Brazil, it was now left up to Ronaldo to pick up where the Brazilian great had left off four years earlier.

Ronaldo had signed with Inter in 1997, luring him away from Barcelona. Ronaldo would go on to influence a generation of Brazilian strikers. He was named FIFA Player of the Year three times and awarded the Ballon d'Or twice. He had been born in Rio and discovered by former Brazilian star Jairzinho, who was coaching São Cristóvão. He played for them starting at age 13 before signing his first big contract four years later with Cruzeiro. To this day, São Cristóvão's concrete stadium features a large painted sign in black that reads: "Aqui Nasceu O Fenômeno." It translates to, "Here Was Born the Phenomenon." The stadium is today named for Ronaldo.

The English may have invented soccer, but the Brazilians reinvented it during the span of decades. If the 1994 team had been more pragmatic and cynical, this team—with its mesmerizing step-overs and fancy footwork that bamboozled defenders—made for some delightful football.

Brazil was coached once again by Zagallo. He had won the tournament twice as a player and managed the great Brazil side that had won it all in 1970. Zagallo had earned the nickname "the little ant" because of his hard work.

Group Stage

The tournament kicked off with the Brazilians recording a hard-fought 2–1 win against fellow Group A side Scotland on June 10 before 80,000 spectators at the Stade de France. Brazil followed up that victory with an emphatic 3–0 win over Morocco six days later at Stade de la Beaujoire in Nantes. Norway, who would finish second in the group to advance to the round of 16, stunned the Brazilians on June 23 in Marseille when Kjetil Rekdal converted a penalty kick in the 88th minute for the unexpected 2–1 win.

Runners-up four years earlier, Italy were favorites to win Group B, but they were barely able to salvage a 2–2 draw against Chile in the group opener on June 11 at Parc Lescure in Bordeaux. The Azzurri got the draw via a Baggio penalty kick in the 85th minute. His kick, in part, exorcised the ghosts that had haunted him since the '94 final. The Italians played better in their next two matches, blanking Cameroon, 3–0, on June 17 at the Stade de la Mosson in Montpellier, and edging Austria, 2–1, six days later in Saint-Denis to finish first in the group ahead of Chile.

Chile, meanwhile, finished second to also advance to the round of 16. The South Americans, playing in their first World Cup since 1982, managed two more draws following the point gained against Italy: 1–1 against Austria on June 17 in Saint-Étienne, followed by another 1–1 draw six days later versus Cameroon. It marked the first time since they had hosted the tournament in 1962 that Chile advanced past the group stage.

France returned to the World Cup as hosts after missing out on both the 1990 and 1994 editions. The 12-year absence did little to hamper their efforts. As hosts, they were considered among the favorites, and a relatively easy group helped pave the way for Les Bleus. The French opened Group C by trouncing South Africa 3–0 on June 12 at the Stade Vélodrome in Marseille. Six days later, the French continued their scoring ways, defeating Saudi Arabia, coached by Parreira, 4–0 at the Stade de France. Thierry Henry scored twice, adding to the goal he had scored against South Africa, and the team, managed by Aimé Jacquet, were off to a flying start.

That strong start was masked by Zinedine Zidane's red card. The French star, the team's playmaker and arguably the most talented player the country had produced since Platini, was ejected in the 70th minute of the Saudi Arabia match after he appeared to purposely dig his cleats into Saudi midfielder Fuad Amin's leg. Jacquet, meeting with reporters after the game, admitted, "You can't let a gesture like that go unpunished." FIFA handed Zidane a two-match ban.

FIFA had been trying for years to eradicate hard tackles, and Zidane's ejection proved that even a superstar wasn't immune from punishment. Nonetheless, the two victories unleashed excitement around the national team in a way never seen before. In a country where soccer was played and watched primarily by the lower socioeconomic classes (upper-crust French society always preferred golf and tennis), the entire nation was cheering for Les Bleus. For the first time, even the French newspapers highlighted soccer over the Tour de France, the famous bicycle race that takes place across the country each June.

France, already through to the knockout stage, closed the group in first place on June 24 with a 2–1 win against Denmark at the Stade de Gerland in Lyon. Emmanuel Petit's goal in the 56th minute proved to be the winning goal. The Danes, nonetheless, finished second to also make it through to the round of 16.

Spain were the favorites to win Group D, but recent history had not been kind to them. La Roja were a proud soccer nation and featured clubs like Real Madrid and Barcelona who routinely dominated European club competition. Nonetheless, that chemistry and talent never worked at the national team level. This time, it was again left up to Clemente to find that successful formula. Twelve of the team's 22 players hailed from either Real or Barca, but again that mattered little.

In its opener on June 13, Spain started the game against Nigeria in good position to win the game. By the time the final whistle blew, it was the Africans who had come out on top. Nigeria's 3–2 win was aided by a late surge in what had been a back-and-forth affair. Down 2–1, the Nigerians roared back with two unanswered goals. The winning goal came in the 78th minute when Sunday Oliseh's slicing right-footed shot found the left corner past Andoni Zubizarreta.

Spain should not have been surprised. Their own futility aside, this was the tournament's "Group of Death," and therefore any of the four teams could advance. Nigeria, coached by Milutinović, was the strongest team from Africa. Nigeria had won the Olympic gold medal two years earlier, and many of their young players had gained valuable experience at that tournament. "I am so happy for the people of Nigeria," Milutinović told reporters afterward while wearing a white tribal robe at the news conference. "They fought all the way against a very tough team."

Spain would manage to play Paraguay to a scoreless draw a week later in Saint-Étienne, then rout Bulgaria 6–1 in Lens on the final match day. But even that cathartic explosion of goals could do little to see them through as Spain finished third. Paraguay, meanwhile, defeated Nigeria 3–1. The South Americans were led by goalkeeper José Luis Chilavert, who followed in the tradition of playing the ball outside the box and often taking free kicks and penalties. The win was good enough for Paraguay to advance as the group's second-place team. Nigeria, who had already clinched a spot in the next round, finished first, and Milutinović's reputation as a miracle worker remained untarnished.

The Netherlands were a lot like Spain in that they were perennial favorites who faltered when it mattered most. The Dutch came into France '98 with a very good squad, highlighted once again by Bergkamp. Despite his ability to score, Bergkamp came up empty in the first Group E game on June 13 against Belgium at the Stade de France. He returned in the second half after being out for six weeks with a hamstring injury. With nine minutes remaining, Patrick Kluivert was shoved by Belgian defender Lorenzo Staelens, then wagged his finger and gave Staelens a jab to the chest with his elbow. Staelens fell to the ground, and Kluivert was red-carded. The game ended 0–0. Mexico, meanwhile, had gotten the better of South Korea 3–1 earlier that day in Lyon to temporarily go to the top of the group.

The Dutch blanked South Korea 5–0 a week later in Marseilles, eliminating the Asians. Bergkamp recorded a goal to get his scoring touch back. Mexico tied Belgium 2–2 in Bordeaux, setting up a final match day with three teams playing for the top two positions in the standings.

The June 25 match in Saint-Étienne between the Netherlands and Mexico turned out to be the most entertaining of the group. The Oranje took the lead after just four minutes with Phillip Cocu, then doubled it with Ronald de Boer in the 18th minute. Mexico mounted a comeback late in the second half, pulling one back in the 75th minute with Ricardo Peláez. It was a Luis Hernández goal in the fifth minute of stoppage time to make it 2–2. At the same time, Belgium, who tied South Korea 1–1 at the Parc des Princes in Paris, finished third after recording three draws.

The draw helped both the Dutch and Mexicans advance. The Netherlands finished first thanks to goal differential, but it was the Mexicans and their never-say-die attitude that got the most attention. "This team has a lot of character to come back in the second half," Hernández told reporters. "From a young age, we all develop a winning attitude. It is in our blood."

Germany headlined Group F, but the return of Yugoslavia, which included players from Serbia and Montenegro, allowed for the war-torn nation to resume its place among the game's top teams. The fraught geopolitics of this group didn't end there with the inclusion of the United States and Iran.

It was the Yugoslavs who opened Group F on June 14 with a 1–0 win against Iran in Saint-Étienne. Iran deserved more, but it was a swerving, 30-yard free kick by Siniša Mihajlović in the 72nd minute that won Yugoslavia the match. The following day, Germany cruised past the United States 2–0 at the Parc des Princes in Paris. The Americans, coached by Milutinović's assistant Steve Sampson, had never won a World Cup game on European soil. The results at this World Cup would only further cement that statistical reality. With MLS still in its infancy, Sampson put French-born defender David Regis on the roster. He'd been naturalized a citizen just weeks before the tournament by virtue of his American wife. Roy Wegerle, a native of South Africa, became a citizen because he, too, was married to an American, while Preki Radosavljević, born in Yugoslavia but becoming a U.S. citizen in 1996 after playing for nearly a decade in the United States, had also been named to the team.

Six days later, Germany and Yugoslavia played to a thrilling 2–2 draw in Lens. It was the match that evening in Lyon between the United States and Iran that drew the most attention, and not for soccer purposes. In 2014, *FourFourTwo* magazine referred to it as "the most politically charged game in World Cup history." Since the overthrow of the pro-Western Shah of Iran, Mohammad Reza Pahlavi, in the 1979 Iranian Revolution and the attack on the American embassy in Iran, the two nations had engaged in hostile relations. The U.S. support of Iraq during the Iran–Iraq War had only further inflamed the situation.

In a pre-match ceremony, the Iranian players gave the Americans white roses as a symbol of peace, and the teams posed together for photos. The game had been a chance to make amends with "the Great Satan," the name used by the Iranian regime to refer to the United States. On the field, the Iranians outplayed the Americans, winning 2–1 and knocking Sampson's team out of the World Cup. FIFA knew the game was a high security risk, and French police made sure to quash any protesters bent on disrupting the game in front of a worldwide audience. The match went off without incident, except for a peaceful protest against Iran's Islamic regime. Several thousand Iranian expatriates living in France smuggled shirts and banners into the Stade de Gerland displaying a photo of Massoud Rajavi, head of an opposition group called the National Council of Resistance. French police in riot gear tried on several occasions to take away the banners, but the fans kept displaying new ones. If only the American players had been so persistent on the field.

Germany went through to the knockout stage after putting together a 2–0 win against Iran on June 25 at the Stade de la Mosson in Montpellier. Yugoslavia, at the same time in Nantes, defeated the United States 1–0 to also advance. Germany and Yugoslavia finished even on points, but Die Mannschaft went through as the first-place team thanks to better goal differential.

England were back at the World Cup after missing out on USA '94, while Romania were looking to better their quarterfinal appearance four years earlier. The inclusion of Colombia didn't make this group any easier for England, but the South Americans would again prove underwhelming.

French police had their hands full in Marseilles as England fans set off two days of violence leading up to the Group G clash on June 15 between the Three Lions and Tunisia. Dozens were injured in clashes on the streets, while inside the Stade Vélodrome it was England who won, 2–0. Two hours later in Lyon, Romania defeated Colombia 1–0 on a goal by Adrian Ilie in the dying seconds of the first half.

The attention may have been on England and its star players like midfielder David Beckham and striker Alan Shearer, but it was Romania who was the first to clinch a spot in the last 16 in Toulouse. With police on high alert outside the Stade de Toulouse, Romania's Dan Petrescu found the back of the net in the 90th minute against England. His left-footed shot went through goalkeeper David Seaman's legs for the 2–1 win.

After Romania won the group following a 1–1 draw against Tunisia on June 26 in Lens, England found a way to advance as well that day by posting a 2–0 victory versus Colombia. The team played with a flair not seen before at the tournament as England manager Glenn Hoddle inserted 18-year-old striker Michael Owen into the lineup. Beckham and fellow midfielder Darren Anderton constantly created space on the right flank. England's opening goal came after 20 minutes when Beckham's cross was cleared by the Colombia backline. The ball found Anderton, who blasted a shot into the top right-hand corner of the net.

Nine minutes later, Beckham scored a goal of his own. After England midfielder Paul Ince was brought down 30 yards from goal, Beckham took the kick and curled the shot over the Colombian wall and past goalkeeper Faryd Mondragon. The win was a good omen for England as they prepared for the knockout round.

Argentina entered a new era post-Maradona. The star's propensity to self-destruct no longer an issue for the Albiceleste, the team could focus on the task at hand. Ariel Ortega, a technically gifted midfielder, was given the number 10 jersey. He would be the first of many Argentines to wear that number and be heralded as the next Maradona. None of them would ever live up to that billing.

Argentina had Batistuta spearheading the attack, and it was his goal against Japan after 28 minutes in Toulouse on June 14 that allowed the Albiceleste to open Group H with a victory. Croatia, however, would be the team who would end up getting the most positive attention at this tournament. After breaking away from Yugoslavia and being recognized by FIFA as an independent nation in 1991, Croatia, wearing their red-and-white checkerboard jerseys, was playing in its first World Cup. A 3–1 win against Jamaica, nicknamed the Reggae Boyz, got them a valuable three points. Led by Robert Prosinečki, Croatia's roster had been built around many players who had played for Yugoslavia at Italia '90. Many of them now featured for some of Europe's biggest clubs, including midfielder Zvonimir Boban at AC Milan and striker Davor Šuker at Real Madrid.

Argentina earned a 5–0 win against Jamaica a week later at the Parc des Princes in Paris as Batistuta recorded a hat trick. It was a stunning offensive display, albeit against a weaker side, but it was a morale booster for a team looking to reach the final. The Albiceleste won the group on June 26, defeating Croatia 1–0 in Bordeaux.

Croatia finished second to also advance to the last 16. It was a wonderful finish for them after reaching the quarterfinals of the European Championship just two years earlier. "I'm full of energy and my optimism is as hard as a granite," manager Miroslav Blažević had told the Associated Press on the eve of the World Cup. "Croatia boasts a class like few other nations." His words would turn out to be prophetic.

Round of 16

The round of 16 featured ten European teams, four from South America, and one apiece from North/Central America and Africa. Italy opened the round of 16 with a win against Norway on June 27 in Marseilles. Norway, a team that had been riding a 17-game unbeaten streak that included a victory over Brazil in the previous round, lost 1–0. Christian Vieri scored his fifth goal of the tournament, and the Azzurri stymied Norway's long-ball attacks throughout the second half. Vieri's goal came after 18 minutes on the counterattack. Luigi Di Biagio sent a long ball to Vieri, who outran defender Dan Eggen to drive a right-footed shot past goalkeeper Frode Grodas. Italy's barrel-chested defender Fabio Cannavaro kept close guard on striker Tore André Flo, sticking to him each time he went for a high ball. Pagliuca made a spectacular diving save on Flo's close-range header in the 71st minute to preserve the win.

Later that day, Brazil crushed Chile 4–1 at the Parc des Princes in Paris, leaving no doubt that the South Americans wanted to retain the title. Two goals from César Sampaio in the first half, the first in the 11th minute and a second 15 minutes later, paved the way for the win. Ronaldo, who spent much of the match roaming free and creating chances, scored a brace himself, the first on a penalty kick in the third minute of stoppage time at the end of the first half and another in the 72nd minute.

France's game against Paraguay on June 28 in Lens brought out a sea of blue, white, and red. France, without the suspended Zidane, had a tough time against Paraguay. The hosts came close to taking the lead after 16 minutes when Bernard Diomède's shot was batted away by Chilavert. France's best scoring chance came five minutes before halftime when Henry put up a nifty chip shot that sailed over the defense and out of reach of Chilavert, only to see the ball bounce off the post. Paraguay, on the other hand, created few scoring chances, resorting to rough tackles and time-wasting techniques. The move earned them jeers from the crowd of 38,000 flag-waving French fans.

The second half featured more of the same with the Paraguayans more than happy to push the game into extra time. They were successful. In the extra session, Les Bleus did their best to try to defeat Paraguay, but Zidane's absence showed. With penalty kicks looming, defender Laurent Blanc finished off Paraguay with a historical goal in the 114th minute. Blanc's golden goal, a volley from point-blank range, was so powerful that even Chilavert couldn't put a hand on it. The goal ended the match and put Blanc in the history books as the first player at a World Cup to score such a goal. "The goal rewarded the better team," Jacquet told reporters. "Often in matches like this, there is injustice at the end, but we got through because of our great defense."

That evening, the Nigerians also yearned to make history at the Stade de France, trying to become only the second African nation since Cameroon in 1990 to reach the quarterfinals. Standing in their way was Denmark. Danish striker Peter Moller wasted no time leaving his mark three minutes into the match, giving his team the lead after unleashing a shot from the top of the box. Moller also had a hand in Denmark's second goal nine minutes later, blasting a free kick from 25 yards out that forced goalkeeper Peter Rufai to block the ball with both hands. The ball rebounded back into play where Brian Laudrup was able to gain possession and score. Denmark led 2–0 at halftime.

Nigeria attempted a comeback in the second half, but Denmark held strong. Substitute Ebbe Sand scored Denmark's third goal in the 60th minute, less than a minute after he had come in for Moller. Rufai's inability to hold on to another shot resulted in a fourth Danish goal: Martin Jorgensen drilled a low shot in from the right that Rufai failed to grab in the 76th minute for the 4–0 lead. Nigeria attempted to claw its way back, but all they could do was score a goal with Tijani Babangida in the 78th minute. The Danes defeated Nigeria 4–1 and were off to the quarterfinals.

On June 29, Germany outclassed Mexico 2–1 in Montpellier with two goals in the final 15 minutes. Down 1–0 after Hernández put Mexico ahead in the 47th minute, the Germans staged a rally. Klinsmann tied the score in the 75th minute, but with temperatures hovering around 90 degrees, the Germans appeared sluggish, while the Mexicans, no strangers to such heat, controlled the pace. The Germans' never-say-die attitude helped them win the game when Oliver Bierhoff's perfect header from 12 yards out with four minutes left to play won them the match.

Later that day in a very humid Toulouse, the Netherlands defeated Yugoslavia 2–1 on Edgar Davids' stoppage-time goal in the 92nd minute. The goal was a fitting way for the gutsy midfielder to make amends with Dutch manager Guus Hiddink. Davids, who played at Juventus, had been recalled to the team following a two-year absence. He had originally been left off the roster after hurling insults at Hiddink following the Dutch's poor showing at the 1996 European Championship.

Croatia advanced on June 30 following a 1–0 win against Romania in Bordeaux thanks to Šuker's penalty-kick goal in the first half of stoppage time. The goal came off a disputed call by Argentine referee Javier Castrilli, who whistled a foul on midfielder Gabriel Popescu inside the box after his leg became tangled with that of Aljoša Asanović as both tried to chase the ball. Popescu protested, but there was no changing Castrilli's mind. Another bad call had determined the outcome of a World Cup game.

That evening, the showdown between old foes Argentina and England in Saint-Étienne was the most anticipated game of the round. The teams had not played each other at a World Cup since that infamous 1986 match. With the Falklands War a distant memory and Maradona not there to stir controversy, the game was free from the tumult some had expected in the days leading to kickoff. Both sides traded penalty shot goals, with Batistuta finding the back of the net after six minutes and Alan Shearer for England just four minutes later. The goal of the game—and possibly the entire tournament—was scored in the 16th minute when Owen embarked on a solo run, something reminiscent of Maradona's second goal against England 12 years earlier. Owen then slotted the ball past goalkeeper Carlos Roa for the 2–1 lead.

The Albiceleste didn't let the goal get them down, tying the score with Javier Zanetti in the first half of stoppage time. The half ended 2–2, but the fireworks continued once the match resumed. Beckham was red-carded by Danish referee Kim Milton Nielsen for kicking Diego Simeone. The Argentine exaggerated the foul by quickly falling to the ground. The game ended 2–2 following extra time. Once again, England faltered on penalties as Roa's save on David Batty's fifth kick gave Argentina the 4–3 win. Beckham had gone from hero to villain in just one game.

Quarterfinals

France returned to Saint-Denis to take on Italy on July 3 to open the quarterfinals. France saw the return of Zidane from suspension, a big plus for Les Bleus, while Italy hoped its defense could help them reach the semifinals for a third straight World Cup.

It became increasingly apparent to the French that their national team, a cultural mix of ethnicities, represented something that transcended sport. Looking back at the team a decade later, author Ian Buruma wrote in the *Globe and Mail*: "The multi-ethnic nature of the 1998 champion was widely touted as a mark not of a long and often bloody colonial past but of national superiority born from the tolerance of the French Enlightenment and the fraternity of the French Revolution."

"The World Cup was a defining moment for the country and for openly questioning who we were as French," said Lilian Thuram. "The team was made up of players of different colors and ethnicities and religions. We were united as a team, a symbol for the entire nation. Politicians embraced us, but it's easier on the soccer field to find equality and win. It's not so easy in society."

Thuram was one of seven Black players on the '98 squad. Prior to the 1960s, the French team did not integrate players from the former colonies of Guadeloupe, Martinique, and French Guiana. That changed, according to Laurent Dubois who authored the 2010 book *Soccer Empire: The World Cup and the Future of France*, in the 1980s when players like Trésor made an impact for the French at World Cup level. "For most of the twentieth century, football has been considered by many in the region to not only be a vehicle for individual success, but also an ideal tool for collective recognition."

Thuram, who had idolized Trésor as a child, had played with Italian club Parma since 1997 and eventually joined Juventus in 2001. Thuram was born in Guadeloupe, and his family relocated to France in 1981 when he was nine. His Paris home is decorated with photos from his playing days and posters of key figures in the fight against racism, most notably Nelson Mandela. Along with Blanc, Marcel Desailly, and Bixente Lizurazu, Thuram formed the backbone of the French defense. These days, Thuram isn't afraid to be political. "Racism isn't something we are born with," he said. "It's something people are taught. It is through politics that we can help change things and fight for equality."

Thuram's teammate Zidane was of Algerian descent, prompting the nickname "Black, Blanc, and Beur"—Black, White, and Arab—to replace the country's flag of blue, white, and red. It was in this spirit of cultural togetherness that France went into the Italy match.

The French did most of the attacking and the Italians the defending. Alessandro Del Piero started instead of Baggio, but Vieri seemed to lose his scoring touch seen in the group stage. Baggio came in for Del Piero midway through the second half, but that did little to change the situation. The game stretched into extra time and remained scoreless after 120 minutes of play. The Italians tried to reverse the curse of the shootout that had plagued them in the last two World Cups. The third time, however, would not be the charm. Goalkeeper Fabian Barthez's save on Italy's second kick by Demetrio Albertini was crucial as France scored its next three kicks. When Luigi Di Biagio's shot crashed against the crossbar, the crowd of 77,000 erupted into cheers. France won the shootout 4–3 to reach the semifinals. "'To lose three times on penalty kicks is a travesty," Baggio observed after the match.

Two hours later in Nantes, Rivaldo scored a brace as Brazil outlasted a fearless Denmark 3–2. At the outset, the Danes took the lead with Martin Jorgensen after just two minutes. The Brazilians reacted, and nine minutes later Ronaldo, in his new role as playmaker, fed the ball to Bebeto. The veteran unleashed a shot that found its way into the lower left corner to tie the score.

Ronaldo didn't stop there. He found Rivaldo in the 27th minute on the left side, and his chip shot over goalkeeper Peter Schmeichel made it 2–1. The Brazilians looked firmly in control for the first time that evening, but the game got nastier as the minutes wore on. Aldair brought down defender Thomas Helveg in the 37th minute, which drew a yellow card from Egyptian referee Gamal Ghandour. Two minutes later, Soren Colding was given a yellow card for fouling Roberto Carlos after slamming the Brazilian in the neck with his forearm.

The Danes exerted greater pressure on the Brazilian backline, which made for a riveting game. In the 50th minute, Roberto Carlos attempted to clear the ball from his own box with a bicycle kick. He missed the ball, which dropped to Laudrup's feet. The Danish striker was unforgiving, firing a shot into the net to make it 2–2. Brazil scored the game winner in the 61st minute when Rivaldo stole the ball in the midfield, ran up the left flank, and blasted a shot from 30 yards out that found the far corner of the net. Speaking to reporters after the game, Zagallo called it a "victory of power and will." It may have been that, but Brazil did not yet look like a team that could win the championship for a second straight time.

Argentina and the Netherlands faced off on July 4 in Marseilles. It was in the 88th minute that Ortega was red-carded for striking six-foot-six Dutch goalkeeper Edwin van der Sar in the jaw. With the teams now at 10 players each (Netherlands defender Arthur Numan had been tossed from the game in the 76th minute for a hard foul), Bergkamp was able to use the extra space to his advantage. Frank de Boer's 60-yard pass was controlled masterfully by the Dutch striker, who brought the ball down to his feet, played it around defender Roberto Ayala, and put a shot past

Roa in the 90th minute for the 2–1 win. The victory set up a semifinal date against Brazil.

"We were in trouble after Numan was sent off, but we were equalized in the number of players," Hiddink told reporters after the game. "All of a sudden, we got a tremendous play from Bergkamp."

The biggest upset of the tournament occurred that evening in Lyon when Croatia crushed Germany, 3–0. A red card made the difference in this game when German defender Christian Wörns was ejected five minutes from the end of the first half for a late tackle on Šuker. That allowed Robert Jarni to score, and the Croats never looked back.

Croatia put the finishing touches on the win with two late goals. Goran Vlaović scored in the 80th minute, and Šuker added another five minutes later to complete the rout. The Croatian players celebrated in the center circle after the final whistle as the majority of the 39,000 fans at the Stade de Gerland cheered them on. France now awaited Croatia in the semifinals.

"This is a historic victory. We are very happy," Croatia manager Miroslav Blažević said after the game. "A Croatian team has never achieved anything this important in soccer."

Semifinals

Marseilles hosted an epic clash on July 7 when Brazil and the Netherlands faced one another. Like many past semifinals, the teams that met were so evenly matched that 90 minutes and another 30 of extra time weren't enough to determine a winner. *New York Times* writer George Vecsey, who would cover eight World Cups in all for the newspaper, made the following observation at game's end: "The Brazilians won their fourth World Cup in 1994 when Taffarel stopped Italy after a dispassionate 0–0 tie in the mid-afternoon California heat, a brutal game time dictated by European television. Tonight's game, played at a civilized hour of 9 p.m., under a near full moon, with a breeze cooling a heat wave, was far superior to the 1994 finale. This was a run-and-shoot battle between the world's great soccer dynasty and the nation that is proud to be called the Brazil of Europe, strong praise for a nation that has never won a World Cup."

It was Brazil who had taken the lead with Ronaldo in the first minute of the second half. The Netherlands responded three minutes from time with Kluivert, the third straight that the Oranje had scored near the end of the match. A scoreless extra time brought with it penalty kicks. In the shootout, Taffarel emerged the hero when midfielder Phillip Cocu, saw his attempt saved. Dunga made his penalty, and Ronald de Boer, twin brother of the Dutch captain Frank, saw his kick smothered by the diving Taffarel to put Brazil in their second consecutive final.

The following evening in Saint-Denis, France tangled with Croatia as the 76,000 inside the Stade de France stood united in their support for Les Bleus. Šuker's goal in the 46th minute gave Croatia the lead after the striker took the ball on his left foot, let it bounce once, and drilled it at Barthez, who charged out of his net. Unfortunately for Barthez, he failed to stop the ball and it went in. The French defense, Lizurazu and Thuram, were out of position on the play. Then the unlikeliest of players stepped up and tied the game: Thuram, who had never scored in 37 appearances for France, tied the score just a minute later.

Jacquet had started Thuram in all 18 games Les Bleus had played between the 1996 European Championship and the World Cup finals. Thuram, one of the greatest defenders at the tournament, added the title of scorer to his resume and energized what had otherwise been a lethargic French side that evening. Thuram did it a second time in the 70th minute when he stole the ball from Jarni, then curled a left-footed shot for what turned out to be the winning goal.

France maintained the tempo until Blanc was shown a red card in the 74th minute following a push on Slaven Bilić that the Croat defender claimed had been a punch to the head. Thuram was placed on the shoulders of backup goalie Bernard Lama after the 2–1 victory and paraded around the field after the game as the crowd cheered wildly. "It was an excellent reward for all the effort he has put in," Jacquet said, referring to Thuram. "The mental discipline he was able to instill into this team is incredible."

Thuram insisted he was no hero that night. "I just scored two goals," he said. "It's 11 players on the team who helped France reach the finals."

Platini's dream final had been realized. The hosts, in their first World Cup final ever, would take on Brazil. Croatia, meanwhile, would take third place after one of the most impressive World Cup campaigns for a first-time finals by a European team since Portugal in 1966.

Final: France vs. Brazil

There were loud screams coming from Ronaldo's room. All of a sudden, his roommate Roberto Carlos ran out into the hallway at the team's hotel outside Paris demanding help.

"If anything, it got worse because, at about four o'clock, he started being sick," he said. "That's when I called the team doctor and told him to get over to our room as fast as he could."

It was the day of the World Cup final, and the Brazilian players had lunch that July 12 at the Chateau de Grande Romaine in Lésigny. After lunch, the players went back to their rooms, which they shared in pairs, ahead of the 9 p.m. kickoff. Ronaldo was with Roberto Carlos, adjacent to the room that had housed striker Edmundo and midfielder Doriva, two players who had seen limited playing time at the tournament.

It was then that Ronaldo started to have a seizure. His body suddenly went into convulsions, and the striker, his teeth clenched tightly, began foaming at the mouth. Roberto Carlos, in a state of panic, began to scream. He frantically started banging on doors seeking help.

"Ronaldo was scared about what lay ahead. The pressure had got to him and he couldn't stop crying," Roberto Carlos said.

Edmundo said he was shocked when he saw the state Ronaldo was in.

"When I saw what it was, I despaired because it was a really strong and shocking scene," he recalled.

Defender César Sampaio was the first person to help Ronaldo. He got to Ronaldo before the doctors did and, with Edmundo holding him still on the ground, put his hand in the striker's mouth to grab his tongue to prevent him from swallowing it.

Ronaldo, who was unconscious for four minutes, was then placed in his bed, where he fell asleep. Edmundo said team doctors decided that the best thing to do next was pretend nothing had happened once Ronaldo woke up from his nap.

"We went back to our rooms and we rested," Edmundo said. "But, you know what I mean, everyone was worried. My room was linked to his, so I saw everything. Every five minutes someone came and stared, and Ronaldo was there, sleeping like a baby."

In a 2014 interview with the BBC, Ronaldo said he has no memory of what happened that afternoon. He speculated that stress ahead of such a big game had possibly gotten to him.

"You cannot disconnect from the competition," said Ronaldo. "It's a lot of pressure."

Ronaldo woke up and was given some tea. Once subdued, Leonardo implored the team medics to tell Ronaldo what had happened. Ronaldo said team doctors "explained to him that he had had convulsions and that you will not play [the final]."

"I said no," Ronaldo recalled.

While the players boarded the bus for the Stade de France at 6 p.m. (minus the usual loud music that typically accompanied the team), Ronaldo was instead taken to the Lilas clinic in Paris. At the same time, Zagallo left Ronaldo out of the starting lineup, replacing him with Edmundo. Ronaldo was added to the list of bench players. The lineups were distributed to reporters inside the stadium, and Ronaldo's exclusion triggered head scratching and puzzled looks. No one outside the Brazilian camp knew of Ronaldo's sudden sickness. The French players thought it gamesmanship on the part of Zagallo to throw them off. There was also speculation that Ronaldo had an injured knee and that had been the reason for him being sidelined.

The Brazilian newspaper *Folha de S. Paulo* later reported that Ronaldo had suffered a nervous breakdown during the tournament. The newspaper said Ronaldo had shown signs of depression in the days leading up to the big game and had even thrown a bike against a wall.

Forty minutes before the game was scheduled to start, doctors gave Zagallo the all-clear following a battery of tests.

"There was no conclusion [to the tests]," Ronaldo said. "I was okay."

Ronaldo said he called Zagallo from the clinic after learning that Edmundo has taken his place.

"I said, 'Zagallo, please. I don't have nothing. I have to play. I went to the hospital. Everything is fine with me.'"

Lidio Toledo, the team doctor, stressed during an investigation conducted by the Brazilian parliament in 2000 the enormous pressure he was put under to let Ronaldo play.

"Imagine if I stopped him playing and Brazil lost," he said. "At that moment I'd have to go and live on the North Pole."

Some players said Toledo could be seen crying after Ronaldo's fit, but he denied it. He said Ronaldo had not lost consciousness. Instead, he said, Ronaldo was conscious and breathing heavily once he got to the player's room.

By now, crowds had filled the streets of Paris and streamed the stadium awaiting the biggest soccer match in the nation's history. As at so many World Cups, the final did not live up to its dramatic overture. It was Zidane, not Ronaldo, who was the star of the game. Corner kicks helped the French take a 2–0 lead. In the 27th minute, Zidane moved into position on a kick from the right by Emmanuel Petit, outjumping Leonardo and heading the ball into the goal. In first-half stoppage time, it was again Zidane who produced a nearly identical header against Taffarel for France's second goal.

Taffarel's exceptional reflexes, one-handed saves, and instant, attack-unleashing throw-outs were a nonfactor against France. Brazil's defense was in disarray, while France's organization and poise with the ball were rewarded in the end. Ronaldo was a nonfactor for much of the game as Brazil tried in vain to stage a recovery after Desailly was given a red card in the 68th minute after getting a second yellow for a foul on Cafu. Petit's last-minute goal on a breakaway sealed the 3–0 win and sparked celebrations along the Champs-Élysées. They were the biggest celebrations since the end of World War II.

France captain Didier Deschamps hoisted aloft the trophy as Platini, wearing a blue jersey under his sports jacket, celebrated alongside the team. The players and the entire nation, both overjoyed and in shock at the enormity of this upset, had done the unthinkable against the best team in the world. France's victory had larger cultural and societal implications, albeit for a temporary period of time, yet another example of the sport's power and grip on nations.

"We had to go through about everything in this competition," Jacquet said after the match. "But we were able to overcome those obstacles. I think it's in adversity and under pressure that France has shown it's such a great team. All those players wanted to see the French flag fluttering above us."

Zagallo admitted afterward that Brazil had suffered from Ronaldo "being unfit to play" and that their confidence had been sapped.

"It was a major psychological blow to our team," he said. "Everyone was very down."

Zagallo, in a sour mood after the game, was repeatedly interrupted by members of the Brazilian press as he tried to answer questions. At one point, Zagallo began shouting and waving his arms in the air before finally storming off.

The Brazil manager would be forced to endure hours of questioning during a subsequent probe, where many of the details surrounding Ronaldo's mystery ailment and what had taken place behind closed doors was made public.

"Faced with this reaction, I chose Ronaldo," Zagallo told investigators. "Now was it his being chosen that caused Brazil to lose? Absolutely not. I think it was the collective trauma, created by the atmosphere of what had happened."

The Brazil manager also said, "If you invert the situation and I didn't put Ronaldo on and then Brazil lost 3–0, people would have said, 'Zagallo is stubborn, he had to put him on, Ronaldo was the best player in the world.' So I think I would do the same again."

Edmundo, however, said it had been Nike—and not Zagallo—who made the call when it came to deciding whether Ronaldo should start. It's true that Nike had exerted enormous influence over the Brazilian team, even being allowed to arrange five friendly matches each year for the team—against relatively weaker nations—since they did not have to play qualifiers as a result of being defending champions heading into France '98. Nike's aim from the start was to sell Brazil jerseys around the world. A clause in the deal that had been kept secret (and was only made public following the parliamentary probe) had stipulated that at least eight first-team regulars had to start in such friendlies. The company's

$160 million deal at the time to sponsor the team had led to speculation that members of the Brazilian FA were no longer calling the shots when it came to the team.

"Nike's people were there 24 hours a day," Edmundo said. "It was as if they were members of the technical staff."

The writer Alex Bellos, in a 2001 article for the *Guardian*, noted: "In Brazil, Nike became a scapegoat for the defeat. When the team arrived back at Rio de Janeiro airport, they were met by a banner that summed up national feeling. A Brazilian flag had been modified so that in place of the slogan 'Order and Progress' was the word 'Nike.'"

The parliamentary inquiry, which centered on Nike's involvement, found no wrongdoing on the part of anyone. Only in Brazil could a lost final result in a political investigation.

Chapter Seven

A New Century

As a teenager growing up in the 1990s, there were a lot of players I admired. One of them was Eddie Pope. A gifted defender, Pope anchored the United States defense for nearly a decade, and his contributions were not always reflected in the box score.

Pope, who represented the United States at three World Cups, was elected to the U.S. National Soccer Hall of Fame in 2011, along with teammates Cobi Jones and Earnie Stewart. The class of 2011 marked the first time all those elected on the players' ballot were African Americans.

"There have definitely been some great African American players. It is important that they are recognized as well," Pope told me at the time. "I looked up to guys like Jimmy Banks and Desmond Armstrong. At the time, it was about just seeing them on TV and thinking that this is something that I can do too. It's hard to express just how important that visual is for African American kids."

Banks and Armstrong were the two African Americans on the 1990 World Cup team. For a then-16-year-old Pope, the lack of inclusiveness on that squad did not deter him from trying to make the team himself someday. By the time he was called up to the senior national team in 1996, Black players had become a regular presence in the lineup. Many Black players of Pope's generation had looked up to Pelé, but the integration of the U.S. team in the ensuing years certainly helped change perceptions.

"I think it has become easier for Black kids now to find role models on the soccer field," said DaMarcus Beasley, who played at four World

Cups. "Now there are many dark-skinned players other than Pelé that Black kids can look up to."

Pope, who played at the 1998, 2002, and 2006 World Cups, made the transition from college (he played at North Carolina) directly to Major League Soccer through the first MLS draft. Without that league, a legacy of USA '94, Pope would never have been able to develop as a player and perform on the sport's largest stage.

"Soccer in the U.S. is growing in general, and therefore it's growing amongst African Americans as well," said Pope. "Having said that, we can do more to get African American kids involved in the sport. I think that more is done for the Hispanic community simply because it's an easier sell."

Tony Sanneh, one of Pope's former U.S. teammates, echoed concerns that more should be done on the grassroots level to ensure that more Black kids play the game in the future. He said the goal of his charity, the Tony Sanneh Foundation, is to get more Black children involved in the game.

About a quarter of players identify as Black in Major League Soccer, hailing from 35 different countries. Seventy players from that list hold a U.S. passport.

"We try to get kids exposed to soccer as early as six and add support in the school system so they stay in it," Sanneh said. "I think the strength of MLS and our national team is that they are also great ways to increase visibility and market [the sport] to African Americans."

2002 WORLD CUP

The tournament entered the new millennium and into uncharted territory. In May 1996, FIFA decided for the first time that the World Cup be contested outside of the Americas and Europe after jointly awarding the competition to Japan and South Korea. The joint bid, also a first, meant that both nations received automatic spots to the finals. The cohosts made interesting bedfellows. At odds historically, Japan and South Korea would have to work together to overcome centuries of tension if they wanted to pull off a great tournament.

At first, South Korea and Japan had been competitors in a bitter bidding war. At FIFA's urging, the two nations combined bids. That was just the first hurdle. Even after FIFA awarded both countries the tournament, problems persisted. Who would host the opener and the final was just one of the issues that needed to be settled. The other was what name would be given to the competition. Following the English alphabetical order, Japan wanted "World Cup Japan/Korea 2002." The South Koreans argued for going with the French alphabet, with the excuse of keeping with FIFA's French origins, and having their country named first in the tournament's official name. FIFA intervened, and a compromise was reached following months of bickering. "Korea/Japan" was the name both sides agreed to go with in the end. South Korea was awarded the opening game; Japan was given the final.

France, the defending champions, Brazil, Argentina, and Portugal were all touted as pre-tournament favorites. France had retained the bulk of its roster and hoped that core of players could deliver once again. Brazil, with Ronaldo at the top of his game, were back after losing the '98 final. Argentina and Portugal, meanwhile, were also top contenders. The following eight teams were seeded for the draw: France, Brazil, Spain, Argentina, Germany, Italy, South Korea, and Japan. Groups A through D were to play in South Korea, while Groups E through H would play in Japan. In addition to the traditional powers, China, Ecuador, Senegal, and Slovenia qualified for their first World Cup. This is how the eight groups looked:

Group A: France, Denmark, Uruguay, and Senegal

Group B: Spain, Slovenia, Paraguay, and South Africa

Group C: Brazil, Turkey, Costa Rica, and China

Group D: South Korea, Portugal, Poland, and the United States

Group E: Germany, Ireland, Cameroon, and Saudi Arabia

Group F: Argentina, England, Sweden, and Nigeria

Group G: Italy, Croatia, Ecuador, and Mexico

Group H: Japan, Belgium, Russia, and Tunisia

As in previous tournaments, there was a "Group of Death" at this World Cup. Group F, featuring Argentina and England, was clearly the biggest group-stage match and a rematch of the 1986 and 1998 quarterfinals, both of which saw the English eliminated. The England versus Sweden game was also an interesting matchup because it pitted England manager Sven-Göran Eriksson against his native Sweden. Nigeria, who had put together solid showings in 1994 and 1998, remained the strongest team from Africa.

For those in the West, the first World Cup outside of the Americas and Europe meant kickoff times at very odd hours. That meant start times in the middle of the night in the Americas and mid-mornings in Europe. By 2002, soccer had become mass-market entertainment. Sepp Blatter wanted to see the World Cup become a truly global event, one of the very few bright spots to his very checkered tenure as FIFA president. There was an eagerness on the part of Japan and South Korea to please. In the end, they would do an extraordinary job as cohosts. It would be a watershed tournament for the number of shock results that would transpire in the group stage and all the way through to the semifinals.

In all, 20 venues were used to host matches, 10 each in South Korea and Japan. The stadiums in Daegu, Suwon, Yokohama, and Saitama all hosted four matches each, while the other 16 stadiums hosted three. For the first time, FIFA allowed teams to take 23 players to the finals, one more than typical, and now allowed for three goalkeepers.

Group Stage

The World Cup opener between France and Senegal was an emotional moment for both South Korea and Japan. President Kim Dae-jung of South Korea and Prime Minister Junichiro Koizumi of Japan drew applause from the crowd of 65,000 following their handshake inside Seoul Stadium. France, as defending champions, opened the tournament on May 31 against the West African nation of Senegal. It was in Seoul that Senegal pulled off a major upset, toppling France 1–0. France's defeat to Senegal set the tone for this World Cup and was a prelude to what would be France's unexpected implosion.

Senegal manager Bruno Metsu, who had a roster of players employed by French clubs but few names fans outside Africa could recall, put together an offensive-minded lineup. The uninspired French were unable to create a solid scoring chance as the Senegalese frustrated Les Bleus at every turn. The barrage paid off. Senegal took the lead after 30 minutes when El Hadji Diouf beat defender Frank Leboeuf on the left and sent the ball into the box. Petit was unable to clear it, and the ball wound up in the direction of Barthez. The loose ball allowed midfielder Pape Bouba Diop to knock it into the net. Diop took off his jersey during a wild goal celebration that included his teammates dancing near the corner kick flag, evoking memories of Cameroon 12 years earlier.

Senegal held off a late French onslaught for the win. It was not lost on the Senegalese players that a defeat against France, who had once colonized the African nation, was somehow part of a larger historical significance. "Between Senegal and France, there is a lot of history," midfielder Salif Diao told reporters. "It's like the children beat the parents."

The French were in trouble. The defeat to Senegal had revealed a plethora of weaknesses. Without Zidane, who sat the game out with a thigh injury, France was not the powerful force it had been in 1998. France showed little improvement in its second game on June 6. Les Bleus were still unable to score after being held to a 0–0 draw with Uruguay in Asiad Stadium in Busan. The South Americans, who had lost 2–1 to Denmark just five days earlier, got a much-needed point. For France, however, they would need a win by at least two goals against Denmark in its last group match to see them through to the round of 16.

Zidane, still nursing a torn thigh muscle, was forced to come off the bench in the hopes of jump-starting the French attack, but his presence wasn't enough on June 11 against the Danes at Incheon Munhak Stadium in Incheon. France was denied the space to move the ball, with the Danes putting on a magnificent defensive display. Scoring two goals would prove an impossible task. Instead, Denmark took the lead after 22 minutes when midfielder Stig Tofting crossed the ball to striker Dennis Rommedahl, who put the ball in the back of the net with a powerful half volley. Jon Dahl Tommasson doubled the lead in the 67th minute after tapping the ball into the goal following a low cross from Jesper Gronk-jaer. Denmark won the game 2–0 and the group, while France had not been able to score a goal in three games and was eliminated in disgrace. "A draw and two losses make it clear. It's hard to explain it," France manager Roger Lemerre said afterward. "I can't do it."

France's loss also gave it the distinction as the first World Cup champion to be booted from the group stage since Brazil in 1966. It would be the start of a trend that saw the defending champions exit future World Cups at the group stage. While Denmark had its way against France, Senegal and Uruguay played to a riveting 3–3 tie at Suwon Stadium in Suwon. Senegal, who only needed a draw to advance, got just that against the Uruguayans. The West Africans, who had stunned the world with their victory over France and 1–1 tie against Denmark, would move on to the round of 16 as the second-place team in the group.

Spain were favorites to win Group B. La Roja opened up their World Cup campaign with a 3–1 win against Slovenia on June 2 at Gwangju Stadium in Gwangju. It marked Spain's first victory in a World Cup opening game since 1950. Spain followed that up with a second victory five days later by the same score against Paraguay at Jeonju Stadium in Jeonju, becoming the first team to qualify for the round of 16. It was a promising start for a nation that had suffered at every World Cup. "With a little bit of luck, we can go a long way, and then, who knows?" Spain manager José Antonio Camacho told reporters before the start of the tournament. "It's about time we did well. Spain has never got the results they deserved at the World Cup. I don't know why. Bad luck at critical moments and a lack of confidence."

Spain won the group following a tough 3–2 victory against South Africa on June 12 at Daejeon Stadium in Daejeon. Down 2–1, Spain mounted a comeback with goals from Real Madrid's goal-scoring sensation Raúl González in the 56th minute and one from Gaizka Mendieta in stoppage time. The win eliminated South Africa, giving Paraguay (3–1 winners against Slovenia in Seogwipo on South Korea's Jeju Island) second place on goal differential. It was a brace by Nelson Cuevas that saw the South Americans advance.

In Group C, Brazil was attempting to reach the final for a third straight tournament with the focus on winning it all. The Brazilians had endured a tough time qualifying for the finals, but the players turned on the pressure once they arrived in South Korea, and its trio of Rs—Ronaldo, Rivaldo, and Ronaldinho—would prove impossible to stop. The other R, Romário, had controversially been left off the roster by manager Luiz Felipe Scolari. The star striker had even tried to talk his way onto the team, holding a news conference and pleading to be chosen. "I've always had dreams, and one of them is to play in one more World Cup, for the simple fact that playing soccer is what I most love to do," Romário said, adding that he wanted to play "for the people who suffer so many problems."

Even Pelé had vouched for Romário's inclusion, saying, "A player who scores goals has always got to be on the team." Scolari was unmoved. Known as "Big Phil," Scolari was a disciplinarian whose job was to manage egos off the field as well as try to restore some of the freewheeling play that had characterized the Brazilian game for decades. As Scolari prowled the sidelines directing his players, Brazil opened the group with a 2–1 victory against Turkey on June 3 at Munsu Cup Stadium in Ulsan. Rivaldo's penalty kick three minutes from time won them the match. But Rivaldo garnered lots of attention for another reason minutes after netting the goal. Upon winning a corner kick, he delayed taking it in a time-wasting effort common among players. A frustrated Hakan Ünsal kicked the ball at Rivaldo in an attempt to get him to restart the match. The ball hit Rivaldo in the knees, but the Brazilian fell to the ground clutching his face and rolling on the ground in pain. South Korean referee Kim Young-joo fell for Rivaldo's theatrics and showed the Turk his second yellow card of the game. Ünsal was ejected as a result, and any chance Turkey had of a late comeback had come to an end. FIFA, after reviewing replays of the incident, fined Rivaldo $7,300 for his unsportsmanlike conduct. Rivaldo later apologized but seemed unfazed by the whole thing. "These things happen in football," he said.

On June 8 in Seogwipo, Brazil tore apart China's defense with Roberto Carlos putting his side ahead, 1–0, after 15 minutes. The Chinese were astutely coached by Milutinović, who had pulled off miracles at the last four tournaments with Mexico, Costa Rica, the United States, and Nigeria. Though he had coached all four of those nations to the knockout round, a defeat to Brazil would mathematically eliminate China. That's what happened when Rivaldo made it 2–0 in the 32nd minute, then a Ronaldinho penalty kick in the first half of stoppage time and a goal from Ronaldo in the 55th minute put Brazil on top, 4–0. The Brazilians would win the group on June 13 in Suwon with a 5–2 rout of Costa Rica, with two goals from Ronaldo in the span of just three minutes. Ronaldo, his toothy grin on full display once again, had scored four goals in three games. "After two years without playing, this is without a doubt a personal victory," Ronaldo said at the conclusion of the Costa Rica match.

In fact, Ronaldo was so confident following the win against China that he exclaimed, "I believe I can now score a goal in every match. I feel great."

If the Brazilians were for real (despite some defensive lapses) after winning the group, so was Turkey, who were playing in the finals for the first time since 1954. A narrow defeat to Brazil, followed by a 1–1 draw against Costa Rica on June 9 in Incheon, and a convincing 3–0 rout of China four days later in Seoul, ensured passage to the round of 16 as the group's second-place team.

Group D proved the opposite and fertile ground for upsets. South Korea stunned Poland, to the delight of 49,000 fans on June 4 at Asiad Main Stadium in Busan, with a 2–0 win. Goals from Hwang Seon-hong in the 26th minute and Yoo Sang-cheol in the 53rd minute lifted the team to victory, the first by South Korea in World Cup history. South Korea's manager Guus Hiddink, who had taken the job the previous year, had physically prepared his team for the rigors of the tournament. That peak physical conditioning proved pivotal against Portugal and Poland, the two teams favored to advance out of the group.

The South Koreans were a well-drilled side, and Hiddink, after guiding the Dutch at the World Cup four years earlier, was looking to make a splash. The lead-up to the tournament had not been so smooth for Hiddink. He had been spotted with his girlfriend on vacation—something that would have gone unnoticed in the West—but South Koreans largely thought it showed that he was unfocused. Jere Longman, writing in the *New York Times* on June 21, observed the following about Hiddink: "In truth, a man who seemed not to be working hard enough had his players working harder than ever. Only two South Korean players are based professionally in Europe. They did not suffer the fatigue of club seasons, as did many from departed giants like France, Argentina and Italy. While other coaches had only weeks to prepare, Hiddink had several months. His players became fit and confident, relentless for 90 minutes, convinced that the collective could benefit from individual flair."

On June 5, the United States defeated Portugal 3–2 at Suwon Stadium in Suwon. The Americans took the lead after just four minutes with John O'Brien when goalkeeper Vitor Baía failed to clear a Brian McBride header. The ball fell to O'Brien, who was standing just a few yards from the goal, and he buried it in the back of the net. The United States served up a one-two punch in the 29th minute when a Landon Donovan cross was deflected off defender Jorge Costa for an own goal. The Americans had more in store for Portugal's lackluster defense. Defender Tony Sanneh crossed the ball in the box for McBride with nine minutes left in the half, putting the ball past Baía with a diving header near the far post. Portugal would score twice, but it wasn't enough. U.S. manager Bruce Arena, not known for being hyperbolic, told reporters that the victory was "probably the biggest win in the modern era" for American soccer.

On June 10, in Daegu, South Korea and the United States played to a 1–1 draw. It was in the 24th minute that O'Brien's long pass from midfield found striker Clint Mathis near the edge of the South Korean box. Mathis unleashed a left-footed shot into the lower-left corner of the net for the lead. The hosts got the equalizer with 12 minutes left to play when Lee Eul-yong served up a free kick from midfield into the box where striker Ahn Jung-hwan was able to outjump the U.S. defense and head the ball past Brad Friedel, who stood rooted on his line, and into the right side of the net.

On the group's final match day, contested on June 14, South Korea won the group via a 1–0 shock win against Portugal at Incheon Munhak Stadium in Incheon. The United States, 3–1 losers against Poland under a heavy rain in Daejeon, would finish second and also advance to the round of 16. "Nobody would have picked out the results in this group," Arena told reporters at the postgame news conference. "It was an unusual World Cup. There will be interesting results ahead of us."

Germany was a traditional power in much disarray by the time the World Cup arrived. They had famously lost 5–1 to England in Munich during qualifying and, like Brazil, had flirted with missing out on the final. Once they arrived in Japan, the team coached by Völler thrashed Saudi Arabia 8–0 on June 1 at the Sapporo Dome in Sapporo to open Group E. The win, punctuated by striker Miroslav Klose's hat trick, provided a big confidence boost, albeit against a very weak opponent. "As a former forward, I like my teams to score goals, though not necessarily eight," Völler said afterward. "We have to stay with our feet firmly planted in the carpet and go on preparing for the next game."

The rout put the Germans in control of the group after Ireland and Cameroon played to a 1–1 draw at Niigata Stadium in Niigata earlier that day. Ireland had become engulfed in a pre-tournament scandal that could have killed their chances of advancing past the group stage. It ultimately did not, but the quarrel, known as the "Saipan incident," between manager Mick McCarthy and star striker Roy Keane is talked about to this day. The team arrived at the U.S. territory ahead of the final to acclimate to the time zone and climate when Keane, the team captain, was sent home early, a decision that divided public opinion in Ireland regarding who was to blame. Keane had questioned Ireland's FA professionalism and problems with team preparations. Keane questioned the conditions of the training field, travel arrangements (which made the players sit in second-class seats, while Ireland FA officials sat in first class), diet, and McCarthy's overall competency as coach.

In an interview with the *Irish Times*, Keane said, "I told Mick I had enough. Basically that was it. We've had discussions already the other night about training facilities. You've got to prepare properly is my attitude."

In his autobiography, Keane said the problems experienced in Saipan had begun the previous year during World Cup qualifying. In a road match against the Netherlands, Keane recalled that the Irish players were eating cheese sandwiches because the more suitable pre-match meal of pasta had not been made available.

Without Keane, Ireland managed a second draw, a 1–1 result against Germany on June 5 at the Kashima Soccer Stadium in Ibaraki. Klose scored again for Germany after 19 minutes, but it was a goal from Robbie Keane, no relation to the temperamental Roy, in stoppage time that salvaged the draw. "What's the point of coming here and going out without a fight?" McCarthy told reporters. "We've given ourselves a chance, haven't we?"

Germany won the group on June 11 following a 2–0 win at Shizuoka Stadium in Shizuoka against Cameroon, a result that eliminated the Africans. The match kept referee Antonio López Nieto of Spain busy and was notable for producing 16 yellow cards, including a red card for each team. One of the most ill-disciplined matches in tournament history saw Klose score his fifth goal at this World Cup 11 minutes from time to put the game away. Ireland, meanwhile, finished second after a resounding 3–0 victory against Saudi Arabia at International Stadium Yokohama, south of Tokyo. The hard rain must have reminded the players of home as Robbie Keane put Ireland ahead after just seven minutes. The rain got stronger in the second half, and Ireland responded with two more goals against a porous Saudi defense. Gary Breen scored in the 61st minute, and Damien Duff tallied a third three minutes from time. After the game, McCarthy avoided answering questions about Roy Keane while praising Robbie and the entire team. "The lads were brilliant," he said.

Over in Group F, Argentina and Nigeria found themselves playing one another in the first round for the second time at a World Cup after they were paired together in 1994. The Albiceleste were expected to finish in the top two spots, with River Plate's Ariel Ortega donning the number 10 shirt as Maradona's heir. Despite that type of hype and offensive power, this was the "Group of Death," and the addition of England and Sweden would make it a tough slog for everyone involved.

Argentina defeated Nigeria on June 2 in Ibraki. Batistuta was once again the key player for the Argentines at a World Cup. England, the other team favored to capture the group, opened their campaign on the same day in Saitama with a 1–1 draw against Sweden. It was the Swedes' 2–1 victory against Nigeria that eliminated the Africans on June 7 at Wing Stadium in Kobe. Henrik Larsson's brace in this one made all the difference.

It was Argentina's clash with England in Sapporo that would help determine the group. The 1986 game still loomed large over these two sides. The 36,000 inside the Sapporo Dome witnessed a wonderful match, although the goals were slow to come. This was the chance for England, and specifically Beckham, to find some redemption. Argentina, coached by Marcelo Bielsa, featured some of the best players the country had developed in the late '90s and early aughts. Bielsa's tactics, meanwhile, would go on to inspire future generations of managers. His 4–1–4–1 system would create a coaching tree that would inspire the likes of Mauricio Pochettino, Gerardo Martino, and Pep Guardiola.

This was the game everyone had been looking forward to at the start of the tournament. Beckham determined the outcome once again—this time in a positive way for the Three Lions—near the end of the first half. Owen was tripped by Mauricio Pochettino in the box, and Beckham shot the penalty kick low in the center past goalkeeper Pablo Cavallero for the 1–0 win. "It's unbelievable. It's been four years," Beckham said after the match. "It's been a long four years."

England would advance to the round of 16 as the group's second-place team on June 12 after a scoreless draw in Osaka versus Nigeria. At the same time in Miyagi, Sweden pulled off the impossible against Argentina, who needed a win to stay alive. The 1–1 draw sent Sweden atop the group as the Argentines, like the French, packed their bags earlier than anyone had expected on the eve of the tournament. "We are so proud that Sweden, little Sweden, has knocked out the favorites," Sweden goalkeeper Magnus Hedman gloated when speaking with reporters after the game. "If we can get through from this group, as we have, then the sky is the limit. Why should anyone stop us now?"

For Batistuta, the defeat marked a bitter end to a national team career that had so many highs, but mostly lows. "I'm frustrated and upset," he said after the game. "I envisioned a different retirement from the national team. We had 25 chances and they put one in."

In a World Cup that would become known for its officiating blunders, Group G had many of them. The Italians, known as slow starters, had to get past their group opponents Ecuador, Croatia, and Mexico as well as a series of bad calls from the referees to get into the round of 16.

The Azzurri opened with a 2–0 victory against Ecuador on June 3 in Sapporo. Two goals from Vieri crushed Ecuador's hopes of earning a win in its first World Cup game ever. Mexico's 1–0 win over Croatia the same day at Stadium Big Swan in Niigata was highlighted by Cuauhtémoc Blanco's penalty kick in the 60th minute.

Italy's second game against Croatia did not go so well for the Azzurri. The Italians were dealt a 2–1 defeat thanks to two bad calls from English referee Graham Poll. To be fair, Poll wasn't the only one to blame. His assistant, Jens Larsen of Denmark, raised his flag on two occasions to signal a stop in play. Vieri had scored a goal that was called back in the 50th minute after Larsen raised his flag, ruling him offside. TV replays showed Vieri was clearly onside. That didn't stop Vieri from scoring five minutes later. He put Italy in front with a header off a cross by Cristiano Doni. Italy manager Giovanni Trappatoni ordered that his team shut down the Croatian defense, as it had done so effectively at past tournaments. Croatia manager Mirko Jozić subbed out midfielder Davor Vugrinec with striker Ivica Olić in the 57th minute. The move changed the course of the game. Sixteen minutes after he had come on, Olić headed the ball into the goal to make it 1–1. Italy no longer looked in control. Croatia exploited Italy's lapse in concentration and took the lead three minutes later. Milan Rapaić's long kick was blocked by defender Marco Materazzi, who had replaced Alessandro Nesta following an injury in the 24th minute. But Materazzi's deflection allowed the ball to sail into his own net past stunned goalkeeper Gianluigi Buffon.

Down 2–1, the Azzurri thought they had managed to snag a point in the game's waning minutes after Materazzi's long-ball pass rolled forward untouched, and past goalkeeper Stipe Pletikosa. But Larsen once again raised his flag, claiming striker Filippo Inzaghi, who was in the box, had fouled defender Josip Šimunič as the ball entered the goal. The contact was minimal, but Poll agreed with his linesman. "For some reason, the referee and the linesman really didn't like us that day," Vieri recalled. "My goal should have stood. I really think it's the referee's job to correct the linesman. I really think we could have won the game. We were unlucky. That loss set the tone for us for the rest of the World Cup."

The Italians had suffered a 2–1 loss to Croatia and now needed at least a draw in their final game against Mexico, 2–1 winners over Ecuador on June 9 in Miyagi, to advance. Italy tied Mexico 1–1 on June 13 at Ōita Big Eye Stadium in Oita thanks to a Del Piero goal five minutes from time. The draw allowed Mexico to win the group and Italy to advance as the second-place team only because Ecuador simultaneously upset Croatia 1–0 in Yokohama. "We played very well the entire game. We certainly didn't deserve a loss against Mexico," said defender Gianluca Zambrotta. "I think we worked hard to score and we were rewarded in the final minutes."

Cohosts Japan had to tangle against Belgium, Russia, and Tunisia in Group H for the chance to get to the round of 16. Much of Japan's hopes rested on manager Philippe Troussier. The Frenchman could pass for a college professor. His sandy brown hair, glasses, and ill-fitting sports coat made it easy to confuse him for one. But Japan's FA didn't hire Troussier for his taste in clothes. Instead, Troussier, one in a long line of soccer players who had average careers, only to find great success as a coach, was brought in to change the fortunes of a nation not known for their soccer pedigree.

Japan came into the tournament as the 2000 Asian Cup champions, an example of the improvements the team had shown since Troussier's hiring in 1998. "Fans in this country are not like those in Europe, where they put teams under enormous pressure to achieve results and can react aggressively if things go badly," Troussier said. "In Japan it is up to the coach and players to create their own pressure—both on themselves and on each other."

Troussier had coached South Africa at the 1998 World Cup, but his handling of Japan had been a bigger success. He earned $1 million at the time of his appointment and had sole discretion over the players he chose and the games the team scheduled. The country had created a talent pipeline after the launch in 1993 of the J-League, a pro domestic competition. The league attracted many foreign stars, including Lineker, Schillaci, and Stoichkov.

Japan's biggest star was Hidetoshi Nakata, a midfielder who signed with Italian club Perugia in 1998. In January 2000, Nakata moved to Roma, helping them win the Serie A title that season. By the time the

World Cup arrived, Nakata was a member of Parma, one of Italy's best clubs at the time. Troussier, however, knew that one player did not make a team. At the World Cup, Japan would need, in Troussier's assessment, a "balance between attack and defense." "Collectively we're very strong," Troussier said on the eve of the tournament. "Our players learn quickly, and they follow tactical plans, but they have to be ready to take more individual responsibility."

At the same time, J-Village, in the city of Fukushima, became a national-team training camp where school-age players could develop their skills. The focus on cultivating homegrown talent had an immediate impact. In 1993, at home, Japan's Under-17 team reached the quarterfinals of the World Youth Championships. In 1999, Japan lost in the final of the World Under-20 tournament. A year later, the team reached the quarterfinals at the Sydney Games.

Group H would also showcase some upsets. Japan played Belgium to a 1–1 draw on June 4 in Saitama, then defeated Russia 1–0 five days later in Yokohama to take control of the group. Japan, helped by the enthusiasm of the crowds, unleashed a wave of nationalism never before seen. In its last group game against Tunisia on June 14 in Osaka, Japan won again. The 2–0 win against Tunisia saw goals from second-half sub Hiroaki Morishima in the 48th minute and Nakata 15 minutes from the end. Japan not only advanced but had also won the group. The victory set off wild celebrations among the 45,000 fans inside Nagai Stadium and throughout the country. "We have written a new page in Japanese football history," Troussier told reporters, "and the World Cup is not over yet."

Belgium would finish second following a 3–2 win against Russia on June 14 at Ecopa Stadium in Shizuoka. The win put Belgium into the round of 16, where they would face Brazil. "It's an honor to meet the great Brazil in the second round of the World Cup," Belgium manager Robert Waseige told reporters. "I never make any forecasts about matches, but it's nice to be able to dream of us beating Brazil."

Round of 16

Although the tournament had featured a number of upsets (and more were to come), the knockout stage opened with a predictable start on June 15 when Germany defeated Paraguay 1–0 in Seogwipo. Oliver Neuville scored two minutes from time to help the Germans advance. The match, one of the most boring so far at the competition, had appeared to be heading hopelessly into extra time until the German striker blasted a shot past Chilavert off a cross from his Bayer Leverkusen teammate Bernd Schneider. Germany's win came as little surprise (even though they failed to get a shot on goal in the first half), but what did shock FIFA and the organizers was the small turnout. Only 25,176 spectators showed up at Jeju Stadium, way short of the 42,000 capacity. Hours before kickoff, organizers began giving tickets away to local schoolchildren and their families, but that wasn't enough to fill the stadium.

Five hours later, England cruised to a 3–0 win against Denmark in Niigata. The Three Lions wasted no time showing the Danes who was the better side that evening. After just five minutes, a poor clearance from Denmark's Martin Laursen allowed Beckham to gain control of the ball and direct it into the box from the left side. Rio Ferdinand headed the ball directly at goalkeeper Thomas Sorensen. The Danish goalie tried to hang on to the ball, but dropped it past the line for the goal. Owen made it 2–0 in the 22nd minute as his shot from six yards out beat Sorensen for the second time. Rain started to fall midway through the second half, but that didn't stop England from tallying a third goal. A poor clearance, this time from Niclas Jensen, allowed the opportunistic Beckham to steal the ball and dish it off to striker Emile Heskey, whose one-time shot eked past Sorensen's left elbow.

On June 16, Senegal pulled the first shocking result of the knockout round in Oita, downing Sweden 2–1 after extra time when Henri Camara netted a golden goal in the 103rd minute. Camara had scored in the 37th minute to tie the game after Sweden had taken the lead with Larsson after 11 minutes. In the day's second match, Spain ousted Ireland 4–3 on penalty kicks in Suwon after the match had ended 1–1. In the shootout, Spain goalkeeper Iker Casillas emerged as the hero when he saved David Connolly's and Kevin Kilbane's attempts, before Gaizka Mendieta bagged the winner. La Roja, who had broken the hearts of its fans so many times before at the World Cup, was in the final eight and had its sights set on the trophy. "We played better than Spain that day," recalled Robbie Keane. "We should have won. That remains one of my regrets. We could have gone far, especially given all the upsets. For me, it remains a great tournament and one of the best Ireland teams at a World Cup."

The United States, meanwhile, found itself pitted against Mexico in one of the biggest regional rivalries in the world. The all-CONCACAF match on June 17 in Jeonju turned out to be a thrilling affair. The Mexicans put pressure on the U.S. backline early on, but it was the Americans who took the lead. Against the run of play, Claudio Reyna ran the ball down the right flank and crossed it to Josh Wolff. The striker linked up well with McBride, who released a wicked shot that beat goalkeeper Óscar Pérez for the 1–0 lead after just eight minutes. The Mexicans dominated possession after the goal and nearly tied the score on a number of occasions, but goalkeeper Friedel put in another top-notch performance. The Americans played tough defensively, using the counterattack to their advantage. In the 65th minute, an Eddie Lewis cross found Landon Donovan near the far post. Donovan, who would emerge as the tournament's best young player, coolly headed the ball past Pérez for a 2–0 victory.

Later that evening, Brazil took on Belgium in Kobe. The game was another example of the increasingly poor officiating that had marred the tournament. The Brazilians were extremely lucky to get the victory after Jamaican referee Peter Prendergast committed a number of mistakes. In the 36th minute, Marc Wilmots jumped in the air over Brazilian defender Roque Júnior to head Belgian Jacky Peeters's cross into the twine. Prendergast disallowed the goal. He argued that Wilmots had pushed Roque Júnior, but subsequent TV replays showed it was a bad call. Wilmots said afterward that Prendergast had admitted to him at halftime that he made a mistake. In the 67th minute, Ronaldinho floated the ball across the box to Rivaldo, who, initially with his back to the ball, controlled it on his chest and sent a spectacular volley off his left foot for the goal and the 1–0 lead. The Brazilians put the game away 20 minutes later when substitute Kléberson ran the ball down the right flank, then put a pass in the path of Ronaldo who side-footed it past goalkeeper Geert De Vlieger for the 2–0 win. "The World Cup starts now," Ronaldo said during a news conference afterward. "Every game is going to be a final."

Japan's fairy-tale tournament, and all the enthusiasm that had carried the team to the knockout round, came to an end on June 18 in Miyagi. Turkey scored the game's only goal in the 12th minute when a Ümit Davala header found the back of the net. Troussier's biggest mistake had been to change his lineup, dumping strikers Atsushi Yanagisawa and Takayuki Suzuki and going with Akinori Nishizawa as a lone forward.

Cohosts South Korea did reach the quarterfinals, pulling off the upset in Daejeon against Italy. It would be a series of poor officiating decisions that would help Hiddink's side. The 39,000 South Korean fans, clad in red and beating drums the entire time, transformed Daejeon Stadium into one of the most hostile places ever for an opponent. Italy took the lead after 18 minutes when Vieri headed in a Francesco Totti corner kick. Up 1–0, Del Piero moved back into the midfield with Vieri operating as sole striker. Alongside Del Piero was the gritty midfielder Gennaro Gattuso, whose job it was to break up the South Korean attack. Despite Buffon's save on Ahn Jung-hwan's penalty kick in the first half, Hiddink's team refused to give up. The Italians, who were missing Nesta and Fabio Cannavaro because of injuries, were trying not to let the ghosts of 1966 get to them. The South Korean players grew bolder as the crowd cheered their every pass. The fans even held up posters with the dreaded message "Remember 1966?"—a reference to the Azzurri's shock defeat to North Korea.

The South Koreans made the Italians pay for a rare defensive lapse in the 88th minute. A cross from the right side bounced off the legs of defender Christian Panucci, putting the loose ball into the path of Seol Ki-hyeon, who drilled it past Buffon for the 1–1 equalizer. A minute later, Vieri had the chance to put the game away, but the Inter Milan striker put the ball over the crossbar from just six yards out. In extra time, South Korea continued to play with its typical upbeat tempo as the Italians struggled to keep up. Referee Byron Moreno of Ecuador, who rarely made a call in Italy's favor, became the game's protagonist. He red-carded Totti 13 minutes into extra time after giving him a second yellow on the night for diving in the box. TV replays showed the decision had been harsh. Trappatoni was livid on the sidelines, complaining and gesturing to FIFA officials near his bench that the call was bogus. With three minutes left in extra time, Ahn, who played with Serie A club Perugia, beat Maldini in the air for the ball and headed it past a diving Buffon to win the game, 2–1. "That was the worst loss of my life," Maldini recalled. "I was totally exhausted. We weren't prepared to lose, but we did."

The following day, Perugia dumped Ahn, saying he had ruined Italian soccer. The poor refereeing would become an excuse to mask some of Trappatoni's failure to field a more attack-minded lineup. The whining reached a crescendo and FIFA's servers crashed after they were inundated with angry emails from Italian fans complaining of Moreno's refereeing. In South Korea, the country was swept up by World Cup fever and the realistic belief that their team could reach the final.

Quarterfinals

For the very first time in World Cup history, teams from five continents—North America, South America, Europe, Africa, and Asia—reached the quarterfinals of the same tournament. The quarterfinals also included four teams—South Korea, the United States, Senegal, and Turkey—that very few would have predicted would get this far into the tournament.

The focus, however, remained on the heavyweights. The biggest clash of the round took place on June 21 and pitted Brazil against England in Shizuoka. Eriksson's team was aware that it had to apply lots of offensive pressure against Brazil or risk losing the game. Owen did just that, scoring in the 23rd minute after faking a hard shot that forced Marcos to fall to the ground. The England striker then put the ball in the goal with ease to Marcos's right for the 1–0 lead. The lead didn't last long. In the first half's stoppage time, Brazil equalized when Ronaldinho's run down the middle forced the English defense to come apart. Ronaldinho's pass to Rivaldo on the right allowed him to place the ball into the goal. Brazil won the game in the second half on a rocket of a free kick from Ronaldinho in the 50th minute.

In the second game of the day, the United States was aiming to reach the World Cup semifinals for the first time since 1930. In order to achieve that, the Americans had to overcome Germany in Ulsan. Arena knew defeating Germany would not be easy, but after overcoming

Mexico, the team exuded a confidence rarely seen by a U.S. side. Another upset could happen, and it almost did. Germany, meanwhile, was aiming to make its tenth appearance ever at a World Cup semifinals. The Germans, who had been criticized back home by the press for their inability to dominate games, suffered a barrage of U.S. attacks throughout the first half. The Germans responded by threatening from set pieces. Michael Ballack headed the ball past Friedel in the 39th minute off an in-swinging corner by Christian Ziege from the right side to take a 1–0 lead.

The Americans continued to test Oliver Kahn in the second half, but the German goalkeeper looked unbeatable. The U.S. team finally broke through the impregnable German backline in the 50th minute, but Scottish referee Hugh Dallas made a bad call—a staple of this tournament—after a shot by defender Gregg Berhalter appeared to cross the line. Cheers erupted among the 38,000 inside Munsu Cup Stadium, but the ball was deflected by Kahn, ricocheting off the forearm of German defender Torsten Frings, over the line, then back at the German goalkeeper. Berhalter looked at the referee, thinking it was a handball, which if called by Dallas would have resulted in a penalty kick. The call never came, though some of the players argued it should have been a goal.

On June 22, South Korea faced Spain in Gwangju. It was another game that ended in an upset as a result of bad refereeing. The cohosts outlasted Spain 5–3 on penalty kicks after the game ended scoreless. This time it was Egyptian referee Gamal Al-Ghandour who made the blunders. Two Spanish goals were called back during regulation, and Al-Ghandour nullified a third in extra time.

The goal that could have won the game for Spain a minute into extra time led Al-Ghandour to make the most scandalous call of the game. Midfielder Sánchez Joaquin strode past the South Korean defense near the right end line, then crossed the ball to the middle of the box where Fernando Morientes headed the ball into the net. Al-Ghandour disallowed the goal because his assistant had raised his flag to signal that the ball had been dribbled over the end line before Joaquin crossed it. Replays showed the ball was in play before the pass. The game went to penalty kicks, and Joaquin suffered more bad luck in the shootout when his kick, Spain's fourth, was saved by goalkeeper Lee Woon-jae. The

South Koreans converted all five of their kicks to complete the upset. South Korea was in the semifinals thanks to Hiddink's master coaching and plenty of help from the refs.

In the last quarterfinal matchup, and the second game of the day, in Osaka, Senegal—the first African nation to reach the quarterfinals since Cameroon in 1990—saw its dreams of advancing to the semifinals shattered by Turkey. The game was resolved four minutes into extra time when second-half sub Ilhan Mansiz scored. He ran down the sidelines in exultation following the goal, his long hair flapping in the wind, as his teammates ran to hug him. Turkey had reached the World Cup semifinals for the very first time.

Semifinals

The tournament, now distilled to just four teams, came down to Brazil and Germany, two of the sport's great powers, and South Korea and Turkey, two minnows looking to rock the game. South Korea had survived two tense encounters, against Italy and then Spain, aided by the referees. In 2015, the Italian daily *Corriere dello Sport* reported that Moreno, who had officiated the South Korea versus Italy match, had been involved in match fixing. The accusations were never proven by authorities or any sporting body. It didn't help, however, that the Ecuadorian FA had suspended Moreno a few months after the World Cup, and again in 2003, for a series of bad calls in the country's domestic competition. In 2010, Moreno was caught smuggling six kilos of heroin, in 10 clear plastic bags tucked into his pants, through New York's Kennedy Airport. He was released after spending 26 months behind bars.

On June 25, in Seoul, South Korean faced off against Germany. Despite the home-field advantage—the 65,000 red-clad South Korean fans made their voices heard once again—it was Germany who would emerge victorious. It was a huge disappointment for the fans, which included a million people gathered in Seoul to watch on giant television screens. The Germans struggled to vanquish South Korea, and it took a Ballack goal 15 minutes from time to do it.

It wasn't all positive for Ballack and Germany. The striker drew his second yellow card of the knockout phase in the 71st minute after committing a foul on Lee Chun-soo, meaning he would miss the final. "My first thought is bitterness," Ballack said. "My dream had been to play in the final. Now it's not meant to be. But the team accomplished quite a feat. We can be proud of ourselves. Prior to the World Cup, few people would have put money on us going to the final. It's nice to prove them wrong. We were realistic enough to believe we would not get this far, yet we've done it."

The following evening in Saitama, Brazil and Turkey met for a second time at this tournament. Turkey, like South Korea, had surpassed expectations—albeit with no help from the referees. Brazil, meanwhile, was where they belonged after summoning *jogo bonito* thanks largely to a fit Ronaldo. As in the first semifinal, the game would be decided by a solitary goal. Ronaldo, in top form, scored the winner four minutes after the restart to reach the final. Scolari was both humble and arrogant after the game. After heaping praise on Turkey in the post-match news conference, Scolari said, "We expected to win by more." Turkey would go on to take third place after a 3–2 win over South Korea, a victory punctuated by Hakan Şükür's goal just 10.8 seconds into the match to record the quickest goal in World Cup history.

Final: Brazil vs. Germany

Brazil's World Cup finale was devoid of the drama that had characterized the hours proceeding the '98 final. The game pitted the offensive Brazilian machine spearheaded by Ronaldo against German defending, powered by Kahn's extraordinary goalkeeping at this tournament. He had conceded just one goal entering the game, although Ronaldo had scored six goals and was looking to add his first World Cup as the tournament's top scorer.

Ronaldo would go on to do just that at on June 30 in Yokohama. Kahn, who had been a fortress the entire tournament, could not stop the dancing Brazilians. The Germans may have shown initiative, but the Brazilians brought the energy. Ronaldo missed a chance after 19 minutes when he was put through by Ronaldinho, but he put his attempt wide. Kahn saved another Ronaldo effort in the 30th minute after Ronaldinho set up his teammate once again. The Brazilians came close to opening the scoring in the 45th minute when Kleberson's long-range effort hit the crossbar.

Brazil put the game away in the second half when Ronaldo finally broke the deadlock in the 67th minute. After regaining possession outside the German box, Ronaldo dished it off to Rivaldo. The Brazilian uncorked a shot that Kahn saved, but failed to hang on to. The onrushing Ronaldo picked up the rebound and slotted the ball home.

With the dependable Kahn defeated, Brazil was riding high. Germany tried to get back into the game, but Brazil's midfield was too strong and its attack relentless in search of a second goal. That second goal arrived 11 minutes from time when Ronaldo summoned all his class to power a right-footed shot for the 2–0 win.

Ronaldo had exorcised the ghosts of four years earlier. He had delivered both personal redemption and in the process a fifth World Cup for Brazil. Ronaldo, who fought back tears after the triumph, said he was "so happy" for helping Brazil capture the title. "We played a great game," he added, "and we brought joy to millions of people."

2006 WORLD CUP

The 2006 World Cup returned to Germany, but the decision wasn't without controversy. The decision in July 2000 to award the tournament to the European nation came after several high-profile Germans were accused of creating a slush fund to bribe FIFA officials to vote their way, the first in a series of allegations to rock FIFA and the World Cup bid process in the ensuing years.

Der Spiegel reported in 2015 that German bid organizers had paid to secure the votes of four Asian members of the 24-person FIFA executive committee. The bribes included the involvement of the then-CEO of Adidas, Robert Louis-Dreyfus, who had created an $8.2 million fund to dole out such secret payments. In 2018, Mohamed bin Hammam admitted to receiving money from the bid. Bin Hammam, a Qatari soccer official and former president of the Asian Football Confederation, was banned from the game for life in 2011 after he was found to have engaged in a series of unethical behaviors.

2000s Innovation: Fan Zones

Soccer has always been a public experience—even for those who couldn't attend a game in person. Throughout the 1930s, people gathered around radios to listen to the World Cup. Since the advent of television in the 1950s, fans have been able to watch games with others inside homes and bars.

The 1998 World Cup in France featured massive public viewings, but they had been organized because many could not score tickets. In 2002, South Korea's long-standing culture of public viewing of sporting events on big screens became one of the lasting legacies of that World Cup. Advances in technology in the early 2000s that allowed for high-quality movie screen broadcasts certainly helped in making this way of watching games ubiquitous.

FIFA Fan Fests—public viewing parties of games on a large screen organized by FIFA and the host nation during a World Cup—are now the norm. Fan Fests followed the success of public viewing at the 2002 World Cup and have become an essential part of the tournament since 2006 in Germany.

In 2014, Fan Fests were organized in each of Brazil's 12 host cities. Some 5 million attended them, with Rio de Janeiro's spectacular Copacabana Beach location attracting nearly a million during the month-long tournament. Fan Fests, featuring live music and entertainment, held four years later at Russia 2018, attracted 7.7 million spectators in the country's 11 host cities.

Argentina supporters crowd into the FIFA Fan Zone in Porto Alegre at the 2014 World Cup in Brazil.
ZUMA PRESS/ALAMY STOCK PHOTO

Bin Hammam was just one in a series of FIFA officials accused of wrongdoing in the years that followed the 2006 World Cup. The vote for which nation would be awarded the tournament, which had also featured South Africa, England, and Morocco, was a contentious affair. South Africa appeared to be the favorite, an effort to award the tournament to an African nation for the very first time. At the time, Asia's four members hinted that they planned to vote for Germany—no surprise given the revelations made public years later—with David Will of Scotland and Charlie Dempsey, president of the Oceania Football Confederation, appearing to be the swing votes.

Germany was awarded hosting duties after receiving 12 votes to South Africa's 11. Dempsey abstained, meaning that his nonvote had guaranteed that the World Cup would return to Germany for the first time since West Germany hosted the 1974 edition. A 12–12 vote would have been a victory for South Africa since Blatter, FIFA's president at the time, had been an open supporter of South Africa's bid and would have broken the tie. Blatter, who had been elected FIFA boss in 2002 after Havelange retired, had spearheaded the move to bring the World Cup outside of Europe and South America. South Africa, meanwhile, would have to wait until May 2004 when they were awarded the right to host the 2010 finals over Morocco, Libya, and Egypt after FIFA only accepted bids from African nations that year.

Dempsey later said he abstained because a vote for either bid would have hurt Oceania's 11 members, although he never explained why that would be the case. The BBC reported that Dempsey had spoken of "intolerable pressure" placed on him by the competing bids ahead of the vote. Dempsey resigned soon after. He died in 2008 at age 87.

The corrupt German bid had also ensnared Beckenbauer, the latest former great-turned-administrator to be accused of wrongdoing. Like Platini at France '98, Beckenbauer was the face of Germany 2006. A FIFA ethics probe that opened in 2016 was looking into Beckenbauer, and three other German officials, for their role in "possible undue payments and contracts to gain an advantage in the 2006 FIFA World Cup host selection and the associated funding" to Bin Hammam, FIFA's ethics committee had said in a statement. In 2021, after much foot-dragging due to Beckenbauer's lawyers claiming the former defender had been too ill to testify, FIFA's ethics judges said they had closed their bribery probe against him because the statute of limitations had expired.

Germany, England, Argentina, Mexico, Italy, Brazil, France, and Spain were the seeded teams and could not meet in the group stage. Here's how the draw shook out:

Group A: Germany, Poland, Ecuador, and Costa Rica

Group B: England, Sweden, Paraguay, and Trinidad and Tobago

Group C: Argentina, the Netherlands, Serbia and Montenegro, and the Ivory Coast

Group D: Mexico, Portugal, Angola, and Iran

Group E: Italy, the Czech Republic, Ghana, and the United States

Group F: Brazil, Croatia, Australia, and Japan

Group G: France, Switzerland, South Korea, and Togo

Group H: Spain, Ukraine, Tunisia, and Saudi Arabia

The groups were evenly balanced, although Group C could easily be considered the "Group of Death." Eight nations qualified for the finals for the first time: Angola, the Czech Republic, Ghana, the Ivory Coast, Togo, Trinidad and Tobago, Ukraine, and Serbia and Montenegro. Serbia and Montenegro separated on the eve of the tournament, but FIFA allowed them to compete together at the 2006 World Cup. The Czech Republic and Ukraine were making their first appearance as independent nations, but they had taken part in the past as part of Czechoslovakia and the Soviet Union, respectively. Serbia and Montenegro had competed as Yugoslavia in the past and as recently as 1998.

Australia qualified for the first time since 1974. Some of the best teams of that decade, such as Turkey, who finished third at the 2002 World Cup, Euro 2004 champions Greece, and 2006 Africa Cup of Nations winners Egypt, all failed to qualify. Belgium failed to qualify for the first time since 1978 and Cameroon for the first time since 1986. For the first time since 1982, all six confederations were represented at the World Cup finals.

As for the venues, Germany had a large selection of suitable stadiums. Organizers settled on 12 stadiums, many of them identified by different names since FIFA had prohibited sponsorship of venues unless those same sponsors had also made a deal with FIFA. For example, the Allianz Arena in Munich was known during the tournament as the FIFA World Cup Stadium. Berlin's Olympiastadion, one of the world's finest venues, would host six matches, including the final.

Group Stage

In the opening match of the World Cup on June 9 in Munich, Germany defeated Costa Rica 4–2 to open Group A, the highest-scoring opening match in tournament history. Just six minutes into the game, Philipp Lahm put the host in front with a curling shot from outside the box that beat goalkeeper José Porras. Costa Rica responded six minutes later with a goal from Paulo Wanchope. In the 17th minute, Germany regained the lead off a Miroslav Klose goal. Klose scored his second of the game in the 60th minute. Germany, coached by Klinsmann and missing Ballack because of an injury, won the game 4–2. In Gelsenkirchen that evening, Ecuador blanked Poland 2–0 at Arena AufSchalke. The back-and-forth play characterized by both matches was a good omen for the tournament in terms of future excitement and goals.

Germany, loaded with talent and playing in front of their home fans, won passage to the knockout stage on June 14 at the Westfalenstadion. The 1–0 win against Poland came in dramatic fashion when substitute Oliver Neuville scored in the first minute of stoppage time on a sliding kick off a wonderful cross from David Odonkor, another sub. "It was a bit lucky, but it was more than deserved," Neuville said afterward. "I should have scored even before."

The following day at Hamburg's Volksparkstadion, Ecuador blanked Costa Rica 3–0. The Ecuadorians showed that a team effort, coupled by the high-flying offense of Agustín Delgado, could translate to wins. On the group's final match day on June 20 in Berlin, it was two first-half goals from Klose that propelled Germany to a 3–0 victory against Ecuador to win the group. Ecuador advanced as the second-place team.

"We wanted to win the group," Klinsmann told reporters after the win. "We scored three victories, we got more confidence and we are growing as a team. Now the real World Cup is beginning. We have fantastic fans and great support and this integration with our fans is great, but we have to keep our feet on the ground."

England were the team to beat in Group B, and the Three Lions didn't disappoint their fans. A 1–0 victory against Paraguay on June 10 at the Waldstadion in Frankfurt did not happen in spectacular fashion—an own goal by defender Carlos Gamarra three minutes into the match—but the three points would prove vital as the group developed. In Dortmund that same day, Trinidad and Tobago and Sweden played to a scoreless draw, a result that mostly benefited tiny T&T.

England's 2–0 won against Trinidad and Tobago on June 15 at the Frankenstadion in Nuremberg earned them passage to the knockout stage. Peter Crouch headed in a cross by Beckham seven minutes from time to give England the goal it needed. Steven Gerrard added a second in stoppage time. "People expected us to walk through this game," Beckham said. "We knew they were going to play 11 men behind the ball. They made it hard for us all game. We knew if we kept to our game plan that we'd break them down." In Berlin that same day, Sweden earned a 1–0 victory versus Paraguay on a goal by Freddie Ljungberg with a minute left to play to keep their hopes of clinching a spot in the round of 16 alive.

England, the eventual group winners, and Sweden pushed Paraguay into third place as a result of narrow victories over the South Americans. In fact, the 2–2 draw between England and Sweden on June 20 at the RheinEnergie-Stadion in Cologne was enough to see both nations through to the next round. Henrik Larsson tied it following a throw-in, getting a touch on the ball and deflecting it into the goal. "We won the group," Eriksson told reporters, "and that's what counts."

Group C, the tournament's "Group of Death," did not disappoint. Argentina opened things up with a 2–1 win against the Ivory Coast in Hamburg. Javier Saviola, who had helped Argentina win the gold medal at the 2004 Olympics in Athens, lived up to the hype—at least he did for this game—when he scored the winning goal after 38 minutes. Juan Román Riquelme, who played at Spanish club Villareal, wore the number 10 jersey. Touted as the next Maradona, he would fall short. It was another player on that 2006 roster named Lionel Messi, donning the number 19 shirt, who would go on to bigger stardom. "He can put up with anything, even with the savior tag that people are already attaching," Maradona told Agence France-Presse when asked about Messi before the World Cup. "The ball remains on the upper part of his foot like it's glued. He's got another gear, and the best part is that he hasn't reached his peak."

The Zentralstadion in Leipzig saw the Netherlands defeat Serbia and Montenegro 1–0 on a goal by Arjen Robben after 18 minutes. The victory ensured that the Argentina-Netherlands game, scheduled for the group's final match day, could decide who would take the group. Argentina defeated Serbia and Montenegro 6–0 in Gelsenkirchen as Maradona watched from the stands. Maxi Rodríguez scored twice, and Messi, who came in as a second-half sub for Rodríguez, tallied one two minutes from time to complete the rout. Argentina's second goal in the 31st minute was not only an amazing display of individual skill, but a sign of how the team's separate parts could work together. The Albiceleste strung together 23 uninterrupted passes among eight players that resulted in a goal. The final pass was by Hernán Crespo, who provided a backheel pass to Esteban Cambiasso. The midfielder hammered the ball in the net for an amazing goal and passage to the round of 16. The Netherlands also booked a place in the knockout round, edging the Ivory Coast 2–1 in Stuttgart. Ruud van Nistelrooy provided the winning goal after 27 minutes.

The most anticipated game of the tournament turned out to be little more than a training session. The Netherlands and Argentina played to a scoreless draw, allowing the Albiceleste to win the group on goal differential. The match was also a chance for Argentina to rest several starters, and manager José Pékerman started Messi and Carlos Tevez for the first time at this tournament. The goals didn't come, but the talent was there. "It shows we have so many quality players," Messi told reporters, "that we can replace other ones and we still have a good chance."

The Group D clash between Mexico and Iran on June 11 in Nuremberg opened the group. The Mexicans were coached by chain-smoking Argentine Ricardo Lavolpe, who bore an uncanny resemblance to Al Pacino in the movie *Scarface*. Mexico opened the scoring after 28 minutes with Omar Bravo, but then gave up an equalizer eight minutes later when Yahya Golmohammadi slammed the ball into the net after the defense failed to clear the ball off a corner kick. The Iranians, looking for their second win ever at a World Cup, could do little as Lavolpe reshuffled his lineup, shifting from a 3–4–3 to a 3–5–2. The attack came to life as the Iranians spent the remainder of the first half soaking up the pressure. While the Mexicans picked up steam in the second half, the Iranians ran out of it. Bravo scored again in the 76th minute, and Antonio Naelson, known by the nickname Zinha, added a third goal 11 minutes from time to give Mexico the 3–1 victory.

That evening, Angola made their World Cup debut against its former colonizer, Portugal, in Cologne. What appeared to be a mismatch turned into a riveting contest. The last time the two teams had met on the soccer field had been five years earlier during a friendly in Lisbon. On that occasion, the Portuguese led 5–1, but the game had to be suspended after Angola had a fourth player red-carded and the game degenerated into a brawl. At Germany 2006, Portugal was only able to win 1–0. Angola might have lost the game, but they won many admirers that evening. The game's only goal came after just five minutes in when Luís Figo galloped past defender Jamba (who went by one name in tribute to the Brazilian players he idolized as a child), then passed the ball to an open Pauleta who side-footed the ball into the goal.

On June 16, in Hanover, the Angolan players put on another surprise showing, only this time they were able to snatch a point away from Mexico. The scoreless draw, which put Mexico's qualification to the next round in jeopardy, gave the Angolans cause for celebration. The next day, Portugal beat Iran, 2–0, in Frankfurt with Figo, now 33 years old and playing his best soccer in years. The Iranian backline, which had looked so lackluster against Mexico, also had to contend with Deco, who missed the game against Angola because of a foot injury. But it was Figo's crosses and a series of passes for his teammates that allowed Portugal to dominate. Figo's pass to Deco gave Portugal the lead in the 64th minute. Another Figo play, this time resulting in a take-down in the box, gave Portugal a penalty kick with 10 minutes left to play. Cristiano Ronaldo, often impeccable from the spot, scored.

Portugal won the group on June 21 after defeating Mexico, 2–1, in Gelsenkirchen, while Angola's dreams of advancing fell apart following a 1–1 draw versus Iran in Leipzig. Angola could have edged out Mexico for second place on goal differential, but the Africans were unable to score more goals. Angola coach Luís Oliviera Gonçalves praised his team after the game. "People were saying we would let in a lot of goals but that didn't happen," he told reporters. "The game was a little bit of bad football, but in the end I think a draw was a fair result."

Group E would be the tightest of them all. The meeting between the Czech Republic and the United States on June 12 in Gelsenkirchen turned into a lopsided affair. The Czechs got on the board after just five minutes when the U.S. backline was too slow to react to defender Zdeněk Grygera, who went on a furious run down the right flank. Grygera's cross was met by the towering Jan Koller—all six foot seven of him—who headed the ball into the net past Kasey Keller. The Czechs doubled their lead with a Tomas Rosicky goal in the 36th minute. Another Rosicky goal in the 76th minute humiliated the Americans, who looked bewildered for much of the 3–0 game.

The Italians, meanwhile, broke with their tradition of being slow starters, defeating Ghana 2–0 that evening in Hanover. The Italian players, distracted by a match-fixing scandal brewing back home, started the game on the defensive but emerged as an offensive threat as the game wore on. Goals by Andrea Pirlo in the 40th minute and a second from Vincenzo Iaquinta seven minutes from time got them the win.

Five days later, Ghana stunned the Czech Republic, putting on a sparkling display for the 2–0 win. The Ghanaians, in the second match of their World Cup debut, had finally played with the flair many expected to see from them, while the Czech Republic lacked the pace and power used to defeat the Americans. Asamoah Gyan put Ghana ahead after two minutes. The Czechs failed to respond, and lone striker Vratislav Lokvenc did little to threaten Ghana's defense. Michael Essien, one of the best playmakers to ever emerge from Africa, created chance upon chance. Gyan missed a penalty kick in the 65th minute, but Ghana got that second goal with eight minutes remaining when Sulley Muntari's powerful shot beat goalkeeper Peter Cech.

That evening at the Fritz-Walter-Stadion in Kaiserslautern, the United States and Italy matched wits in a game the Azzurri were expected to dominate. The Italians never took charge, and the plucky Americans were able to remain competitive in a game that was rich in controversy but meager in quality. The Americans started strong, but it was Italy that took the lead after 22 minutes when Alberto Gilardino's header off a Pirlo free kick found the back of the net. The Italians could have killed any U.S. chance of a comeback, but that second goal never came. Worse, the Azzurri complicated matters for themselves five minutes later by giving up a bizarre own goal following a Bobby Convey free kick from the right sideline. The ball hit defender Cristian Zaccardo in the leg, then took an awkward bounce and spun into the net for the own goal. The game took on an even odder twist after that. A minute after the U.S. equalizer, the Italians were down a man when midfielder Daniele De Rossi elbowed Brian McBride in the face. Uruguayan referee Jorge Larrionda pulled out a red card, and the AS Roma player was out of the game. De Rossi walked off the field as the U.S. team's medical staff stitched up McBride's bloody face. Seconds before the end of the first half, Larrionda pulled out his red card once again, sending off U.S. midfielder Pablo Mastroeni following a two-footed tackle on Pirlo. Both sides were even with 10 men.

The second half featured more rough tackles and theatrics. Two minutes after the interval, the Italians gained the numerical player advantage after Eddie Pope was given a second yellow card and ejected after a tackle on Gilardino. The call seemed unjustified, particularly since Pope had won the ball on the play. Marcello Lippi's men, unable to put the one-man advantage to good use, responded by putting in Del Piero to replace Zaccardo and Iaquinta for Luca Toni. Del Piero had two clear scoring chances, but Keller saved them both and the game ended 1–1.

Ghana advanced as the group's second-place team on June 22 after defeating the United States 2–1 in Nuremberg. Italy, meanwhile, won the group that same day in Hamburg, eliminating a 10-man Czech side 2–0 thanks to goals from defender Marco Materazzi and striker Filippo Inzaghi. "This team has terrific spirit, probably the most fighting spirit I have had in any team," Lippi told reporters. "We deserve to qualify. We played two great games to beat Ghana and Czech Republic. They are two very difficult teams."

An hour later, a cloud fell over the win as Italian FA prosecutor Stefano Palazzi recommended that Juventus, AC Milan, Fiorentina, and Lazio be demoted to Serie B, the country's second division, for their involvement in a match-fixing scandal, known as Calciopoli, that was starting to overshadow much of the work the Italians had accomplished on the field at this tournament. On the eve of the World Cup, several recorded telephone calls revealed a network of cozy relationships between several team managers and referees dating back to the 2004–5 season. The transcripts from these phone taps resembled something out of a gangster movie. Juventus general manager Luciano Moggi was at the center of the scandal, though he has always maintained his innocence. Moggi was eventually banned for life from any involvement in the game. After the World Cup, Juventus was stripped of the 2004–5 title (which was left unassigned) and the 2005–6 title (subsequently awarded to Inter Milan). As punishment, the team was relegated to the second division. AC Milan, Fiorentina, Lazio, and Reggina were all given point deductions to follow the subsequent season.

As is the case with every World Cup, all eyes were set on Brazil. The defending champions—if you believed the Nike ads—were the team to beat in Group F and possibly even among all the finalists. In an environment of such high expectations, there was no room for error. Anything short of winning the trophy would be seen as a defeat for the Brazilians. Winning another title was entirely possible given the talent of Brazil's roster. Carlos Alberto Parreira was back coaching the team after the triumph at USA '94 and was relying on the so-called "Magic Quartet" with Ronaldo, Ronaldinho, Kaká, and Adriano forming the frontline. "Brazil is considered the favorite because of the success it has had in the past," Parreira told a news conference before the start of the World Cup. "But the tournament is treacherous. Being the favorite off the field doesn't count for much. On the field, everyone is equal."

Brazil learned that 11 solo artists did not necessarily make an orchestra. Problems were evident. Ronaldo had injured himself midway through the season with Real Madrid. He reported to Brazil's training camp overweight and sluggish. Ronaldo's own website listed his weight at 190 pounds—21 pounds more than four years earlier. The striker had also complained of blisters—five of them on his left foot—in his never-ending saga of excuses for why he was in such poor shape.

In Brazil's debut on June 13 against Croatia in Berlin, the Seleção were far from peak form. While Kaká and Ronaldinho appeared in top shape, Ronaldo and Adriano were not. What resulted was a lethargic match in which the Croatian attack showed plenty of potential, but ultimately never threatened the Brazilian goal. The only goal of the game came from a fierce shot fired by Kaká in the 44th minute from long range. Despite the 1–0 defeat, Croatia's fans lit red flares in honor of their team's positive performance. Brazil had won—but barely.

The previous day, Australia, marking its return to the finals after a 32-year absence, used its stamina to defeat Japan 3–1 in Kaiserslautern. Hiddink had imposed a tough regimen on the team, all in the hopes of developing the players' stamina in time for the finals. Hiddink's plan worked, and the Socceroos, down 1–0 at halftime, scored three unanswered goals in the game's waning minutes to grab a 3–1 victory.

Japan, in search of a win after falling apart to Australia, were looking for a victory against Croatia. The teams squared off on June 18 in Nuremberg with the Croatians also in desperate need of points if they wanted to remain in contention for a spot in the final 16. Japan, coached by former Brazilian great Zico, ran out of steam early, and so did the Croatians. The game ended scoreless, but Croatia could have won the game in the first half after Darijo Srna saw his penalty kick blocked by Japan's goalkeeper Yoshikatsu Kawaguchi. That evening in Munich, Brazil played Australia in another game that would end in a victory for the defending champions. Brazil's 2–0 win gave it the points needed to advance, but it was unconvincing. Second-half goals by Adriano and Fred got them the win, but Ronaldo had been contained by the Aussie defense and became a nonfactor as the game wore on.

Australia joined Brazil in the round of 16 following a 2–2 draw against Croatia on June 22 in Stuttgart. The sides played an intense match—and participated in yet another World Cup game where the protagonist turned out to be the referee. Australia needed Brazil to beat Japan (they would, 4–1, in Dortmund) and at least earn a draw against Croatia to advance out of the group. England's Graham Poll, one of the most respected referees in the world, had a lousy day. He failed to award Australia two penalty kicks, and he red-carded Croatia's Josip Šimunič in stoppage time after showing him a third yellow card just three minutes after he had been booked a second time, an offense that should have gotten the player booted from the game. Australia played a strong game, but the match descended into anarchy in the final 10 minutes thanks to Poll's abysmal performance. Down 2–1, the Aussies battled back, as they had against Japan, and the stamina and determination infused in them by Hiddink came through in the end. Harry Kewell scored 11 minutes from time off a Mark Bresciano cross to make the score level and earn a 2–2 draw. John Aloisi looked offside on the play, but Poll let the goal stand, to the delight of the yellow-clad Australian fans, which made up a majority of the 52,000 in attendance at Gottlieb-Daimler-Stadion. Australia was through to the second round, while Croatia—and Poll on orders from FIFA—were sent home early.

Group G opened June 13 with South Korea downing Togo 2–1 in Frankfurt. Ahn Jung-hwan scored the game winner in the 72nd minute for the South Koreans, who were no longer the powerful and hard-running team that had finished fourth just four years earlier at home. Togo, playing in its first World Cup finals, had seen its preparations undermined by a pay dispute with the country's FA that forced their German-born manager Otto Pfister to walk off in frustration a day before the match, only to return hours before the game and resume his place on the bench.

On the same day, France and Switzerland squared off in Stuttgart. Both sides conspired to play what turned out to be one of the dullest games at the tournament. The teams had played each other in the qualifying rounds, tying each other on both occasions—0–0 in Paris and 1–1 in Berne—and could do no better at the World Cup. France, who had not scored in four straight World Cup games dating back to the 1998 final, would need offensive firepower if it hoped to get far.

Five days later in Leipzig, manager Raymond Domenech's team finally had something to cheer about when they faced off against South Korea. France scored first with Henry after nine minutes, but Les Bleus' failure to score again hurt them in the end when Park Ji-sung grabbed the equalizer nine minutes from time to earn a 1–1 tie. Zidane's indolent style appeared to stifle the team's midfield, but Domenech insisted on keeping the Real Madrid star in the game. David Trezeguet, on the outs with Domenech, replaced Zidane in the 90th minute, but there was no time for France to do anything. Worse yet, Zidane, who had announced a few months earlier that he would retire after the tournament, collected a second consecutive yellow card and was forced to miss France's final group game against Togo. A place in the next round seemed highly doubtful for France, while the South Koreans had three points and were in good position to advance.

Switzerland eliminated Togo on June 19 following a 2–0 victory in Dortmund. Pfister's resignation over bonuses, followed by his swift return, created an unsettled mood in the Togo camp. This time, the players threatened not to show up against Switzerland. FIFA intervened and settled the dispute, trying to avoid the embarrassment a no-show would have caused. Togo certainly could have played better, but a series of wasted opportunities and the off-the-field shenanigans were too much for the team to endure. A goal from Alexander Frei in the 16th minute and a strike by Tranquillo Barnetta with two minutes left was enough for the Swiss to win the game.

France finally showed what it was made of on June 23, blanking Togo 2–0 in Cologne. Without Zidane, Domenech's team appeared more likely to score, although a scoreless first half was anything but promising. The second half was another story. France grabbed the lead in the 55th minute with Patrick Vieira, who celebrated his 30th birthday with a goal. Trezeguet got the start alongside Henry, and the French imposed their game on the Africans. Vieira was impeccable in the back. He added to his birthday gift six minutes after he scored, heading the ball in for Henry to make it 2–0. France finished second in the group and clinched a berth to the round of 16, joining first-place Switzerland, who had defeated South Korea 2–0 in Hanover.

Spain, as expected, dominated Group H from the early going. La Roja blanked Ukraine 4–0 on June 14 in Leipzig, then followed up that win with a 3–1 drubbing of Tunisia five days later in Stuttgart thanks to two goals from Fernando Torres. Spain, with six points, was guaranteed a spot in the last 16. Whether Spain would finally be able to break from the shackles of early elimination and reach the final remained a mystery. For now, the team was playing to the potential that manager Luis Aragonés had heaped on them on the eve of the competition.

The fight for second place was between Ukraine, Tunisia, and Saudi Arabia. Ukraine rebounded from their defeat to Spain, downing Saudi Arabia 4–0 on June 19 in Hamburg. AC Milan striker Andriy Shevchenko, back in top form after his abysmal showing against Spain, ignited his team's attack, even scoring a goal. A 1–0 victory in Berlin against Tunisia on June 23, via a Shevchenko goal on a penalty kick in the 70th minute, helped them finish second and through to the round of 16. The decision by referee Carlos Amarilla of Paraguay ultimately decided the match.

Rob Hughes, writing in the *International Herald Tribune* the following day, noted the sly way in which Shevchenko had won the penalty.

Whether or not it was a soft penalty is a matter of opinion. To my eye, Shevchenko deliberately took the route between Ali Boumnijel, the 40-year-old Tunisian goalie, and the defender, Karim Haggui, that was bound to lead to contact. When he fell, there was no Tunisian foul, but possibly the referee felt some electricity of his own. Perhaps he ruled that the nudging and pushing that always happens in these circumstances had caused a delayed loss of balance. Whatever, he pointed to the penalty spot. Haggui didn't so much protest as beg the arbiter to reconsider. But officialdom seldom does, and with the face of an executioner, Shevchenko claimed his prize.

Round of 16

Teams from Europe dominated the round of 16. Unlike 2002, there would be few surprises as teams whittled down to just two on the road to the final. Europe featured 10 teams, while Brazil and Argentina were also there.

The all-European matchup between Germany and Sweden got things off on June 24 in Munich. A strong crowd of 66,000 greeted the home team. Propelled by that and by the gulf in talent, Germany progressed to the quarterfinals thanks to a Lukas Podolski brace in the opening 12 minutes. Sweden, down to 10 players after Teddy Lučić received two yellow cards in the first half, blew a chance at a comeback. In the 52nd minute, Larsson won a penalty kick that could have cut the lead in half, but his attempt went high over the bar.

While the Germans were finding cohesion, Argentina was giving its fans heart attacks. It took extra time in Leipzig for the Albiceleste to find a 2–1 victory over Mexico following a brilliant blast from Rodríguez. The attacking midfielder chested down a long, arcing pass from Sorín near the right corner of the penalty box and volleyed a left-footed shot to the far corner of the goal past goalkeeper Oswaldo Sánchez. It was a shot no goalie could save. It was little consolation for the Mexicans after they had played a competitive match. "I had not decided to shoot it, but the ball fell right in front of me," Rodríguez said after the game. "It's one of those shots that can go into the stands or in the goal."

England, in its quest to reach the final, got past Ecuador 1–0 on June 25 in Stuttgart. It was another individual effort—this one from Beckham—to power the Three Lions to the quarterfinals. Beckham bent a 30-yard free kick just in the 60th minute, lifting England to victory. It was an ugly win, but that didn't matter at this stage of the competition. England's disjointed outing was in part due to the sweltering 95-degree temperatures. "We've got to overcome it because there will be other days like this," Beckham told reporters. "We make things hard for ourselves. We don't keep the ball as well as we can do."

The same score resolved the contest between Portugal and the Netherlands. Portugal survived with a 1–0 win (via a goal by Maniche after 23 minutes), but would have to play against England in the quarterfinals without Deco and Costinha, who were red-carded after both teams ended the game with nine players amid a sea of pushes and shoves.

The players and referee Valentin Ivanov of Russia made a mess of this one, as unsportsmanlike conduct became the norm as the game wore on. Ivanov handed out 16 yellow cards and four red. "I think in the second half we only played 20 or 25 minutes of football," Dutch manager Marco van Basten said after the game. "There was little playing time with all the injuries and the players going down all over the place. What is also regrettable is that the refereeing has such an influence on such an important match."

Italy also won by a 1–0 margin against Australia on June 26 in Kaiserslautern. The Socceroos played the Azzurri tightly, stifling Italy's attack the entire game. The Italians, however, spoiled any notion of another Hiddink team overachieving at a World Cup. It was a controversial Totti penalty kick in stoppage time that made the difference and saw the Azzurri though to the quarterfinals. The penalty kick came after defender Fabio Grosso fell to the ground after Lucas Neill slid into him. Grosso clumsily tried to leap over him, but instead found the turf. Referee Luis Medina Cantalejo of Spain whistled a penalty kick, and the underdogs from Down Under were out.

In the day's second game, Ukraine and Switzerland ended scoreless after 120 minutes of action. When extra time failed to produce a goal, the game went to a shootout—the first at this tournament. In a shootout highlighted by poor shooting accuracy and strong goalkeeping, Switzerland's Pascal Zuberbühler saved the opening kick by Shevchenko. Switzerland, however, failed to take advantage. Ukraine goalkeeper Oleksandr Shovkovskyi saved the first and third penalties from Marco Streller and Ricardo Cabanas, respectively, while Tranquillo Barnetta's kick hit the crossbar in his team's second attempt to see Ukraine win 3–0. Switzerland became the first team in World Cup history to exit the tournament without giving up a goal.

In Dortmund, Brazil did not disappoint in its outing against Ghana. The Brazilians managed a 3–0 victory on June 27, with Ronaldo opening the scoring after just five minutes. Ghana made it a close game by keeping Brazil off the scoreboard for the rest of the half, but Adriano's strike in stoppage time killed off the game. Brazil added another goal with Zé Roberto six minutes from time.

In the last round-of-16 game, France defeated Spain 3–1 in Hanover. The French, so criticized at various stages of this competition, scored two late goals to put this one away. It was a strong display by Les Bleus, spearheaded by Patrick Vieria and Zidane, to set up a quarterfinal clash against Brazil.

Refereeing controversies once again took center stage. Referee Roberto Rosetti of Italy blew for a foul when Henry went down after a tackle by Spain defender Carles Puyol, a play that resulted in a Vieria goal. Spain manager Luis Aragonés, fuming after the match, told reporters, "Their second goal came from a free kick that wasn't a foul and we were punished by a refereeing error."

Quarterfinals

Germany hosted Argentina on June 30 in Berlin to open the quarterfinals. Against the host nation, Argentina played an authoritative match—perhaps even its best soccer at this tournament—and took the lead in the 49th minute through Roberto Ayala's header following a corner kick. However, the Albiceleste endured some trouble as the second half wore on. Goalkeeper Roberto Abbondanzieri was replaced in the 71st minute with backup Leo Franco following an injury. Seven minutes earlier, the Boca Juniors goalkeeper received a blow to the hip from Klose and, despite extensive treatments by team medics, was forced to exit the match.

The move changed the course of the game. The Germans, seeking the tying goal with a greater sense of urgency and cheered on by 72,000 fans, created several chances. In the 80th minute, on one such play, Ballack crossed the ball to Tim Borowski. The Werder Bremen midfielder passed the ball to Klose, who then directed his header past Franco to tie the score. Extra time failed to yield a goal, forcing a shootout. The Germans proved once again that they have no equals when it comes to winning a shootout, scoring all four of their kicks. Argentina missed two of them as Ayala and Juan Cambiasso saw their attempts saved by goalkeeper Jens Lehmann. Following the game, a melee erupted on the sidelines. As the punches flew, Argentina's Leandro Cufré was shown a red card. Frings was also subsequently suspended for his involvement. The incident was an unfortunate end to what had been an enthralling match.

In Hamburg that evening, Italy had little trouble eliminating Ukraine. The Azzurri took just six minutes to score when Gianluca Zambrotta picked up a cheeky backheel from Totti, blasting it into the net with a low shot from outside the box. Toni added two goals, in the 59th and 69th minutes, to give Italy a 3–0 win. The players dedicated the win to former Italy defender Gianluca Pessotto after he survived a fall from a fourth-story window at Juventus's headquarters in Turin just three days earlier. Since he was holding a rosary, it was widely believed to be a suicide attempt. The plunge coincided with widening investigations regarding match-fixing allegations. Though not implicated in the scandal, Pessotto was said to be depressed with his role as the club's team manager. He suffered multiple fractures and internal bleeding as a result of the fall. He was released from the hospital a month later. At the end of the game, Italian players posed behind a banner expressing support for their friend with the message: "We are with you, Pessotto."

On July 1, England and Portugal met in Gelsenkirchen. Penalty-kick shootouts had been a disaster for England in the past, and when the game ended scoreless, a look of despair came over the players' faces. History repeated itself for the Three Lions. England had played with 10 players for much of the second half after Wayne Rooney was shown a red card in the 62nd minute. The England striker stomped on Carvalho's groin as the player lay on the ground. Referee Héctor Elizondo of Argentina had no choice but to show him a red. Rooney's exit was another blow to England's effort after Beckham was forced to leave the game just 10 minutes earlier following an ankle injury. In the shootout, Ricardo was able to save three of England's attempts as Portugal prevailed 3–1 to reach the semifinals at a World Cup for the first time since 1966.

The final quarterfinal was perhaps the most anticipated of the round. Brazil and France squared off in Frankfurt. The game's only goal came in the 57th minute when Zidane, off a quickly taken free kick, found an unmarked Henry. The striker, who beat his marker after Roberto Carlos had stopped to tie his shoes, volleyed the ball home for the 1–0 win. France, who beat Brazil at its own game by playing a joyful brand of craft soccer, was through to the semifinals. "Since he's going to retire, he's fully invested in this game," Domenech said of Zidane. "He doesn't have to calculate anything. Every moment is perhaps his last one."

For Parreira, the defeat meant humiliation and his subsequent resignation. A sluggish Ronaldo and sloppy defending had done Brazil in.

Individual brilliance doesn't always make for a talented team—an issue that had plagued the Brazilians in the past. "I wasn't prepared for defeat," Parreira told reporters. "It never crossed my mind we wouldn't come to the final. It's a very hard moment."

Semifinals

With Brazil eliminated, the four semifinals saw Germany among the favorites to win it all. Host nations had traditionally done well, and Klinsmann's team had looked stronger with each passing round.

Standing in Germany's way was rival Italy. The Azzurri did what they often did best at the World Cup by combining strong defense and counterattacks. The July 4 game in Dortmund was a stalemate for much of the contest, both teams evenly matched and somewhat afraid of exposing themselves too much in order to avoid conceding a goal.

The game ended scoreless, but the Italians appeared rejuvenated in extra time. With a minute left to play in extra time, Pirlo played the ball to Grosso. The defender one-timed the ball with his left foot as the ball curled past the left post. The goal sent Grosso, his teammates, and Italian fans everywhere into ecstasy. Not to be outdone, Italy added a second two minutes later in stoppage time. Cannavaro broke up the German attack, then powered the ball forward. Gilardino then fed a pass to Del Piero, who chipped the ball into the goal for the 2–0 win. Germany, meanwhile, would take third place. Klinsmann stepped down as manager to spend more time with his family.

In the second semifinal the following day, France edged Portugal 1–0 in Munich. Once again, Zidane made the difference for Les Bleus, converting a penalty kick after 33 minutes to put his nation back into a World Cup final for the second time in eight years. "Now that we are here, after all the effort we have made, we will try and bring it home," Zidane told reporters after the game. "It won't be easy. It will be difficult, but we have the weapons to do it. We have the will to do it."

Final: Italy vs. France

Italy and France did battle in the final just six years after the sides met at the 2000 European Championship. On that occasion in Rotterdam, Italy, 30 seconds away from pulling off a 1–0 win, conceded the equalizer in stoppage time. A golden goal by Trezeguet won France the trophy. The World Cup rematch was played on July 9 in Berlin's Olympiastadion before 69,000. The Italians were favored, but Zidane's performances against Spain and Brazil made France a legitimate contender for the final prize. Many had predicted a scoreless tie—given the strong defenses—but they would be mistaken.

Zidane put France ahead after seven minutes after Florent Malouda was brought down by Materazzi. Referee Elizondo pointed to the spot, apparently fooled by Malouda's dramatic fall. Zidane stepped up to take the shot, cheekily chipping the ball to Buffon's left, which hit the underside of the crossbar and bounced to the ground just inches past the line for the goal. A seemingly relieved Zidane raised his arms in relief, jogging away as his teammates hugged him. The old magician had conjured up one more trick. In the process, Zidane, who was playing in his last game, had made history, joining Brazilians Pelé and Vavá and Germany's Paul Breitner as the only players to ever score in two World Cup final games.

The Italians, down for the first time at the tournament, quickly reacted. Materazzi made amends for conceding the penalty when he headed the ball off Pirlo's out-swinging corner kick, towering over the French defense to tie the score in the 19th minute. The Italians nearly took the lead in the 36th minute when Toni's header, off another Pirlo corner kick, hit the crossbar.

The game went to extra time. Trezeguet, the hero six years earlier, was subbed in for Franck Ribéry in the 100th minute, but he was to become the villain here. Zidane came back to life again in extra time, bursting into the box with a powerful header that was tipped over the bar by Buffon. The play, the stuff of highlight reels, would be overshadowed by another Zidane header of a different sort.

Zidane, in a moment that can only be described as insanity, charged toward Materazzi, head-butting the Italian defender in the chest. Materazzi fell to the ground the moment Zidane thrust his head into him. Elizondo did not see the infraction, but Buffon ran toward him to point out the offense. Elizondo consulted his assistant, but it was the fourth official, Luis Medina Cantalejo of Spain, stationed in between the Italian and French benches, who saw the head butt.

Questions arose immediately afterward as to whether Cantalejo had seen TV replays on a small monitor placed along the sidelines. If he had, Cantalejo would be the first referee ever to use instant replay. FIFA said afterward that TV technology was never used as part of the decision that led to Zidane's red card. In fact, the majority of those in the stands had not seen the incident. How else could it be explained that the decision to eject Zidane was greeted by a chorus of jeers?

Zidane did not argue the decision and slowly made his way into the tunnel to the dressing rooms, his head slumped down as he walked past the podium where the World Cup trophy was sitting. The image of Zidane walking past the trophy, so close and yet so far away from his grasp, a defeated man in his last game, was surreal. Speaking for the first time since the incident three days after the game, Zidane said in an interview on Canal Plus, a French television network, that Materazzi cursed at him and mentioned his sister. "I tried not to listen to him, but he repeated them several times," Zidane said about Materazzi's taunts. "Sometimes words are harder than blows. When he said it for the third time, I reacted." For months, Materazzi vehemently denied Zidane's account, but he eventually admitted to making an inappropriate comment about the Frenchman's sister. The incident was a sad ending to another emotion-filled World Cup.

The game would need a shootout to determine a winner. Pirlo, Materazzi, De Rossi, Del Piero, and Grosso all scored for Italy in the shootout. The winning kick—off of a ferocious left-footed shot by Grosso that flew into the upper right corner of the goal past Barthez— sent the Italian players into hysterics. The Italians won a fourth World Cup, and Cannavaro celebrated by planting a kiss on the trophy before proudly lifting it toward the sky in a sea of white confetti. For Italy, beset by a scandal back home, the victory was further evidence that the country remained a perennial soccer power.

CHAPTER EIGHT

European Sweep

BEFORE DANNY JORDAAN WAS GIVEN THE TASK OF HEADING SOUTH Africa's 2010 World Cup organizing committee, he was a fervent anti-apartheid advocate. As he watched his beloved nation split further down racial lines, Jordaan realized sports could serve a role in mending deep divisions.

A former teacher and businessman, the affable Jordaan was elected to the South African parliament in 1994—the same year apartheid ended and Nelson Mandela was elected the country's first Black president—and worked arduously toward trying to unite the country through sport.

"The 2010 FIFA World Cup would leave a substantial economic and tourism legacy for South Africa with the once-in-a-lifetime marketing opportunity expected to make South Africa a more widely known and understood tourism destination," Jordaan told me on the eve of the tournament. "This is the year when as a nation, we will open our doors, hearts and sporting spirits to the world. This is our time. This is our year."

Legacy can be a tough thing when it comes to World Cups. Host nations build lots of stadiums, but those often come at the expense of hospitals and schools. Take Soccer City Stadium. The venue is located in Soweto, on the edge of Johannesburg, where dirt roads and shantytowns share space with highways and shopping malls. The stadium itself—built in the shape of a calabash, a gourd used to cook meals—would turn into a melting pot of nationalities throughout the competition.

"I am tired, but no more than all the men and women who helped make this World Cup a success," Jordaan told me on the day of the 2010

World Cup final. "South Africans made this dream a reality after so many years of hard work."

I, too, was tired after my 17-hour flight to Johannesburg from New York, which had included trips to picturesque Cape Town and exotic Durban. As for Jordaan, the ensuing years weren't great for him. In 2015, he admitted to paying Jack Warner $10 million to help support soccer development, denying it had been to help secure the rights to host the World Cup.

The payment was essentially a bribe, the kind of thing that had come to characterize the way business was conducted by FIFA officials. Two years later, he was accused of having allegedly raped a former parliamentarian some two decades earlier. Jordaan, who was never charged with a crime, denied the allegations.

2010 WORLD CUP

An African nation was finally awarded a World Cup as part of FIFA's short-lived policy to rotate the tournament throughout the world in an effort to break the Europe–South America lock on hosts. The policy was abandoned in 2007, but not before South Africa was awarded hosting rights.

The successful South African bid was a victory for a nation that for much of the previous century had been banned from international competitions in all sports because of apartheid. After successfully hosting and winning the Rugby World Cup in 1995, then-president Nelson Mandela set his sights on soccer's biggest prize. Mandela served 27 years in prison for conspiring to overthrow the government but was released in 1990 just as the country prepared to end its segregationist policies.

The aim of the World Cup was to boost the nation economically, but primarily to promote South Africa as a tourist destination even as it had to deal with a growing crime problem. Despite maintaining a low profile during the tournament itself due to his ailing health, Mandela made his final public appearance during the World Cup final, where he received loud applause.

The tournament would be played in 10 venues—five new stadiums were built for the occasion, while five existing ones were upgraded—at a cost of $1.3 billion. The country also improved its public transportation system and major roadways, an ambitious project whose legacy was meant to last decades after the event. While the renovations benefited the country, many of the stadiums remained underutilized once the World Cup concluded.

Ahead of the World Cup finals draw, FIFA based its eight seeded teams on the October 2009 FIFA World Ranking, in addition to the host nation. No two teams from the same confederation were to be drawn in the same group, except allowing a maximum of two European teams in a group. Here's how the eight groups were composed:

Group A: South Africa, France, Uruguay, and Mexico

Group B: Argentina, Nigeria, South Korea, and Greece

Group C: England, the United States, Algeria, and Slovenia

Group D: Germany, Australia, Serbia, and Ghana

Group E: The Netherlands, Denmark, Japan, and Cameroon

Group F: Italy, Paraguay, New Zealand, and Slovakia

Group G: Brazil, North Korea, the Ivory Coast, and Portugal

Group H: Spain, Switzerland, Honduras, and Chile

As the quality in international soccer rose, so did the World Cup group stage. D and G were both considered the tournament's "Group of Death." While both were tricky, few surprises would ensue. Groups F and H, in the end, would unexpectedly prove to be two of the most competitive.

The altitude of several venues would affect games, although FIFA had downplayed it as a factor during the bidding process. Six of the 10 venues were more than 3,900 feet above sea level. Both Johannesburg venues—Soccer City Stadium and Ellis Park—were the highest at approximately 5,740 feet. The final would be played at Soccer City. "The time for Africa has come," South Africa's president Jacob Zuma said on June 11 at Soccer City before the opening match. "It has arrived."

What had also arrived was international fame for the *vuvuzela*, a relatively inexpensive horn made of plastic that South African fans loved to blow during games. The monotone noise emitted from the horns sounded more like an elephant in heat and made for an annoying sound for those inside the stadiums as well as for fans at home through their TVs. Some had called for the horns, about two feet in length, to be banned, but instead they became one of the symbols of this World Cup.

Group Stage

The hosts opened Group A, and the tournament, versus Mexico at Soccer City before 84,500 fans. South Africa were coached by Carlos Alberto Parreira, who was hoping to bring some Brazilian flair to the team though his coaching. The crowd, many blowing on *vuvuzelas*, was treated to a favorable start for the team nicknamed Bafana Bafana (the Zulu phrase meaning "The Boys, The Boys") when they opened the scoring in the 55th minute after Siphiwe Tshabalala tallied from a pass by Kagiso Dikgacoi. Mexico spoiled the party when captain Rafael Márquez equalized following a corner kick in the 79th minute. "We are still in the competition. I can't ask for more from the boys," Parreira said. "They did not disappoint us. I'm very happy."

The enthusiasm surrounding South Africa—both among the players and the millions throughout the country—took a hit on June 16 at Loftus Versfeld Stadium in Pretoria. Uruguay, a stronger and more talented side, got the best of the hosts. Diego Forlán, aggressive on the ball throughout the contest, scored twice as La Celeste cruised to a 3–0 victory. The following day in Polokwane, Mexico upset France 2–0 at Peter Mokaba Stadium, sending Les Bleus' chances of advancing into a tailspin. For the second straight game, France played with no cohesion and had failed to score a goal.

During halftime, striker Nicolas Anelka unleashed a verbal attack against Domenech in the dressing room. Domenech had criticized Anelka, who had not recorded a shot on goal in 429 consecutive minutes for France, for being out of position during the opening half. *L'Equipe* reported that Anelka exploded in rage. Domenech responded by subbing

Anelka from the game. The following day, Anelka was asked to apologize by the French FA. When he refused, Anelka was thrown off the team.

The decision caused shockwaves. On June 20, on the eve of the decisive France–South Africa match, the team's problems were laid bare before hundreds of fans and TV cameras from throughout the world there to watch the players practice. The players refused to train at their scheduled afternoon session in Knysna, on the country's southern coast, to protest the decision to ban Anelka. Captain Patrice Evra got into a skirmish with fitness coach Robert Duverne, which resulted in the players retreating to the team bus. The day culminated with Domenech reading aloud a statement from the players: "All the players without exception want to declare their opposition to the decision taken by the FFF to exclude Nicolas Anelka from the squad. At the request of the squad, the player in question attempted to have dialogue but his approach was ignored. The FFF has at no time tried to protect the squad. It has made a decision without consulting all the players, on the basis of the facts reported by the press."

The French FA fired back, calling the players' actions "unacceptable." It was a humiliating state of affairs, something that culminated with France's 2–1 defeat to South Africa two days later at Free State Stadium in Bloemfontein. The result failed to see South Africa through to the second round, the first host nation in World Cup history not to advance to the knockout stage. Nonetheless, the games had been a boon for South African unity and nationalism. For France, the dishonor was complete and highlighted one of the most disgraceful exits in tournament history. The French daily *Le Parisian* did not spare the team: "To have the worst soccer team at the World Cup was almost unbearable. To also have the most stupid is intolerable." Uruguay won the group, followed into the round of 16 by Mexico, who went through on goal differential after being tied for second with South Africa.

Argentina was drawn into Group B with some familiar foes. The Albiceleste had faced South Korea in the group stage back in 1986, while they had played both Nigeria and Greece during the opening round in 1994. Argentina and Nigeria had both been in the same group at the 2002 World Cup.

The team was coached by Maradona, while his heir Messi roamed the midfield. Of all the players to be dubbed the "next Maradona," Messi is the only one to live up to that billing. Both men possessed a powerful left-footed shot—although Messi did not have a penchant for being self-destructive.

In 2006, Maradona told the BBC that Messi was not only "the best player in the world," but also his heir. "I have seen the player who will inherit my place in Argentine football and his name is Messi," he said, adding, "I see him as very similar to me."

Both men—short and agile—were also wonderful dribblers and able to create goals as well as score them. Where Maradona's success included winning the World Cup for his country and leading Napoli to two Serie A titles, Messi had a greater range of opportunities at Barcelona. By 2010, Messi had already captured four league titles with the Catalan giants and two Champions Leagues, which by now had become the barometer most players measured themselves by.

It was at Ellis Park on June 12 that Argentina opened the tournament against Nigeria. It took six minutes for Argentina to take the lead after an unmarked Gabriel Heinze dived forward to head Juan Sebastián Verón's corner kick. Messi had several chances to score after that, but goalkeeper Vincent Enyeama's heroics kept the score close. The Argentines emerged victorious 1–0.

South Korea emerged as the second-place team in the group via a hard-fought 2–2 tie against Nigeria on June 22 at Moses Mabhida Stadium in the eastern coast city of Durban overlooking the Indian Ocean. It was the first time South Korea had advanced past the group stage on foreign soil. This might not have been the same team that had gone on a deep run at home in 2002, but South Korea had shown that it could claw back even when falling behind.

England came into Group C with high hopes of winning it. After all, the Premier League was the world's best and most lucrative domestic competition, but that did not automatically translate into success for the national team. Their three group-stage opponents, the United States, Algeria, and Slovenia, appeared more than manageable. So much so that the *Sun*, the London-based tabloid, went with the headline "EASY" following the draw as the word spelled out England, Algeria, Slovenia, and Yanks. It would be anything but once the Three Lions arrived in South Africa.

England, coached by former Italian international Fabio Capello, featured Steven Gerrard and Frank Lampard, two of the best attacking midfielders in the world. The English opened the tournament on June 12 against the United States at Royal Bafokeng Stadium in Rustenburg. The Americans had defeated England 1–0 back at the 1950 World Cup, but very few expected any sort of repeat of that grand upset this time around. As expected, England controlled the game from the start and was rewarded with a goal in the fourth minute. An unmarked Gerrard made a run into the box and beat goalkeeper Tim Howard with the outside of his right foot.

The Americans responded by leveling the score in the 40th minute when what appeared to be a harmless shot by Clint Dempsey, who played in England with Fulham, was mishandled by goalkeeper Robert Green. The 1–1 draw was a big result for the United States, while England walked away wondering what could have been. The United States followed that draw with another one. This time it was a hard-fought 2–2 against Slovenia, where the Americans could have secured all three points. U.S. fans were well represented in the stands among the 46,000 in attendance at Ellis Park after more than 130,000 of the 2.8 million World Cup tickets put up for sale had been purchased by Americans, the highest total of any country outside South Africa. What they witnessed was Slovenia jumping out to a 2–0 lead. "We all spoke about first of all believing that we could do it. That was the first thing that was said, and the second was that we need to score as early as we can," U.S. midfielder Landon Donovan said. "We knew if we did that we'd have a chance to get back in the game."

The second half was a new game. It was Donovan who tallied in the 48th minute after blasting the ball into the roof of the net from close range, a shot that caused goalkeeper Samir Handanović to flinch. The goal, from just six yards out, was the culmination of a play that saw Donovan dribble the ball freely along the right flank and into the box, before shooting it into the net from a tight angle for one of the most improbable-looking strikes in tournament history. "In the end, I decided to take a touch, aim high, and aim at his head. I don't think he wanted to get hit from there," Donovan said.

Following a series of chances for the United States, the Americans scored in the 82nd minute on a toe poke from Michael Bradley, who was set up on the right side by Jozy Altidore. The U.S. comeback was complete, and the Americans looked to have salvaged a draw. But the inspired Americans scored what appeared to be the go-ahead goal five minutes from time, but Maurice Edu's volley was disallowed by referee Koman Coulibaly of Mali. The blown call caused confusion as celebration turned to head-scratching. "Who knows what it was? I'm not sure how much English he spoke or if he spoke English," Donovan said. "We asked him several times in a non-confrontational way. He just ignored us."

Speculation was that the Americans had been tugging the shirts of several Slovenian players in the box the moment the goal was scored. The shirt tugging—a common practice on set pieces and corner kicks—had been done by players on both sides. With no other conceivable reason, the call remained a mystery. The FIFA practice of using a diverse referee pool at the World Cup was admirable, but in this case Coulibaly's only prior experience had been at the Africa Cup of Nations. A game of this magnitude was too much for him to deal with in the end.

England would advance as the second-place side after a 1–0 win against Slovenia at Nelson Mandela Bay Stadium in Port Elizabeth. A U.S. win in its final group match on June 23 against Algeria in Pretoria would qualify them to the last 16. The scoreless draw that was playing itself out between the United States and Algeria would see the Americans eliminated. After almost giving up another early goal, the Americans saw Dempsey's goal disallowed for being offside in the 21st minute. Dempsey came close a second time in the 57th minute when his shot hit the post, then he pounced on the rebound before sending it wide.

The United States was rewarded with a goal—and a 1–0 win—that helped them win the group in dramatic style. In the game's dying minutes, the Americans, in full desperation mode, lunged forward in search of a goal. After Howard made a save, he tossed the ball forward to Donovan in the midfield. Donovan, going at full speed, found Altidore in the box. Altidore then passed the ball over to Clint Dempsey, who attempted a shot. That's when Algerian goalkeeper Raïs M'Bohli made a save, but the ball bounced off him and into the path of Donovan.

Whether you were one of the 36,000 in attendance that night or watching on television, it is a moment—a goal—that will live on in the memory of fans forever, and on YouTube for those who weren't born yet. It's the moment Donovan ran toward the ball at full speed, slotting it into the net with a powerful and precise right-footed shot. The goal set off celebrations on the field, in the stands, and in millions of American homes and bars. "My favorite memory from that goal was turning the corner and looking up and seeing first Stuart Holden's face running toward the corner flag, followed by like 30 people—including staff and coaches and everyone—and just kind of meeting at the corner flag to celebrate," Donovan recalled. "That was a really cool moment."

Donovan's teammates recalled the last-gasp goal and celebration with fondness. "I remember running towards Landon and all of a sudden there were a pile of players on top of me. It was a great moment," Holden said. "It really was unbelievable."

"I didn't run towards him because I had no energy left," Howard added. "I was just exhausted. All I could do was hunch down on the ground at that moment. It was a relief."

The United States won a World Cup group for the first time since 1930. More than a decade later, the goal remains an internet phenomenon. For the first time in America's soccer history, one goal meant so much to a nation continuing to grow its love for the game. It seemed, for a moment anyway, that the United States was no different than Brazil. It was a collective moment where a nation could celebrate the success of its soccer team.

Group D, considered the "Group of Death," featured Germany, Serbia, Australia, and Ghana. Germany did not disappoint, blanking Australia 4–0 on June 13 in Durban. Five days later in Port Elizabeth, the Germans did disappoint, losing to Serbia 1–0 on a Milan Jovanović goal after 38 minutes. The Serbs, who had lost to Ghana 1–0, brought equilibrium to the group following their upset of the Germans. The two sides that would advance would be decided on the final match day on

June 23. Germany took on Ghana at Soccer City, while Australia played Serbia simultaneously at Mbombela Stadium in the northeastern city of Nelspruit (known as Mbombela since 2014).

The Germans came into the match in need of points, something it isn't typically accustomed to, and found the back of the net with Mesut Özil in the 60th minute. Özil's delicious left-footed shot from the top of the box curled past a gaggle of players and into the goal. It was enough to give Germany the win and the three points needed to go through as the group winners. Ghana also won that day by virtue of Australia's 2–1 victory against Serbia.

Ghana would finish second, edging the Socceroos on goal differential, as the continent rejoiced at seeing an African nation through to the last 16. In a game that had featured a clash of half-brothers—defender Jérôme Boateng of Germany and midfielder Kevin-Prince Boateng of Ghana— both teams went into their respective dressing rooms happy. Ghana would ultimately be the only African nation to advance to the round of 16.

Meanwhile, Group E was one of firsts. It would be the first time that the Netherlands, Denmark, Japan, and Cameroon would meet during a World Cup group stage. The technically superb Dutch had a lineup loaded with stars, including captain and defender Giovanni van Bronck-horst, midfielder Mark van Bommel, and strikers Klaas-Jan Huntelaar, Robin van Persie, and Arjen Robben.

The Netherlands opened the group on June 14 against Denmark at Soccer City. There were positives and negatives to emerge from the Dutch win. A 2–0 victory to start the group stage is an enormous plus, but they hadn't played well. The goals came from the most unusual places. An own goal by Denmark's Daniel Agger in the 46th minute and one from Dirk Kuyt five minutes from time sent the orange-clad fans in the stands, a majority of the 84,000 in attendance, into wild celebration. In the dressing room, the Dutch were much more introspective. "We didn't play that well and we won 2–0," Dutch midfielder Wesley Sneijder told reporters. "I say, if you don't play your best game, win it."

The Oranje followed up the win with another on June 19, this time a 1–0 result against Japan in Durban. Japan, 1–0 winners against Cam-eroon to open their World Cup campaign, kept the game close. Japan's midfield spent much of the time breaking up the Dutch's passing game, a disruption that led to fewer scoring chances for the side coached by Bert van Marwijk. Like all superior technical sides, the Dutch found a way to score after catching a break. In the 53rd minute, Sneijder's powerful shot deflected off goalkeeper Eiji Kawashima for the 1–0 win.

The Dutch won the group, posting a 2–1 win against Cameroon on June 24 at Cape Town Stadium in Cape Town. With second place still in the balance, the Japan-Denmark clash in Rustenburg would decide who else would advance from Group E. The group—more competitive than many had expected—was punctuated by Japan's 3–1 upset of Denmark. The Danes, in need of a win to advance, wilted as Japan showed both defensive and offensive dominance.

Italy were the favorites to take Group F, but the start of a new decade had brought with it better soccer across the globe. With more upsets frequent, the defending champions had the easiest group in the first round with Paraguay, Slovakia, and New Zealand. The Azzurri, coached once again by Marcello Lippi, had more World Cup appearances than the other three nations in Group F combined.

The Italian defense remained the envy of the world with Buffon in goal and his Juventus teammate Cannavaro in front of him. But a great goalkeeper and strong defense wasn't enough, as the Italians opened the tournament on June 14 with a 1–1 draw against Paraguay in Cape Town. Buffon was forced to leave the game at halftime with a back injury as the Italians salvaged a point following a De Rossi goal in the 63rd minute.

Six days later in Nelspruit, Italy—for the second straight game—fell behind when New Zealand's Shane Smeltz found the back of the net after just seven minutes past backup goalkeeper Federico Marchetti. An Iaquinta penalty kick in the 29th minute gave Italy the draw in a game they should have won.

The group remained wide open going into the final match day. New Zealand was in position to advance to the second round if it could defeat Paraguay on June 24 in Polokwane. The Italians would also move on if they beat Slovakia at the same time at Ellis Park. "We are always daring to dream," New Zealand manager Ricki Herbert told reporters. "At the World Cup, anything is possible."

Despite a valiant effort by New Zealand, a scoreless draw against Paraguay saw the South Americans through as the group winners. Italy and Slovakia, meanwhile, played an epic match. Slovakia imposed its game and jumped out to a 2–0 lead with two Róbert Vittek goals. "We didn't dominate," Vittek recalled. "I think we were better."

Italy could have gone through with another draw. It looked as if that could happen when Antonio Di Natale scored nine minutes from time. Down 2–1, the Italians pushed forward, and Slovakia took advantage of it by scoring a third goal with Kamil Kopúnek in the 89th minute. Second place remained on the line, and the Italians pulled another one back in stoppage time with Fabio Quagliarella, Italy's best player that evening.

Slovakia won 3–2, a result that eliminated the Italians. The Italian players, some of them in tears, walked off the field in shock. Lippi, criticized for calling up too many old players, apologized profusely for his failure in the post-match news conference and for not even coming close to delivering back-to-back titles. After France in 2002, the defending champions failed to advance out of the group stage. "I really believed that the men I chose would have been able to deliver something different," he said. "I guess this time around I was just not capable to motivating the men as I should have."

Group G, the tournament's other "Group of Death," saw Brazil as the favorites to advance, but second place remained wide open as Portugal, the Ivory Coast, and relatively unknown North Korea also aimed to reach the round of 16. The Brazil-Portugal match was one of the most anticipated of the first round.

While arguments over whether the Brazilians played enough of a free-flowing style that was to the liking of its fans, the Seleção, coached by former captain Dunga, boasted one of the world's leading playmakers in midfielder Kaká of AC Milan fame, while strikers Luís Fabiano and Adriano were proven finishers. Goalkeeper Júlio César led a stingy defense anchored by Lúcio.

The Brazilians opened the group on June 15 in Port Elizabeth. A 2–1 win against North Korea gave the impression of a much tighter contest. After a scoreless first half, Brazil got its scoring mojo back in the 55th minute when right back Maicon scored from a tight angle. Midfielder

Elano followed that up with a second goal in the 72nd minute. North Korea, making its return to the finals for the first time since 1966, scored a consolation goal in the 89th minute with Ji Yun-nam.

Five days later at Soccer City, Brazil dominated the Ivory Coast 3–1 to the delight of many in the crowd of 84,500 to see the South American giants through to the second round. Luís Fabiano netted a brace, and Elano scored his second of the tournament. Joy was diminished when Kaká was red-carded two minutes from time for a second yellow card after elbowing Ivory Coast striker Abdul Kader Keïta in the chest. He fell to the ground clutching his face theatrically, forcing referee Stéphane Lannoy of France to eject the playmaker.

Portugal, who could not get past a scoreless draw against the Ivory Coast in its opener, demolished North Korea 7–0. Cristiano Ronaldo, winner of the Ballon d'Or in 2008 for the first time in his career as Europe's best player, got a goal as Portugal saw goals from six players—including a brace from midfielder Tiago Mendes—to gain the goal-differential advantage in the battle for second place.

Portugal would advance as the group's second-place team after a scoreless draw on June 25 against Brazil. They played a grinding, low-quality game for all to see. It was pragmatic and it did get the job done for both teams, but there was no show for everyone who had expected a great game.

Spain won the European Championship in 2008. In doing so, it became only the second nation to win all its group-stage matches and the first team since Germany in 1996 to win the tournament undefeated. From the start of 2007 to the end of 2009, La Roja had gone undefeated in 35 straight matches, a world record at the time. The backbone of the team was comprised of players from Barcelona and Real Madrid, teams on the rise in those years. Players like Carles Puyol of Barcelona and Sergio Ramos of Real Madrid formed the team's defensive bulwark, while the midfield featured talent and passing galore with Xavi, Andrés Iniesta, and David Silva. The Barca trio lent support to strikers David Villa and Fernando Torres.

The team had conquered Europe under Aragonés. His *tiki-taka* style—highlighted by intricate midfield passing and a possession game aimed at wearing down opponents—was retained by his successor Vicente del Bosque ahead of the World Cup.

The glue that kept this collection of largely Barca and Real players together was captain Iker Casillas. A veteran goalkeeper, Casillas had played at two World Cups and served as the link between the older players and the new generation just coming onto the senior national team. That glue seemed to come apart in Durban on June 16 in Spain's Group H opener against Switzerland, a 1–0 win by the Swiss on a Gelson Fernandes goal in the 52nd minute. "This is of course not a good sign, certainly not a good sign, that we start off this way," Del Bosque told reporters. "I think it's our duty to cope with this and to approach the next two matches by trying to win."

A Spain win on June 21 against Honduras was imperative. The Central Americans, 1–0 losers to Chile in their opener, also needed a victory at Ellis Park to stay alive. Spain's artistry and offensive prowess came through in the end when Villa scored a brace—a goal in each half—to down Honduras 2–0. Chile, 1–0 winners against Switzerland that same day, were through to the round of 16.

La Roja entered the final match day on June 25 knowing that a win versus Chile would see them advance out of the group. The two nations had shared a first-round group at the 1950 World Cup. Spain won the group at that edition, something it was trying to repeat 60 years later. No stranger to having to win big games, Spain dominated Chile in Pretoria as Villa and Iniesta found the back of the net. The victory put Spain in first place in Group H with six points thanks to goal differential. Chile finished second and would play Brazil.

Round of 16

The tournament's remaining 16 teams broke down this way: six from Europe, five from South America, two from Asia, two from North/Central America, and one from Africa. It was Ghana, Africa's lone representative, that South Africans and the entire continent rallied around during the knockout stage.

Nelson Mandela Bay Stadium in Port Elizabeth was the setting for the opening match of the round of 16 on June 26 between Uruguay and South Korea on a rain-swept field. La Celeste came into it as the favorites, but the South Koreans gave them a close game. In the eighth minute, Luis Suárez scored to give Uruguay a 1–0 lead. Uruguay adopted a defensive posture after the goal, but Lee Chung-yong equalized in the 68th minute on a close-range header following a free kick.

South Korea had a real chance of winning the game, but Suárez scored the winner 10 minutes from time with a spinning shot from the edge of the 18-yard box—one of the prettiest goals of the tournament—that found the back of the net after the ball hit off the inside of the post. "I couldn't believe it," Suárez said after the game. "I couldn't believe that the ball was going in."

Uruguay's 2–1 win seemed improbable as the team had struggled during the group phase. Uruguay had reached the last eight and were poised to regain some of their past glory. The same score would prove fatal for the United States against Ghana. The 35,000 fans in Rustenburg largely backed the Ghanaians, and their *vuvuzelas* served as a victorious soundtrack.

Boateng put Ghana ahead after five minutes, but the Americans again clawed back and drew level in the 62nd minute on a Donovan penalty kick. The 1–1 game was headed to extra time. Just three minutes into the first half of extra time, Ghana took the lead again, this time for good, when Asamoah Gyan's powerful strike beat Howard.

There was no late American comeback this time around. Ghana won 2–1 to become just the third African nation—behind Cameroon in 1990 and Senegal in 2002—to reach the quarterfinals. "We fought for the continent. We fought for Ghana," midfielder André Ayew said afterward. "We made a lot of people proud."

Germany against England in Bloemfontein on June 27 was a rekindling of one of the game's best rivalries. The Three Lions, trying to forge into the semifinals for the first time since 1990, gave Germany a close game—at least for 45 minutes—until an officiating decision impacted the match. Die Mannschaft took a 2–0 lead with goals from Klose in the 20th minute and the second from Podolski 12 minutes later.

England, however, powered forward and cut the lead in half with a Matthew Upson goal in the 37th minute. The match reached a decisive turning point when Lampard's lob a minute later struck the crossbar, then dropped to the turf more than a foot over the goal line. Uruguayan referee Jorge Larrionda did not award the goal. "I saw the ball in the net," Capello said after the game. "I no understand this decision."

The no-goal call proved crucial. Instead of being tied at two, Germany took a 2–1 lead into the second half. It was there that the Germans, with their clinical passing, made it 3–1 with Thomas Müller in the 67th minute off a three-on-two counterattack. Müller scored his second of the game three minutes later to put the game away. The Germans rejoiced in their 4–1 victory, but Lampard's goal that was never properly awarded became the storyline of the round. "What I saw on the television, the ball was behind the line," Germany manager Joachim Löw told reporters. "It must have been given as goal."

At Soccer City later that evening, Argentina and Mexico squared off once again after the sides met in the last 16 just four years earlier in Germany. The Albiceleste had won that match, and they won this one as well in Johannesburg. Carlos Tevez scored twice—the first goal spectacularly and the other controversially—to power Argentina to a 3–1 win.

Again, the game was marred by bad refereeing. The controversial Tevez goal came after 26 minutes with the game deadlocked at 0–0. Argentina took the lead when Messi fed the ball to Tevez clearly in an offside position. Tevez stroked the ball into the net—and using a type of gamesmanship that his manager Maradona would be proud of—celebrated as if nothing was wrong. Italian referee Roberto Rosetti let the goal stand. "At first I thought he was saying that it was not a goal, then I saw the signal and I started celebrating," Tevez said after the game. "I was happy. I know I was offside. I know it was selfish, but as long as they say it was a goal it is all right for me and the team."

Blatter took the unprecedented step of publicly apologizing to both England and Mexico, reopening talks about the use of goal-line technology that would be implemented for the first time at a World Cup four years later. "I deplore when you see the evident referees' mistakes," Blatter told reporters. "It has not been a five-star game for referees. I'm distressed by the evident referees' mistakes."

In Durban, the Netherlands squeaked past Slovakia on June 28 by a score of 2–1, while Brazil blanked Chile 3–0 at Ellis Park. While the Dutch had struggled, the Brazilians had not. Both results, predictable on the eve of each game, had eliminated two teams who hoped to go on Cinderella runs.

The following day in Pretoria, Paraguay and Japan played 120 minutes of scoreless soccer. In the shootout, the first one at this World Cup, Paraguay converted all five of their attempts to down Japan 5–3. Japan defender Yuichi Komano saw his shot hit the crossbar. The mistake unleashed celebration among the Paraguayan players. "Everyone knows it's unfair to have it decided by a penalty shootout, but that's the way it is," Paraguay manager Gerardo Martino told reporters. "I just think we were lucky during the penalty shootout."

In the final round-of-16 match, Spain edged Portugal 1–0 in Cape Town. Villa's goal, his fourth of the tournament, after 63 minutes was the only thing that separated the sides in what was a largely tense affair between two of Europe's best teams. Portugal may have featured an iron-clad defense, but few teams were able to break down Spain's intricate passing game and midfield domination. "When we play like this," Del Bosque told reporters, "it's difficult for our opponents to control us."

Quarterfinals

The quarterfinal round was dominated by European nations—at the expense of South American ones—with the Brazilians joining the tournament's other favorites crashing out of the competition. Brazil ultimately succumbed to the Netherlands on July 2 in Port Elizabeth, exiting in the quarterfinals for the second straight World Cup.

While Brazil's elimination was the headline, it shouldn't take away from the Dutch and the supremacy they exhibited that evening. Not since 1974, during the days of Cruyff, had the Netherlands defeated Brazil at a World Cup. The Brazilians, who had never faced a strong team at this tournament until this round, dominated in the first half. That domination, following Robinho's goal after 10 minutes, fell apart in the second half.

The Dutch stormed back after the break as Wesley Sneijder recorded a brace. In the 53rd minute, Sneijder's 30-yard shot pierced the net to tie the score. Defender Felipe Melo certainly didn't help his team's cause when he interfered with his goalkeeper Júlio César on the play.

It was Sneijder again who found the back of the net in the 68th minute, heading the ball home following a Kuyt corner kick for the game-winning goal to make it 2–1. Things got worse for Brazil five minutes later when Felipe Melo was red-carded for stomping on Robben's hamstring. Down a player, Brazil's offense was feeble as the Dutch searched in vain for a third goal that never came.

The Netherlands would face Uruguay in the semifinals after the South Americans eliminated Ghana at Soccer City. That game highlighted just how cunning this sport can be at times. Trickery has always been part of the game. Maradona elevated it to an art form in 1986. Suárez would do the same in 2010.

In Johannesburg, Ghana nearly pulled off a shocker against Uruguay. But it was not meant to be. After the game ended 1–1, the teams played an uneventful extra time—until two minutes from the end. As penalty kicks loomed, a scramble in front of the Uruguay goal caught goalkeeper Fernando Muslera out of position. That's when Dominic Adiyiah's header was cleared off the line by Suárez swatting the ball away—a play some have called the "Second Hand of God." Had Suárez not intervened, the goal would have sent the Black Stars to the semifinals. Instead, Suárez was ejected and a penalty kick awarded to Ghana. Suárez had given his team a lifeline with no time left on the clock, sacrificing himself for the good of his team.

Amid the loud sounds of *vuvuzelas* blaring, Gyan went to the spot to take the kick. Suárez, watching from the tunnel entrance that led to the field, celebrated as the shot caromed against the crossbar. "The way it finished was incredible," Forlán recalled. "Suárez, instead of scoring a goal, had saved one."

As the ball bounced off the bar and behind the goal, Gyan was left holding his head as the final whistle sounded, sending the match to penalties and the crowd into stunned silence. Muslera proved the hero in the shootout as Uruguay advanced 4–2. The victory had nothing to do with skill. Instead, it showcased the ability of players to improvise, even resorting to fraud, in order to win. "This is a sporting injustice," Ghana manager Milovan Rajevac told reporters after the match. "But I have to congratulate Uruguay . . . they are the lucky ones."

Argentina and Germany renewed their rivalry on July 3 in Cape Town. Maradona's side, impressive for much of the tournament, crashed out as the Germans scored four goals, the third time they had done so at this World Cup. Müller set the tone early when his header after just three minutes gave the Germans the lead. Klose would record a brace in the second half as Argentina's backline struggled to stop the bleeding. After Brazil, another South American giant had fallen.

Germany's 4–0 win had exposed Maradona's limited coaching experience as well as the inability of Messi to step up in big games for the Albiceleste. It would be a recurring story line for Messi in the ensuing years. It was an outcome few would have predicted, but one that put the Germans through to the semifinals. "I think we made it easy for them," Maradona told reporters after the game. "They got easy control of the ball. Germany had more ideas, lots of them, and more than they ever have before at this tournament."

The Germans would face Spain, 1–0 winners against Paraguay after Villa scored seven minutes from time. It was a slim margin, but for La Roja it was the first time since 1950 that they had reached the World Cup semifinals. Both Paraguay and Spain missed penalty kicks, a game highlighted more by offensive misfire than precision.

Spain's precision game led to the goal. Iniesta avoided two defenders, then passed the ball to his right. Pedro, a second-half substitute, got a shot that went past goalkeeper Justo Villar, but was denied by the post. Villa grabbed the rebound off that left post before putting the ball into the net for the game's only goal. "He is always right there with the ball before anyone else," Del Bosque said afterward.

Semifinals

Uruguay, in the best position to win a World Cup since 1950 despite the suspension of Suárez, took on the Netherlands in the first semifinal on July 6 in Cape Town. Against Brazil, the Dutch allowed their opponents to take the initiative offensively. Against Uruguay, the Netherlands took on a more aggressive posture. It paid off in the form of a goal after 18 minutes when captain Giovanni van Bronckhorst scored off a wonderful shot from 35 yards out.

The goal served as motivation for Uruguay. The Celeste equalized with Forlán in the 41st minute. Dutch goalkeeper Maarten Stekelenburg misjudged the power and trajectory of the shot, and Forlán's attempt from 25 yards made it 1–1. It had not been the first time at this tournament that a long-range effort had resulted in a goal. Aside from the power and skill of the players, many had blamed the ball for all these goals. The Jabulani, the official World Cup ball manufactured by Adidas, featured a textured surface intended to improve aerodynamics. What it did was also draw the ire of many players, particularly goalkeepers, who complained the ball was inadequate.

The ability or not of this experimental ball to easily fool goalies, Uruguay should have been better prepared for the Dutch response in the second half. The Netherlands found the back of the net twice more—with Sneijder in the 70th minute and Robben's header three minutes later—to put the game out of reach. Despite the 3–1 lead, Uruguay was never out of the game. They scored what turned out to be a consolation goal in stoppage time, but time had run out on Uruguay.

The Dutch prevailed 3–2 and reached the final for the first time since 1978. "This is great, but the thing is we're not there yet," Van Marwijk told reporters.

The following day in Durban, Spain, who like the Netherlands were the other great team never to win a World Cup, also reached the final. Spain's passing game forced the Germans into a defensive game. As in Spain's previous two matches, the game was resolved by a single goal. Spain won a corner kick in the 73rd minute. The corner, taken by Xavi, found Puyol and his curly mop of hair. The Spanish defender met the ball in the air and headed it past Manuel Neuer. Spain won 1–0 to reach its first World Cup final in history. "We have been waiting so many years to have success," Del Bosque told reporters afterward. "I believe Spain deserves to be triumphant."

Germany would capture third place and spend the next four years rebuilding a team that could compete for the title. Müller, who would finish as tournament top scorer with five goals and three assists, had emerged as a budding star. The Bayern Munich star would play a key role in Germany's future soccer success. "It's an honor of course, but at the end of the day, I'd rather have had the World Cup itself," he told Bayern's official team website following the World Cup.

Final: Spain vs. Netherlands

A nation who had never before lifted the World Cup would be crowned champions in Soccer City. Not since France won the title in 1998 had that been the case. It was also the first time since 1978 that neither team in the final had ever won the World Cup.

Soccer City, teeming with 85,000 fans and the sound of *vuvuzelas* one last time, was prepared for the all-European final between Spain and the Netherlands. The sides had never before met one another at a World Cup or European Championship. The teams were evenly matched, and a close game was expected given the talent on both sides of the ball. What ensued was a rough-and-tumble game that kept referee Howard Webb of England busy.

What the fans also witnessed that evening was a wave and a smile from Mandela. The former South African president, in poor health at the time of the World Cup, had been notably absent from public view throughout the tournament. Fans inside Soccer City rose with excitement and greeted Mandela with thunderous applause. The 92-year-old Mandela, sporting a fur hat as temperatures plunged into the 50s that evening, and his wife Graça Machel waved as a car drove them around the field.

The 1986 final between Argentina and West Germany had featured a total of six cards. Spain and the Netherlands exceeded that number, accumulating 14. The statistic highlighted the game's physical style and the tactics the Dutch employed in order to break up the Spanish *tiki-taka*. It worked as Spain failed to get on the score sheet, but the game suffered overall as players crashed into one another and fouls became more commonplace than shots on target (just 13 overall). After the match, Van

Marwijk admitted that the fouls "may be a sad thing for a final, but it is not our style."

The game's most egregious foul was committed after 28 minutes when Xabi Alonso was booted in the ribs by Nigel de Jong, who should have gotten a red card. Instead, Webb handed him a yellow for his kara-te-style kick, and the teams remained even as the match headed, inevitably it seemed, into extra time.

The Spanish retaliated with fouls of their own, but found the man advantage in the 109th minute when Dutch defender John Heitinga was red-carded after receiving a second yellow following a foul on Iniesta. The man advantage was just what Spain needed. A series of passes and a midfield buildup allowed Iniesta to score the winning goal four minutes from time. His right-footed half volley was low to Stekelenburg's right. The goal finally saw Spain raise the World Cup. "I can't quite believe it yet," Iniesta said afterward. "It's something absolutely incredible. I simply made a small contribution to a match that was very tough, very rough."

The Spanish players piled on top of Iniesta as the crowd cheered. It was a fourth straight 1–0 win for Spain to become the first European nation to win the World Cup away from its home continent. It was a combination of skill and patience that led Spain to the title. The final had been a disappointment, but overall the tournament was a rousing success. It is an achievement Africa as a whole will be proud of for decades to come.

2014 World Cup

The tournament returned to Brazil for the first time in 64 years. For Brazil, this World Cup was a chance for redemption, an opportunity to erase the bad memories of the Maracanazo. The World Cup was returning to the game's "spiritual home" and marked the first time since 1978 that the tournament would take place in South America.

The tournament also featured every World Cup–winning team since the first one held in 1930: Argentina, Brazil, England, France, Germany, Italy, Spain, and Uruguay. Bosnia and Herzegovina were the only debutants in 2014, joining the list of 32 nations that qualified for the finals. The competition also featured goal-line technology for the first time following the officiating blunders that characterized the 2010 tournament. Aided by 14 cameras, the ball was outfitted with a microchip that transmitted data to determine whether it had crossed the line for a goal. The referee, equipped with a watch that vibrated if a goal was scored, could then make the correct call. The Adidas Brazuca—following the controversy over the Jabulani—reduced the number of panels to six and was tested for two years in order to meet the players' approval.

In addition to an improved ball, FIFA approved the use of vanishing spray by the referees for the first time at a World Cup. The water-based spray—which disappeared within minutes of application—was used by match officials to mark the minimum 10-yard distance players must stand when a free kick is taken. FIFA also tried to quell criticism swirling around Brazil's hot temperatures by allowing brief cooling breaks—one per half after the 30th minute—if temperatures exceeded 90 degrees during games.

While FIFA had control over what occurred on the field, it was worried about what had been going on off it. A year before the World Cup, many Brazilians had grown frustrated and upset at the staggering amount of money the government had spent on stadiums and other infrastructure projects related to the tournament. During the Confederations Cup the year before, thousands of Brazilians had taken to the streets to decry the cost overruns and the government's neglect of schools and hospitals. At the same time, Blatter criticized the hosts, telling a gathering of Swiss reporters in January 2014 that Brazil was behind in its preparations. "No country has been so far behind in its preparations since I have been at FIFA even though it is the only host nation which has had so much time—seven years—in which to prepare," Blatter told the Swiss newspaper *24 Hueres*.

While Brazilian officials admitted to spending $14 billion on the tournament ($4.2 billion on the 12 stadiums alone), Brazil's tourism minister, Vinicius Lages, tried to downplay the negative figures, saying that more than 3.1 million Brazilians and 600,000 visitors were expected to travel throughout Brazil for the World Cup. That would inject $4 billion into the country's economy.

The spiraling costs—$3 billion more than had been budgeted—highlighted the corruption and mismanagement that often comes with the staging of such a large sporting event. Despite the demonstrations, the country's sports minister, Aldo Rebelo, was confident Brazil would host a wonderful tournament. "Through the World Cup, Brazil will offer not only the material conditions to hold a great event, but above all, will show how warmly the Brazilian people welcome visitors from around the world," he said. "I believe that those who visit us during the World Cup will appreciate this distinguishing feature that is so characteristic of our people."

Spain, the defending champions, added another European Championship to its trophy case in 2012. Brazil were the heavy favorites given their history and for playing at home, while Argentina, with Messi in his prime, were expected to also contend for the title. Germany, meanwhile, had introduced a possession game into their system. With a midfield featuring Bastian Schweinsteiger, Sami Khedira, and Toni Kroos, the Germans looked formidable. Özil and Müller provided support and allowed Germany to impose its will on opponents. The final draw brought with it the following eight groups:

Group A: Brazil, Croatia, Mexico, and Cameroon

Group B: Spain, the Netherlands, Chile, and Australia

Group C: Colombia, Greece, the Ivory Coast, and Japan

Group D: Uruguay, Costa Rica, England, and Italy

Group E: Switzerland, Ecuador, France, and Honduras

Group F: Argentina, Bosnia and Herzegovina, Iran, and Nigeria

Group G: Germany, Portugal, Ghana, and the United States

Group H: Belgium, Algeria, Russia, and South Korea

Scolari, back for another run as Brazil manager after winning the World Cup with the team in 2002, exuded confidence in his players in the months leading up to the finals. In an interview with the Spanish sports daily *Marca*, Scolari took a shot at Spain, the reigning world champions and a favorite to repeat after winning the 2012 European

Championship. "I believe in my team," he said. "We need to have respect for the other contenders, but there are teams that have won a World Cup and believe they're the best. We have won five."

Group Stage

Anti–World Cup protests had reached their height the summer before the World Cup. Protests grew louder again in the weeks before the June 12 Group A opener, and police in riot gear had to be called in just hours before kickoff to quell the protesters that had gathered at the Arena de São Paulo in São Paulo.

Brazil opened the tournament on June 12 against Croatia. The Europeans came into the match missing their star striker, Mario Mandžukić, suspended after receiving a red card in the team's final qualifier versus Iceland. Despite that, they took the lead after 12 minutes when Ivica Olić's cross was deflected into his own net by Marcelo. The own goal deflated the hopes of the 62,000 in attendance, but only temporarily. Neymar equalized in the 25th minute off a 25-yard shot. Brazil's class shined though in the second half. Neymar completed his brace in the 71st minute, scoring on a penalty kick after it had been awarded to Brazil following Dejan Lovren's foul on Fred in the area. The contact appeared minimal, but the call stood. Brazil put the game away in stoppage time with Oscar for the 3–1 win.

Five days later, Brazil had the chance to clinch a spot to the next round at the Estádio Castelão in Fortaleza, but a scoreless draw against Mexico, 1–0 winners against Cameroon in their opener, allowed Croatia to remain in contention. Their 4–0 victory against Cameroon at the Arena da Amazônia in the city of Manaus—spearheaded by Mandžukić's two goals—made the group competitive going into the final match day. Cameroonian officials said they were investigating allegations that seven players had been involved in fixing the result. FIFA said there was no evidence of any match fixing.

Mexico's 3–1 victory against Croatia at the Arena Pernambuco in Recife put them through to the round of 16 as the group's second-place team. Brazil won the group, not surprisingly, as they cruised to a 4–1 win against Cameroon.

In Group B, Spain, the defending champions, remained among the world's best teams. Even the best teams, history has shown, can falter at a World Cup. Spain was spared no favors, opening the tournament in a rematch of the 2010 final. It was the first time in World Cup history that the previous edition's finalists met in the group stage.

If the Dutch feared that history would repeat itself on June 13 at Arena Fonte Nova in Salvador, those worries were alleviated in the second half. Spain took the lead after 27 minutes when Diego Costa was tripped in the box by Stefan de Vrij. Xabi Alonso scored the penalty kick for Spain for the 1–0 lead. The Dutch equalized with a minute left in the first half when Robin van Persie scored off a diving header from 15 yards out that got past Casillas off his line. Four goals from the Dutch in the second half exposed Spain's messy and confused defense as both van Persie and Robben scoring twice to get the tournament off to a rollicking start for the Oranje. "Hopefully, this is the start of a great tournament," Kuyt observed afterward.

Chile and Australia, who met on the same day at the Arena Pantanal in Cuiabá, were also hopeful that either one of them could compete for a knockout-round spot. The South Americans were the ones to dominate, grabbing a 3–1 win. Chile's match against Spain was do-or-die for both teams, and for different reasons. Chile was trying to remain perfect, while La Roja were in desperation mode after their shellacking. The June 18 game at the Maracanã saw the Chileans upset Spain 2–0 with two first-half goals from Eduardo Vargas in the 20th minute and Charles Aránguiz two minutes before the interval. Spain's passing game was no match for the talented Chileans, who effectively broke down La Roja's midfield with their own pace and skill.

Spain became the fifth defending champions to be knocked out in the group stage. Many were surprised at the outcome, including the Spanish camp. "I would never have thought that we would exit the tournament after the first round," Del Bosque told reporters. "We started sluggishly and were really not brave enough. It's a pity because I didn't expect it."

The Netherlands, 3–2 winners against Australia, won the group with a 2–0 victory against Chile on June 23 in São Paulo. A Dutch win was far from expected, especially after they were without the suspended van Persie due to yellow-card accumulation, while the defeat saw Chile finish second. It was the most competitive match to date for the Netherlands.

Group C—dubbed the "Group of Life" because all four teams had an equal chance of advancing—saw Colombia get off on the right foot by defeating Greece 3–0 on June 14 at Estádio Mineirão in Belo Horizonte. The South Americans—without star striker Radamel Falcao who had suffered a torn ACL six months earlier—emerged as the Cinderella story. Colombia defeated the Ivory Coast 2–1 and Asian champion Japan 4–1 to reach the round of 16. James Rodríguez's three goals—one in each game—put Colombia on the path to success. The 22-year-old's prowess would also work out well for him after Spanish club Real Madrid decided to sign him later that summer. "It is a huge success to see Colombia reach this level, but we can't start thinking ahead of time or what will happen later on," said Colombia manager José Pékerman.

With Colombia dominating the group, the three remaining teams fought for second. Greece would be the ones to do it, qualifying for the knockout stage in dramatic style after scoring the game winner in the third minute of stoppage time during its game against the Ivory Coast on June 24 in Fortaleza. The 2–1 victory came via a Giorgos Samaras penalty kick.

Group D turned out to be more interesting. It featured three former World Cup winners—Italy, Uruguay, and England—along with Costa Rica. Although no one expected much from the Central American nation, it would be all anyone was talking about after stunning Uruguay 3–1 in its opener on June 14 in Fortaleza. The Ticos then edged out Italy 1–0 a week later in Recife to advance to the round of 16. "It was a beautiful match. The people of Costa Rica deserve this day," rejoiced Costa Rica coach Jorge Luis Pinto after the game.

With England once again putting in a subpar showing (it would finish last in the group with one point after managing just a draw against Costa Rica), second place would come down to the showdown between Italy and Uruguay. With Italy needing only a draw to advance, it had a slight advantage going into the game on June 24 in Natal.

The Azzurri looked slow—especially in its attack—and striker Mario Balotelli was taken off at halftime. The Italians then went down a man after midfielder Claudio Marchisio was red-carded in the second half following a high tackle on Arevalo Ríos. With the Italian attack incapable of scoring, it was Uruguay who got on the scoreboard when defender Diego Godín's header in the 81st minute put them ahead. The goal turned out to be the game's only goal, but all eyes were on Luis Suárez. The striker—known for having bitten opponents on two previous occasions—was caught on video sinking his teeth into the shoulder of Giorgio Chiellini. The Italy defender tried in vain to get the attention of match officials, even pulling down his jersey to show his teeth marks, but the game went on.

Uruguay was through to the round of 16, but Suárez's World Cup would be over. He was handed a four-month ban from all competitive matches for both club and country. In addition, Suárez was suspended for nine competitive international matches, meaning he would also sit out the 2015 Copa America.

In Group E, France was attempting to redeem itself after a poor showing and internal squabbling in 2010. With Switzerland, Honduras, and Ecuador all vying for a spot in the knockout phase, the French showed their superiority. France comfortably defeated Honduras 3–0 on June 15 at Estádio Beira-Rio in Porto Alegre (highlighted by the fact that goal-line technology was used for the first time ever at a World Cup after Karim Benzema's 48th-minute shot came back off the post and rolled across the line before hitting goalie Noel Valladares) and Switzerland 5–2 five days later in Salvador. The French, so flawless in their performance, featured a Karim Benzema in great form, prompting coach Didier Deschamps to say, "We were almost absolutely perfect."

Switzerland finished runners-up, defeating Honduras 3–0 on June 25 in Manaus. The Swiss, traditionally a second-tier European team with little international success, proved tougher than its Central American opponent. A hat trick by Xherdan Shaqiri—with goals in the 6th, 31st, and 71st minutes—helped the Swiss advance.

Argentina was the favorite in Group F. Messi was the one everyone was looking to again after a disappointing 2010 tournament. The

Barcelona playmaker was still at the top of his game despite sitting out part of the Liga season with an injury. It was no surprise then that Argentina became Messi-dependent from the start and needed him to score decisive goals. Argentina took all nine points, edging out Bosnia and Herzegovina 2–1 on June 15 at the Maracanã and overcoming Iran 1–0 six days later in Belo Horizonte. Messi scored the winning goal in both games. His strike against Iran in the first minute of stoppage time, a curling left-footed shot from 25 yards out, was memorable. "We have a genius who is called Messi and we are fortunate that he is Argentine. Iran made it difficult for us, but with Messi everything is possible," said Argentina manager Alejandro Sabella.

Argentina's 3–2 victory over Nigeria (who went through nonetheless as runners-up) on June 25 in Porto Alegre assured the South Americans first place. Against Nigeria, Sabella switched from his 5–3–2 formation to a 4–3–1–2, with Messi as the playmaker alongside strikers Gonzalo Higuaín and Ezequiel Lavezzi. Again, a Messi brace proved to be the difference. His four goals in three games made him only the second Argentine since Maradona to score that many goals in a World Cup group stage. Indeed, Messi was out of this world, and he was showing it. "Messi is from Jupiter. He is an amazing player," hailed Nigeria coach Stephen Keshi.

Group G, the tournament's "Group of Death," featured Germany, Portugal, Ghana, and the United States. The Americans, without Donovan who had unexpectedly been dropped from the team by manager Jürgen Klinsmann on the eve of the tournament, needed a victory against Ghana in its opener in Natal if it had any hope of advancing. Clint Dempsey wasted no time putting the U.S ahead, scoring after just 30 seconds following a dazzling run in the box. Needing just four touches, Dempsey got past two players before depositing the ball into the net.

The Americans were hoping the goal would be enough to grab the win. Instead, the U.S. defense gave up a goal in the 82nd minute when Andrew Ayew knocked the ball inside the left post and past Tim Howard to tie the score. The United States had spent much of the second half fending off attacks and struggled to create any offense. That all changed on a set piece. With four minutes left in the game, defender John Brooks, on as a halftime substitute, headed home the winner off a Graham Zusi corner kick. An incredulous Brooks celebrated—his hands on his head and a look of shock on his face—as his teammates piled on top of him.

The Americans knew they would have to work even harder in their second match versus Portugal. On June 24, in Manaus, Klinsmann's men took on a Portugal side that featured an injured Ronaldo and little else in the way of a supporting cast. Nevertheless, Portugal took the lead with Nani after just five minutes following a poorly cleared ball by Geoff Cameron. Both sides appeared sluggish for stretches of the first half, and the heat and humidity of the jungle made it unbearable at times. In the 39th minute, referee Néstor Pitana of Argentina whistled for a water break—the first in World Cup history. The United States had struggled in the first half but dominated the start of the second. Jermaine Jones tied the score in the 65th minute when his 27-yard shot off the right post found the back of the net.

With the game tied 1–1, the Americans hit their stride. Ronaldo, who had been named FIFA's Player of the Year in January, was invisible for much of the time, and the U.S. midfield, spearheaded by Zusi and Kyle Beckerman, helped move the ball forward. The one player the United States could rely on was Clint Dempsey. He came up big once again, creating space and making sure he was always in a position to score. Ever the opportunist, the Seattle Sounders striker took a cross from Zusi in the 81st minute and scored his second goal of the tournament to give the United States a lead. A victory would have automatically put the Americans through to the second round. Instead, Portugal's Silvestre Varela, off a perfectly placed Ronaldo cross, scored past Howard for the tying goal in the fifth minute of stoppage time. The game ended 2–2, and the U.S. party was postponed.

The final U.S. group game against Germany would be decisive. Win and go through, while a draw or a defeat were still possibilities the United States could bank on depending on the outcome of the Portugal-Ghana match. As for Klinsmann and whether or not he and Löw would play for a draw, the former German international said, "Our goal is to go to the next round so we will do everything in our capabilities to go into the next round. I'm not thinking about what goes on in other peoples' minds and situations. It's about what's important to us, so we're going to take our game to Germany and give everything we have, give them a real fight."

The June 26 match in Recife was marred by heavy rain the day before. With the weather appearing to worsen just hours before kickoff, the streets surrounding the stadium and throughout the fifth-largest Brazilian city were knee-deep in water. Thousands braved the waterlogged streets to get to the game. The 12-hour downpour may have flooded streets, but FIFA assured everyone that the match would go on as scheduled. The stadium's drainage system ensured that the game could go on, and an inspection of the pitch by the match officials confirmed that no delay would occur.

Rain could not keep away the thousands of American fans—and their "I believe that we will win" chant that had permeated stadiums in the country's previous two games. Aside from the growing number of Americans in Brazil, the following back home had grown to levels never before seen for soccer. Bars, restaurants, and public parks had become places for people to gather. Although many may have never watched soccer before, it seemed—temporarily, at least—that World Cup fever had caught on. On the field, the Americans lost 1–0, but they managed to reach the round of 16 after Portugal defeated Ghana 2–1 in the group's other game played simultaneously in Brasilia.

Top-seeded Belgium was the team to beat in Group H, although they struggled against Algeria on June 17 at the Estádio Mineirão in Belo Horizonte. In an era where no team could be considered a pushover, the Algerians jumped in front after 25 minutes on a penalty kick by Sofiane Feghouli after the striker had been fouled in the box. Two Belgian goals in the second half turned Belgium's fortunes around. It was Dries Mertens's goal 10 minutes from time that gave his side a 2–1 win.

Belgium advanced to the round of 16 following a 1–0 at the Maracanã against Russia. It was Divock Origi's goal two minutes from time, scoring from 10 yards out after Eden Hazard's pass split the defense, catching five defenders flat-footed, as Belgium earned all three points. "We didn't play a very good match," Hazard said. "The last 10 minutes were good. That's all."

Belgium's 1–0 win on June 26 in São Paulo against South Korea put it in the same exclusive club (alongside the Netherlands, Colombia, and

Argentina) of teams that had gone 3–0 in the first round. "This is truly a historic achievement for Belgium," manager Marc Wilmots said.

In the battle for second, Algeria defeated South Korea 4–2 in Porto Alegre on June 22 and needed just a 1–1 draw against Russia four days later to advance to the knockout round of a World Cup for the first time in the country's history. The Russians, led by famed Italian coach Fabio Capello, fell flat—something of an embarrassment for the highest-paid manager at the tournament and for the World Cup's next host nation. Although his team had failed miserably, Capello praised the level of play demonstrated at the tournament throughout the first round. "In my career, I have never seen a World Cup at this level. The quality is absolutely incredible, the pace is so intense," he said. "It's without doubt the best World Cup of all."

Capello was not exaggerating. The first round had produced attacking soccer and some surprises. With the exception of Honduras and Ecuador, every team from North/Central and South America had reached the knockout stage. Playing in South America to mostly partisan crowds had certainly helped. CONCACAF, in particular, was the big winner. Cinderella side Costa Rica had won Group D, and Mexico finished second in Group A, losing out to Brazil only on goal differential for first place.

There had been nearly as many goals in Brazil in 2014 after the first round (136 for an average of 2.83) than in all of the 2010 World Cup (145 for an average of 2.27). Costa Rica and Mexico, along with Belgium, were three of the 16 teams that advanced to the knockout stage to concede the fewest goals—just one. That statistic said a lot, especially in a tournament dominated by so many goals. Although teams would play a little more defensively in the second round, the matches were still highlighted by teams looking to score. In the end, the tournament would produce 171 goals for an impressive average of 2.67 goals per match, which equaled the record set at France '98.

Round of 16
The 16 remaining teams included some pre-tournament favorites, such as Brazil, Argentina, Germany, and Belgium. It also included some

potential Cinderella sides like Colombia, Chile, Costa Rica, and the United States.

The round of 16 opened in Belo Horizonte on June 28 with the all–South American clash between Brazil and Chile. Brazil had played Chile in the knockout round of the World Cup on three previous occasions, all won by Brazil, including at the same stage at the 2010 tournament. The 58,000 in the crowd gave Neymar and his teammates loud cheers and they reciprocated with a goal in the opening 18 minutes. David Luiz was credited with the goal after replays appeared to show it had deflected off Gonzalo Jara.

Chile, a team not afraid to take the game to the Brazilians, used their strong midfield and wing play to make plays in the Brazilian half. Turnovers forced Brazil to chase the game, and that's how Chile was able to drawl level. Chile's midfield did all they could to thwart Neymar, chopping him down every chance they got as referee Howard Webb was later criticized by Scolari for not doing enough to protect the Brazilian star.

Brazil regained control of the game in search of a winning goal that never came. Tied at one, the match went to extra time and would be resolved via a shootout. Brazil prevailed 3–2 on penalties, but Chile had given them a tough game. At every World Cup until this point where Chile had reached the knockout stage, they had been eliminated by Brazil. Millions throughout the country breathed a sigh of relief. "We needed this," goalkeeper Júlio César told reporters after the game. "I just hope that the next games don't go to penalty kicks again because our family members and relatives might have a heart attack."

The day's second match was another clash between Latin American sides with Colombia and Uruguay meeting at the Maracanã. Uruguay, without the suspended Suárez, struggled as Colombia's James Rodríguez put on a one-man clinic to help his side advance to the quarterfinals against Brazil.

Rodríguez scored both of Colombia's goals. His first came in the 28th minute, where after controlling the ball on his chest he unleashed a left-footed 25-yard volley that went into the net past Muslera after hitting the crossbar's underside. It was the goal of the tournament and made Rodríguez into a star. Rodríguez's second goal came in the 50th minute when he scored with his right, this time after receiving a headed pass from Juan Cuadrado. The 2–0 win put Colombia in the World Cup quarterfinals for the first time. "We're very happy because we're making history," Rodríguez told reporters. "We want to do even more."

The Netherlands and Mexico match in Fortaleza on June 29 didn't start off well for the Dutch. Following a scoreless first half, Mexico took the lead five minutes after the break with a Giovani dos Santos goal. The striker scored from outside the box when Mexico regained possession after a poor Dutch clearance.

Mexico came within two minutes of pulling off an upset, but some late-game Dutch heroics changed the outcome. A Dutch corner two minutes from time was headed by Klaas-Jan Huntelaar for Wesley Sneijder who equalized with a blast from 16 yards. The Dutch completed the comeback in stoppage time. Robben was tripped in the penalty area by Márquez. Robben, who had a reputation for diving, made the fall look even more dramatic than it was. Referee Pedro Proença of Portugal whistled a penalty kick, and Huntelaar, who had come into the game later in the second half, scored for the 2–1 victory.

Mexico's petulant manager Miguel Herrera, who had spent the entire game stomping and fuming on the sidelines, did more of that in the post-match news conference. "The penalty was an invented one," Herrera said. "It was the man with the whistle who eliminated us from the World Cup."

Costa Rica and Greece met for the first time at a World Cup in the day's second match in Recife. It was another close match after a scoreless first half. Bryan Ruiz gave Costa Rica the lead in the 52nd minute. Costa Rica were reduced to 10 men in the 66th minute when Óscar Duarte was ejected after picking up a second yellow. Costa Rica tried to stave off the Greeks, but Sokratis Papastathopoulos equalized in stoppage time from close range after goalkeeper Keylor Navas had made the initial save. A scoreless extra time ushered the tournament's second shootout to determine who advanced to the quarterfinals.

In the shootout, Navas emerged as the hero, saving Theofanis Gekas's shot before Michael Umaña scored the winning penalty for Costa Rica for the 5–3 win. Costa Rica continued its dream run and consolidated itself as the tournament's Cinderella team after advancing to the quarterfinals for the first time in history. "It was a dream for us to get this far," Navas told reporters. "The dream has become a reality." On June 30, European teams advanced at the expense of African ones. France defeated Nigeria 2–0 in Brasilia, while Germany needed extra time to eliminate Algeria 2–1 in Porto Alegre.

Argentina took on Switzerland on July 1 in São Paulo. It took a Di María goal, off a Messi pass, with two minutes left in extra time for the 1–0 win. Argentina advanced to the quarterfinals thanks to Messi's brilliance. "At times I was nervous because we couldn't score a goal, and any mistake could have knocked us out of the World Cup," Messi told reporters. "When you are here, you don't have an easy opponent."

In the final round-of-16 match, Belgium and the United States produced a wild match in Salvador. The Belgians dominated the game, but the United States was able to produce a few chances that an upset seemed to be a possibility. The game remained scoreless thanks largely to Howard, while striker Chris Wondolowski missed a chance from a few yards in stoppage time.

The Belgians won the game with two goals in extra time—the first by Kevin De Bruyne in the 93rd minute and a second by Romelu Lukaku in the 105th. Two minutes later, Julian Green pulled one back, while the United States came close to tying the score with six minutes to go, but goalkeeper Thibaut Courtois came up with the big save on a shot from Dempsey. Belgium advanced 2–1 despite Howard's 15 saves, the most recorded in a World Cup match since FIFA started to keep track in 1966. For a second straight tournament, the United States had nothing to be ashamed of at a World Cup.

Quarterfinals

The round opened between Germany and France, two of Europe's best teams, in a game that reignited a World Cup rivalry like few others. The biggest clash between these two giants, specifically the '82 and '86 semifinals, saw Germany win both those contests. In 2014, the victor was Germany once again. The game's lone goal on July 4 came after 13 minutes when a Mats Hummels header off a Toni Kroos free kick led the

Germans to a 1–0 win at the Maracanã. In doing so, Germany advanced to the semifinals to become the first team to reach four consecutive World Cup semifinals, breaking the previous record of three shared by West Germany (1966–1974 and 1982–1990) and Brazil (1970–1978 and 1994–2002).

In the day's second game, Brazil took on Colombia in Fortaleza. The home side took the lead when after seven minutes Neymar's corner kick turned into a close-range goal by Thiago Silva. Brazil doubled its lead in the 69th minute when David Luiz scored off a long-range free kick that went over the Colombia wall. The Colombians pulled one back 10 minutes from time when James Rodríguez scored from a penalty kick. With two minutes left to play, Juan Camilo Zúñiga kneed Neymar in the back, an injury that forced the Brazilian to be subbed out. A subsequent medical evaluation found that Neymar had suffered a fractured vertebra, forcing him to miss the remainder of the competition.

The following day, the remaining two quarterfinals were played. Argentina had the better of Belgium at the Estádio Nacional Mané Garrincha in Brasilia. A Higuaín goal in the opening eight minutes turned out to be the game's only goal as Argentina marched off to the semifinals. Joining them would be the Netherlands, who struggled mightily against Costa Rica in Salvador.

The crossbar (twice) and post conspired to keep the Dutch from scoring. When the woodwork wasn't getting in the way, goalkeeper Keylor Navas made a series of great saves to keep his side in the game. A scoreless 90 minutes meant the game would go to extra time. After the teams failed to score, a penalty-kick shootout was needed to determine which side advanced.

In a move that was both bold and seldom ever used, Dutch manager Louis van Gaal subbed out goalkeeper Jasper Cillessen with the rested and taller Tim Krul, who at six foot two would use his incredible reach to power the Dutch to new heights. The Netherlands buried all of their kicks, while Costa Rica saw two of their attempts saved by Krul for the 4–3 victory. "We thought it all through," Van Gaal told reporters after the win. "We all thought Tim Krul was the best keeper to stop penalties."

Semifinals

The semifinals opened on July 8 with the much-anticipated Brazil-Germany match in Belo Horizonte. The Brazilians, without the injured Neymar and captain Thiago Silva through suspension for yellow card accumulation, were a step away from the final. In Brazil's path stood a German team seemingly ready to take on any opponent. By the time the evening was through, Brazil had suffered its worst defeat ever at a World Cup and the most lopsided outcome ever in the semifinals.

Germany's 7–1 demolition of the hosts put it through to the final and was the reward for years of hard work. For Brazil, it signaled the end of an era. After just 11 minutes, an unmarked Müller scored from Kroos's out-swinging corner. The goal was enough to unhinge the backline. With the Brazilian defense in shambles, Germany scored again 12 minutes later with Miroslav Klose. The goal, his 16th at a World Cup, made Klose the tournament's all-time leading scorer, surpassing Ronaldo. Two more goals by Kroos—in the 24th and 26th minutes—and another from Sami Khedira in the 29th put the Germans ahead 5–0 at halftime. The game was over after just a half, and Brazil's shambolic defending was to blame.

Germany added two more goals in the second half, with striker André Schürrle in the 69th and 79th minutes, before Oscar pulled one back for Brazil for the 7–1 final. For Brazil, a World Cup at home had ended in failure. Instead of a Maracanazo, the Brazilians had suffered what has come to be known as the Mineirazo. "After losing the semifinal to Italy in 2006, we know how Brazil, the players, Scolari, and the fans feel, so we have to be modest and humble and take the next step," Löw said. "The emotions are great. We won, we've made it to the final. We coped with the passion of the Brazilians and we knew that if we played to our capabilities we thought we would win—but we couldn't have expected this result."

As for Brazil, the outcome was a shock, something Scolari took full responsibility for in the post-game news conference. "It's the worst moment of my soccer career and the worst day of my soccer life. But life goes on. Who is responsible for this result? I am! It's me," he said. "The blame for this catastrophic result can be shared between us all, but the person who decided the lineup, the tactics, was me. It was my choice. We tried to do what we could, we did our best, but we came up against a great German team. We couldn't react to going behind. We got disorganized and panicked after the first goal and then it all went wrong for us."

The other semifinal, played the following day in São Paulo between Argentina and the Netherlands, was the opposite of the Germany-Brazil match. Instead of a goal deluge, fans got a drought. The game ended 0–0 after 90 minutes, and extra time was needed. Argentina had the clearest chance to score in the 115th minute when a long ball was lobbed into the path of substitute Rodrigo Palacio, but his header was too weak and Cillessen produced an easy save.

The game went to penalties, where Argentina goalkeeper Sergio Romero proved decisive. His saves put Argentina on top, 4–2, in the shootout, catapulting them to the World Cup final for the first time in 24 years. His saves on Ron Vlaar's spot kick before making a stunning one on Sneijder's kick proved decisive. Van Gaal could not muster up magic this time. They had been able to stop Messi but could do little offensively to win the game. Romero admitted that winning via a shootout had been more the product of luck than skill. "You can dive and not make it, like their goalkeeper did," he said. "I had confidence, and thank God things turned out well."

While the Netherlands would go on to take third place and Rodríguez of Colombia to finish as the tournament's top scorer with six goals, the final was set: Germany versus Argentina.

Final: Germany vs. Argentina

Germany was looking to win its first World Cup as a unified nation, while for Argentina it was Messi's big chance to come out of Maradona's shadow and lead his country to an international title. With Brazilians rooting for Germany (and against their biggest South American rivals), it looked as if the Europeans would have the edge in terms of fans. Nonetheless, Argentines continued to flood into Rio de Janeiro, despite not having tickets to the game. No matter. These fans were there to drink and dance. They wanted to soak up the enthusiasm of the World Cup and cheer on their team in the streets and in front of the large screens set up on Copacabana Beach. Indeed, Brazilian authorities estimated that there were some 100,000 Argentina fans, many with no place to stay and opting to sleep in their cars parked along the picturesque Avenida Atlântica. In the days leading up to the final, Argentine fans gathered in large groups along Rio's streets, taunting locals with a song featuring several incendiary lyrics that had become famous during the tournament:

Brasil, decime qué se siente tener en casa a tu papá.
Te juro que aunque pasen los años, nunca nos vamos a olvidar,
Que el Diego te gambeteó, que Cani te vacunó, que estás llorando
desde Italia hasta hoy,
A Messi lo vas a ver, la Copa nos va a traer, Maradona es más grande
que Pelé.

That translates to:

Brazil, tell me how it feels, to have your daddy in your house.
We'll never forget how Diego dribbled past you, how Cani [Claudio
Caniggia] killed you off in Italy,
We're going to see Messi, he's going to bring us the Cup, Maradona is
much better than Pelé.

With Brazil's failure one of the biggest story lines to come out of the tournament, Germany and Argentina met on July 13 at the Maracanã before 75,000 fans. The teams seemed energized from the start, with both looking to score early. The naturally frenetic start even brought with it a goal by Higuaín in the 30th minute off a Lavezzi cross, but he was deemed offside by Italian referee Nicola Rizzoli.

Messi looked to be a factor, but the Germans did a great job containing him. On the other side of the field, Argentina defender Javier Mascherano was doing his part to stop Müller and his teammates. The biggest moment of the first half, however, was when Germany's Christoph Kramer suffered a blow to the head after just 16 minutes. Despite the renewed focus on concussions, Kramer, visibly dazed, received medical treatment and was allowed to reenter the match. It wasn't until the 31st minute that Löw replaced Kramer with Schürrle. The fact that

Rizzoli did nothing to ensure Kramer's safety will forever be a blemish on a game that was both well played and properly officiated.

Extra time seemed like a real possibility, and a feeling of urgency overcame both teams. The Germans dominated possession, with Özil and Kroos linking up well in an attempt to create a scoring chance. Not to be outdone, Messi tried to score, but his attempt in the 75th minute went wide. Kroos responded with a long-range shot of his own in the 82nd minute, but that kick was also off target. With two minutes left to play, Löw made a change that would affect the outcome of the match. Out came Klose, and in his place entered striker Mario Götze.

The game ended scoreless. The final would once again go to extra time. The teams appeared relatively equal in the extra session. However, the second period of overtime was where Germany would get the victory. As the Argentines grew more frustrated, the game became increasingly tense. Bastian Schweinsteiger, the midfield workhorse who had fought for nearly every ball, took a beating from the Argentines and had to receive medical treatment for an open cut to his face. The Germans continued to maintain possession and scored in the 113th minute. The goal came together well and was executed beautifully. Götze did a fabulous job of controlling a pass from Schürrle and slotting a one-time shot past Romero. "I just took the shot and didn't know what was happening," Götze recalled.

The goal unleashed joy from German and Brazilian supporters and tears from the many Argentines in the stadium. "We always knew that we would need 14 players during this match and everyone in top shape, and all the players had to be ready. It was good that we had played who could come on and make an impact, and [Mario] Götze is a miracle boy, a boy wonder. I always knew he could decide the match," said Löw. Germany had won a fourth World Cup title to become the first European nation to win the tournament in South America.

Götze had become the unlikely hero of a World Cup that was full of surprises. In the course of five weeks, the tournament had featured entertaining games and thrilling goals. Despite pre-tournament fears, Brazil had avoided any major embarrassments (except for its national team's shocking collapse). In the end, Brazil 2014 would go down as one of the greatest World Cups in history.

21st-Century Star: Lionel Messi

Considered the best player of his generation alongside Cristiano Ronaldo of Portugal, Messi has won a record seven Ballon d'Or awards—yet he has never been able to get away from the shadow of Diego Maradona after failing to win the World Cup in four tournament appearances.

National team career: Messi has made the most appearances in Argentina's history as well as being the team's all-time top scorer. At youth level, he won the 2005 FIFA World Youth Championship, finishing the tournament with both the Golden Ball and Golden Shoe awards. He won an Olympic gold medal at the 2008 Beijing Games. He was made Argentina captain in 2011. He led Argentina to the 2014 World Cup final, where they lost to Germany. After announcing his international retirement in 2016, he reversed his decision and played at the World Cup two years later. He led the team to the 2021 Copa America, winning his first-ever trophy for his country.

Club career: Messi moved to Spain at age 13 to join Barcelona. Messi made his debut in 2004 at age 17 and established himself as a key member of the club. He helped the team win the Champions League in 2006. Three seasons later, Messi helped Barca win the treble, culminating with his winning his first Ballon d'Or at age 22. He also had helped the team win the Champions League in 2011 and 2015. In all, he won 10 La Liga titles for Barcelona, the last one in 2019, before signing with Paris Saint-Germain in August 2021.

Argentina's Lionel Messi celebrates with his teammates after beating Brazil in the 2021 Copa America final.

SHUTTERSTOCK

Honors: Messi has been awarded the Ballon d'Or in 2009, 2010, 2011, 2012, 2015, 2019, and 2021. He won the FIFA Golden Ball as the best player at the 2014 World Cup. He is a seven-time winner of the Trofeo Alfredo Di Stéfano, as the Spanish league's best player, and a six-time winner of the European Golden Shoe as the continent's top scorer, the last one in 2019.

2018 World Cup

The tournament came to Russia in 2018 and marked the first time that a World Cup would be played in both Eastern Europe and Asia. This World Cup—like past ones—was a showcase for both the country and President Vladimir Putin's political power in the post–Cold War era. After cruising to a fourth straight victory at the polls earlier in the year, the tournament allowed both Putin and Russia to put their best foot forward.

In an effort to strike a unifying tone at the tournament's opening ceremony, Putin told the crowd gathered at Moscow's Luzhniki Stadium: "There are billions of people on the planet who are devoted football fans. And wherever we live, no matter our traditions, we all are united as one team by our love for this spectacular, dazzling, uncompromising game."

On the field, Iceland and Panama qualified for the very first time, while 20 nations that had participated at Brazil 2014 were back. The finals, however, were known for their notable absences. Italy did not qualify for the first time since 1958, nor did the Netherlands, who had qualified for the last three World Cups and finished third just four years earlier. Four defending continental champions—2017 Africa Cup of Nations winners Cameroon, Copa America champions Chile, Oceania winners New Zealand, and Gold Cup champions the United States (for the first time since 1986)—also failed to qualify.

Russia, Germany, Brazil, Portugal, Argentina, Belgium, Poland, and France were the tournament's eight seeded teams. Groups D, E, and F were all considered "Groups of Death," which made for a competitive first round. This is the result of the draw and the composition of the eight groups:

Group A: Russia, Saudi Arabia, Egypt, and Uruguay

Group B: Portugal, Spain, Morocco, and Iran

Group C: France, Australia, Peru, and Denmark

Group D: Argentina, Iceland, Croatia, and Nigeria

Group E: Brazil, Switzerland, Costa Rica, and Serbia

Group F: Germany, Mexico, Sweden, and South Korea

Group G: Belgium, Panama, Tunisia, and England

Group H: Poland, Senegal, Colombia, and Japan

The big innovation was the use of video assistant referees, or VARs. Shortly after the International Football Association Board decided to allow the use of video assistant referees in the laws of the game in 2018, FIFA moved quickly to implement their use in international competition. From a centralized location in Moscow, the VAR team had access to all broadcast cameras in addition to two offside cameras. The team reviews the plays and remains in contact with the referee via an earpiece. The referee still made the final call.

The use of instant replay was used in just four cases during the course of a match: to determine the validity of a goal, in the awarding of a penalty kick, on direct red-card incidents, or in cases where the referee may have given a yellow or red card to the wrong player. The World Cup became the first tournament where VAR was used in every game. Both praised and hated, VAR would be used to determine several key incidents during the tournament.

Twelve venues in 11 cities would host the games. Nine new stadiums were built, while three were renovated. Moscow featured two venues: the new Spartak Stadium and the renovated Luzhniki. A football temple that has become as popular as the ornate Saint Basil's Cathedral in Red Square, the Luzhniki would host some of the World Cup's most memorable matches, including the July 15 final.

On the eve of the tournament, Alexei Sorokin, head of the 2018 World Cup Local Organizing Committee, said the Luzhniki was the perfect place to host games of such magnitude: "This is an excellent, modern stadium that has been recently revamped, fully rebuilt, preserving elements of its former looks with overhauled technologies," Sorokin told the Russian news agency TASS. "Of course, it is unique in many respects—this is an excellent blend of memory, history, and modern technologies. It is convenient and comfortable for watching football matches."

Group Stage

Russia opened the tournament on June 14 at Luzhniki Stadium before 78,000 fans against Saudi Arabia. The hosts recorded the biggest opening-game win since Italy defeated the United States 7–1 in 1934, recording a 5–0 victory as Putin looked on with delight. Going into the World Cup, the Russian prospects appeared dim. The team had failed to win one game out of seven leading up to the tournament. Any fears the Russians would be humiliated in Group A were cast aside as Yury Gazinsky scored after just 12 minutes on an Aleksandr Golovin cross. Putin and Gianni Infantino smiled after the goal and shrugged as they sat with Saudi crown prince Mohammed bin Salman. Putin even reached over to shake the prince's hand as if to rub it in.

Ahead 2–0 at halftime, the Russians scored again in the 71st minute when Artem Dzyuba, who had come into the game just 89 seconds earlier, headed the ball in off a Golovin pass. Golovin, who had two assists, tallied a goal of his own in the fourth minute of stoppage time with a superb free kick over a wall of Saudi players to make it five on the day. The win ended a 16-year drought for the Russians at a World Cup. The Saudis would end the match without a shot on target. Russia coach Stanislav Cherchesov said after the game that he was "relaxed today because I know my players. It is a pleasure to work with them. Every coach depends on the players, this is why I am relaxed. Why do I have to be stressed? I would like to underscore that we are grateful to our squad with how they fulfilled our goals, how they played in a relaxed game under the pressure stemming from this being an opening match."

In the group's other game, played the following day at Ekaterinburg Arena in Yekaterinburg, Uruguay defeated Egypt 1–0. For the South Americans, the victory was the first in their opening game for the first time since 1970. While Suárez looked abysmal and Edinson Cavani a lot livelier—he came close twice to scoring—Uruguay would get its goal in the 89th minute. Egypt, without Mohamed Salah after he was injured in the Champions League final won by Real Madrid against Liverpool, featured a lackluster offense.

The group's second match day on June 19 saw Russia all but clinch a spot to the knockout round—a goal that appeared unattainable on the eve of the tournament—following another resounding victory. With Salah back in the lineup for Egypt, the Africans were expecting a better performance at Saint Petersburg Stadium in St. Petersburg. Instead it was the upstart Russians who dominated with a 3–1 win. Up 1–0 thanks to an own goal by Ahmed Fathy, the Russians put the game away in the second half by netting twice in a span of three minutes via Denis Cheryshev and Dzyuba. All Salah could do was score on a penalty kick late in the game with his side already down by three goals.

The following day, Uruguay's 1–0 victory against Saudi Arabia—on a Suárez goal—at Rostov Arena in the city of Rostov-on-Don officially put the South Americans, as well as the Russians, through to the second round. The June 25 matchup between Russia and Uruguay at Samara Arena in Samara was to determine who would win the group. The Russians had momentum on their side and home support that had reached a frenzied pitch in the days leading up to the game. The 41,970 fans in attendance made their voices heard, but it wasn't enough as Uruguay earned an easy 3–0 win against a 10-man Russian side following Igor Smolnikov's red card in the 36th minute. The attacking duo of Cavani and Suárez was paying dividends for veteran manager Óscar Washington Tabárez. The two-time World Cup winners looked strong. The Russians, while failing after facing their toughest test at this tournament, remained optimistic heading into the knockout phase. "I like how my team played after we lost one player," Cherchesov said. "We were rather aggressive."

In Group B, the Iberian derby between Spain and Portugal on June 15 was one of the most anticipated games of the opening round, and the two nations did not disappoint. At Sochi's Fisht Olympic Stadium, La Roja's passing game and Ronaldo did battle in what resulted in an enthralling 3–3 draw. In the never-ending debate over who was better— Ronaldo or Messi—the Portuguese tried to use this match to tell the world that Ronaldo is the greatest of all time (GOAT). After scoring Portugal's goal just four minutes into the game, Ronaldo celebrated by rubbing his chin, implying he was the GOAT. The celebration was in reaction to Adidas's "GOAT" promotion featuring Messi with a real goat.

Ronaldo scored twice more, including an exquisite free kick two minutes from time to give Portugal a 3–3 draw. It's true that Spain controlled large portions of the game, but even double-marking Ronaldo proved fruitless. "When I play against a player like Ronaldo, these things can happen," Spain manager Fernando Hierro said. "It's very fortunate for whatever team has Cristiano Ronaldo."

The draw was a relief for Spain given the drama that had unfolded days earlier. The Spanish FA fired manager Julen Lopetegui for taking a job with Real Madrid without letting officials know in advance. Hierro, a former player and Spain's sporting director, replaced Lopetegui despite no significant previous coaching experience. "It wasn't an easy situation," Hierro admitted. "When you have this staff and these young players, they make it much easier."

Five days later, both Portugal and Spain managed to record 1–0 wins. Portugal edged Morocco with Ronaldo scoring the game's only goal after four minutes at Luzhniki Stadium. Spain, meanwhile, did the same, defeating Iran at Kazan Arena in Kazan. Diego Costa's goal in the 54th minute put Spain into a tie for first place in the group alongside Portugal. Again, the Spanish dominated possession, but Iran had given them fits all evening. Hierro summed up the game this way afterward: "We have four points. We were happier after the match against Portugal, but we only had one point."

Spain managed to win the group on the final match day, salvaging a 2–2 draw against Morocco with a goal by Iago Aspas in stoppage time. It really did seem that Morocco would pull off the upset at Kaliningrad Stadium in Kaliningrad, but the goal was awarded after it was reviewed by VAR for potentially being offside. As a result, Spain won the group. "Until the last minute, we weren't sure who was going to finish first and second," Hierro recalled. "And I have to say we were lucky to finish first."

At the same time at Mordovia Arena in Saransk, Portugal could do no better than a 1–1 draw against Iran. It was enough to see Portugal through to the round of 16 as the group's second-place team. Iran came close to winning the match—and as a result the group—after goalkeeper Ali Beiranvand's clutch save in the 53rd minute thwarted a Ronaldo penalty kick that would have put Portugal ahead 2–0.

Instead, Iran tied the score with a Karim Ansarifard penalty kick in stoppage time. The 42,000 inside the stadium audibly gasped when

Mehdi Taremi's attempt moments later hit the side netting. Portugal escaped with the draw, while Iran left the tournament with their heads held high. "Every match in the World Cup is difficult," Portugal manager Fernando Santos observed after the game. "Those thinking it would be easy for Portugal were certainly not on the same field with us."

In Group C, France, among the pre-tournament favorites, defeated Australia 2–1 on June 16 in Kazan. After a scoreless first half, a struggling France were able to break the deadlock thanks to a decision by referee Andrés Cunha of Uruguay after he overturned his own decision and awarded a penalty kick. The decision came after defender Josh Risdon of Australia tackled Antoine Griezmann in the box. Cunha did not originally whistle a penalty kick. After French players complained, Cunha went to consult the video replay. It was the first time VAR was used in a World Cup game. After several tense moments, Cunha overturned his own decision and whistled for a penalty kick to be taken. Griezmann converted to give France a 1–0 lead in the 58th minute. Replays showed Risdon had made light contact with the Les Bleus striker.

Four minutes later, Australia tied the score after Cunha whistled a penalty for the Socceroos following a handball in the box. The infraction was obvious and no VAR was needed. Mile Jedinak scored from the spot to level the score. The use of technology didn't end there. France took the lead nine minutes from the end when Paul Pogba saw his shot hit the crossbar and drop over the line. While the French players held off celebrating, Cunha indicated the ball had crossed the line after goal-line technology signaled the ball had crossed the line, lifting France to a 2–1 victory. France, despite all its attacking talent, looked lackluster in its opener.

The same day, Denmark managed a 1–0 win over Peru thanks to a counterattacking strike from Yussuf Poulsen in the 59th minute. With 40,000 Peruvians traveling to Russia during the course of the tournament to support their team, they outnumbered Danish supporters among the crowd of 40,502. In goal, Kasper Schmiechel proved effective as Peru struggled to get the ball past him following six attempts. Peru featured captain Paolo Guerrero in the lineup after the striker had initially been banned from the World Cup after testing positive for a cocaine byproduct that was in a cup of tea he drank. The 34-year-old, who has denied any wrongdoing, appealed to a Swiss federal court—the final instance in the sporting judicial system—which on May 31 agreed to lift the suspension. Nonetheless, his appearance wasn't enough to help Peru. "It's good to have a good goalkeeper, let me put it that way," Denmark coach Age Hareide told reporters. "He is acrobatic and a very quick goalkeeper. He had a fantastic performance, and we needed it. You have to acknowledge the performance of Kasper."

Five days later in Samara, Denmark and Australia played to a 1–1 draw, while France eliminated Peru 1–0 at Ekaterinburg Arena in Yekaterinburg. Far from convincing, the French scored the winner in the 34th minute from Kylian Mbappe. At just 19 years and 183 days, Mbappe became the youngest player to score for France at a World Cup, while also helping his side reach the knockout round in the process. Born just months after France won the World Cup in 1998, Mbappe said after the game: "I've always said that the World Cup is a dream for any player. It is a dream come true and I hope I will have more like this."

The group's final match day on June 26 saw Peru eliminate Australia 2–0—rewarding the 44,000 mostly Peruvian fans at Fisht Stadium—and ending a winless run of eight World Cup games that stretched back to the 1978 World Cup. "Many people made the impossible trip to be here," Peru striker André Carillo, who scored Peru's first goal, said after the game. "I am happy to give them the victory. We are proud of them." Meanwhile, at Luzhniki Stadium, the 78,000 in attendance were treated to a scoreless draw between France and Denmark. The stalemate suited both sides ahead of the knockout stage.

What many predicted to be one of the toughest groups at the tournament turned out to be just that. Argentina struggled for most of its first three Group D matches, while Croatia, Iceland, and Nigeria all tried to take advantage of that sudden vulnerability. Argentina had struggled in qualifying, and friendlies leading up to the finals did nothing to quell concerns that coach Jorge Sampaoli was not up to the task. A 6–1 defeat to Spain in March sent Argentina fans reeling.

The pressure on Messi to deliver a World Cup title for his country, just like Maradona had, didn't help. While Messi remained the fulcrum for this team, there were other players—in defense, midfield, and attack—who are also expected to have big tournaments. Sampaoli went with Messi, Paulo Dybala, Sergio Agüero, and Gonzalo Higuaín. Only two of these players, Agüero and Higuaín, were pure strikers. Higuaín would get the start as the lone striker. A strong forward at club level for Napoli, and later at rivals Juventus, the forward had often come up short when Argentina needed him most. In both Copa America finals against Chile, in 2015 and 2016, Higuaín had flubbed scoring chances early on that could have changed the course and outcome of those matches. Argentina also lost the World Cup final four years earlier after Higuaín squandered a clear chance early on.

Luck wasn't on the Albiceleste's side when starting goalkeeper Sergio Romero was ruled out of playing with a knee injury ahead of the tournament. Making things worse, the team's backup goalkeeper the past two years, Nahuel Guzmán, was originally left off the squad. Sampaoli called in Guzman—even after the goalkeeper's father had gone after the manager on social media following the initial exclusion. Sampaoli would give the starting job to Chelsea backup Willy Caballero.

Argentina got off to a positive start against Iceland when Agüero put his side ahead after just 19 minutes. The game would end in frustration for the Argentines, however, when Iceland—playing a disciplined defensive style in its first World Cup game ever—got the equalizer just four minutes later thanks to Alfred Finnbogason. Making matters worse, a Messi penalty-kick attempt denied by goalkeeper Hannes Halldórsson in the second half would deal the Argentines a psychological blow early in the competition.

Later that day, Croatia powered itself to a 2–0 win against Nigeria. An own goal in the 32nd minute and a penalty kick converted by Real Madrid midfielder Luka Modric in the 72nd minute put the game away. Croatia had not played a pretty game (Modric's penalty kick was Croatia's first shot on goal and only one of two clear scoring attempts), but it was enough to power the team to first place in the group. "A win is a win is a win. It doesn't matter how you score," said Croatia manager Zlatko Dalić. "What matters is that you score!"

The June 21 game pitting Argentina and Croatia was already a must-win for both sides. With only the top two teams advancing from the first round, neither could afford to drop points given that the group remained wide open. The game at Nizhny Novgorod Stadium in Nizhny Novgorod would expose Argentina's vulnerabilities while further propelling Croatia's status as one of the tournament's dark horse sides. With Maradona watching from the stands, Croatia swept Argentina aside after a Caballero attempt to clear the ball following an errant back pass from defender Gabriel Mercado allowed Ante Rebić to volley the ball into the net. Caballero's massive blunder in the 53rd minute set the tone for the rest of the game. In a desperate bid to score an equalizer, Sampaoli removed Agüero and put the scoring onus on Higuaín, Dybala, and Cristian Pavón. With Argentina exposing itself in the back and in midfield, Croatia found a second goal in the 80th minute. With Modric unmarked, the midfielder unleashed a shot from 25 yards out to beat Caballero. In stoppage time, Ivan Rakitic, a teammate of Messi's at Barcelona, beat Caballero for a third time as Croatia moved on to the knockout phase.

Argentina, now in last place in the group, needed a victory against Nigeria in its final game—coupled with a Croatia victory against Iceland—to advance to the knockout round. Nigeria had defeated Iceland 2–0 and were very much alive in the competition. The days leading up to the game were full of drama and anxiety as tumult reigned inside the Argentina camp with Sampaoli increasingly coming under fire and speculation that the Argentine FA could fire him at any moment. Argentina's players, with just days before the Nigeria game, were in revolt after a failed coup attempt to oust their manager. The days prior to the game were fraught with anger and frustration within the Argentine camp after the country's FA confirmed it had no plans to sack the embattled Sampaoli. The headline in *Clarin*, one of the country's largest newspapers, summed it up best: "Sampaoli continues, but the players aren't responding."

Tensions had risen just a day after their humiliating loss to Croatia when it was reported that a secret meeting was held, spearheaded by Messi and Javier Mascherano, that involved asking Sampaoli to step down to be replaced by technical director and 1986 World Cup star Jorge Burruchaga. The mood was glum inside the Argentine camp, with the players no longer listening to their coach despite the team holding training sessions in the days leading up to the game. However, Claudio

Tapia, the head of the Argentine FA, said the coaching staff and players had come up with a peace agreement after meeting at the team's base camp in Bronnitsy, located in suburban Moscow, and deciding to "get together and move forward."

With Messi looking for his first goal at the tournament, Argentina came out aggressive against Nigeria on June 26 in St. Petersburg. Not only did Argentina get the win it needed—and help from Croatia in the form of a 2–1 win versus Iceland—but Messi scored an exquisite goal after just 14 minutes from a long pass from defender Éver Banega. The wild enthusiasm that followed, led by an animated Maradona in the stands, swung the momentum in Argentina's direction. While Messi, who later hit the post off a free kick, and Banega controlled the game in the first half, the rest of the team did not look up to the task.

Behind 1–0 at halftime, Nigeria scored the equalizer in the 51st minute after they were awarded a penalty kick following a Mascherano foul in the box. Victor Moses put the ball past Franco Armani, a goal that would deal a blow to Argentina's hopes of qualifying to the next round. The South Americans needed a win or suffer a humiliating elimination. Once again, with the game on the line, Higuaín put an easy chance over the crossbar. With Argentina pushing forward and Sampaoli encouraging his players from the sidelines, Argentina grabbed the winner with four minutes left to play from an unlikely source when defender Marcos Rojo slotted home a volley with his right foot into the bottom corner. The goal unleashed delirium among the 64,468 in attendance, including Maradona. The former Argentine legend had to be taken to the hospital after the game after suffering chest pains. The final whistle saw Argentina through to the knockout stage as the players huddled around Messi.

"The most important thing for Leo is his human side. He cries. He suffers. He's happy when Argentina wins. I know him," Sampaoli said afterward. "Many people say Leo does not enjoy playing for Argentina, but I do not agree. He enjoys and suffers like all the other players and that makes him even bigger."

In Group E, Brazil was expected to sail through to the next round, but was stunned in its opener when it could only get a 1–1 draw against Switzerland on June 17 at Rostov Arena in Rostov-on-Don. The Brazilians took the lead after 20 minutes when Philippe Coutinho curled in a brilliant right-footed shot to take the lead. The Swiss tied the game in the 50th minute when an unmarked Steven Zuber headed home a Xherdan Shaqiri corner kick. Neymar was a nonfactor for long stretches, fouled 10 times by the Swiss throughout the match.

The Brazilians got the win five days later at Saint Petersburg Stadium in St. Petersburg, blanking Costa Rica 2–0. It didn't come easy as Brazil scored twice in stoppage time. The first goal came in the first minute of stoppage time when Coutinho was able to poke the ball into the goal. Neymar added a second six minutes later when he volleyed home from close range a Douglas Costa cross. For Brazil, the win was more gritty than stylish.

Brazil won the group on June 27 after defeating Serbia 2–0 at Spartak Stadium. Switzerland, meanwhile, finished second following a 2–2 draw versus already-eliminated Costa Rica. For the first time since 2006, Switzerland had avoided defeat in each of their three group-stage games at a World Cup.

The good news of advancing was overshadowed by yellow cards for captain Stephan Lichtsteiner and fellow defender Fabian Schär—both their second of the tournament—that meant both would have to sit out the round of 16. "This is certainly not an ideal scenario," Swiss midfielder Blerim Džemaili told reporters. "We don't need to look at who's not there, we need to look at who will be able to play."

Germany was the seeded team in Group F and heavy favorites to advance. Instead, it would be the worst-ever performance by Die Mannschaft at any level. Mexico pulled off the upset in its opener on June 17 at Luzhniki Stadium. Mexico scored the game's only goal in the 35th minute following a wonderful play. Javier Hernández's played a one-two with Andrés Guardado, allowing him to break free of Mats Hummels inside the German half. With the ball fed to Hirving Lozano down the left, the speedy striker cut inside and hit a low, right-footed shot for the goal. "I don't know if it's the biggest victory in our history, but one of the biggest for sure," Lozano said. "My teammates and I did some great work. We all ran our hearts out."

The following day, Sweden defeated South Korea 1–0 at Nizhny Novgorod Stadium in Nizhny Novgorod. With Sweden and Mexico temporarily at the top of the group, Germany was in a must-win situation going into its June 23 match against Sweden in Sochi. The Germans did not disappoint this time, squeezing out a 2–1 victory via a dramatic stoppage-time goal from Kroos. The midfielder tapped a free-kick short to teammate Marco Reus before kicking the return pass into the top right corner to keep his nation's World Cup hopes alive.

All four teams had a chance to advance heading into the final match day. In the end, it would be Sweden and Mexico who would advance to the round of 16. Sweden's 3–0 win against Mexico on June 27 at Central Stadium in Yekaterinburg allowed them to win the group. Mexico, meanwhile, benefited from South Korea's stunning 2–0 win against Germany in Kazan.

In defeat, Germany finished last in the group and became the fourth defending champions to be eliminated from the group stage at a World Cup in the last five tournaments, following France in 2002, Italy in 2010, and Spain in 2014. For Germany, it also marked the end of a cycle. "We deserved to be eliminated," Löw told reporters. "For us, this is a huge disappointment. But we have young players who are talented and have the potential to go forward. It happened to other nations before. We need to draw the right conclusions."

Belgium, a dark horse to win the tournament, and England dominated Group G over Tunisia and Panama. In the group opener on June 18, Belgium routed Panama 3–0 in Sochi, while England edged out Tunisia 2–1 at Volgograd Arena in Volgograd. While Belgium dominated thanks to two Romelu Lukaku goals, England, as usual, struggled and was only able to grab the win via a Harry Kane strike in stoppage time. Unmarked at the far post, Kane—ever opportunistic in the box and one of the world's best players for his predatory skills—redirected a header into the net. The England captain and Tottenham star had been double-teamed and fouled the entire match. After he was dragged down on two occasions, the referee refused to consult with VAR. England's energetic start and Kane's imposing game were rewarded in the end. "Maybe there was a bit of justice at the end," Kane said.

Five days later, Belgium defeated Tunisia 5–2 at Spartak Stadium. Two goals apiece from Lukaku and Hazard lifted the team to success. In Nizhny Novgorod, England romped Panama 6–1, confirming the enthusiasm in the Three Lions camp, to record its biggest margin of victory at a World Cup. A Kane hat trick and two goals from John Stones lifted England to the win. The victory allowed Belgium and England to reach the final 16 even before the sides met in the final group match.

With both sides resting players ahead of the knockout stage, Belgium defeated England 1–0 on a goal from Adnan Januzaj. Although Belgium coach Roberto Martínez admitted before the June 28 game that "the priority was not to win," the players were content to have won the group.

Neither team really wanted to win the game or the group. The defeat benefited England as Belgium advanced to what most consider the tougher side of the knockout-round bracket that included Brazil, Mexico, France, Argentina, Uruguay, and Portugal. England had made eight changes to its starting lineup for the game—but the players made it clear they wanted to win every game. "We're disappointed we couldn't do that. . . . I thought it was quite an even game," said midfielder Eric Dier. "We created some good chances. We needed to finish one of them. That was all that was missing."

Poland, who were the seeded side in Group H, returned to the World Cup for the first time since 2006. Colombia, meanwhile, had lit up the tournament four years earlier with Rodríguez's goals. Senegal and Japan, relatively unknown sides, rounded out a group that was relatively even. Any one of these four teams could advance, leading some to brand it the "Group of Life."

While Colombia and Poland were favored by some to advance, no one was ruling out plucky sides such as Japan and Senegal. That was proven in the group's opening game on June 19 when Japan shocked Colombia 2–1 in Saransk. It marked the first time that Japan had recorded a World Cup victory on European soil—thanks to a goal from Yuya Osako in the 73rd minute—after Los Cafeteros were reduced to 10 men after just three minutes. Carlos Sánchez was red-carded—the first of the tournament—after he handled the ball in the box. Shinji Kagawa scored on the ensuing penalty, a lead that held for just 33 minutes when Juan Quintero's free kick tied the score.

Japan joined Mexico, Switzerland, and Iceland in earning unexpected results at this tournament. The win came as a surprise also because Japan had changed coaches shortly before the tournament. "If we had actually won the World Cup, we would have had a parade on the main street of Saransk," Japan manager Akira Nishino said. "However, it is just one win, three points. We'll save our celebrations."

On June 24, Colombia rebounded with a 3–0 win against Poland in Kazan to keep its World Cup hopes alive. On the same day in Yekaterinburg, Japan came from behind twice to draw Senegal 2–2. The game showcased the attacking styles of both nations, but also their defensive lapses. Keisuke Honda's equalizer for Japan in the 78th minute put him in the history books as the first from his country to score at three World Cups. The results meant Poland was the only team eliminated ahead of the group's final match day. Japan left nothing to chance. Even though they would play Poland, Nishino would need to impose its style—even though a draw would be enough to advance—in order to reach the last 16. "We need to be able to play to our full potential rather than being reactive to the opposition's strength," he said ahead of Japan's June 28 game against Poland.

Colombia won the group with a 1–0 against Senegal, while Japan scrapped by despite a defeat by the same score. In the end, Japan finished second after finishing with a 1–1–1 record with four goals for and four conceded—an identical record as Senegal—but advanced by virtue of having collected fewer yellow cards. The tiebreaker was controversial, but enough for Japan in the end. It also ensured that no African team reached the final 16 at Russia 2018.

Round of 16

The knockout stage opened with the much-anticipated France-Argentina match on June 30 in Kazan. Argentina had limped into the round of 16, while France had started to look like contenders for the ultimate prize. What ensued was a topsy-turvy affair that produced seven goals. It was Mbappe's brace in a four-minute span starting in the 64th minute that buried the Argentines.

The encounter was ridden with fouls as Argentina grew more desperate as the minutes waned on. The game's eight yellow cards—five of them collected by Argentina—were a reflection of this. France won 4–3, and Messi, unable to create much, had been dumped out of the World Cup prematurely once again. "Of course, as I've already and always said, in the World Cup you have all the top level players so it is an opportunity to show what you can do and what your abilities are," Mbappe told reporters. "There is no better place than a World Cup."

In the nightcap, Ronaldo also exited the tournament early as Uruguay edged Portugal 2–1 in Sochi. Cavani stole the show, and his brace, his first goal coming after just seven minutes, was enough to get the South Americans through to the quarterfinals as the defense kept Ronaldo, limited to one shot on goal, off the score sheet.

The World Cup was now without its two GOATs, but that mattered little. The elevated play and ability of players like Mbappe and Cavani to grab the spotlight and overshadow the more-established superstars made for an exciting and unpredictable tournament. "The truth is, it was really exciting," Cavani said afterward. "There aren't words to describe this."

Russia and Spain faced off on July 1 in a highly anticipated match. Spain's *tiki-taka* had not worked as well as in years past. Opponents had grown wise to it. The Russians certainly had, absorbing pressure after Spain's possession game failed to penetrate the backline. Spain dominated in what turned out to be a frustrating match for them after Hierro's side completed more than 1,000 passes with 74 percent possession—but could only produce one goal. Spain led in the 12th minute after captain Sergio Ramos helped force Sergei Ignashevich to divert a crossed ball into his own goal. An error at the other end put Russia back in the game. Gerald Piqué handled the ball in the box off a corner kick. Dzyuba scored on the ensuing penalty in the 41st minute to tie the score.

That's where the goals came to an end, but the heroics were just getting started. After 120 minutes, the match headed to a shootout. On penalties, goalkeeper Igor Akinfeev made two saves—on Spain's third and fifth shots—and lifted the hosts to a 4–3 win. The decisive save came when Akinfeev used his left foot to stop Iago Aspas's left-footed shot. The save unleashed celebrations throughout Moscow that stretched throughout the massive country of 145 million people and 11 time zones. The unexpected win led to an outpouring of celebration and public displays of patriotism not seen since the end of World War II. As vehicular traffic leading to Red Square came to a halt and fans streamed into the street, the chants of "Ro-si-ya! Ro-si-ya!" filled the skies of the massive capital. "I'm not the man of the match. The man of the match is our team and our fans," Akinfeev said, referring to the cheering from of the 78,000 fans inside Luzhniki Stadium.

The day's second clash in Nizhny Novgorod also produced a thriller between Croatia and Denmark. Denmark, who came into the game on an 18-game unbeaten streak, scored after just 57 seconds with Mathias Jorgensen who stabbed home a shot after a long throw-in caught the Croatian defense flat-footed. Croatia didn't lose its nerve, tying the score just three minutes later when Mandžukić took advantage of a scramble in the penalty area to fire home the ball. The evenly matched sides traded shots as possession remained even. Nonetheless, it was the goalkeeping that kept the came close.

Tied at one, the game went to extra time. It all seemed to come unraveled for Denmark in the 113th minute after Modric passed a ball to Ante Rebić who, after rounding Schmeichel and looking certain to score, was upended by Jorgensen. Modric's penalty kick, however, was saved by Schmeichel, the son of former Denmark goalkeeper Peter Schmeichel who was in the crowd for the game. The momentum swung in Denmark's favor as the teams entered the shootout.

Schmeichel was still oozing confidence, as his two saves in the shootout showed, but those heroics were canceled out by Croatia's Danijel Subašić. Christian Eriksen's first kick slammed against the post, while Subašić made saves on both Lasse Schöne's and Nicolai Jorgensen's attempts, lifting his side 3–2 in a heart-stomping win. "He was a hero tonight," Dalić added. "He saved three penalties in a shootout. You don't see that every day."

Mexico was trying to break its jinx of failing to reach the quarter-finals. Standing in their way was a Brazil side that raised their game on

July 2 in Samara. The exception to that was Neymar. His constant play-acting and rolling around on the ground reached new, farcical heights as Mexico played a strong first half. Neymar's overreaction to a Miquel Layún foul near the touchline earned the Brazilian striker internet ridicule that would stick with him for the remainder of the tournament. "I'm here to win. I hope I can improve always," Neymar told reporters after the match.

Mexico's pressing game fell apart in the second half as Brazil got on the board. In the 51st minute, Neymar helped draw the Mexican backline out of position. In typical Brazilian style, Neymar backheeled the ball to Willian, then back to Neymar who put the ball into the goal. Two minutes from the end, Brazil put the game away when a Neymar attempt was parried by Guillermo Ochoa and Roberto Firmino grabbed the rebound to clinch a spot in the quarterfinals.

The day's second game in Rostov-on-Don would produce another fun encounter. Japan, who had sneaked into the knockout stage, were the underdogs going into this game—although no one told Belgium. The wild and chaotic game would produce a memorable second half. Japan jumped out to a 2–0 lead within a span of four minutes. Frustrated, Belgium attempted a comeback that was thwarted by the post following a Hazard shot, while a Lukaku header from close range failed to change the score.

Martínez made two key substitutions in the 65th minute, putting in Nacer Chadli and Marouane Fellaini. The move would be a stroke of coaching genius. Japan naively continued to play, as opposed to locking down its defense, and Belgium's experienced players took advantage. "It's a test of character. It's a test of the team," Martínez told reporters after the game. "You have to see how the substitutes react, how the whole team reacts." The reaction paid off in the 69th minute when Japan's defense failed to clear a high ball that fell to Jan Vertonghen. The Tottenham defender took advantage of it, sending a looping header into the goal at the far post. Five minutes later, off a Hazard cross, Fellaini headed the ball into the goal to draw the game level. "When we were up 2–0, I really wanted to score another goal and we did have opportunities," Nishino recalled. "We were to some extent controlling the game, but Belgium upped their game when they had to."

What was expected to be a mismatch was instead a close game. With a quarterfinal berth and a meeting with Brazil on the line, the Red Devils initiated another attacking play that started with Courtois and ended 10 seconds later on the other side of the field with a brilliant Chadli goal in the fourth minute of stoppage time. After Courtois made a save following a corner kick, he rolled the ball to De Bruyne, who dribbled the ball to Thomas Meunier on the right. Meunier flicked the ball across the area toward Lukaku, who let it roll by for Chadli. The sub then tapped the ball with his left foot from just seven yards to grab the improbable win. In doing so, Belgium became the first team to overturn a two-goal deficit in a World Cup knockout game since West Germany defeated England in extra time at the 1970 tournament. The game saw Belgium extend its undefeated streak to 22 games. The final whistle unleashed tears among the dejected Japanese players, while Martínez and his players hugged one another. In the post-game news conference, Martínez was already looking ahead to Brazil, saying, "I think we can enjoy it from the first minute. When you're a little boy, you dream of facing Brazil in the World Cup."

Sweden stayed alive on July 3 following a 1–0 victory against Switzerland in St. Petersburg. Although Sweden was not as resolute, a goal by striker Emil Forsberg in the 67th minute proved to be enough against a Swiss side that came into the game never having won a World Cup knockout match. The win sent Sweden to the quarterfinals for the first time since 1994.

The day's second game was a tasty affair between England and Colombia at Spartak Stadium. Enthusiasm had grown back in England that the Three Lions could win their first World Cup since 1966. It was, however, a song from the 1996 European Championship called "Three Lions"—and its chorus "It's coming home"—whose lyrics could be heard in pubs throughout the country and at games. As the game got underway, England fans nestled among the 44,000 inside the venue chanted away:

> It's coming home. It's coming home. It's coming,
> Football's coming home,
> Everyone seems to know the score,
> They've seen it all before,

They just know, they're so sure,
That England's gonna throw it away, gonna blow it away,
But know they can play, 'cause I remember
Three Lions on a shirt,
Jules Rimet still gleaming,
Thirty years of hurt, never stopped me dreaming.

The dreaming continued after Kane scored on a penalty kick in the 57th minute to break the scoreless deadlock. The decision to award a penalty came when Carlos Sánchez wrestled Kane down in the box. In scoring, Kane became the first player for England to tally at least one goal in six straight appearances for England since Tommy Lawton in 1939. Another stoppage-time goal at this World Cup saw Colombia storm back to tie the score in the 93rd minute when an unmarked Yerry Mina scored off a play initiated from a corner kick that got past Jordan Pickford.

The contentious game was marred by fouling, with U.S. referee Mark Geiger at risk of losing control of the proceedings after he showed Wilmar Barrios a yellow card, rather than a red, following a head butt against Jordan Henderson. England defender John Stones called Colombia the "dirtiest team I've ever come up against," adding that his side's ability to rise above provocation was a sign of its growing maturity. Colombia, without Rodríguez due to a calf injury, resorted to a more defensive style and tactical fouls in an effort to break up England's possession game. But England's fine abilities from set pieces remained a threat, and Kane's penalty kick further proved that talking point.

After 120 minutes, the game went to a shootout. England had never won a shootout at the World Cup in three previous editions. England delivered a victory its fans would never forget. The 4–3 win was punctuated by Eric Dier's decisive kick after Colombia's Mateus Uribe's attempt hit the crossbar and Carlos Bacca saw his kick saved by Pickford. "It was like an out of body experience," Dier later said. "I just tried to stay in the moment."

Quarterfinals

France defeated Uruguay 2–0 on July 6 in Nizhny Novgorod, sending Les Bleus to the semifinals for the sixth time in their history. Without the injured Cavani, Uruguay was unable to generate the offense needed to beat a very talented French side. The midfield looked sharp with Paul Pogba finally starting to show his potential at this tournament. Raphael Varane gave France the lead on a header in the 40th minute. Off a free kick, Griezmann sent the ball from the right side, and Varane raced across the area. He got his head to the ball and sent it into the far corner. France doubled the score in the 61st minute when Griezmann's shot was deflected by Muslera into the net after failing to make what appeared to be an easy save. For Griezmann, it was his third goal of the tournament. "I was playing against a lot of friends," said Griezmann, who was teammates with Uruguay defenders Diego Godín and José Giménez at Atletico Madrid, "so I think it was normal not to celebrate."

France would face the winner of Brazil-Belgium, a clash of titans between two nations favored to lift the trophy. The offensive trio of De Bruyne, Lukaku, and Hazard proved tough for Brazil's defense in Kazan. Brazil maintained most of the possession, but it was Belgium that made the most of its three attempts. In the end, Belgium would emerge victorious 2–1 in a nervy affair. An own goal from Fernandinho put Belgium ahead after just 13 minutes. De Bryune doubled the lead with Brazil's defense failing to keep up with the Red Devils' counterattacking pace. A header from Renato Augusto in the 76th minute reopened Brazil's chances, with Martínez's team locking itself in its own half in an effort to grind out the win.

Wave after wave of Brazil attacks were thwarted with Neymar growing increasingly frustrated as the game wore on. Neymar limited his playacting versus Belgium but did get a yellow card after diving in the box. In stoppage time, a last-gasp attempt by Neymar resulted in a brilliant save from Courtois, his eighth of the game. The victory sent Belgium to the semifinals and a date with France. "Sometimes you have to accept that Brazil has this finesse, that quality, that they're going to break you down, and we just refused to accept that," Martínez said. "This is something special."

England's dream of bringing the World Cup home remained alive on July 7 as the Three Lions needed minimal effort to dispose of plucky Sweden. They took the lead after 30 minutes when Harry Maguire scored on a header off an Ashley Young corner. England killed off the match in the 59th minute when a Jesse Lingard cross was met by Dele Alli's header, putting an end to an emphatic 2–0 win. "We knew set plays would be key," Maguire said. "Also that little ball that Jesse sent in for Dele, that was great! We worked on that in practice."

In reaching the semifinals for the first time since 1990, England was able to do something that David Beckham, Frank Lampard, and Steven Gerrard had failed to do in the decades since that World Cup. With chants of "football's coming home" as fans streamed out of Samara Arena, the players exited the dressing room with a confidence not seen among England players in a generation.

The quarterfinal stage concluded the same day in Sochi as Russia, along with a country brimming with enthusiasm, took on never-say-die Croatia. Having gone further than anyone had ever expected, Russia hoped the strategy that eliminated Spain would work again. But Dalić's side, although tired, remained energized under the leadership of Modric and his abilities at midfield. The sides traded goals in the first half— Cheryshev in the 31st minute and Andrej Kramarić—to end the match 1–1 in regulation.

Extra time produced more drama as Croatia took the lead in the 101st minute on a header from Domogoj Vida. Russia, however, buoyed by the home support among the 44,287 at Fisht Stadium, tied the game. The Brazilian-born Mario Fernandes's header, off a free kick, sailed past Subašić and sent the crowd into a frenzy. The game ended 2–2 and would be decided by a shootout. On penalties, Akinfeev could not duplicate his previous heroics. Akinfeev made one save during the shootout, and nearly a second on Modric's attempt after the shot deflected off his hand, off the post, and into the net. In the end, Rakitic's goal helped Croatia emerge victorious, 4–3. In winning, Croatia became the second team—after Argentina in 1990—to win two penalty shootouts at a World Cup. It also marked the second time in Croatia's history that it had reached the semis after a phenomenal run 20 years earlier in France. As for Russia, the team's epic run propelled the game to new heights. After the game, Cherchesov said Putin called before and after the game to rally the players. "He congratulated us on a very good game," he said. "He said what we showed on the field was great."

Semifinals

For the first time in tournament history, neither Germany, Argentina, nor Brazil had reached the semifinals. Furthermore, the semifinals featured four European nations for the first time since 2006, another indication of the power and money associated with clubs that take part in domestic leagues in England, Germany, Spain, Italy, and France.

The talented and much-hyped France opened the semifinal round on July 10 against Belgium in St. Petersburg. A lively first half surprisingly produced no goals. Belgium, more a collection of stars than a unified force, struggled to penetrate France's defense. France's offense, meanwhile, always posed a major threat, and goals were expected from them as the second half began.

Samuel Umtiti's header in the 51st minute put France into their third World Cup final. Deschamps, speaking to the press after the match, highlighted the defense for getting his side past Belgium. "We had to defend really low sometimes because this Belgian team had great technical qualities," he said. "The idea was not to give them any space, because they can be like lightning bolts if you give them the space like we saw in their match against Brazil."

The following day at Luzhniki Stadium, surging England and Cinderella side Croatia faced off in the second semifinal. The game had plenty of action and drama, something made evident after Kieran Trippier put England ahead after just five minutes via a tantalizing free kick that beat the diving Danijel Subašić. It was a stroke of genius for Trippier, who scored his first World Cup goal of his career. The goal should have come as no surprise. Dead-ball situations had become the way to score at this tournament. England's run had been dominated by scoring off set pieces. Overall, 30 percent of the tournament's goals had come on free kicks and corners, outpacing the previous high of 23 percent (in 2002 and 2006) among the five most recent World Cups.

Croatia tied the score in the 68th minute after Kyle Walker attempted to head the ball clear. Instead, Ivan Perisic jumped and from behind raised his left boot over Walker's head to put the ball past Pickford. The game, tied at one, went to extra time. For Croatia, it was the third straight match of the knockout rounds to last 120 minutes. Mandžukić scored the winning goal in the 109th minute after Walker made another defensive lapse, deflecting a Josip Pivarić cross in an attempt to block it. The ball went into the air, and Perisic outjumped Trippier to head the ball. Mandžukić reacted by placing a left-footed shot to the left of Pickford.

Football was not coming home. Croatia became the first team to avoid defeat after falling behind in three consecutive World Cup knockout matches. Asked if fatigue would be a factor in the final, Rakitic observed, "We still have lots of energy in the tank."

Final: France vs. Croatia

The title match on July 15 at Luzhniki Stadium was set. France, with its brash and flashy young stars, pitted against the mentally tough and blue-collar Croatia. While France were slight favorites going into the match, Croatia had to deal with the issue of fatigue. The Croatians had played a full 90 minutes more than France after contesting three consecutive 30-minute overtimes. The final was also a rematch of the 1998 World Cup semifinals, which France won, 2–1.

The game was fantastic for long stretches. With 78,000 fans looking on, France started the game preferring to play on the break. In response, Croatia dominated the ball in the opening stages with Modric and Rakitic controlling the midfield. Nonetheless, France took the lead in the 18th minute after Griezmann dived to win a free-kick 30 yards out on the right side of the penalty area. Mandžukić flicked the ensuing delivery into his own net, the first-ever own goal in a World Cup final.

Croatia responded impressively and equalized 10 minutes later from another dead-ball situation. After France failed to clear, the ball fell to Perisic, who took one touch past N'Golo Kante before firing into the bottom corner. With Croatia once again beginning to take control, France retook the lead in the 38th minute, this time from the penalty spot after Perisic handled the ball in the box. Referee Néstor Pitana initially awarded a corner kick but reversed his decision following a VAR consultation. The decision impacted the rest of the match. "In a World Cup final, you do not give such a penalty," Dalić said.

Croatia came out quickly in the second half but were undone by Les Bleus' excellent counterattack shortly before the hour mark. Pogba unleashed Mbappe with a stunning cross-field diagonal before arriving at the top of the box to score. His first effort was blocked, but he picked up the rebound and curled past a wrong-footed Subašić. Mbappe's goal in the 65th minute killed the match. The 19-year-old, who became the first teenager to score in a World Cup final since Pelé in 1958, controlled Lucas Hernández's cutback before drilling past Subašić into the bottom corner.

At the other end, goalkeeper Hugo Lloris's error in the 69th minute—after he tried to knock the ball past an onrushing Mandžukić, only to hit it straight at his leg and into the net—gave some life to Croatia's attack, but as it had all tournament, the French defense held firm. There would be no Croatia comeback as France powered to a 4–2 win to capture its second World Cup in history. Amid a heavy downpour—mixed with gold confetti—that soaked the players, the French celebrated into the night. It was a wonderful ending to an exceptional month of soccer.

The six-goal game was the most in a final since England beat West Germany 4–2 in 1966. Like the 1998 team, this France roster was loaded with immigrant talent and players of African descent. Once again, the country had come together, under the leadership of Deschamps, to win soccer's biggest prize. "We did not play a huge game, but we showed mental quality," Deschamps said. "And we scored four goals, anyway."

Chapter Nine

Rising Out of the Desert

Storm clouds gathered over Moscow as thousands of France and Croatia supporters exited the Luzhniki Stadium and made their way down the long pedestrian avenue that connects to the Sportivnaya metro station. For the 78,000 in attendance, including Russian president Vladimir Putin, the 2018 World Cup final on July 15 had capped off the month-long soccer festival and a successful tournament for the hosts. By the time the fans started departing the stadium, France was already celebrating its second World Cup triumph under a heavy downpour.

Once the game was over and the confetti cleaned up, the pressure moved away from the players on the field and immediately transferred to Hassan Al-Thawadi, the man who heads Qatar's 2022 World Cup organizing committee. After Russia's successful hosting, Al-Thawadi knows his country has big shoes to fill. In fact, two days before the final, FIFA president Gianni Infantino even went so far as to call Russia 2018 "the best World Cup ever."

The World Cup's future remains a point of contention, while its recent past not so much. Russia, for example, exceeded expectations, both on and off the field, as the country worked arduously to shatter stereotypes. The team had gone far in the competition, an astonishing achievement, eliminated by Croatia in the quarterfinals following a penalty-kick shootout. Now the ball goes to Qatar. In many ways, the small nation—the first Middle Eastern state to host a World Cup—has an even harder task before it. "We're excited and what we saw in Russia has made us even more excited," Al-Thawadi said.

Doha has a little bit of Las Vegas to it. The city is opulent, a place built out of a desert where money is no object. A modern train system connecting venues will make it easy to travel.

Qatar has never been to a World Cup. Instead, the World Cup is coming to them. With the countdown toward the finals underway, the country's efforts to put together a world-class tournament—in addition to a national team that can compete on football's biggest stage—has come into greater focus. Is Qatar, a nation of just 300,000 people, in over its head? Qatar 2022's motto is "Expect Amazing." Will it be?

For starters, the tournament will be played throughout November and December for the first time in its history. Alcohol will only be served in designated areas, given that it is a Muslim nation, and the government does not recognize same-sex marriage or civil partnerships.

"We're embracing it," Al-Thawadi said of the pressure Qatar faces. "When we bid to host the World Cup, we knew there was no platform like football to change people's perceptions, to bring people together from different walks of life, and different cultures and to break down stereotypes. That was our message from the very beginning."

Since FIFA awarded the tournament to Qatar in 2010—a controversial decision tainted by allegations of corruption and bribery—the country has been dogged by scandal. Human rights groups have said that the estimated two million foreign workers who have streamed into the country during the past decade—mostly from India, Pakistan, Nepal, and Bangladesh—have been poorly paid and often mistreated. Some 6,500 workers, according to the *Guardian*, have died building the venues and other infrastructure projects connected to the coming tournament. Qatari officials have refuted that figure, saying just three have died from work-related injuries.

FIFA, not surprisingly, has come to Qatar's defense, saying the country's World Cup organizing committee "have always maintained transparency around these fatalities." In a statement, they tried to explain away the situation by adding that it "remains a challenge to fully safeguard workers from health hazards that may not be directly associated with their work on site."

2020s Innovation: Stadium Air-Conditioning

Soccer fans could experience a cool breeze at the World Cup in Qatar. Beneath each seat and along the field, vents will provide cold air should temperatures rise to unbearable levels during games. First designed in 2009 by air-conditioning expert Saud Ghani, an engineering professor at Qatar University, the system was made so that games could be played in one of the hottest places on the planet.

"When we were preparing our submission for the World Cup in 2022, we wanted a unique bid that would stand out among other bidding countries," he told FIFA.com in 2019. "Most countries would usually present their stadiums as a design idea and not a technology. We presented our stadiums in a new way—as a technology."

Saud's cooling technologies will be used at all eight World Cup stadiums in Qatar in 2022. The method allows venues to cool two hours before a game. "The most important thing to cool effectively is that you don't want the outside wind to enter the stadium," Ghani said. "That's why the size and design of the stadium have to be studied and altered accordingly so that they block warm air from entering the stadium."

No matter the weather outside, organizers said all venues will be cooled to a comfortable 64 to 75 degrees Fahrenheit. Although the temperatures will be much cooler during the winter compared to the summer when the World Cup is typically played, Qatari officials have said the cooling system is aimed at allowing the country to host sporting events of all varieties during any season.

A view from inside Al Janoub Stadium, one of eight venues in Qatar that will be used at the 2022 World Cup.
SHUTTERSTOCK

FIFA's Corruption Woes

The sport's international governing body has had a very tough few years, proving that it is indeed one of the most corrupt organizations on the planet. In 2015, 17 years after France hosted the World Cup, investigators discovered that France '98 had been awarded to them by FIFA's executive committee as a result of bribes. It was just the start of what would be a years-long uncovering of wrongdoing, both by investigative journalists and law enforcement officials, into the backroom machinations over at FIFA.

Chuck Blazer, who hailed from the United States, cooperated with the FBI and Swiss authorities following his arrest in 2011 for failing to pay taxes. Blazer, an eccentric figure and a fixture in American soccer for decades, had served as a member of FIFA's executive committee for six years until 2013. He admitted before a New York judge in 2013 that he and others had taken bribes in return for votes. "I and others on the FIFA executive committee agreed to accept bribes in conjunction with the selection of South Africa as the host nation for the 2010 World Cup," Blazer told the judge in a closed-door session in November 2013.

Giving a few people so much power, with little or no oversight, is what led to bribes and other crimes in relation to nations bidding for the World Cup. Blazer, who had been instrumental in Russia getting the 2018 World Cup, admitted to U.S. authorities that he had abused his position to fund a lavish lifestyle that included two apartments in New York's Trump Tower—one of them for his cats. Nicknamed "Mr. 10 Percent" due to the commission he demanded as CONCACAF general secretary each time a TV deal was signed, Blazer hid much of his wealth in offshore accounts. It was only after the FBI and the Internal Revenue Service began to look into Blazer's activities on American soil—he had not filed any tax returns between 2005 and 2010—that the larger web of FIFA corruption came into focus.

Blazer had documented his travels in a blog, which included photos of him on a private jet with Nelson Mandela and Putin. He was eventually charged with tax evasion and money laundering and given a lifetime ban from FIFA. The crooked sports executive-turned-whistleblower shook the foundation of soccer's governing body to its core. As for the

2018 World Cup in Russia, FIFA found in June 2017 that the country's organizing committee had done nothing corrupt—although a cloud of suspicion still hovered over them after it was determined that Russian officials had destroyed computers and emails related to the bid.

Blazer, who died from cancer in 2017, became an FBI informant, bringing down many FIFA officials with him who had taken part in financial wrongdoing. He was critical in helping to expose the illicit behavior that brought about reforms aimed at reducing such corruption. Blazer and Jack Warner, a businessman, were both accused of soliciting and accepting bribes over the selection of the host nation for the 1998 World Cup. According to the indictment put forth by the U.S. Attorney's Office in New York, Blazer traveled with Warner, a high-ranking CONCACAF official at the time, to Africa in 1992 at the invitation of the Moroccan bid committee. The African nation's bid committee allegedly offered a $1 million bribe payment to Warner in exchange for his secret ballot on the executive committee for Morocco to host the '98 tournament.

In 2004, according to the indictment, the Moroccan bid committee secretly offered Warner another $1 million payment if he supported the country's bid for the 2010 World Cup. South Africa won the right to stage the 2010 World Cup after missing out on the 2006 tournament to Germany. The Moroccan bribe offer was outmatched by South Africa, which promised to arrange $10 million to the Caribbean Football Union, headed by Warner.

South Africa was selected over Morocco to host the World Cup. Blazer and Warner indicated afterward that they had voted for South Africa. The $10 million bribe was transferred in three payments to bank accounts in New York controlled by Warner in the name of two regional soccer associations. Warner then pocketed the money, the indictment said.

The FIFA corruption that was exposed had taken root in the 1980s and coincided with an infusion of cash as a result of TV revenue, ticket sales, and marketing stemming from the World Cup. Havelange's presidency stretched for much of this period of increased revenue. His term ended in 1998, replaced by his mentee Sepp Blatter.

In 1999, the Dutch newspaper *De Telegraaf* reported that Havelange, who also served as an International Olympic Committee member, had accepted gifts of diamonds, bicycles, clothing, porcelain objects, paintings, and art books in connection with Amsterdam's failed bid for the 1992 Summer Games. "I remember it very well because he had special wishes, wishes which were in conflict with the IOC laws," Peter Kronenberg, who headed the press office of the Amsterdam Olympic Games 1992 Foundation, told the newspaper.

Havelange, who died in 2016 at age 100, was also implicated in other alleged acts of corruption that came to light after his term had ended. The creation of International Sport and Leisure (ISL) to help market the 1986 World Cup under Havelange eventually met its demise in 2001 after it was looted by officials. It was revealed that from 1989 to 2001, ISL paid $204 million in "personal commissions" to sports executives and others involved in the marketing of TV rights. A 2008 trial in Germany revealed that the payments were bribes and that ISL was essentially a piggy bank for high-profile FIFA officials.

In 2006, British investigative reporter Andrew Jennings reported that Havelange had urged officials to secretly repay the commissions they had received once he learned that investigators were looking into it. In 2011, Jennings told Brazil's Senate that Havelange may have amassed upwards of $50 million in bribe money through a front company. An IOC ethics committee was announced that same year to investigate claims that Havelange received a bribe of $1 million in connection with ISL. The probe was prompted by Jennings's claims in a TV broadcast called "FIFA's Shame," an episode of *Panorama* broadcast on the BBC. As a result, Havelange resigned as a member of the IOC, citing health concerns. The probe was eventually closed.

Havelange's crime partner was his son-in-law Ricardo Teixeira, who served as head of the Brazilian FA from 1989 to 2012. A financier, Teixeira had no experience as a sports administrator. It had been his family bond with Havelange that allowed him to run things as well as pocket millions in bribes, investigators argued. In 2012, Teixeira was also named by Swiss prosecutors as being a beneficiary of ISL money from 1992 to 2000. A year before France '98, Havelange had given ISL the exclusive marketing rights to FIFA tournaments, which included the men's and women's World Cups. ISL was then given the exclusive TV and radio rights to the 2002 and 2006 World Cups. In return, FIFA paid ISL $1.4 billion. Havelange, Teixeira, and others pocketed "commissions"—kickbacks for their wheeling and dealing—as a result of awarding ISL such tournaments, according to Swiss authorities. Some of this wrongdoing had taken place under Blatter's tenure as president, something that would eventually lead to his resignation after Blazer turned on his fellow executive committee members.

The awarding of World Cups to Russia in 2018 and Qatar in 2022 triggered raised eyebrows when Blatter made the announcement in December 2010. The awarding of the tournament, especially to Qatar, had come just days after the BBC broadcast the *Panorama* exposé on FIFA claiming that senior officials such as Teixeira, Nicolás Leoz of Paraguay, and Issa Hayatou of Cameroon had accepted bribes during the 1990s.

In February 2011, FIFA's ethics committee upheld three-year and one-year bans imposed respectively upon executive committee members Amos Adamu of Nigeria and Reynald Temarii of French Polynesia for breaches of ethics rules following a *Sunday Times* investigation into wrongdoing during the awarding of the 2018 and 2022 World Cups. Two of the twenty-four members of FIFA's executive committee were suspended as a result of the *Sunday Times'* reporting. Five more ExCo members—including Blazer—were either banned or forced to resign after charges that they had pocketed bribes were made public.

Unable to ignore the growing criticism, FIFA hired former U.S. attorney Michael Garcia to commission a report aimed at uncovering the internal issues plaguing the 2018 and 2022 bids. Following a two-year investigation, Garcia submitted a 349-page report in September 2014 to Hans-Joachim Eckert, FIFA's head of adjudication on ethical matters. But Eckert refused to make the report public and instead released his own 42-page summary.

Eckert's summary was criticized, and Garcia described it as "materially incomplete." After unsuccessfully appealing for FIFA to publish the report in full, Garcia resigned. In 2017, the German newspaper *Bild* said it had obtained a copy of the report and planned to publish it. FIFA, in an effort to preempt the newspaper, released the report. Russia's bid, according to Garcia, was found not to have fully reported all its contacts with executive committee members, as required by FIFA rules, but was cleared of offering any excessive gifts or "undue influence." Qatar, meanwhile, had influenced members to vote for their bid, but Garcia stopped short of saying they had bought votes.

Overall, Garcia found what he called in the report a "culture of entitlement" that typified FIFA officials. He also said that holding a vote for two different World Cups at the same time had made FIFA vulnerable to collusion. He found that Blatter was more indulgent and generous toward executive committee members than the disapproving statements of wrongdoing he had made in public. While Garcia praised Blatter for introducing reforms, he wrote, "As head of FIFA, however, President Blatter bears some responsibility for a flawed process that engendered deep public skepticism, and for presiding over an executive committee whose culture of entitlement contributed to many of the issues this report identified."

The report confirmed what many had already suspected. In 2015, U.S. prosecutors, with help from Swiss authorities, arrested seven FIFA officials in a predawn raid of the Zurich hotel Baur au Lac where they were staying. The officials, along with seven others, were indicted on charges that included wire fraud, racketeering, and money laundering. "They held important responsibilities at every level, from building soccer fields for children in developing countries to organizing the World Cup. They were expected to uphold the rules that keep soccer honest, and protect the integrity of the game," U.S. attorney Loretta Lynch told reporters on May 27, 2015, after the 166-page indictment was unsealed. "Instead, they corrupted the business of worldwide soccer to serve their interests and enrich themselves. This Department of Justice is determined to end these practices, to root out corruption, and to bring wrongdoers to justice."

Seven months later, 16 other officials were charged in connection with the widening scandal. The arrests were largely praised, although Blatter said the charges had been retribution for the United States not being chosen to host the 2022 World Cup. FIFA eventually launched a probe of Blatter and banned him from all soccer activities until the year 2028. In his place, FIFA members elected Gianni Infantino in February 2016 with the mandate of cleaning up the embattled organization. Whether soccer's governing body actually became less corrupt remains a matter of debate. The fallout, however, included Blatter getting banned from the sport through 2028.

The World Cup Grows

FIFA decided to expand the World Cup to 48 teams from 32 in time for the 2026 tournament, which will be hosted by the United States, Canada, and Mexico. The vote took place on June 13, 2018, during FIFA's annual congress in Moscow and was open to all member nations. Each FIFA member was allowed to cast a ballot, taking the power away from the select few who sat on the executive committee who used to decide World Cup hosts.

The U.S./Canada/Mexico bid received 134 ballots, while Morocco received 65. Mexico will become the first nation to host three World Cups, while the United States will become the first country to host both men's and women's World Cups twice each—having hosted the 1994 men's and the 1999 and 2003 women's World Cups.

The United Bid proposed a World Cup hosted in 16 cities, with the final to be played at MetLife Stadium just outside New York City. The bid forecast revenues of $14 billion, twice the amount presented by Morocco. For FIFA, an organization that lost significant sponsorship income as a result of the 2015 scandals, the push was to have the U.S.-led bid win the hosting rights sweepstakes.

FIFA—the largest nonprofit in the world—had in 2018 revenues of $4.6 billion and cash reserves of $2.7 billion. The men's World Cup represents 93 percent of FIFA's earnings. Money aside, the outcome of the vote was proof that different federations could come together, build a bid, and win. "They could also dream of hosting a World Cup," then–U.S. Soccer president Carlos Cordeiro told reporters, referring to FIFA members. "That will be the legacy for the future."

Pelé, the always smiling spokesman whom FIFA likes to trot out whenever possible to promote the game, suffered a series of health setbacks during the COVID-19 pandemic. In his place, the now retired Brazilian star Ronaldo and his toothy smile filled in as international ambassador. Ronaldo was trotted out many times in 2021 as FIFA tried to argue that the men's and women's World Cups should be held every two years rather than four.

"This format is almost 100 years old—the World Cup being held every four years—and the world has changed, has evolved greatly, the speed of information is insane, so I think that in today's generation, where everything happens so fast, to improve and have a World Cup every two years would be a great opportunity to engage the youth that may be going into different areas, into other sports," Ronaldo told reporters in September 2021. "So, I think it's a great opportunity for us to continue to evolve and attract more people interested in football."

It was a controversial plan. Opponents said it would water down the tournament; yet FIFA argued that it would allow smaller countries the chance to participate and grow the game. The plan was never put to a vote.

What the 2022 World Cup Will Look Like

In January 2019, FIFA president Gianni Infantino said they were exploring the possibility of having neighboring countries host matches during the 2022 tournament, but the plan never came to fruition. "If we can accommodate some of the neighboring countries in the Gulf region which are very close by to host a few games in the World Cup this could be very beneficial for the region and the entire world," Infantino told reporters.

The United Arab Emirates, Saudi Arabia, Bahrain, and Egypt all launched a diplomatic and trade boycott of Qatar in 2017 that complicated any prospect of sharing the tournament. The countries have accused Qatar of supporting terrorism, which it denies.

Middle Eastern nations aren't the only ones upset with Qatar. Norway, upset with Qatar's human rights record, had threatened to boycott the World Cup. At an extraordinary congress called by the Norwegian FA, 368 delegates voted for a motion rejecting a boycott, while 121 were in favor. It was just one example of the possible activism teams and individual players could employ once they arrive in Qatar.

The 32-team tournament will once again feature eight groups of four. As a result, four matches will be played each day (at 1 p.m., 4 p.m., 7 p.m., and 10 p.m. local time) during the group stage, which will span a 12-day period and see winners and runners-up progress to the round of 16.

The tournament kicks off on November 21 at the Al Bayt Stadium in Al Khor with a match that will feature the host country. The final will be played on December 18 at Lusail Stadium in Doha. Kickoff is scheduled for 6 p.m. local time.

Here is a preview of what we can expect from several key nations at the upcoming World Cup:

Argentina

Winners of the 2021 Copa America, Argentina finally won a major tournament for the first time since capturing the South American title in 1993. The victory also allowed Lionel Messi to win a title with his country after so much club success at Barcelona. In attack, Lautaro Martínez did an exceptional job playing alongside Messi. He's quick and consistent and can provide goals when needed. His success at Inter Milan has translated well for the national team, something that can blossom in the lead-up to the World Cup if he can stay healthy. Nicolás Otamendi has been the defensive anchor, providing experience on a back line that features lots of young players.

Belgium

The Red Devils looked poised to win the Euros, but they fizzled out in the quarterfinals amid talk that their golden generation had come to an end. It's possible that the Belgians have run out of gas, and an older team at the next World Cup doesn't necessarily mean they will win it. Nonetheless, striker Romelu Lukaku is one of the best, and midfielder Kevin De Bruyne may still have something left in the tank to get to the finish line.

Brazil

Losing the Copa America final at home to rivals Argentina left Neymar in tears. The Brazilian striker will be looking to win a major trophy of his own, with the five-time World Cup champions always a favorite on the eve of the tournament. Neymar, who has said this upcoming World Cup could be his last, is just one piece of the Brazilian puzzle that needs to come together. In attack, the youngster Vinicius Júnior of Real Madrid is expected to take part in his first World Cup. He is Neymar's heir apparent. The pair could be joined up front with winger Rodrygo, who also plays for Real Madrid.

Denmark

The second team (after Germany) to qualify for the World Cup out of Europe, Denmark was a semifinalist at the 2020 European Championship, a surprising run after their star player Christian Eriksen collapsed and nearly died as a result of cardiac arrest during his country's opening match versus Finland. It remains unclear if the talented playmaker will be forced to sit out the World Cup due to ongoing health reasons or whether he can make a full recovery and represent Denmark again.

England

The Three Lions go into Qatar 2022 as one of the pre-tournament favorites. The team has grown immensely under manager Garett Southgate. England finished fourth at the last World Cup and as runners-up at the Euros. Striker Harry Kane remains largely underrated, while England's new generation of players, spearheaded by Jadon Sancho, hope to lead the team to a trophy for the first time since being crowned world champions in 1966.

France

Thinking that France can win the World Cup for a second straight time isn't much of a stretch. They are, after all, the defending champions and feature Kylian Mbappe, one of the planet's best strikers. Les Bleus didn't look so strong at the 2020 European Championship. France's stock had dropped. By October 2021, it was France who showed that they are the frontrunners to repeat as World Cup champions. France's UEFA Nations League triumph put them back in top position. In the semifinals against Belgium, France scored three unanswered goals to record an epic 3–2 come-from-behind victory. In the final, France, down 1–0 to Spain, scored twice late in the game (including off a controversial Mbappe goal 10 minutes from time) for the 2–1 win.

Germany

The Germans, under new manager Hansi Flick, have hit the reboot button now that the Joachim Löw era has come to an end. His reign included guiding the Germans to the World Cup title in 2014, although they have done little else since then. The Germans always find a way to make an impact at any tournament. They have the tradition and the players to go far once again. Kai Havertz is the team's midfield lynchpin, and striker Serge Gnabry will be called on to step up their game.

Mexico

Losing in the final of both the CONCACAF Nations League and the Gold Cup in the summer of 2021 triggered some introspection on the part of Mexico manager Gerardo "Tata" Martino and Mexican soccer, from the FA on down to TV pundits, as a whole. But Mexico remains a competitive side and have seemingly settled to playing Martino's 4–3–3 formation as their depth has been evident throughout qualifying. Veteran midfielder Andrés Guardado and striker Hirving Lozano have been key, as goalkeeper Guillermo Ochoa continues to give the team reassurance in the back.

Netherlands

The Dutch, currently coached by the veteran Louis van Gaal, have never won a World Cup, but they have made a very large impact on the tournament throughout the years. In 2022, the Dutch could find themselves contending for the title of world champion after finishing runners-up three times in their history. Striker Memphis Depay has all the qualities and talent to lead the Netherlands to a deep run. He remains one of the world's best forwards, but certainly his stock will rise if he can help the Dutch win a World Cup.

Qatar

The host nation, which will make their World Cup debut, has a relatively young and modest soccer pedigree. Qatar has played in 10 Asian Cup tournaments, winning it once in 2019 with Sudanese-born striker Almoez Ali scoring nine goals. Not having to qualify for 2022 meant that Qatar didn't get the chance to play competitive matches. Instead, Qatar was invited to play at the 2019 Copa America, where they finished last in Group B with a 0-1-2 record behind Colombia, Argentina, and Paraguay. In 2021, they were invited to participate in the Gold Cup, where they won Group D with a 2-1-0 record. Qatar bowed out in the semifinals, losing 1–0 to the United States. Nonetheless, Ali finished as the tournament's top scorer with four goals.

Spain

Manager Luis Enrique turned some heads when he named a team at Euro 2020 without any Real Madrid players. The experiment to focus on a new generation worked as La Roja reached the semifinals, losing to Italy in a shootout. In midfield, Spain has two of the most promising players in Pedri and Gavi. The duo have the skill to replicate the success of Xavi and Andrés Iniesta. Named the best young player at the recent Euros, Pedri has pace and artistry. He's key when Spain have the ball, which is often given its penchant for possession.

United States

After missing out on the 2018 World Cup, the United States will try to make a go of reaching the finals this time around. The Americans had a wonderful 2021, beating rivals Mexico in two straight finals to capture the CONCACAF Nations League and Gold Cup. Led by striker Christian Pulisic, the Americans have a new generation of stars playing at the highest levels throughout Europe. These standouts include midfielder Weston McKinnie (Juventus) and striker Sergiño Dest (Barcelona). They have made manager Gregg Berhalter hopeful this team can compete at the highest levels for the next decade.

Appendix

World Cup Statistics and Records

Finals

1930	Uruguay 4, Argentina 2	Montevideo, Uruguay
1934	Italy 2, Czechoslovakia 1 (extra time)	Rome, Italy
1938	Italy 4, Hungary 2	Paris, France
1950	Uruguay 2, Brazil 1	Rio de Janeiro, Brazil
1954	West Germany 3, Hungary 2	Bern, Switzerland
1958	Brazil 5, Sweden 2	Solna, Sweden
1962	Brazil 3, Czechoslovakia 1	Santiago, Chile
1966	England 4, West Germany 2 (extra time)	London, England
1970	Brazil 4, Italy 1	Mexico City, Mexico
1974	West Germany 2, Netherlands 1	Munich, West Germany
1978	Argentina 3, Netherlands 1 (extra time)	Buenos Aires, Argentina
1982	Italy 3, West Germany 1	Madrid, Spain
1986	Argentina 3, West Germany 2	Mexico City, Mexico

1990	West Germany 1, Argentina 0	Rome, Italy
1994	Brazil 0, Italy 0 (Brazil wins 3–2 on penalty kicks)	Pasadena, USA
1998	France 3, Brazil 0	Saint-Denis, France
2002	Brazil 2, Germany 0	Yokohama, Japan
2006	Italy 1, France 1 (Italy wins 5–3 on penalty kicks)	Berlin, Germany
2010	Spain 1, Netherlands 0 (extra time)	Johannesburg, South Africa
2014	Germany 1, Argentina 0 (extra time)	Rio de Janeiro, Brazil
2018	France 4, Croatia 2	Moscow, Russia

INDIVIDUAL RECORDS

Most championships
   3, Pelé (Brazil, 1958, 1962, 1970)

Most appearances in a World Cup final
   3, Cafu (Brazil, 1994, 1998, 2002)

Most different teams played
   2, Luis Monti (Argentina, 1930; Italy, 1934), Robert Prosinečki, Robert Jarni (Yugoslavia, 1990; Croatia, 1998, 2002)

Most tournament appearances
   5, Antonio Carbajal (Mexico, 1950–1966), Lothar Matthäus (Germany, 1982–1998), Rafael Márquez (Mexico, 2002–2018)

Most goals scored
   16, Miroslav Klose (Germany, 2002–2014)

Most goals scored in a single tournament
   13, Just Fontaine (France, 1958)

Most goals scored in a single match
5, Oleg Salenko (Russia) versus Cameroon in 1994

Most hat tricks
2, Sándor Kocsis (Hungary, 1954), Just Fontaine (France 1958), Gerd Müller (West Germany, 1970), Gabriel Batistuta (Argentina, 1994 and 1998)

Most assists overall
10, Pelé (Brazil, 1958–1970)

Most assists in a single tournament
6, Pelé (Brazil, 1970)

Most matches played
25, Lothar Matthäus (Germany, 1982–1998)

Most knockout games played
14, Miroslav Klose (Germany, 2002–2014)

Most minutes played
2,217, Paolo Maldini (Italy, 1990–2002)

Most shutouts
10, Peter Shilton (England, 1982–1990), Fabien Barthez (France, 1998–2006)

Most consecutive minutes without conceding a goal
517, Walter Zenga (Italy, 1990)

Most matches coached
25, Helmut Schön (West Germany, 1966–1978)

Most matches won
16, Helmut Schön (West Germany, 1966–1978)

Most tournaments won
2, Vittorio Pozzo (Italy, 1934–1938)

Most tournaments
6, Carlos Alberto Parreira (1982, 1990–1998, 2006, 2010)

Most nations coached
5, Bora Milutinović (Mexico, 1986; Costa Rica, 1990; United States, 1994; Nigeria, 1998; China, 2002), Carlos Alberto Parreira (Kuwait, 1982; United Arab Emirates, 1990; Brazil, 1994, 2006; Saudi Arabia, 1998; South Africa, 2010)

Most cards all-time
7, Javier Mascherano (Argentina, 2006–2018)

Most yellow cards all-time
7, Javier Mascherano (Argentina, 2006–2018)

Most red cards all-time
2, Rigobert Song (Cameroon, 1994, 1998), Zinedine Zidane (France, 1998, 2006)

TEAM RECORDS
Most matches played
109, Germany and Brazil

Fewest matches played
1, Indonesia (as Dutch East Indies)

Most wins
73, Brazil

Most losses
27, Mexico

Most draws
21, Italy, England

BIBLIOGRAPHY

Throughout this book I have attempted to document primary sources, which are sufficiently identified in the text. Quotes without attribution include news conferences and interviews that I conducted throughout the years. The purpose of this section is to identify the many sources—books, magazines, websites, television broadcasts, studies, and archival material—used in the writing of this book.

BOOKS

Agnew, Paddy. *Forza Italia: The Fall and Rise of Italian Football*. London: Ebury Press, 2008.

Atherton, Martin. *The Theft of the Jules Rimet Trophy: The Hidden History of the 1966 World Cup*. London: Meyer & Meyer Sport, 2008.

Bayle, Emmanuel, and Patrick Clastres. *Global Sport Leaders: A Biographical Analysis of International Sport Management*. London: Palgrave Macmillan, 2018.

Bellos, Alex. *Futebol: The Brazilian Way of Life*. London: Bloomsbury, 2014.

Bongers, Michel, and René Bremer. *Kapitein van Oranje: De memoires van Jan Zwartkruis als bondscoach van het Nederlands Elftal*. Amsterdam: Bellucic, 2008.

Burns, Jimmy. *Maradona: The Hand of God*. London: Bloomsbury, 2010.

Burns, Jimmy. *La Roja: How Soccer Conquered Spain and How Spanish Soccer Conquered the World*. London: Bold Type Books, 2012.

Dubois, Laurent. *Soccer Empire: The World Cup and the Future of France*. Berkeley: University of California Press, 2010.

Foer, Franklin. *How Soccer Explains the World: An Unlikely Theory of Globalization*. New York: Harper Perennial, 2010.

Glanville, Brian. *The Story of the World Cup*. London: Faber & Faber, 1997.

Grimaldi, Mauro. *Vittorio Pozzo: Storia di un Italiano*. Rome: Società Stampa Sportiva, 2001.

Harris, Harry. *Pelé: His Life and Times*. London: John Blake, 2018.

Holt, Nick. *The Mammoth Book of the World Cup: The Definitive Guide, 1930–2018*. London: Constable & Robinson, 2019.

Jamrich, Klara, and Rogan Taylor. *Puskas on Puskas: The Life and Times of a Footballing Legend*. London: Robson Book, 1997.

Jawad, Hyder. *Four Weeks in Montevideo: The Story of World Cup 1930*. London: Seventeen Media & Publishing, 2009.

Keane, Roy. *Keane: The Autobiography*. London: Michael Joseph, 2002.

Leblond, Renaud. *Le Journal de Jules Rimet*. Paris: First, 2014.

Maradona, Diego. *Maradona: The Autobiography of Soccer's Greatest and Most Controversial Star*. New York: Skyhorse, 2011.

Martin, Simon. *Sport Italia: The Italian Love Affair with Sport*. New York: I. B. Tauris, 2011.

Mason, Tony. *Passion of the People? Football in Latin America*. London: Verso, 1995.

Murray, Scott, and Rob Smyth. *And Gazza Misses the Final*. London: Constable & Robinson, 2014.

Muylaert, Roberto. *Barbosa: Um Gol Silencia o Brasil*. São Paulo: SESI-SP Editora, 2019.

Rimet, Jules. *L'Histoire Merveilleuse de la Coupe du Monde*. Paris: Union Européenne d'éditions, 1954.

Taylor, Matthew. *The Leaguers: The Making of Professional Football in England, 1900–1939*. Liverpool: Liverpool University Press, 2005.

NEWSPAPERS

A Bola
American Oggi
Belfast Telegraph
Clarin
Correio Paulistano
Corriere della Sera
Corriere dello Sport
Dagens Nyheter
Daily Express
Daily Mail
Daily Mirror
L'Equipe
Folha de S. Paulo
La Gazzetta dello Sport
Globe and Mail
O Globo
Guardian
El Heraldo de Madrid
Imparcial
Independent
International Herald Tribune
Irish Times
Liverpool Daily Post
Los Angeles Times
Marca
La Nazione

New York Times
News of the World
Pagina 12
El País
Le Parisien
Il Popolo d'Italia
La Prensa
El Sol
Sun of London
Sunday Times
De Telegraf
Telegraph
El Tiempo
Times of London
24 Heures

WIRE SERVICES
Agence France-Presse
Associated Press
Reuters
TASS
United Press International

MAGAZINES
Der Spiegel
Esquire
FourFourTwo
France Football
Guerin Sportivo
Marca
Nation
Newsweek
Sports Illustrated
World Soccer

WEBSITES
AS.com
BBC.com
ESPN.com
FanSided.com
FCBayern.com
FIFA.com
ForeignPolicy.com

Goal.com
History.com
MLSSoccer.com
Netflix.com
Sport.es
TalkSport.com
TheseFootballTimes.co
UEFA.com
USSoccerPlayers.com
WorldCup1930Project.blogspot.com

TELEVISION NETWORKS
Al Jazeera
British Broadcasting Corporation
Canal Plus
El Trece
France Bleu
ITV
Radio y Televisión Argentina
RAI Radio Televisione Italiana
Sky Sports
SporTV
TyC Sports

REPORTS AND STUDIES
Brawling in Berne: Mediated Transnational Moral Panics in the 1954 Football World Cup
FIFA Official Report World Cup 1982
FIFA Official Report World Cup 1986
FIFA World Cup Italia '90 Official Report
Montevideo 1930: Reassessing the Selection of the First World Cup Host
Report of Conadep (National Commission on the Disappearance of Persons)
When Football Went Global: Televising the 1966 World Cup

ARCHIVAL INFORMATION
Archives Nationales de France
General Archive of the Nation (Argentina)
Hungarian National Archives
Istituto Luce
Italian Football Federation
Library of Congress
National Archives of Brazil

Index

ABOUT THE AUTHOR

Clemente A. Lisi is a journalism professor at The King's College in New York. His work has appeared at ABC News Digital, Goal.com, the *New York Daily News*, the *New York Post*, *These Football Times*, and USSoccer-Players.com.